Treating Concurrent Disorders

Treating Concurrent Disorders

A Guide for Counsellors

Edited by W.J. Wayne Skinner

Centre for Addiction and Mental Health
Centre de toxicomanie et de santé mentale

A Pan American Health Organization /
World Health Organization Collaborating Centre

Library and Archives Canada Cataloguing in Publication

Treating concurrent disorders : a guide for counsellors / edited by W.J. Wayne Skinner.

Includes bibliographical references.

ISBN: 978-0-88868-499-8 (PRINT)

ISBN: 978-0-88868-868-2 (PDF)

ISBN: 978-0-88868-869-9 (HTML)

ISBN: 978-0-88868-870-5 (ePUB)

1. Dual diagnosis—Treatment. 2. Dual diagnosis—Patients—Rehabilitation.

I. Skinner W. J. Wayne, 1949- II. Centre for Addiction and Mental Health.

RC564.68.T74 2005 616.86'06 C2004-907421-0

Printed in Canada

This publication may be available in other formats. For information about alternate formats or other CAMH publications, or to place an order, please contact Sales and Distribution:

Toll-free: 1 800 661-1111

Toronto: 416 595-6059

E-mail: publications@camh.net

Online store: http://store.camh.net

Website: www.camh.net

This book was produced by the following:

Development: Caroline Hebblethwaite, CAMH
Editorial: Sue McCluskey, CAMH; Nick Gamble, CAMH; Michelle Maynes, CAMH
Design: Mara Korkola, CAMH; Nancy Leung, CAMH
Typesetting: Theresa Wojtasiewicz
Print production: Christine Harris, CAMH
Marketing: Arturo Llerenas, CAMH

2449 / 09-2010 / PM 055

To our clients and their families
And in memory of Tom Franklin, Joan Bresher and Blenos Pederson

Acknowledgments

To our colleagues in the Concurrent Disorders Service and beyond—for their support, advice and their inspiring example in working with clients with complex problems—many thanks.

To Peter Coleridge, Nevin Coston and Betty Dondertman, for their patient and loyal support for a project that took longer than we imagined, a special acknowledgment.

While each chapter in this book has its authors, a project like this is, in fact, authored by many people whose hidden contributions have been no less essential. Among them, it is important to credit and thank Michelle Maynes, Anita Dubey, Sue McCluskey and Nick Gamble. For layout and design, full credit is due to Mara Korkola and Nancy Leung.

Thanks to Christine Bois, Nady el-Guebaly, Mary Jane Esplan, Allan Furlong, Karen Leslie, Neil Rector and Zindal Segal for commenting on parts of the manuscript.

And finally, for her commitment to this project, which has been heroic, and for the skill, sensitivity and wise counsel with which she, as project manager, has guided us through this long journey, there are not enough thanks and praises that I can extend to Caroline Hebblethwaite, *sine qua non.*

Contents

vii **Acknowledgments**

xiii **Preface:** Approaching Concurrent Disorders
WAYNE SKINNER

1 **Introduction**
WAYNE SKINNER

PART I: ASSESSMENT

17 **1** Identifying, Assessing and Treating Concurrent Disorders: The Client–Counsellor Relationship
WAYNE SKINNER

29 **2** Screening and Assessing for Concurrent Disorders
JUAN C. NEGRETE

53 **2 APPENDIX 1** Screening and Assessment Tools

77 **2 APPENDIX 2** Toxicology Tests

85 **3** Using Motivational Interviewing with Clients Who Have Concurrent Disorders
LORNA SAGORSKY AND WAYNE SKINNER

PART II: PRACTICAL APPLICATIONS

113 **4** A Program Model for Integrated Treatment: The Concurrent Disorders Service
ANDREA TSANOS

129 **4 APPENDIX** Concurrent Disorders Service: Inclusion and Exclusion Criteria

137 **5** Integrated Group Psychotherapy for Clients with Concurrent Disorders
ANDREA TSANOS, SUZANNE MORROW AND VICKI MYERS

163 **6** Group Therapy for Severe Mental Illness and Concurrent Substance Use Disorders
ANDREA TSANOS, VICKI MYERS AND SUZANNE MORROW

189 **7** Adapting Dialectical Behaviour Therapy to the Treatment of Concurrent Substance Use and Mental Health Disorders
SHELLEY McMAIN

193 **8** Dialectical Behaviour Therapy for People With Concurrent Borderline Personality and Substance Use Disorders
SHELLEY McMAIN, SHIRA GREEN, LAUREN DIXON AND HARRIET WEAVER

215 **9** Concurrent Anger and Addictions Treatment
LORNE M. KORMAN

235 **9 APPENDIX** Violence and Anger History Interview

249 **10** Treating Concurrent Substance Use and Eating Disorders
CHRISTINE M.A. COURBASSON AND PATRICK D. SMITH

PART III: APPROACHES AND TECHNIQUES

271 **11** Metacognitive Therapy for Concurrent Alcohol Use and Anxiety Disorder
TONY TONEATTO

287 **12** Interpersonal Group Therapy for Concurrent Alcohol Dependence and Interpersonal Problems
JAN MALAT AND MOLYN LESZCZ

311 **13** The Impact of Concurrent Disorders on the Family
CAROLINE P. O'GRADY

331 **14** Concurrent Disorders: A Framework for Working with Couples and Families
GLORIA CHAIM AND JOANNE SHENFELD

349 **15** Concurrent Disorders in Young People
BRUCE BALLON

369 **16** A Concurrent Disorders Capacity-Building Initiative in a Clinical Program for People with Schizophrenia
ANDREA TSANOS AND MARILYN HERIE

397 **16** APPENDIX 1 Concurrent Disorders Capacity-Building Activities

399 **16** APPENDIX 2 The Training and Support Needs Questionnaire

403 **16** APPENDIX 3 Minkoff Symposium, 2001

405 **About the Authors**

Preface

Approaching concurrent disorders

WAYNE SKINNER

A single problem can be difficult enough to address, but when people have more than one, and perhaps many problems, even understanding how these problems relate to and affect each other can be a challenge.

Addiction and mental health workers know that many, if not most, of our clients have problems beyond those that brought them into treatment. Difficulties with interpersonal relationships, employment, finances, housing or the law often go hand-in-hand with substance use and mental health problems. We also know that when people present with either a substance use or mental health problem, their risk of having both kinds of problem is increased. Studies show that about half of the people with either a mental health or substance use disorder have had problems in the other domain at some point in their life (Health Canada, 2002; Kessler et al., 1996; Regier et al., 1990).

When people with co-occurring substance use and mental health problems seek help, the treatment they receive is too often directed at only one of these problems. Helping clients to address one key problem can sometimes start a process of change that goes on to have far-reaching positive effects; other times this approach does little to improve clients' overall situation, and may even make both problems worse. To understand how we can best help a client, we need to look at that person as a whole, and see how that person's problems overlap, disguise or exaggerate one other. Only then we can begin to offer help that is effective.

Although many people have noted the interdependency of substance use and mental health problems over the years, the notion of integrating the treatment of these co-occurring problems is recent. Clients seeking help for these "concurrent disorders" have almost always had to go one place for mental health treatment and another for substance use treatment, often with little or no connection between the services. Only in the past 20 years have clinicians and researchers begun to develop and implement more comprehensive treatments for these clients.

Now that the need for integrated treatment for concurrent disorders is being more widely recognized, there is much to be done. Some clinical practices have been developed, and some of these practices have been supported by research, but much more needs to be discovered.

In this book, we draw on our understanding of existing research and "expert consensus" literature, and also on what we have learned through our work with clients here at the Centre for Addiction and Mental Health (CAMH). Our goal in sharing our understanding and experience is to allow others to take advantage of the gains that we have made, and to join us in pursuing further knowledge in this area.

If you work with clients who have substance use or mental health problems, you are undoubtedly already working with people who have concurrent disorders. If you are committed to understanding and working with clients as whole persons, then you need to understand what these problems are, how they co-occur and how you can help.

Leaving this work to specialists in concurrent disorders is not enough. People in all kinds of helping roles can provide support—people who work in the addiction and mental health systems, obviously, but also people working in other domains, such as criminal justice and corrections, health care, child welfare and family service, employee assistance programs and education.

With this book, our goal is to take information about concurrent disorders beyond academic and scientific discourse, and to make it accessible to a wider range of readers. We hope that counsellors across a diverse range of services will be better able to work with this client population, and that people with co-occurring substance use and mental health problems will get the comprehensive care they need.

DEFINING CONCURRENT DISORDERS

In Ontario, "concurrent disorders" is the term used to refer to co-occurring addiction and mental health problems (see "Defining the Terms," below). The term covers a wide array of combinations of problems, such as anxiety disorder and alcohol abuse, schizophrenia and cannabis dependence, borderline personality disorder and heroin dependence, and bipolar disorder and problem gambling. These problems can co-occur in a variety of ways. They may be active at the same time or at different times, in the present or in the past, and their symptoms may vary in intensity and form over time.

Note that the term "concurrent disorders" as we define it here does not include co-occurring mental health problems without substance use problems, or co-occurring substance use problems without mental health problems. Such co-occurrences do of course exist, but are not the subject of this book.

Also, our primary focus in this book is on co-occurring mental health and substance use problems, although other behavioural addictions, such as problem gambling, may also be associated with mental health problems.

Defining the terms

Here in Ontario, the Ministry of Health and Long-Term Care uses the term **Concurrent Disorders** to describe co-occurring addiction and mental health problems. Other terms are used in other places and by different groups. The following list should help to clarify the confusion.

Dual Diagnosis/Dual Disorders: outside of Ontario, these terms are often used to describe what we call concurrent disorders. Much of the literature that comes from the U.S. uses these terms, and focuses on severe mental illness and co-occurring substance use problems. In Ontario, dual diagnosis is used to describe co-occurring developmental delay and mental illness.

Comorbid Disorders: Comorbid is a medical term used to describe the presence of more than one significant health problem in a person.

Mentally Ill Chemical Abusers (MICA) and Chemically Abusing Mentally Ill (CAMI): MICA is used to describe people whose primary problem is mental illness, who have co-occurring substance use problems; CAMI refers to people whose primary problem is substance use, who also have mental health problems. Both terms originate in the U.S. literature.

Substance-Abusing Mentally Ill (SAMI): SAMI is used to describe people with serious and persistent substance use and mental health problems.

Double Trouble and Double Jeopardy: These terms are sometimes used by people with co-occurring substance use and mental health problems to refer to their own struggles.

Co-occurring Disorders: This is the term used by the Substance Abuse and Mental Health Services Association (SAMHSA) in their 2002 report to the U.S. Congress.

SETTING THE CONTEXT

Much of the research in concurrent disorders has focused on people with severe mental illness—in particular, on people with psychotic disorders. The excellent work of

Drake, Mueser, Minkoff and others has provided a solid base for work with this population. Their work tends to follow the disease model of addiction, which emphasizes an abstinence-based treatment approach.

Despite the clear value of abstinence as an ideal goal, most experts in the field acknowledge that a relapse to drug use and, in some cases, not even being able to interrupt or reduce drug use, are realities with this client population, and that there is a need to continue to work with these clients even (or especially) when they are not abstinent. Looking at concurrent disorders in this way has helped people realize that these are chronic, recurring problems, and that there usually are no quick remedies. Across North America, this approach has led to the development of integrated treatment approaches and community-based care, and to a greater emphasis on open-ended case management and psychosocial rehabilitation of these clients.

When we look at people whose co-occurring substance use and mental health problems are mild to moderate, there is much less research to draw from. However, we know that, while 2.4 per cent of people in general have severe, persistent mental illness (Standing Senate Committee on Social Affairs, Science and Technology, 2002), mild to moderate mental health issues, especially depression and anxiety, are over-represented among people with substance use problems. Substance use problems also range widely in severity, with the majority of problems falling into the mild to moderate range of the spectrum. For example, it is estimated that there are four times as many people with a "drinking problem" as there are people with severe "alcohol dependence" (Institute of Medicine, 1990).

By including people whose problems fit within the mild to moderate range in our approach to concurrent disorders, our goal is not to take attention away from those with severe mental illness or addiction, but rather to extend the scope of our concern to the full set of people affected by co-occurring substance use and mental health problems. Even when problems are less severe, they still have a profound effect on the person, and on families, friends and colleagues.

A benefit of working with people whose problems are mild to moderate is that there is a greater chance of improved outcome. Less severe problems are often easier to treat. And while building social support and hopefulness about positive change is often a primary challenge when working with people with severe addiction and mental health problems, people whose problems are mild to moderate generally have higher levels of support and motivation. The presence of such factors is predictive of more positive results.

BEST PRACTICES

In *Best Practices: Concurrent Mental Health and Substance Use Disorders* (Health Canada, 2002), experts review and comment on the existing scientific literature, and provide consensus where literature does not exist. The document provides opinions from stakeholders, including clients, and is a summation of what we know and don't know, with a large nod to what we don't know.

Constructing a best practice model is an ongoing task of bringing together evidence-based knowledge, and of creating protocols of care that we can justify on the basis of the research and what we know produces better outcomes. That task has begun, and in some areas, such as assessment and screening, there is strong evidence of the best approach. In other areas, however, we don't yet have the knowledge to be able to say, "Here's what you should do . . . ." We can talk about what we do; we have materials that we can share; but we can't say they have been rigorously evaluated. This is not unlike many other domains of health care practice.

There is some crossover between our book and Health Canada's *Best Practices*. Some chapters in this book are written by people who also contributed to that document. The goal here, however, is to offer more detailed and practical information, revealing how we work to provide specialized services to clients. Some of what we present here does not yet have a best practice literature to support it, but it is included to encourage dialogue and contribute to knowledge- and skill-building in these practice areas, where clinical services are needed, in spite of the lack of a strong scientific literature.

THE BIOPSYCHOSOCIAL–SPIRITUAL MODEL

To help us understand the problems of people with concurrent disorders, we think in terms of the biological, psychological, social and spiritual factors involved in the emergence of these problems and—even more importantly—how these four vectors can become pathways to change and recovery.

For example, if a person has psychosis, or is severely depressed, medication works on the biological level to reduce symptoms. Another person, whose anxiety or anger causes out-of-control behaviours, might be able to manage better with cognitive-behavioural strategies learned in psychotherapy. For someone else, social issues may trigger distress or depression that could be improved with interpersonal therapy. And for another, spirituality can provide a pathway for recovery, as people who join 12-step fellowships such as Alcoholics Anonymous often report.

Our service has evolved in response to the needs of a set of clients in a particular urban and regional context. Over the past decade, we have committed ourselves to working with a heterogeneous client population, recognizing that outside our service there are no real options for integrated treatment for most clients with complex problems. Our treatment services have been determined by the real clients in our clinic, rather than by a theoretical model of concurrent disorders. Our inclination has been to accept all comers.

As such, our approaches have been our best practice efforts to respond to the needs of a particular clinical population. We are fortunate to be able to draw on evaluation material that has allowed us, along with emerging knowledge, to review and reshape our activities. This is very much a continuing task, so that this book presents a picture of where we stand now, with a nod toward the past and our development, and a glance toward the future and where we see our work evolving.

ATTITUDE AND STIGMA

Most of us—and this includes professionals as well as lay people—at some point in time will experience negative feelings and thoughts that we will project onto people with substance use or mental health problems. These feelings reflect attitudes that have been formed through the influence of our families, our society, our personal experiences and our own level of understanding. Negative feelings such as fear, moralism, pity, derision and even contempt may be subtle or strong, but, either way, they can have immense power to shape and construct the perceptions we hold of the person toward whom they are directed.

It is not incorrect to describe the effects of these feelings and attitudes as hurtful. In time, these hurtful effects are shaped not just by the external attitudes of others toward people with substance use or mental health problems, but also by the internalized attitudes people with these problems have toward themselves. The mark left by these negative feelings, or stigma, can be more long-lasting than the illnesses themselves.

Attitudes change slowly. Much progress has been made toward people's accepting mental health problems as illnesses, but less so with addiction. Although both can be chronic and relapsing health problems, people tend to make a distinction between the two. Some mental health workers, for example, may see people's psychiatric problems as real illnesses, and their substance use problems as intentional behaviour. Addiction workers, on the other hand, may firmly believe that most people can recover from substance use problems, but think people with serious mental health problems are not capable of significant change. As more mental health and addiction workers learn to work with clients with co-occurring problems, and their understanding of the relationship between substance use and mental health problems increases, client care will become more responsive and effective.

The chapters in this book are intended to serve as an introduction to each of the different aspects of identifying, understanding and treating concurrent disorders. The first part provides an introduction to the field, the second looks at the programs offered here at CAMH, and the third offers some theoretical and therapeutic perspectives. The concluding section looks at what is being done here to expand the capacity of our concurrent disorder services, and what can be done in services outside CAMH to better serve these clients.

For many years, addiction and mental health service providers have worked with clients with concurrent disorders, often not having the knowledge, skill, resources or supports to work effectively with such complex problems. In that sense, the tradition has been to work with this population *in spite of* their co-occurring problems. With the work that has been done to develop more collaborative, integrative approaches to treating concurrent disorders, and with the insights into the inclusive approach to care offered in this book, we hope our readers will be better prepared to welcome the challenges and opportunities of working with these clients, and to work with them not in spite of their co-occurring problems, but *because of* them.

REFERENCES

Health Canada. (2002). *Best Practices: Concurrent Mental Health and Substance Use Disorders.* Ottawa: Minister of Public Works and Government Services Canada, Cat. #H39-599/2001-2E.

Institute of Medicine. (1990). *Broadening the Base of Treatment for Alcohol Problems.* National Academy Press: Washington.

Kessler, R.C., Nelson, C.B., McGonagle, K.A., Edlund, M.J., Frank, R.G. & Leaf, P.J. (1996). The epidemiology of co-occurring addictive and mental disorders: Implications for prevention and service utilization. *American Journal of Orthopsychiatry, 66*, 17–31.

Regier, D.A., Farmer, M.E. & Rae, D.S. (1990). Co-morbidity of mental disorders with alcohol and other drug abuse. Results from the Epidemiological Catchment Area (ECA) study. *Journal of American Medical Association, 264*, 2511–2518.

Standing Senate Committee on Social Affairs, Science and Technology. (2002). *The Health of Canadians—The Federal Role: Final Report on the State of the Health Care System in Canada.* Ottawa: Senate of Canada.

Substance Abuse and Mental Health Services Administration (SAMSHA). (2002). Report to Congress on the Prevention and Treatment of Co-occurring Substance Abuse Disorders and Mental Disorders. Retrieved December 1, 2004, from www.samhsa.gov/reports/congress2002/

Introduction

WAYNE SKINNER

The study of co-occurring substance use and mental health problems, or concurrent disorders, has emerged as a dynamic space, where knowledge and practice are constantly evolving. This sets the stage for lively debates among researchers, the community of professionals who work in addiction, mental health and concurrent disorders, as well as people who are affected by concurrent disorders: clients and their families. Although concurrent disorders—variously known as dual diagnosis, co-occurring disorders or dual disorders—as a discipline is just over two decades old, many clinicians have been attempting for much longer to provide comprehensive care for clients who have substance use and mental health problems.

Over the past 20 years, researchers and clinicians have worked to find common ground between the substance use and mental health systems, each of which had developed strong traditions and treatment approaches, usually funded and operated quite separately from one another. The earliest evidence-based work in the area of co-occurring substance use and mental health problems focused on people with severe mental health disorders. We now recognize that the topic of concurrent disorders encompasses a full range of co-occurring substance use and mental health problems.

MENTAL HEALTH PROBLEMS

The *Diagnostic and Statistical Manual of Mental Disorders* (DSM-IV; American Psychiatric Association, 1994) lists 16 major diagnostic classes of psychiatric disorders. Differential diagnosis requires that the therapist fit mental health problems into one or more categories based on whether the problems meet a defined set of criteria. This can be a difficult task, particularly when behaviours are the result of a complex interaction between substance use and mental health problems. In the first stages of a treatment relationship, it may be useful to take a dimensional approach that looks at problems on a continuum of severity. One advantage of this approach is that it includes symptoms that may be causing distress but that might not meet DSM criteria.

In our clinical work we find it useful to group behaviours into four dimensions:

- *psychosis*: involving problems of cognitive and perceptual organization
- *impulsivity*: including problems of anger and aggression, including risk of harm to self and others
- *mood*: including depression and affective instability
- *anxiety*: involving the problematic inhibition of responses.

Personality disorders (called Axis II disorders in DSM) can also be accommodated in this model. The DSM-IV identifies three clusters of personality disorders:

- *Cluster A* (called the "odd" cluster in earlier versions of the DSM) belongs in the psychosis dimension, and includes diagnoses of schizoid, schizotypal and paranoid personality disorders.
- *Cluster B* (previously called the "dramatic" or "impulsive" cluster) belongs in the impulsive dimension, and includes antisocial, narcissistic, histrionic and borderline personality disorders.
- *Cluster C* (previously called the "anxious" cluster) can be found in the anxiety dimension, and includes compulsive, avoidant and dependent personality disorders.

FIGURE I-1

A dimension approach to mental illness

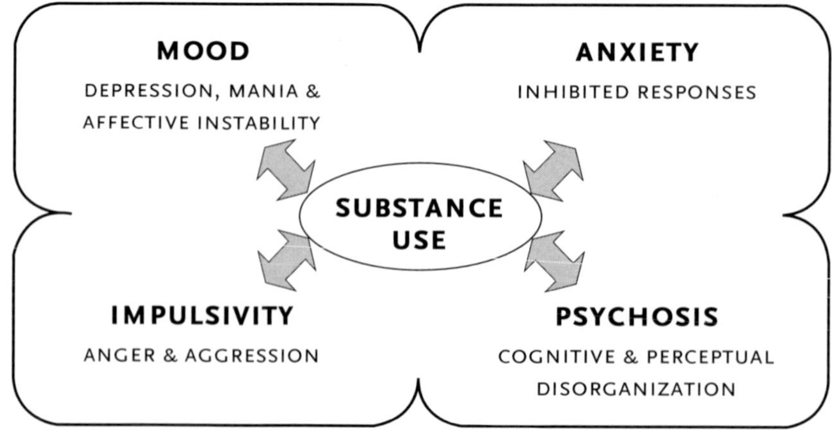

The dimensional approach allows the counsellor to explore the dimensions in which the mental health problems are evident, regardless of whether they are Axis I or Axis II disorders.

SUBSTANCE USE PROBLEMS

We also find it helpful to take a dimensional approach to substance use, by grouping different substances into one of three broad groups, according to their effect on the body and the brain.

- *stimulants*: substances that excite and stimulate mental processes
- *depressants*: substances that dampen and mute mental processes
- *hallucinogens*: substances that alter and distort perceptual and sensing processes.

The number of substances that can be placed in any of these groups is formidable. Yet, from our clinical perspective, *most* clients' primary problems are with:

- alcohol
- cocaine and the amphetamines
- opioids (including heroin and pharmaceutical opioids)
- cannabis
- prescription tranquillizers.

FIGURE I-2

A dimension approach to substance use

STIMULANTS
ACTIVATE & EXCITE MENTAL (AND OTHER) PROCESSES

MENTAL HEALTH

HALLUCINOGENS
ALTER & DISTORT SENSORY PROCESSES

DEPRESSANTS
MUTE & DAMPEN MENTAL (AND OTHER) PROCESSES

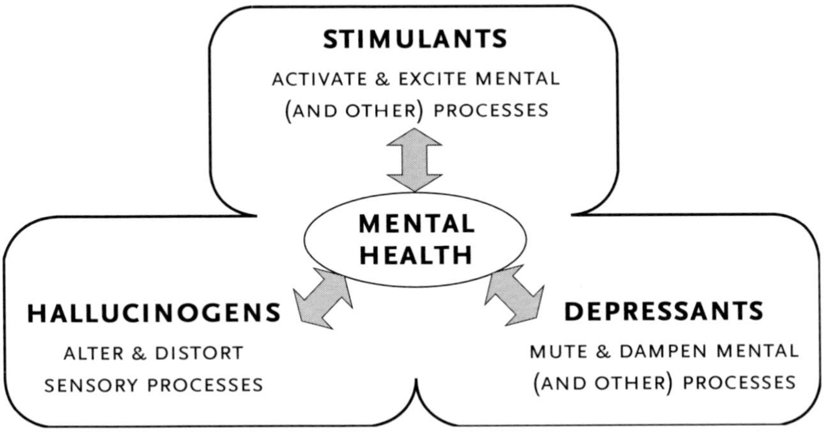

Although, when looking at concurrent disorders, tobacco is not usually identified as the substance for which clients are seeking help, nicotine needs to be identified as problematic. Its prevalence among people who have concurrent disorders is disturbingly high, and its use will seriously affect the health and life course for many clients.

TABLE I-1

Dimensional approach for grouping mental health and substance use problems

DIMENSION	VERBAL BEHAVIOUR	MENTAL HEALTH PROBLEM		SUBSTANCE USE PROBLEM
		AXIS I: MENTAL HEALTH DISORDERS (EXAMPLE)	AXIS II: PERSONALITY DISORDERS (EXAMPLE)	SUBSTANCE-INDUCED DISORDERS (EXAMPLE)
PSYCHOSIS (COGNITIVE-PERCEPTUAL ORGANIZATION)	"weird talk"	schizophrenia, other psychotic disorders, mania	schizoid, schizotypal, paranoid	substance-induced psychotic disorder (e.g., cocaine-induced paranoia), substance-induced delirium
IMPULSIVITY (ANGER/AGGRESSION)	"threat talk"	impulse control disorders, gambling, sexual paraphilias, bulimia, alcohol or other drug abuse/dependence	antisocial, borderline, narcissistic, histrionic	substance-induced impulse control disorder (e.g., amphetamine-induced sexual disorder)
MOOD (DEPRESSION & AFFECTIVE INSTABILITY)	"sad" talk, laconia, "manic/grandiose" talk	depressive disorders, dysthymia, bipolar disorders	affective features often present in personality disorders	substance-induced mood disorder (e.g., heroin-induced depression)
ANXIETY (INHIBITION)	"fear talk"	anxiety disorders, panic disorders, phobias, obsessive-compulsive disorder	avoidant, dependent, obsessive-compulsive	substance-induced anxiety disorder (e.g., cannabis-induced anxiety disorder)

THE RELATIONSHIP BETWEEN SUBSTANCE USE AND MENTAL HEALTH PROBLEMS

Having a mental health problem increases the risk of having a substance use problem, just as having a substance use problem increases the risk of having a mental health problem (Health Canada, 2002). As well, substance use can cause behaviours that mimic symptoms of mental health problems. These substance-induced problems improve as substance use is decreased or stopped.

Factors that affect the relationship

The nature of the relationship between substance use and mental health has been a topic of concern among clients, families and professionals for years. Are the substance use behaviours causing psychiatric symptoms? Are the mental health issues leading people to use substances to get relief from their troubled mental states? Unfortunately, the relationship between co-occurring mental health and substance use problems is usually much more complicated than simple cause-and-effect:

- There can be, for example, *predisposing* factors that affect vulnerability to certain problems.
- There can be *precipitating* factors that relate to the initiation or onset of problems.
- And there are usually *perpetuating* factors that shape the way problems continue.

Even when one problem was clearly present before the other, the problems may interact, and the relationship between them may change over time.

Interaction models

Degenhardt et al. (2003) suggest four types of models to explain concurrent disorders:

- *Common factor models* explain that the same set of factors can contribute to increased risk both of substance use and mental health problems. These risk factors may be biological (genetic or disturbances in neurotransmitter function), related to temperament, social or environmental.
- *Secondary substance use models* hold that mental health problems increase the chances of developing a substance use disorder. The self-medication hypothesis, which holds that people use substances to relieve symptoms of mental health problems, is one well-known example of a secondary substance use model. This explanation appears to be more relevant when considering problems related to mood, anxiety and impulsivity than to psychosis. For example, there is evidence that people use alcohol to help them cope with anxiety problems (Thomas et al., 2003). Other theories include alleviation of dysphoria hypothesis; multiple risk factor model; supersensitivity model; and iatrogenic (problems caused by treatment) vulnerability.

- In *secondary mental health models,* substance use may precipitate mental health problems in people who would not otherwise have developed them. For example, cannabis use may precipitate psychotic symptoms in people who are already vulnerable (Hall & Degenhardt, 2000).
- *Bidirectional models* take the view that one problem increases the person's vulnerability to developing problems in the other area. For example, a person who has severe substance use problems may have problems holding a job. This in turn may increase the person's risk of developing depression.

It is also possible—if not common—to find co-occurring disorders that are largely independent of one another. That is, they are both present, but their interactive effect is weak.

Determining the functional relationship between substance use behaviour and mental health problems often shapes the counsellor's expectation (e.g., of what will happen if the client stops substance use). If the client is experiencing problems directly linked to substance use, stopping or reducing use is likely to lead to improvement in mental health symptoms. On the other hand, if the client is using substances to get relief from distressing mental states or from difficult situations, getting him or her to stop use could worsen the client's subjective experience of distress.

Concurrent substance use and mental health problems also vary in severity. Most mental health services are directed toward helping people who have severe mental illnesses. It is the substance use problems of this population that have had the most influence on the ways that mental health providers have approached concurrent disorders. On the other hand, the addiction treatment system works with people whose substance use problems usually range from moderate to severe. There, the prevalence of mood, anxiety and anger problems has informed the ways that addiction professionals have viewed concurrent disorders (Prim et al., 2000). Thus the treatment setting, and the identified characteristics of the population seeking help in that setting, influence the choice of screening, assessment and treatment approaches.

The four-quadrant framework, developed by the U.S. National Association of State Mental Health Program Directors (NASMHPD) and National Association of State Alcohol and Drug Abuse Directors (NASADAD) Joint Task Force, and adopted by the Substance Abuse and Mental Health Services Administration (Substance Abuse and Mental Health Administration, SAMHSA, 2003), illustrates the range and severity of concurrent disorders within both the mental health and the substance use treatment populations. The framework relates systems of care to problem severity and is intended to help substance use and mental health providers "organize the range of services that can best meet the needs of the individuals with multiple symptoms and varying degrees of severity" (SAMHSA, 2003, p. 59).

Most people with concurrent disorders have mild to moderate substance use and mental health problems. The population-base view (Figure I-3, below) suggests that all levels of the health care system are involved in treating concurrent disorders. There is overlap between these settings, and people may move back and forth based on their stage of recovery.

FIGURE I-3

A population view

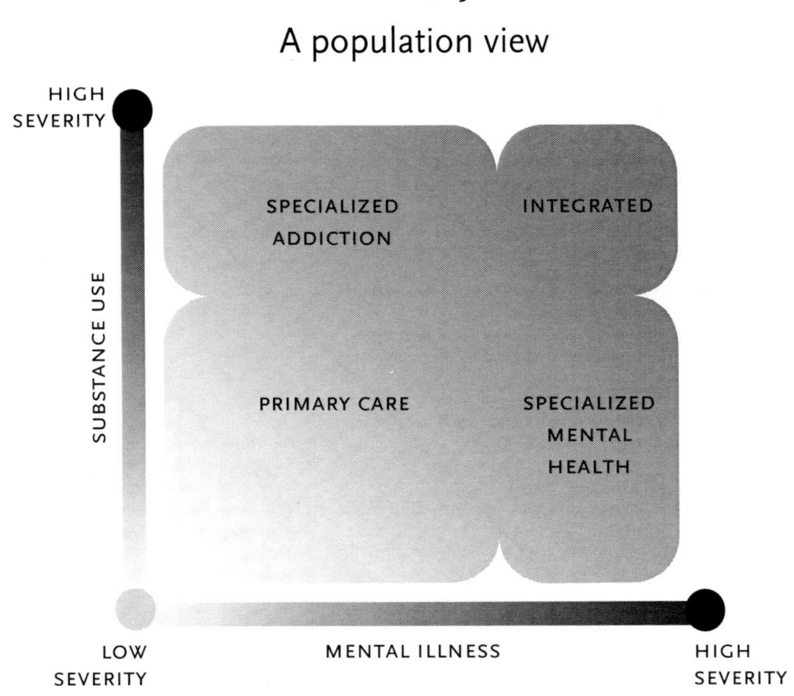

CONCURRENT DISORDERS TREATMENT

Whereas, in the past, substance use and mental health services were often part of separate treatment systems, it is now increasingly recognized that care, for many clients, needs to involve both systems and be delivered in ways that are co-ordinated and collaborative. Treatment for concurrent disorders can be provided at different levels of co-ordination (the choice of level is often determined by the level of severity of the substance use and mental health problems, and the availability of services in a community).

- *consultation*: informal linkages between substance use, mental health and other social service agencies
- *collaboration*: formal links between agencies; can be appropriate for clients who have one moderate and one severe problem (e.g., staff from a mental health and a substance use agency working together to design and implement a treatment plan)
- *integration*: integrated programs providing substance use and mental health treatment within a single treatment setting. Comprehensive integrated program models have been developed in response to the needs of clients with severe mental illness.

FIGURE 1-4
Type of care

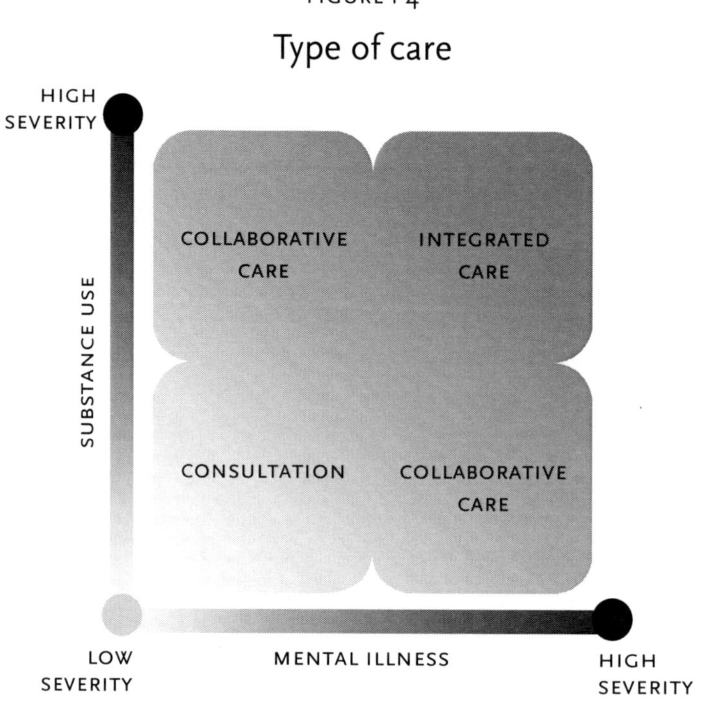

Integrated treatment

Integrated treatment is founded on the assumption that there is a close relationship between substance use and mental health problems and that one problem shouldn't be treated in isolation from the other. The concept was developed to respond to the difficulties clients had when navigating between the substance use and mental health systems. Drake and Mueser (2000) suggest that integrating treatment services shifts the responsibility for navigating and negotiating the complexities of diverse treatment approaches from clients/consumers to the people and agencies that deliver the services.

Broadly defined, integrated treatment is "any mechanism by which treatment interventions for [concurrent disorders] are combined within the context of a primary treatment relationship or service setting" (SAMHSA, 2003, p. 59). One clinician or treatment team takes overall responsibility for blending treatment and support interventions into one coherent package (Drake et al., 2004).

Much of the literature on integrated treatment has concentrated on clients who have substance use and severe mental health problems, particularly psychotic disorders. The needs of this population led to an emphasis on treating substance use and mental health problems simultaneously and within the same treatment program. The definition of integrated treatment has since been widened to also include approaches that involve co-ordination among staff from two or more agencies. This expanded definition also allows for staging of treatment interventions within one co-ordinated treatment plan. Because the approach is co-ordinated and consistent, the treatment should appear seamless to the client (Health Canada, 2002).

PROGRAM/SERVICE-LEVEL INTEGRATION

In integrated programs or services, substance use and mental health treatments are delivered by one team of clinicians and support workers in the same treatment setting (Health Canada, 2002). Most integrated programs that have demonstrated good outcomes include:

- staged interventions
- assertive outreach
- motivational interventions
- counselling
- social support interventions (Drake et al., 2001).

SYSTEM-LEVEL INTEGRATION

If all integrated care required that clients be served in a single program, current service systems would have to be rebuilt from the ground up. As mental health and addiction providers and funders realize the need to work more effectively with clients with complex problems, they are turning to improvements that do not require the creation of a new treatment system. Existing systems can offer improved treatment for the full continuum of concurrent disorders if they establish links among treatment programs, some of which have the capacity to deliver both substance use and mental health treatment, and others that co-ordinate services among two or more agencies, allowing each agency to customize treatment to suit the population it serves (Health Canada, 2002).

COMPONENTS OF AN INTEGRATED SYSTEM

With the recognition of the high rates of co-occurrence of substance use and mental health problems comes an expectation that all substance use and mental health programs will develop at least a basic level of skill at identifying, assessing and working with clients with concurrent disorders.

Kenneth Minkoff (2001) describes four levels of agency capability, based on program categories from the American Society of Addiction Medicine. Using his model, but adapting his terminology to the language of concurrent disorders we are using here, the levels are as follows:

1. Concurrent Disorders Capable—Addictions Program: welcomes people with co-occurring disorders whose conditions are sufficiently stable, so that neither symptoms nor disability significantly interferes with standard treatment. Makes provision for concurrent disorders in program mission, screening, assessment, treatment planning, psychopharmacology policies, program content, discharge planning, and staff competency and training.

2. Concurrent Disorders Capable—Mental Health Program: welcomes people with active substance use disorders for mental health treatment. Makes provisions for concurrent disorders as above. Incorporates integrated continuity of case management and/or stage-specific programming, depending on type of program.
3. Concurrent Disorders Enhanced—Addictions Program: program enhanced to accommodate people with subacute mental health symptomatology or moderate disability. Enhanced mental health staffing and programming, increased levels of staffing, staff competency and supervision. Increased co-ordination with continuing mental health or integrated treatment settings.
4. Concurrent Disorders Enhanced—Mental Health Program: mental health program with increased substance-related staffing skill or programmatic design. For example: day treatment units, providing addiction programming in a psychiatrically managed setting; intensive case management teams, providing premotivational engagement and stage-specific treatment for the most impaired and disengaged individuals with active substance disorders; comprehensive housing or day programs, providing multiple types of stage-specific treatment interventions and substance-related expectations.

Approaches to treatment

Treatment for concurrent disorders needs to include:
- screening both for substance use and for mental health problems
- comprehensive assessment
- psychosocial and pharmacological interventions
- a plan for continuing care and support (SAMHSA, 2003).

However, because the population is heterogeneous, no one set of interventions will be effective for all clients with concurrent disorders (Kavanagh et al., 2003).

Evidence-based care

DEFINITIONS

Research using randomized controlled clinical trials is the gold standard for validating the effectiveness of a treatment intervention in a given population. The next best evidentiary base is research using quasi-experimental designs (comparison groups assigned by randomization), followed by open clinical trials (no independent comparison group). While the evidence base for concurrent disorders interventions is growing, very little in this domain meets that gold standard yet (SAMHSA, 2003).

The (U.S.) Institute of Medicine (2000) has suggested that, where results from randomized clinical trials are not available, it is appropriate to use the following criteria to evaluate treatment approaches:

- *best research evidence*: clinically relevant research, often from the basic health and medical sciences, but especially from patient-centred clinical research, into the accuracy and precision of diagnostic tests (including the clinical examination), the power of prognostic markers, and the efficacy and safety of therapeutic, rehabilitative and preventive regimens
- *clinical expertise*: the ability to use clinical skills and past experience to identify and treat each client's unique state and diagnosis, to assess the individual risks and benefits of potential interventions, and to do so within the context of the patient's personal values and expectations
- *patient values*: the preferences, concerns and expectations each patient brings to a clinical encounter, which must be integrated into clinical decisions if they are to serve the patient.

EVIDENCE FOR TREATMENT INTERVENTIONS

When we consider the evidence that supports approaches to helping people with concurrent disorders, we need to look at subpopulations. Best practices guidelines published by Health Canada (2002) concluded that there was sufficient evidence to support dividing subpopulations into groups who have co-occurring substance use and:

- mood and anxiety disorders
- severe and persistent mental health disorders
- personality disorders
- eating disorders
- other mental health disorders.

For each group, the report reviewed the evidence for:

- what sequencing of substance use and mental health interventions was most effective
- what treatment approaches were most effective.

Despite the high prevalence of concurrent mood, anxiety, impulsivity and substance use problems, and depression and substance use problems (20 to 30 per cent of the general population), there is still very little evidence on appropriate treatment interventions for this group (Kavanagh, 2003). The stronger body of concurrent disorders research with clients with severe mental health problems (which occur in two to three per cent of the general population) needs to be extended to the other domains, where better evaluated treatments could help inform concurrent disorders treatment practices.

Within the concurrent substance use and severe mental illness subgroup, better evidence exists for overall approaches (integrated treatment, stage-wise treatment, motivational techniques) than for any specific treatment intervention (Drake et al., 2004). We need to know more about what components of integrated treatment are the most helpful to clients. The capacity to provide support, beyond episodes of care from which clients are discharged, appears to be an important feature in producing effective outcomes, avoiding relapses and helping clients live more successfully in the community.

Customizing the helping response to the client's stage of treatment and recovery, combined with a pragmatic harm-reduction orientation, appears to enhance engagement and lead to better working relationships between client and counsellor, and to better outcomes (Roth, 1999).

In the end, even as the research knowledge base is evolving, we, as helping professionals, need to start from where we find ourselves. Some clinical questions cannot wait for an evidence-based solution (Goldman et al., 2001). The evidence-building task is more a continuing journey than a destination. Each new contribution to the literature is an occasion for reflection and re-evaluation of existing practices. Counsellors who work with people with concurrent disorders need to combine the best available evidence with clinical expertise, empathy, respect and common sense. And ultimately, because we work *with* people affected by concurrent disorders—clients and their families—we need to pass the test that they set: that they value our work because, in the face of addiction and mental health problems, it helps them live the lives they want for themselves.

REFERENCES

American Psychiatric Association. (1994). *Diagnostic and Statistical Manual of Mental Disorders* (4th ed.). Washington: Author.

Degenhardt, L., Hall, W. & Lynskey, M. (2003). What is co-morbidity and why does it occur? In M. Teesson & H. Proudfoot (Eds.), *Comorbid Mental Disorders and Substance Use Disorders: Epidemiology, Prevention and Treatment* (pp. 10–25). Sydney, Australia: National Drug and Alcohol Research Centre.

Drake, R.E., Essock, S.M., Shaner, A., Carey, K.B., Minkoff, K., Kola, L. et al. (2001). Implementing dual diagnosis services for clients with severe mental illness. *Psychiatric Services, 52*(4), 469–476.

Drake, R.E. & Mueser, K.T. (2000). Psychosocial support to dual diagnosis. *Schizophrenia Bulletin, 26*(1), 105–117.

Drake, R.E., Mueser, K.T., Brunette, M.F. & McHugo, G.J. (2004). A review of treatments for people with severe mental illnesses and co-occurring substance use disorders. *Psychiatric Rehabilitation Journal, 27*(4), 360–374.

Goldman, H.H., Ganju, V., Drake, R.E., Gorman, P., Hogan, M., Hyde, P.S. et al. (2001). Policy implications for implementing evidence based practices. *Psychiatric Services 52*(12), 1591–1597.

Hall, W. & Degenhardt, L. (2000). Cannabis use and psychosis: A review of clinical and epidemiological evidence. *Australian and New Zealand Journal of Psychiatry, 34*, 26–34.

Health Canada. (2002). *Best Practices: Concurrent Mental Health and Substance Use Disorders.* Ottawa: Minister of Public Works and Government Services Canada, Cat. #H39-599/2001-2E.

Institute of Medicine. (2000). *Crossing the Quality Chasm: A New Health System for the 21st Century.* Washington, DC: National Academy Press.

Kavanagh, D.J., Mueser, K.T. & Baker, A. (2003). Management of comorbidity. In M. Teesson & H. Proudfoot (Eds.), *Comorbid Mental Disorders and Substance Use Disorders: Epidemiology, Prevention and Treatment* (pp. 78–120). Sydney, Australia: National Drug and Alcohol Research Centre.

Minkoff, K. (2001). *Behavioral Health Recovery Management Service Planning Guidelines Co-occurring Psychiatric and Substance Use Disorders.* Chicago: Illinois Department of Human Services.

Prim, A.B., Gomex, M.B., Tzolova-Iontchev, I., Perry, W., Vu, H.T. & Crum, R.M. (2000). Mental health versus substance use treatment program for dually diagnosed patients. *Journal of Substance Abuse Treatment, 19*(3), 285–290.

Roth, D. (1999). *Towards Best Practices: Top Ten Findings from the Longitudinal Consumer Outcomes Study 1999.* Columbus, OH: Ohio Department of Mental Health. Retrieved February 2, 2005, from: http://www.mh.state.oh.us/offices/oper/tbp2.pdf

Substance Abuse and Mental Health Administration. (2003). *Report to Congress on the Prevention and Treatment of Co-occurring Substance Abuse and Mental Disorders.* Washington, DC: Author.

Thomas, S.E., Randall, C.L. & Carrigan, M.H. (2003). Drinking to cope in socially anxious individuals. *Alcoholism: Clinical and Experimental Research, 27*(12), 1937–1943.

Part I

Assessment

Chapter 1

Identifying, assessing and treating concurrent disorders: The client–counsellor relationship

WAYNE SKINNER

Only connect.
—*E.M. Forster,* Howard's End

Most texts that discuss ways to identify, assess and treat concurrent disorders concentrate on methods, techniques, tools and instruments. The interpersonal dimensions of working in this area are given, at best, a passing nod. This is understandable: co-occurring substance use and mental health problems are complex and diverse, with patterns of illness and recovery that are dynamic and elusive. To be as helpful as possible, the counsellor needs many resources to understand the client's problems. When clients present with complex problems and histories, the clinician's first consideration tends to be, "What tools will help me screen for substance use and mental health problems and, then, assess comprehensively?"

However, if one is preoccupied with technique, it is easy to forget that the fundamental task for the counsellor is to work with the client and the other people who can play an important role in producing healthy outcomes. This chapter addresses the role of the client–counsellor relationship, serving as a background for the following chapter, which discusses instruments and techniques.

Note: The term client can be used here to refer not only to the narrow description of someone with a diagnosis of a substance use disorder or mental illness, but also to the broader set of people who are affected by substance use and mental health problems, including people who are not formally involved in the health care system. The term also extends to those who are affected by other people's mental health and substance use problems. While the context for a counsellor's involvement with this wide range of people varies, the helping role applies, no matter what the situation.

Evidence of the importance of the client–counsellor relationship

Evidence suggests that the client–counsellor relationship has more influence on engagement and improved outcomes than the methods, tools and instruments we employ (Hubble et al., 1999). Clients coming into treatment facilities for assessment indicate that the warmth and welcoming attitudes of the staff—rather than client perceptions of the staff's skills—are the most important factor in making clients want to return to use the service (Health Canada, 2002).

In a cross-cultural meta-analysis of therapy outcome literature, Asay and Lambert (1999) report that the single most important factor that the counsellor can influence is the therapeutic relationship; this relationship explains 30 per cent of the variance in treatment outcome. Technique and method, which counsellors tend to focus on in their training, was only half as powerful, accounting for just 15 per cent of the outcome variance in therapy. The other factor that the therapist can influence, expectancy (the belief that things will improve or be adequately addressed), accounted for 15 per cent of the variance—the same as technique and method. That leaves 40 per cent of the variance to extratherapeutic factors relating to the client's personal strengths and weaknesses, social supports and environmental resources.

Too often, clinicians have assumed that clients with severe, persistent substance use and mental health problems are too compromised to benefit from the therapeutic relationship in the way healthier clients are. We are now seeing that the opposite is true. Where clients face overwhelming challenges, a respectful, continuing, supportive relationship with a health care provider not only helps people to get through hard times, but also to accomplish positive change.

CHARACTERISTICS OF THE CLIENT–COUNSELLOR RELATIONSHIP

Other research offers information about the interpersonal dynamics between clients and their counsellors (Bachelor & Horvath, 1999):

- For therapy to be successful, a positive client–counsellor relationship is necessary.
- The client–counsellor relationship is usually formed early—within the first few contacts.
- The client's perceptions of the relationship are more relevant to treatment outcomes than are those of the counsellor.
- Counsellors contribute to the relationship by using active listening, respect and responsiveness to build a climate of safety, trust and dependability.
- Clients contribute by becoming active participants, so that a shared view of the work together is developed.
- It is not whether conflict arises (it will), but how it is handled that makes the difference for the future relationship.

KEY CONSIDERATIONS FOR BUILDING A SUCCESSFUL CLIENT–COUNSELLOR RELATIONSHIP

Phases of treatment

One widely used model in concurrent disorders treatment was proposed by Osher and Kofoed (1989). This model divides the process of treatment into four phases:

- engagement
- persuasion
- active treatment
- relapse prevention.

Phases of treatment: Alternative terminology

As useful as these phases are in conceptualizing different components of treatment, their terminology contains some problems:

- Engagement is described as a phase (implying a beginning and an end).
- Persuasion implies that it is a task for the counsellor.
- Relapse prevention is too limited a term for all post-treatment tasks.

ENGAGEMENT

"Engagement" is undoubtedly the start point. As a connection with the client that allows a working alliance to emerge, engagement allows any subsequent helping activity to happen. However, engagement does not end once it is established; it continues as long as the counsellor and client are working together.

PERSUASION OR PREPARATION?

"Persuasion" can be seen as an internal process, in which a person becomes convinced of something about which he or she had an earlier view that is now seen as deficient or wrong. However, particularly in the context of the therapeutic process, the term also rather unfortunately carries the implication that it is the counsellor's task to persuade the client that the client is ill and needs to be in treatment.

An alternative approach is to see this second phase as preparation. In a preparation, rather than persuasion, phase, the counsellor and client work together to:

- understand the client's goals and concerns
- explore what will be the focus of their work together
- look at resources and supports
- decide on the plan of action.

RELAPSE PREVENTION OR CONTINUING CARE?

"Relapse prevention" is a good description of one key task after the active treatment phase is completed, but it is just one of the essential tasks of continuing care. The term "continuing care and support" acknowledges that people with concurrent disorders should be entitled to a team of resources that take an ongoing, respectful and proactive interest in supporting them and their families. Continuing care does not necessarily mean that the client and counsellor must continue to meet regularly, but that, from the counsellor's perspective, the door is always open and the client is welcome, even if the last contact was some time ago.

Using these more descriptive terms, the four phases of treatment would then be:

- engagement
- preparation
- active treatment
- continuing care and support.

Building a working relationship: Connect, understand, proceed

The task of building a relationship between client and counsellor can be summarized in three key concepts: connect, understand and proceed.

For counsellors, every contact with a client is an opportunity to connect in some way. Types of client contact can differ, of course; seeing a client who has been admitted because of a crisis and is heavily medicated is different from seeing the same client later when he or she is well enough to attend a scheduled appointment. But whatever the circumstance, the counsellor must always give priority to the task of connecting with the client.

As the counsellor and client build a working relationship, they negotiate together how to proceed—what to do next, what the longer-term goals are. Even when the client is not able to co-participate in care in the moment (e.g., an involuntary admission because of extreme psychosis or intoxication), the counsellor works respectfully and supportively with the client to address immediate needs and to prepare the ground for future work together.

Attitudes, values and beliefs

When working with people who have concurrent substance use and mental health problems, counsellors need to be willing to explore and acknowledge their own attitudes, values and beliefs about substance use and mental health problems, and the people who are affected by them.

Ongoing, active involvement with clients who have profound problems, in often overwhelming circumstances, affects the counsellor not only professionally but also personally (Skinner & Paterson, 2004). Counsellors need to develop self-awareness of the ways in which their work affects them, and develop strategies for coping and self-care, including supervision and peer support.

PRACTICAL WAYS TO BUILD THE CLIENT–COUNSELLOR RELATIONSHIP DURING SCREENING AND ASSESSMENT

Engaging clients

All too often, the work of engagement is taken for granted. Usually, clients arrive at addiction or mental health programs in active crisis or otherwise seeking help. While counsellors must certainly know how to respond to any client's presenting needs, they must also know how to ensure that the client feels welcomed, respected, listened to, understood and willing to continue. Such engagement puts the counsellor in the best position to negotiate with the client about what to do and how to do it.

This process of connecting and understanding is useful at every stage in the helping process. Often, problems that arise in treatment result from breakdowns in this seemingly simple process. This approach could be described using Figure 1-1: Connect, Understand, Proceed, below:

FIGURE 1-1

Connect, understand, proceed

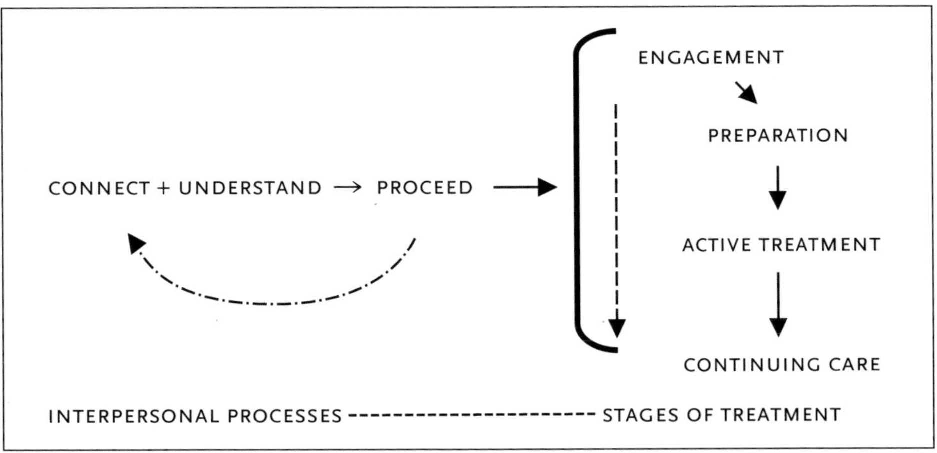

Connecting with clients

It is often assumed that all clinicians are rich in interpersonal skills and that they use these skills when they work with clients. Staff often display the caring and attentive human qualities that make a client feel welcome, safe, comfortable and respected. Indeed, these qualities are often relied on to counterbalance environments, processes and structures that are not client-friendly.

However, evidence, both from clients and from clinical research, suggests that these skills—when clinicians possess them—are underused (Miller & Rollnick, 2002; Roth, 1999). The screening and assessment procedures used in many agencies tend to focus on formal data collection and documentation. In such circumstances, it is easy to forget to look for the unique qualities of each client. As a result, the diverse characteristics of people who have concurrent disorders are reduced to a category that is processed in a rote manner.

THE FIRST MEETING

In the initial contact, whether by phone or in person, counsellors must be particularly attentive, responsive and respectful. This contact is about more than setting an appointment date or collecting information—it is the client's first introduction to you and to the setting in which you work. Clients should leave feeling that the person they spoke with was friendly, knowledgeable, helpful and approachable.

Consider the pace of the interaction. Does it include a greeting? Do you check to see if the client has any questions? Is there a friendly sign-off? Do you ask the client if he or she wants to be reminded to call and make an appointment? (This could raise issues of confidentiality for some clients, who will usually request not to be called.)

Clients should be greeted and introduced to people by name. In all activities, whether an intake or screening appointment or a comprehensive assessment, the counsellor or staff person should give the client an overview of what will be involved and how long it will take, and should ask whether the client has any special needs or concerns.

IMMEDIATE NEEDS NOT SPECIFIC TO THE CONCURRENT DISORDERS

Clients often have very practical concerns that, while they are not necessarily the purpose of the appointment or contact, must also be given priority, such as:

- shelter and housing
- food
- physical health care
- interpersonal crises.

To address these concerns, the counsellor may take direct action or see that the client is connected with community resources that can help. Supporting the client through any crisis is important in itself, and helps build the ongoing connection. Helping the client with practical issues related to physical health (e.g., wounds, infections, dental health) often provides an immediate and very tangible way of showing concern for the client. Roth (1999) concludes that it is the perception of clients/consumers that their needs are met that best predicts positive outcomes, rather than the amounts and types of services received.

TRAUMA

People who seek treatment for concurrent disorders often have a history of sexual, physical, psychological or emotional trauma. More than 50 per cent of women with serious mental illness report some form of physical or sexual abuse, and the incidence is higher for those with concurrent disorders (Substance Abuse and Mental Health Services Administration, 2003).

Asking about possible traumatic experiences should be a routine part of exploring a client's history. Trauma may be an underlying or contributing cause of many of the behaviours and problems that are seen as indications of substance use and mental health problems, including:

- physical problems such as chronic pain and sleep disorders
- impaired sense of self
- relationship difficulties
- problems with memory
- expressions of distress such as suicidal impulses and self-inflicted harm
- mental health problems such as dissociation and depersonalization (Haskell, 2001).

Our experience is that not all clients with trauma histories want to deal with trauma explicitly. Often the most useful first step is to address safety issues, such as helping clients to find a safe place to live. However, some clients seek safe opportunities to talk about their experiences. One of the challenges for counsellors is to know what the scope of their own professional competence is. Where possible, clients with trauma issues should work with qualified, professionally trained therapists who are experienced in providing specialized trauma therapy.

When there are no specialized services available, counsellors should listen and respond with validating statements that acknowledge the client's experience. Counsellors can:

- reframe "symptoms" as "adaptations" or "coping strategies" to trauma
- explain that reacting to and coping with trauma is a normal response to an abnormal event
- offer support by providing information on posttraumatic stress and effects of violence
- help clients to find resources for basic needs such as food, shelter, clothing, physical health and income support.

A lack of specialized services to which clients can be referred means that many counsellors are left in a very lonely and unsupported situation. To be able to have clear limits, to be able to practise self-care, and to be able to draw on collegial support are key ingredients to professional self-management in situations where the optimal resources are not available (Haskell, 2001).

HARM REDUCTION

Counsellors need to respect the client's ambivalence about change—avoiding pushing for premature action and change can contribute to the client's willingness to stay connected to the helping relationship. Rather than push for a large change in behaviour, the counsellor and client can together find a smaller step that the client is able and willing to do.

Related to this is an openness to using harm reduction principles. If clients are injecting drugs, do they have access to clean needles? If they are smoking crack, do they need safer equipment? If they are sexually active, do they have condoms? To connect successfully with clients and help them over the long term, counsellors must accept them as they are, and show concern about their health and safety, even when clients do not want to change risky behaviours. This creates a positive context for the counsellor to encourage and support the client toward healthier options. It recognizes that the pace of change, especially with clients who do not immediately want active treatment, is gradual and incremental.

Another element in working from a harm reduction perspective is to be willing to reach out and connect to the most vulnerable people affected by substance use and mental health problems: those who are marginalized and unable or unwilling to participate in conventional treatment approaches (e.g., clients who are homeless, or clients who have severe substance use or mental health problems). Such clients tend to shy away from traditional services, which require that the client be stable and organized enough to attend scheduled appointments and keep to a structured routine. Finding ways of connecting to and supporting these populations is a particularly important challenge for counsellors to address, given that this population has the highest risk of experiencing serious effects from their problems.

SOCIAL SUPPORT

Besides working to build the counsellor–client connection, counsellors may want to engage and involve other social supports, such as:

- family members with whom the client wants to connect
- peer supports
- other community resources related to leisure, work or recreation.

This includes offering the client information about mutual aid options such as Alcoholics Anonymous, Rational Recovery, Double Trouble Groups and other peer-based supports that can provide fellowship and valuable ongoing support in dealing with substance use and mental health problems.

Understanding the client

An essential function of an assessment is to evaluate the client within a framework that helps determine the client's problems and what services the client may be eligible for. Procedures, tests, instruments, algorithms and decision trees can help the clinician to evaluate these factors.

"Understanding the client" includes this function of assessment, but extends beyond it. It also means understanding clients on their own terms:

- how they see the problem
- the solution they want
- the goals they would like to achieve
- the resources they feel they can draw on
- the strengths that they can draw on
- their sense of their own deficits, barriers, limitations and other negatives that could interfere with reaching their desired outcome.

Understanding has four components:

- subjective: the story as seen through the eyes of the client, without a mediating or interpretive lens being put upon it
- collateral: the information, observations and comments that people who know the client offer to the counsellor
- impressionistic: the clinical observations and questions that the counsellor and other professionals involved in the client's care have
- objective: the client's signs and symptoms as measured, using objective instruments such as screening and assessment tools or diagnostic frameworks such as the DSM.

The challenge in understanding at the screening and assessment stages is to have enough information to be able to confidently proceed to the next stage. The goal of screening is to look for indications that there is a problem that needs to be assessed more comprehensively. The goal of assessment is to determine if the person is eligible and appropriate for a treatment intervention.

Proceeding with the treatment plan

An effective client–counsellor relationship should be the logical consequence of the work done between the client and counsellor in connecting and understanding. When the client and the counsellor make a plan that both agree on and can commit to, and that is based on the client's perceived needs and goals, the more the client feels that the counsellor has an empathic awareness of his or her issues and concerns, and the more willing the client will be to consider taking action and work with the counsellor to follow the plan.

Challenges

Sometimes during screening and assessment it becomes apparent that the program doesn't have the resources to help the client. In such cases, one option is to refer the client to an agency that has more appropriate resources.

However, some communities have no specialized services to draw upon to assess and treat complex cases. In others, the waiting lists for specialized services are too long. Programs and services may have admission criteria that exclude clients with concurrent disorders. Finding psychiatrists or clinical psychologists who can provide psychiatric diagnoses can be a challenge in many communities. These factors make it difficult to get the comprehensive assessment that can inform a fuller understanding of the client and the best options for treatment and other services and supports.

It might be treatment resources that are lacking, so that, while the counsellor understands what would be most helpful, an appropriate program does not exist or is not available in a timely way, if at all, for the particular client.

Solutions at the individual program level often depend on the ability of the worker to make connections with other providers to construct care plans that are uniquely crafted for that client. These connections may be informal (e.g., a phone call asking for advice) or more formal (e.g., inter-agency staff meetings to discuss treatment plans).

Whether the decision is to continue to work with the client or to refer to another program, screening, assessment and treatment should appear to the client to be seamless. It is easy to lose clients during transitional points in the process. Even when counsellors are convinced that they are not the right fit for a client, they need to take responsibility for finding someone to take over care, for managing the transition and for following up to ensure that the new arrangement works.

At the systems level, agency leaders need to advocate and negotiate agreements at the service level for the complex needs of clients. Finally, government funders need to support and to facilitate the alignment of the substance use and mental health systems to develop helping responses that work for clients affected by concurrent disorders.

Taking a person-centred approach

Counsellors need to develop a person-centred approach, starting at the beginning—at the very first stages of the client's involvement with the health care system. The following advice draws on work by Donovan and Moss (2002), Hayes et al. (1999), Miller and Rollnick (2002), Mueser et al. (2003), Rowan and O'Hanlon (1999) and White and Epston (1990):

- Figure out who your client is—is it the person with the substance use and mental health problems, a family member, the court, the referral source?
- Identify and acknowledge the client's point of view.
- Find out what the client wants. Is it the same as what others involved (family, friends, employer, court, probation) are looking for?
- Identify and affirm the person's strengths, competencies, interests and resources.
- Think small—keep the big picture in mind, but look for the small steps that move things in the right direction.
- Remember the person is not the problem, and separate the person from the problems.
- Be aware (and beware) of other people's evaluations.
- You want the client to be committed to the helping process: commit yourself to the client.
- Change happens—especially if you believe in it!

As much as counsellors need skill and expertise, Rowen and O'Hanlon (1999) advise professionals to cultivate a "beginner's mind": "In the beginner's mind there are many possibilities, in the expert's mind there are few" (Suzuki, 1975, p. 21). Couple a beginner's mind with willingness to work at the practical level with the client, and you put yourself in a strong position to realize the transformative potential of the helping relationship.

As stated earlier, the following chapter complements this discussion; it covers ways to approach the technical task of screening and assessing clients for concurrent disorders.

REFERENCES

Asay, T.P. & Lambert, M.J. (1999). The empirical case for the common factors in therapy: Quantitative findings. In M.A. Hubble, B.L. Duncan & S.D. Miller (Eds.), *The Heart and Soul of Change: What Works in Therapy* (pp. 33–56). Washington, DC: American Psychological Association.

Bachelor, A. & Horvath, A. (1999). The therapeutic relationship. In M.A. Hubble, B.L. Duncan & S.D. Miller (Eds.), *The Heart and Soul of Change: What Works in Therapy* (pp. 133–178). Washington, DC: American Psychological Association.

Donovan, D. & Moss, H. (2002). *Dual Disorders: Counselling Clients with Chemical Dependency and Mental Illness* (3rd ed.). Center City, MN: Hazeldon.

Haskell, L. (2001). *Bridging Responses: A Front-Line Worker's Guide to Supporting Women Who Have Post-Traumatic Stress.* Toronto: Centre for Addiction and Mental Health.

Hayes, S., Strosahl, K. & Wilson, K. (1999). *Acceptance and Change Therapy: An Experiential Approach to Behavior Change.* New York: Guilford.

Health Canada (2002). *Best Practices: Concurrent Mental Health and Substance Use Disorders.* Ottawa: Minister of Public Works and Government Services Canada, Cat. #H39-599/2001-2E.

Hubble, M.A, Duncan, B.L. & Miller, S.D. (Eds.). (1999). *The Heart and Soul of Change: What Works in Therapy.* Washington, DC: American Psychological Association.

Miller, W.R. & Rollnick, S. (2002). *Motivational Interviewing: Preparing People for Change.* New York: Guilford Press.

Mueser, K., Noordsy, D., Drake, R. & Fox, L. (2003). *Integrated Treatment for Dual Diagnosis: A Guide to Effective Practice.* New York: Guilford

Osher, F.C. & Kofoed, L.L. (1989). Treatment of patients with psychiatric and psychoactive substance use disorders. *Hospital and Community Psychiatry, 40,* 1025–1030.

Prochaska, J. & DiClemente, C. (1984). *The Transtheoretical Approach: Crossing the Traditional Boundaries of Therapy.* Homewood, IL: Dow Jones/Irwin.

Roth, D. (1999). Towards Best Practices: Top Ten Findings from the Longitudinal Consumer Outcomes Study 1999. Columbus, OH: Ohio Department of Mental Health. Retrieved February 2, 2005, from http://www.mh.state.oh.us/offices/oper/tbp2.pdf.

Rowan, T. & O'Hanlon, W.H. (1999). *Solution-Oriented Therapy for Chronic and Severe Mental Illness.* New York: Wiley & Sons.

Skinner, W. & Paterson, J. (2004). Ethical and professional issues. In S. Harrison & V. Carver (Eds.), *Alcohol and Drug Problems: A Practical Guide for Counsellors* (pp. 73–89). Toronto: Centre for Addiction and Mental Health.

Substance Abuse and Mental Health Services Administration (SAMHSA). (2002). *Report to Congress on the Prevention and Treatment of Co-occurring Substance Use and Mental Disorders.* Washington, DC: Author.

Suzuki, S. (1975). *Zen Mind, Beginner's Mind.* New York: Weatherhill.

White, M. & Epston, D. (1990). *Narrative Means to Therapeutic Ends.* New York: W.W. Norton & Company.

Chapter 2

Screening and assessing for concurrent disorders

JUAN C. NEGRETE

INTRODUCTION

The previous chapter reminded us that the effectiveness of the helping process is largely determined by our abilities to form positive working relationships that recognize the client's goals and address practical issues that lead to even small improvements in everyday life. In this chapter, we will see that part of the expert role of the counsellor is to develop an accurate and useful understanding of the client's problems and strengths. This understanding is usually pursued with increasing detail in the screening and assessment process.

While screening and assessment are often thought of as front-end events that get worked out and set the stage for active treatment, we must also consider them to be continuing and ongoing activities, particularly when trying to understand and help clients with the complex problems resulting from concurrent disorders. Screening and assessment are about the larger process of learning from the client, and about the client, through collateral input and objective measures, so that the helping task is informed by the best information available.

Screening is a preliminary step, often the first one in the evaluation of substance use and mental health problems. It refers to procedures, usually simple and brief, that are used systematically to detect and flag indicators of the probable presence of substance use and mental health problems deserving of a more complete assessment.

However, screening is not only the initial event of flagging issues for more comprehensive exploration. It also refers to ongoing monitoring of the clinical course of substance use and mental health disorders already diagnosed and treated. Systematic or random testing for substance use or medication compliance is an example of this approach, as are rating scales that look at changes in client self-report or objective measures. A core theme of this book is that co-occurring substance use and mental health problems should be more the expectation than the exception. Regular screening for both those conditions should be a standard component of the clinical protocols in mental health and addiction services.

Informal screening can be effected by asking such opening questions as, "Have you ever felt the need to cut down on your drinking?" or "Has there been a time when you were unable to fulfil your daily obligations because you lacked energy or were feeling dejected?" Positive answers to these questions point to the need for a more specific examination of possible problems; in these examples, the questions probe substance use problems and depression—two conditions that commonly co-occur.

Unfortunately, addiction workers do not always feel required or able to screen for the presence of other mental health disorders, and many mental health clinicians do not systematically ask basic screening questions for substance use disorders when conducting psychiatric examinations.

Assessment is the general name given to processes that aim to recognize—with a greater degree of clinical accuracy—the exact nature of the client's situation, including:

- a clinical diagnosis of the problems, including the duration and severity of problems
- the particular characteristics of these problems (i.e., their individual presentation)
- client strengths and social supports
- the client's readiness to engage in treatment
- the specific needs for intervention and treatment planning.

Assessment is also the process that gathers the information clinicians need to make an informed decision about the most appropriate focus of the therapeutic effort, both in the short and long terms. This chapter describes some of the best established practices for screening for substance use and other mental health disorders and discusses the challenge of performing valid and sound clinical evaluations of people who have concurrent disorders.

The choice of screening and assessment processes, methods and tools is influenced by:

- the resources available—one of the most important factors being the limited availability of psychiatrists and clinical psychologists who can make a diagnosis
- characteristics of treatment population.

IDENTIFYING SUBSTANCE USE: CASUAL OBSERVATIONS AND PURPOSEFUL SCREENING

In identifying substance use problems, screening usually takes the form of one or more of the following:

- clinician observation
- narrative reports
- screening questionnaires, and
- toxicology screening.

Clinician observation

In health care and social service settings, clinicians should be aware of a number of health and social factors that are often related to substance use disorders. The following pointers are not definitive or specific evidence of substance use disorders, but indicate the need for further investigation.

REASON FOR FIRST CONTACT

Front-line practitioners should pay attention to the problems or events that caused the person to come to their attention in the first place. Events and problems that could indicate mental illness, substance use problems or both include:

- incidents of domestic violence, physical aggression or public disturbance
- suicide attempts
- accidents, falls, burns, frostbite, fractures or other suspicious injuries
- truancy, vagrancy, homelessness, social isolation or family abandonment.

PATTERN OF SERVICE UTILIZATION AND HELP-SEEKING BEHAVIOUR

Health care workers should take notice of:

- impromptu visits and erratic compliance with follow-up plans
- frequent change of health care providers or concurrent visits to different providers
- frequent requests for medical certificates to justify—often retrospectively—an absence from work, courses, exams or court hearings
- repeated problems with prescriptions for psychotropic medications (prescriptions are lost, cannot be renewed by the regular physician or have been miscalculated)
- insistence on getting specific prescriptions—usually opioids or tranquillizers mentioned by name as the only ones that help.

The possibility of substance use problems should also be considered when clients with severe mental health problems are missing clinic appointments, not taking their prescribed medication or being seen unusually often in the emergency room. Such patterns are often observed in people with co-occurring severe mental illness and substance use problems.

TYPE AND NATURE OF THE HEALTH COMPLAINTS

The range of health problems that can be induced by or related to substance use is extensive. The presence of the following health problems should alert health care and social support workers to the possibility of a substance use problem (Brick, 2004):

- fatty liver, non-viral hepatitis, cirrhosis of the liver or hepatitis B and C

- vomiting blood
- HIV infection
- cellulitis, injection site abscesses
- infectious phlebitis (inflammation of a vein) or endocarditis (inflammation of the heart valve)
- septicemia (blood poisoning)
- lesions in the nasal septum
- fainting spells or loss of consciousness
- delirium
- seizures
- illusions and hallucinations.

An examination for probable substance use disorder is also suggested by the presence of other complaints that are less specific to substance use, such as:

- recurring nausea, heartburn or diarrhea (alcohol)
- chronic running nose (cocaine)
- chest pain or tachycardia in otherwise healthy young persons (cocaine)
- chronic fatigue and other long-lasting or recurring disabilities of unclear origin.

Finally, the following complaints may indicate drug-seeking behaviour:

- chronic pain of undefined origin and the request for opioid analgesics
- repeated episodes of acute pain that require emergency opioid analgesia (e.g., renal colic or migraine-like headache)
- recurring reports of chronic depression or anxiety that does not seem to respond to treatment (benzodiazepines)
- chronic insomnia requiring long-term drug therapy (sedative-hypnotics).

INCIDENTAL FINDINGS IN HEALTH CARE SETTINGS

Incidental observations that should alert clinicians to inquire about substance use problems include:

- accidental trauma due to impaired function
- evidence of repeated traumatic injury in the form of non-surgical scars or several bruises sustained on different occasions
- fortuitous radiology findings of old fractures or sub-periosteal hematomas, usually in the rib cage, shin bones and skull
- needle marks in arms, legs, feet, neck or breasts
- evidence of a pre-existing high tolerance for anesthetics, opioid analgesics or sedative-hypnotics
- routine blood work that shows abnormal liver function, a high mean corpuscular volume (MCV) figure, high blood lipids, hyper- or hypoglycemia
- immunology positive for viral hepatitis or HIV (see Appendix 2: Toxicology Tests for information on biological markers).

However, such observations can also indicate other psychiatric conditions, such as borderline personality disorder, psychomotor hyperactivity and other impulse control disorders. For example, manifestations of such disorders commonly include multiple scars and injuries, which may be the result of self-mutilation, parasuicidal behaviour or accident proneness, which can certainly occur in the absence of intoxication.

Narrative reports and screening questionnaires

Collateral sources of information

Information provided by collateral sources (family, friends, other health care and social service workers) can help to identify a substance use problem. The usefulness of the collateral reports varies with the degree of contact that the person providing them has with the client, and with the person's ability or willingness to disclose the information. Siblings of people who have mental illnesses, in spite of their frequent contact, tend to contribute less than other third parties (Carey & Simons, 2000). Mental health workers who act as case managers for clients who have mental illnesses have proven to be highly reliable sources of information (Carey & Correia, 1998). Brief rating scales have been developed to help these clinicians estimate clients' degree of alcohol (Alcohol Use Scale) or other substance (Drug Use Scale) use (Drake et al., 1996).

Self-reports

The patient/client's own report is often the best evidence that can be gathered in the substance use screening and assessment process. But the subject of substance use must be approached carefully. Because of social stigma and personal feelings of guilt and shame, it is unsurprising that some people are defensive when asked about substance use.

Many self-report questionnaires have been developed and validated for the purpose of determining whether someone is likely to have a substance use disorder. These questionnaires, which present a carefully considered and well-validated set of questions, are particularly useful, because they can be self-administered by the client before or during a clinical assessment. They are generally brief—requiring no more than a few minutes to complete—and the clinician has the option of giving the client a print version or simply asking the questions in the course of an interview.

Although some questionnaires are specifically designed to uncover other drug problems, the largest number of substance use screening instruments addresses problem alcohol use. Only a few of these screening questionnaires have undergone proper evaluation of their psychometric properties among people with severe mental illness.

Questionnaires are listed in the body of the chapter. For those that are commonly used (their names appear in bold typeface), more detailed information is provided in Appendix 1: Screening and Assessment Tools.

ALCOHOL

Tools used to screen for alcohol use problems include:

- the *Michigan Alcoholism Screening Test* (**MAST**) and its variants—the 13-item Short MAST (SMAST) and the Brief MAST (bMAST)
- the ***CAGE***
- the *Alcohol Use Disorders Identification Test* (**AUDIT**).

Several other short screening questionnaires currently in use have not yet been studied for their psychometric properties with people with concurrent disorders:

- the ***TWEAK*** and the ***T-ACE*** (developed to test pregnant women)
- the *RAPS-QF* (used in emergency rooms and trauma centres)
- the *RUFT-Cut* (useful with older adolescents seen in a hospital's emergency department).

OTHER DRUGS

One questionnaire used to screen for illegal substances and prescription drugs is the *Drug Abuse Screening Test* (**DAST**).

COMPOSITE DRUG AND ALCOHOL SCREENING INSTRUMENTS

Instruments have been developed to screen for problems with alcohol *and* other drugs. Some of these instruments are simple variants of the well-proven alcohol tests, such as the *Michigan Assessment–Screening Test for Alcohol and Drugs* (MAST/AD). A modification of the CAGE was tested with older adults and found to be very sensitive in the detection of alcohol and other drug use disorders (Hinkin et al., 2001). The ***CRAFFT*** was specifically designed to screen for both alcohol and other drug use disorders among adolescents.

Problems with accuracy of self-report screening instruments

People with concurrent disorders might be reluctant to disclose all the details about their substance use and its effects on their lives. A strong client–therapist relationship helps to counteract this tendency. Clinicians can use information from family members and other contacts to help evaluate information provided by clients (Mueser et al., 2004).

In an attempt to bypass the minimization and lack of accuracy that can invalidate the responses in self-reports, screening questionnaires have been developed that detect the problem in a less direct manner; others include components to measure reliability of answers. Among these are:

- the *MacAndrew Alcoholism Scale—Revised* (**MAC-R**), which is part of *Minnesota Multiphasic Personality Inventory*
- the *Substance Abuse Subtle Screening Inventory* (**SASSI-3**).

Substance use screening for people with severe mental illness

People who have severe mental health problems often experience adverse consequences at lower levels of substance use than the general population (Rosenberg et al., 1998). Some of the signs that indicate a possible substance use problem—for example, problems with social relationships and employment—are also associated with severe mental health problems (Mueser et al., 2004). Many self-report questionnaires require a degree of cognitive functioning that may not be present when people have severe mental illness (Kavanagh et al., 2003).

To date, the *Dartmouth Assessment of Lifestyle Instrument* (**DALI**) is the only substance use screening instrument that is designed specifically for use with people who have severe mental health problems.

Toxicology screening

(Detailed information about toxicology screening tests is provided in Appendix 2: Toxicology Tests.)

The most conclusive evidence of substance use is found in the person's body. Toxicology screening, which measures substances of abuse in body fluids and hair, is a widely common way to identify and monitor substance use disorders. Toxicology screening is a routine procedure for acute emergencies such as suicidal overdoses, coma, respiratory depression, seizures, chest pain, cardiac arrhythmia, cerebral vascular accidents, delirium or acute psychosis, where it is imperative to find out if a psychoactive substance is playing a causal role. These tests are a reliable method of establishing exactly which substances have been used and in what amounts.

However, the following caveats must be considered when toxicology tests are used to explore the presence of a substance use disorder.

The presence of a substance does not determine dependence

The mere presence of a substance in blood, breath, urine, saliva, sweat, gastric lavage fluid or hair does not reveal the pattern or the nature of use, nor can it determine whether the person is dependent on the substance. However, some toxicology results can be taken as valid evidence of a pattern of chronic and heavy use.

For example, if a person has a high blood concentration reading of a substance, yet does not exhibit the intoxication effects proportionate to the dose, this likely indicates a well-established state of neuroadaptation (tolerance), one of the hallmarks of dependence. This is particularly true for central nervous system depressants such as ethanol, sedative-hypnotics and opioids. Finding blood alcohol levels of 150 mg per dL or more in a person who does not show the signs or symptoms of inebriation is generally accepted as reliable evidence that the person has a history of drinking excessively.

Rates of elimination differ for each substance

Not all of the psychoactive substances commonly misused are equally amenable to detection through toxicology screening. Some, such as ethanol or the opioid Fentanyl, are eliminated rapidly and can only be detected for a few hours after use. Others, such as cannabinoids and long-acting benzodiazepines or barbiturates, remain detectable for much longer.

The results must be interpreted carefully
A positive screening must be judged in context and against the type of substance it has detected. Legal substances, such as alcohol or prescription psychotropics, may be found in persons who do not have a diagnosable substance-related disorder. However, a positive screen for alcohol from a sample taken early in the morning indicates that the person drank heavily the previous evening, or was drinking through the night or in the morning—all strong indications of an alcohol use problem. Similarly, a positive screen for benzodiazepines, barbiturates or methadone, in a person who does not have a prescription for these medications, indicates a likely substance use problem.

IDENTIFYING MENTAL HEALTH DISORDERS

In identifying mental health problems, screening usually takes the form of dimensional screens and diagnostic screens.

Dimensional screens

People who have substance use problems—whether or not they have another concurrent mental health disorder—frequently experience psychological distress, often as a direct consequence of intoxication, withdrawal or both (i.e., substance-induced disturbance). They have been found to score consistently higher than the norm on self-rating procedures that measure current psychological complaints in a general, non-categorical manner. Examples of such instruments are:

- the ***Brief Symptom Inventory*** (53 items)
- the *General Health Questionnaire* (**GHQ-12**).

Both of these instruments require respondents to rank, on a five-point scale, the severity of each symptom they report.

These scales are highly sensitive to point-in-time "symptoms," and the scores have been seen to vary greatly, depending on the status (i.e., active use, withdrawal, sustained abstinence) of the respondent at the time of administration (Pinard et al., 1996). While questionnaires such as these yield valid evidence that the respondent is experiencing active distress at the time of the evaluation, they do not attempt to establish which diagnostic categories or specific disorder is causing the distress. The symptom reports have limited permanence and often do not detect the presence of an independent co-occurring mental illness.

Diagnostic screens

Another approach to the initial psychiatric evaluation is to administer actual diagnostic questionnaires or short structured interviews that follow a succinct schedule of questions.

The *SCID Screen Patient Questionnaire* (**SSPQ**) is a screening tool based on the Structured Clinical Interview for *DSM-IV*™ (**SCID**). It is designed to flag problems that should be followed up by a full SCID interview or clinical evaluation.

The **CIDI-Auto** (the computer-based version of the *Composite International Diagnostic Interview*) and the *Schedules for Clinical Assessment in Neuropsychiatry* (**SCAN**) are intended to provide diagnoses. These instruments can take 90 minutes or more to administer.

Several instruments have been developed to help identify mental health disorders in health care settings, mostly by non-specialized clinicians. These questionnaires are meant to guide the clinical examiner by screening for initial evidence of psychiatric disturbance; their administration is usually to be followed by a medical evaluation. The most frequently used of these instruments are:

- *the Quick Psychodiagnostics Panel* (**QPD**)
- *the Symptom Driven Diagnostic System for Primary Care* (**SDDS-PC**)
- *the Primary Care Evaluation of Mental Disorders* (**PRIME-MD**)
- *the Psychiatric Diagnostic Screening Questionnaire* (**PDSQ**).

COMPREHENSIVE ASSESSMENT OF CONCURRENT DISORDERS

When screening results suggest that a person might have co-occurring substance use and mental health problems, it is recommended that the client have a formal assessment. The usual form in which this occurs is an interview with a health care professional (doctor, psychiatrist, psychologist, nurse) who can make mental health diagnoses. The complete clinical evaluation of concurrent disorders involves:

- precisely identifying the disorders (clinical diagnoses)
- estimating the severity and individual characteristics of these conditions, to determine the person's particular needs and an appropriate treatment approach
- assessing for additional problem areas that can affect treatment planning and effectiveness (e.g., the person's physical health, occupation, housing, social support, legal issues and family relations).

Arriving at a clinical diagnosis

An accurate and comprehensive diagnosis of concurrent disorders is crucial to effective care, but it is often very hard to make; many effects of substance use and substance withdrawal mimic the symptoms of mental health problems and vice versa. Many clients have stories of being inappropriately or insufficiently diagnosed, and their course in care and treatment outcomes has been negatively affected, to the extent that some client rights advocates debate the value of diagnosis at all.

Particularly if a client is offered pharmacotherapy, diagnostic accuracy is crucial, as it determines the drug therapy options open to the doctor to prescribe to the client. Another risk is under-diagnosis—the clinician may reach one diagnosis that explains the client's symptoms, while, in fact, more than one problem is active. In addition, diagnosis in mental health and substance use affects the client's eligibility for different programs and entitlements to supports, financial assistance, housing and other benefits.

Information obtained through screening procedures, even when clearly revealing and fairly specific, does not constitute a proper clinical assessment. Both the evidence of substance use problems and the manifestations of other mental health problems must be systematically explored to determine their nature and significance.

A complete assessment always includes the formulation of a clinical diagnosis that is based on the guidelines currently in force. The American Psychiatric Association's fourth edition of the *Diagnostic and Statistical Manual of Mental Disorders* (DSM-IV) (American Psychiatric Association, 1994) is most frequently used in North America, while the World Health Organization's *The ICD-10 Classification of Mental and Behavioural Disorders* (ICD-10) (World Health Organization, 1992) has been widely adopted in other parts of the world.

Both manuals include *substance use disorders* (*dependence* and *abuse* in the DSM-IV; *harmful use*, in the ICD-10) and *substance-induced disorders* (Mental and Behavioural disorders due to Psychoactive Substance use, in the ICD-10). These disorders encompass a wide array of behaviours that are the expression of brain disturbances experienced during intoxication or withdrawal (e.g., mood, anxiety, psychotic, sleep, sexual and cognitive disorders). One of the key diagnostic challenges is to figure out if the symptoms the client is experiencing are related to substance use behaviour or are manifestations of co-occurring mental illness.

SUBSTANCE USE

The diagnosis of *substance dependence* is made when a minimum set of three, from a list of nine (DSM-IV) or seven (ICD-10), manifestations of the disorder are present within a period of 12 months. Those symptoms are considered to be expressions of the following basic phenomena:

- a process of progressive neuroadaptation (tolerance, withdrawal) to the effects of the substance
- a loss of capacity to moderate or control the frequency and amount of use
- the exaggerated priority that substance use has acquired in the person's life
- the persistence of use despite the person's awareness of its harmful consequences.

For substance use to be considered a clinical problem, it must minimally be associated with psychological distress or functional impairment.

A diagnosis of *substance abuse* (DSM-IV) or *harmful use* (ICD-10) applies to maladaptive patterns of use that lead to significant impairment or distress, as indicated by least one of the following:

- recurrent neglect of obligations and responsibilities
- repeated instances of reckless or hazardous use
- continuing use in spite of legal, social or interpersonal problems.

For a diagnosis of substance *abuse*, the person must not show symptoms of tolerance or withdrawal, or evidence of inability to exert voluntary control on his or her substance use; otherwise the proper diagnosis would be substance *dependence*.

In a clinical interview, it is hard to elicit enough details to be certain that all necessary criteria have been met to make a valid diagnosis of substance use disorder. The difficulty is compounded when examining clients who have concurrent mental health disorders, because they can be unable or unwilling to share information.

Provisional diagnosis

In addition, some mental health disorders can present with symptoms very similar to those that would be found in intoxication or withdrawal states (e.g., diaphoresis, tremors, insomnia, tachycardia, dilated pupils, fatigue, psychomotor restlessness, perceptive distortions, impaired concentration, or attention or memory problems). Similarly, some behavioural criteria in the substance dependence diagnostic list—such as progressive social withdrawal, abandonment of previous interests and activities, or personal neglect—could result from psychiatric impairment rather than substance use. These caveats must be considered when attempting to determine the extent of the patient's substance use problems without any collateral information or the objective evidence provided by toxicology screening.

A definitive conclusion about the true magnitude of a substance use problem in people with co-occurring mental health problems (e.g., chronic psychoses, bipolar disorder, borderline personality disorder) is sometimes possible only after long-term observation, data gathering and evaluation, including the reports of case managers and other front-line care providers.

MENTAL HEALTH

Clinical practice can be complicated by unreliable symptom reports and questionable psychiatric diagnoses in people who have substance use problems. People who are intoxicated or in withdrawal may have symptoms that mimic mental health disorders. Such substance-induced symptoms—while they have no real permanence or diagnostic significance—may linger for some time after cessation of use.

Differentiating between substance-induced and independent mental health problems

The relationship between mental health and substance use problems in a person can vary, making it impossible to offer a step-by-step guide to reaching a diagnosis (see Introduction). However, looking at the following parameters can help guide a differential diagnosis between substance-induced and independent mental health disorders:

- the sequential order in which the symptoms appeared
- whether the symptoms improve significantly if the person abstains from substance use
- whether the mental health problems recur when the person is not using substances
- how the substance use and mental health problems change over time.

Particularly when a client is in active distress, the clinical team does not have the luxury to wait until the relationship between the mental health and substance use problems is completely clear. Care can be started on the preliminary diagnosis. The client's response to treatment provides additional evidence that can help the clinician decide whether the preliminary diagnosis is correct. If it is not, the treatment team can see if interventions indicated by other possibilities are more effective.

Sequential order of appearance of symptoms

Clearly, a mental health disorder can be deemed to have been caused by substance use only if the latter was present before the onset of the former. But this seemingly obvious rule is hard to apply, because the use of psychoactive substances tends to start earlier than the expected age of first emergence of many mental health disorders. The DSM-IV guidelines stress that a diagnosis of substance-induced disorder should be made only when a direct temporal connection can be established between the development of psychiatric symptoms and earlier states of intoxication or withdrawal.

Not all mental health problems that occur after substance use problems emerge are the result of substance use—however, all diagnoses of substance-induced mental health symptoms must show that the substance use problem precedes the mental health issues.

Significant improvement of symptoms during sustained abstinence

The DSM-IV suggests that, on average, the spontaneous remission of substance-induced problems can be expected to occur within four weeks of sustained abstinence from the substance. This timeframe must be interpreted cautiously: it does not apply equally to every type of psychiatric symptom or to all substances of abuse. Alcohol or cocaine-induced psychoses, for instance, usually remit in matter of days, not weeks. By contrast, some benzodiazepine-induced disturbances, such as anxiety or sensory-perceptive changes, might last much longer than four weeks after withdrawal.

Recurrence of psychiatric symptoms in periods of remission of the substance use disorder

Periods of abstinence from the substance can offer insight into how independent the two disorders are from one another. For example, if a reduction or cessation in substance use correlates with a return of mental health problems, it suggests that the mental health problems may be triggering the substance use behaviour, as the client tries to find relief from these symptoms. Even when mental health disorders (e.g., psychosis) occur at the same time as severe substance use problems, it would be risky to diagnose a substance-induced disorder if there is a significant family history of mental health problems.

Cross-sectional, single interview assessments are often insufficient to determine whether mental health problems are substance-induced or "primary." The client usually needs to be re-evaluated after a period of abstinence of several weeks. The most helpful information comes from a reliably gathered sequence of the clinical history—an inquiry that meticulously examines the onset and course of each diagnostic parameter in relation to intoxication and withdrawal states.

The *Psychiatric Research Interview for Substance and Mental Disorders* (**PRISM**) was designed to provide clear guidelines for differentiating between the effects of substance use and independent psychiatric problems (Hasin et al., 1998; Hasin et al., 1996).

Longitudinal assessment

Assessment should be seen as an ongoing process, one that extends over a period of time, including a period of abstinence or significant reduction in use. One of the strongest recommendations made by experts in the field is for assessment to be conducted over more than one interview and to include multiple sources of information (Health Canada, 2002).

The *Longitudinal, Expert, All Data* procedure (LEAD) is an approach to overcoming the limitations of single interview assessments. (Kranzler, 1997). The LEAD was proposed as the set of information that should serve as the gold standard when validating other assessment methods.

The client's substance use and other mental health disorders are well-identified through this longitudinal approach, particularly because it allows the clinician to judge the disorders' stability over time, through all the changes in substance use and mental health status.

The diagnoses arrived at by the LEAD have been found to have fair to good validity and permanence (Kranzler, 1997), based on:

- multiple observations by expert clinicians
- data gathered in medical and other service records over time
- information from front-line care providers and other collateral sources.

Assessing individual characteristics

When assessing individual characteristics, clinicians look at:

- the severity of the client's substance use problems (including substances used, and quantity and frequency of substance use)
- the client's individual vulnerability (factors that can jeopardize or interfere with treatment effectiveness)
- the client's own expectations about the effects of the substances used
- the client's readiness to engage in treatment and effect change in substance use behaviour
- the severity of the client's mental health symptoms
- additional considerations.

SEVERITY OF THE SUBSTANCE USE PROBLEMS

Obtaining information about the severity of the substance use and associated functional problems is an important step in determining short-term and long-term treatment needs, objectives and appropriate interventions. The DSM-IV nomenclature provides for some clinical estimation of severity status when diagnosing a substance use disorder (e.g., dependence that is active, in partial remission or in full remission). However, instruments have been developed that provide a more precise, quantitative rating. Quantitative ratings are useful as an initial measure of severity; when repeatedly applied, they also help track the course of the disorder and evaluate treatment outcome.

Other publications offer comprehensive listings of instruments that rate severity (Allen & Columbus, 1995; Donovan, 1999; National Institute on Drug Abuse, 1994). The following instruments have been used for, or should be reasonably valid in, measuring severity of substance use problems in people with concurrent mental health disorders.

Measuring severity of alcohol problems

- The *Alcohol Dependence Scale* (**ADS**) inquires about recent occurrence of the most frequent and severe symptoms of alcoholism.
- The *Severity of Alcohol Dependence Questionnaire* (**SADQ**) asks clients to rate how often they experience each of a list of symptoms of alcohol withdrawal or tolerance.
- The *Alcohol Use Scale* (**AUS**) helps clinicians classify the level of severity of a client's alcohol use problem, using information collected over a six-month period.

Measuring severity of other drug problems

Several substance-specific scales are available. The severity of opioid dependence, for instance, can be quantified with instruments that measure the subjective distress (i.e., self-rating) or the objective signs (i.e., examiner's estimate) of the withdrawal state.

These scales include:

- *Subjective Opiate Withdrawal Scale* (**SOWS**)
- *Objective Opiate Withdrawal Scale* (OOWS)
- *Clinical Institute Narcotic Assessment* (CINA)

- *Halikas-Crosby Drug Impairment Rating Scale for Cocaine* (**HC-DIRS-C**)
- *Minnesota Cocaine Craving Scale (***MCCS***)*
- ***Cocaine Craving Scale***
- *The Marihuana Screening Inventory* (**MSI-X**).

COMPREHENSIVE ASSESSMENT OF SUBSTANCE USE SEVERITY

Measuring severity by evaluating and ranking multiple substances used

People who have substance use disorders rarely have a single-substance consumption pattern (Health Canada, 2002). Effective assessment tools must evaluate not only the types of primary substances that are being used, but also explore the presence of other substance-related problems.

Several standardized quantitative approaches yield comprehensive ratings of the complete substance use profile. Such evaluation can help summarize the client/patient's overall status at admission to treatment. Standardized evaluation:

- helps in formulating treatment plans and selecting the most appropriate therapy approach
- establishes an objective correlation between problem ratings and treatment outcome
- provides a common problem description that can be adopted by all players in the field
- quantifies patient/client status at follow-up.

Measuring quantity and frequency of substance use

A quantitative measure of substance use at the initial assessment can:

- help evaluate the severity of a substance use problem
- help assess treatment outcome
- create the foundation for measuring change over time
- when reviewed periodically, provide a useful longitudinal understanding of the client's substance use and other potentially addictive behaviour.

Note that quantity and frequency cannot be used as absolute reference points with people who have concurrent disorders. For example, for clients who have severe mental health problems, we must look at the functional effects of any substance use, rather than assume that small amounts and infrequent use have few negative consequences (Mueser et al., 2004).

The following tools offer a comprehensive profile of substance use:

- The *Addiction Severity Index* (**ASI**) is a semi-structured interview that yields quantitative scores of severity in seven separate problem areas: a) medical status, b) employment status, c) alcohol use, d) drug use, e) legal status, f) family/social relations and g) psychiatric status.
- The *Substance Dependence Severity Scale* (**SDSS**) is a semi-structured clinical interview that evaluates diagnostic symptoms and use pattern for alcohol, cocaine, heroin, stimulants, methadone, other licit opioids, sedatives, cannabis, other hallucinogens and two "other drugs" categories (e.g., inhalants).

- The *Maudsley Addiction Profile* (**MAP**) is a multidimensional instrument that quantifies major problems presented by people with substance use disorders, including in the area of psychological health. The authors intended it mainly for treatment outcome research, but it does offer clinicians a well-structured schedule to measure substance use problems in other circumstances.
- The *Global Appraisal of Individual Needs* (**GAIN**) is a structured tool for the comprehensive assessment of substance use problems. It obtains and integrates data on the respondent's background and treatment arrangements, substance use, physical health, risk behaviours, mental health, environmental factors, legal/justice problems and vocational/occupational status.

Timeline Followback (TLFB) is one of the best known and most widely used clinical methods to record client self-report information on substance use (Sobell & Sobell, 1996). In addition to the data on substance use, the method can chart events related to substance use or to mental health impairment, such as work days missed, visits to or stays in health care facilities, homelessness or occurrence of risk behaviours (Carey et al., 2001; Mueser et al., 1995). The TLFB has been tested and found satisfactory with respondents who have mental illnesses (Carey, 1997); however, the reliability of responses is enhanced when using it over a shorter time (i.e., one week) than the one-month period suggested in the original user's manual.

INDIVIDUAL VULNERABILITY

One of the principles of effective treatment is understanding the client's unique issues, so that individualized plans of care can be developed. Some assessment tools help identify factors that can jeopardize or interfere with the person's chances of engaging in the necessary process of change and of remaining relapse-free after the change has been achieved. Some of these instruments provide quantitative ratings of particular vulnerabilities that can inform treatment planning. When used repeatedly as a follow-up assessment, these ratings can also measure the progress made in treatment. Such tools include the following:

- The *Inventory of Drinking Situations* (**IDS**) is available in a long (IDS-100) or a short version (IDS-42). It helps clients become more aware of the possible motivations that drive their drinking behaviour and provides the evaluator with a map of situations in which the client is at elevated risk.
- The *Inventory of Drug Taking Situations* (**IDTS**) is a complementary instrument, which profiles the client's degree of risk in different types of situations—again, helping not only to understand where problems have occurred, but also to know what to target when helping the client.

MEASURES OF EXPECTANCY

Assessment should also look at the client's own expectations about the effects of the substances used. Measures of expectancy are essential when designing individualized cognitive treatment approaches. The following instruments yield expectancy scores:

- *Alcohol Expectancy Questionnaire* (AEQ)
- *Alcohol Beliefs Scale* (ABS)
- *Comprehensive Effects of Alcohol Scale* (CEOA)
- *Cocaine Expectancy Questionnaire* (CEQ)
- *Cocaine Effect Expectancy Questionnaire—Likert* (CEEF-L)
- *Marihuana Effects Expectancy Questionnaire* (MEEQ).

Information on these instruments can be found in Donovan's (1999) "Assessment Strategies and Measures in Addictive Behaviors."

READINESS TO ENGAGE IN TREATMENT AND EFFECT CHANGE IN SUBSTANCE USE BEHAVIOUR

Evaluating the degree of motivation for change is now widely accepted as a regular component of therapy for substance use problems. It has also been included in concurrent disorders treatment guidelines (Minkoff, 2001). Several procedures measure readiness for change in people with substance use problems. Some have been specifically tested in people who have concurrent disorders.

Tools that measure motivation for change are meant to assess the patient/client's readiness to undergo therapy for substance use disorders; the use of such tools with people who have concurrent substance use problems and mental illness has yielded inconclusive results.

Ziedonis and Trudeau (1997), for instance, studied the effectiveness of one method of evaluating motivation for change in people with psychosis. While they elicited answers that permitted them to place people at a well-defined stage of change, those who qualified for the more advanced "action" and "maintenance" levels were no more likely to be involved in treatment for their substance use disorder than were those in the "pre-contemplation" and "contemplation" stages.

Motivational enhancement is a constructive way of communicating with clients about substance use behaviours, as well as other issues, such as medication compliance. When using the stages of change as a measurement tool, note that motivational readiness does vary over time and across substance use behaviours. For example, a client might be ready to take action on stopping cocaine use but does not want to stop smoking tobacco or cannabis.

Self-report instruments

- The *University of Rhode Island Change Assessment Scale* (**URICA**) yields four summary scores corresponding to the stages in the transtheoretical model of change.
- *The Stages of Change Readiness and Treatment Eagerness Scale* (**SOCRATES**) evaluates motivation for change in alcohol use (version 5A) and drug use (version 5D).

Clinician-administered instruments

- The *Substance Abuse Treatment Scale* (**SATS**) assesses the level of substance use treatment involvement in patients with co-occurring substance use and mental health disorders. This instrument was designed to be consistent with a model of dual diagnosis treatment that recognizes eight stages: pre-engagement, engagement, early persuasion, late persuasion, early active treatment, late active treatment, relapse prevention, and remission or recovery.

SEVERITY OF MENTAL HEALTH SYMPTOMS

In addition to making categorical diagnoses, the clinical evaluator can use quantitative scales to rate the severity of mental health symptoms. Severity rating establishes a baseline against which to measure the changes that take place in treatment. Some severity scales cover a wide spectrum of symptoms, such as:

- the *Brief Psychiatric Rating Scale* (**BPRS**)
- the *Positive and Negative Syndrome Scale* (**PANSS**).

Both of these instruments yield quantitative values and have been widely used to rate symptoms in people with psychosis and concurrent substance use problems. (Margolese et al., 2004).

These instruments must be administered by clinicians with training in mental status examinations. Also, as with any clinical assessment interview, clients who are under the influence of, or in withdrawal from, alcohol or other drugs often provide invalid ratings.

Severity of symptoms: Specific disorders

Other instruments measure specific disorder syndromes. Some of the most widely used are:

- the *Young Mania Rating Scale* (YMRS) (Young et al., 1978), which rates the severity of the symptoms of mania in the three core dimensions of hedonism, dysphoria and activation
- the *Hamilton Depression Rating Scales* (**HAM-D**) in the longer (21 and 17 items) and the more recent and shorter (seven items) versions (McIntyre et al., 2002)
- the *Montgomery-Asberg Depression Rating Scale* (**MADRS**).

Self-Report

Among the most widely used disorder-specific self-administered rating scales are:

- the *Beck Depression Inventory* (**BDI**)
- the *Beck Anxiety Inventory* (**BAI**).

ADDITIONAL CONSIDERATIONS IN THE CLINICAL MANAGEMENT OF CONCURRENT DISORDERS

Psychosocial functioning

In addition to the evaluation parameters already discussed (severity of substance use, individual vulnerability, expectations, treatment readiness and severity of mental health problems), clinicians also need to assess other predictors of better treatment outcomes, including the client's:

- general medical condition
- family and social situation
- housing
- legal status
- occupation.

Some treatment and rehabilitation programs for people with concurrent disorders have incorporated interventions aimed at helping the patient/client obtain and maintain low-risk housing and stable employment (Drake et al., 2001).

The American Society of Addiction Medicine (ASAM) treatment placement guidelines are often used to help rate the severity of the client's situation (Mee-Lee, 2001). The ASAM evaluation grid assesses six dimensions or problem areas for the client:

- intoxication and withdrawal risks
- readiness for treatment
- risk of relapse
- general health
- psychiatric status
- environmental support that he or she can count on in recovery.

Deciding on appropriate treatment arrangements

The main purpose of assessment is to gather information that guides the choice of appropriate therapeutic interventions. The ASAM Patient Placement Criteria (Mee-Lee, 2001) recognize five levels of service for treating substance use problems, in a rank order of increasing complexity and sophistication:

- early intervention
- outpatient treatment
- intensive outpatient/partial hospitalization services
- residential inpatient treatment
- medically managed intensive inpatient treatment.

There is a range of specific levels of care within these broad categories.

This ranking of services may not reflect the structure of care outside the United States and is limited to the placement choices available in the American addiction treatment system. Also, it does not include options within the mental health services. The treatment of people with concurrent disorders is usually offered within several models of care (Drake et al., 2001):

- sequential treatments
- parallel treatments
- integrated treatments.

Sequential treatments

In sequential treatments, one of the problems is treated first and, only after the first, the other. This is usually an undesirable approach, for the presence of the untreated coexisting disorder is likely to jeopardize the treatment of the targeted disorder, particularly when, for example, a person with a severe mental illness is referred for addiction treatment first.

However, sequential treatment may be the most rational approach for patients with milder affective disorders or anxiety (e.g., social phobia, panic disorder) who must stop their pattern of frequent intoxication before some state-of-the-art therapies (e.g., cognitive-behavioural approaches) can be implemented.

Parallel treatments

In parallel treatments, both problems are treated at the same time but separately, in two disconnected systems of care. Parallel treatment is often the only possible arrangement to deal comprehensively with the concurrent disorders. However, as with sequential treatments, people who have severe mental illness may have problems in accessing and benefiting from addiction programs, which are usually intensive, time-limited and not flexible enough to accommodate them. Moreover, the client may be unable to adjust to and synthesize the very different philosophies that guide the therapy in the two systems of mental health and substance use services. Indeed, the person risks being exposed to conflicting messages.

Nonetheless, parallel care can be feasible when:

- The person is less psychiatrically disturbed.
- The person needs specialized mental health interventions that are available only in a limited number of places (e.g., for eating disorders, sexual paraphilias, pathological gambling, OCD, ADHD).

Integrated treatments

When the substance use and the mental health disorders are treated conjointly and under a single program leadership, this is known as integrated treatment. This model is particularly useful for people who have a concurrent substance use disorder and severe and persisting mental illness. A body of scientifically gathered evidence supports this approach over any other options for treating people who have concurrent substance use disorders and severe mental illness (Mueser et al., 2004).

DECIDING BETWEEN SEQUENTIAL, PARALLEL AND INTEGRATED TREATMENTS

The severity of the mental health disorder and the substance use disorder (as well as what services are available in a region) largely determines which approach is the most appropriate:

- When the mental illness is severe, there is little choice but to refer the patient to a mental health program, hoping that it would provide the addiction treatment as well.
- When the mental health disorder is not severe, clinicians have more options. Such patients may benefit from substance use programs with little or no psychiatric input.

Recent discussion of the systems-level implications of concurrent disorders has led to suggestions that integrated approaches (all services given by one provider) may be harder to effect than integrative strategies that bring mental health and substance use providers together in collaborative programming for clients with co-occurring problems (Health Canada, 2002).

DECIDING BETWEEN RESIDENTIAL AND OUTPATIENT TREATMENT

The decision to refer the patient for inpatient as opposed to outpatient (ambulatory) treatment is usually based on the following criteria:

- There is a history of severe withdrawal events and need for withdrawal management under round-the-clock nursing or medical supervision.
- The pattern of substance use is so entrenched that the person will find it extremely difficult to alter it if not removed from his or her usual environment.
- The person is in poor general health, will need active or intensive medical care, or has disabilities that impede attendance to ambulatory programs.
- The person has significant psychiatric pathology (e.g., high anxiety, strong suicidal urges, severe cognitive impairment, psychotic disorganization) that requires intensive treatment.
- The conditions at home are too unfavourable (e.g., aloneness, lack of support, presence of others who are still using, social chaos).

Residential care is also the option when there is a need for a prolonged stay in therapeutic communities that provide comprehensive milieu therapy. It may be the right decision for people who have concurrent disorders who have not made progress as outpatients and who present with psychiatric disorders that are best treated in controlled environments (e.g., Cluster B personality profiles, chronic psychoses non-responsive to ambulatory care) (Drake et al., 2004).

THE NEED FOR A PERSON-CENTRED, CONTINUING CARE APPROACH

Beyond access to residential care for crisis, beyond re-evaluation and stabilization, and beyond intensive treatment programming, work in concurrent disorders must focus on models of care that are continuing, comprehensive and collaborative, that go beyond a narrow frame of client and counsellor to include family, peer and community support. Screening and assessment become invaluable practices, not just at the start of care, but as ways of monitoring progress, preventing relapse and keeping the focus on client needs, satisfaction and life goals. The more that treatment activities point the client positively and hopefully toward improved functioning and recovery, the more the client will use them constructively (Trainor et al., 2004).

REFERENCES

Allen, J.P. & Columbus, M. (Eds.). (1995). *Assessing Alcohol Problems: A Guide for Clinicians and Researchers.* NIAAA Treatment Handbook Series 4. Rockville MD: National Institute on Alcohol Abuse and Alcoholism, NIH Publication No. 95-3745.

American Psychiatric Association. (1994). *Diagnostic and Statistical Manual of Mental Disorders* (4th ed.). Washington, DC: Author.

Brick, J. (Ed.). (2004). *Handbook of the Medical Consequences of Alcohol and Drug Abuse.* Binghamton, NY: The Haworth Press.

Carey, K.B. (1997). Reliability and validity of the Timeline Follow-Back interview among psychiatric outpatients: A preliminary report. *Psychology of Addictive Behaviors, 9,* 26–33.

Carey, K.B. & Correia, C.J. (1998). Severe mental illness and addictions: Assessment considerations. *Addictive Behaviors, 23*(6), 735–748.

Carey, K.B. & Simons, J. (2000). Utility of collateral information in assessing substance use among psychiatric outpatients. *Journal of Substance Abuse, 11*(2), 139–147.

Carey, M.P., Carey, K.B., Maisto, S.A., Gordon, C.M. & Weinhardt, L.S. (2001). Assessing sexual risk behavior with the Timeline Follow-Back (TLFB) approach. *International Journal of STD & AIDS, 12,* 365–375.

Donovan, D.M. (1999). Assessment strategies and measures in addictive behaviors. In B.S. McCrady & E.E. Epstein (Eds.), *Addictions: A Comprehensive Guidebook* (pp. 187–215). New York: Oxford University Press.

Drake, R.E., Essock, S.M., Shaner, A., Carey, K.B., Minkoff, K., Kola, L. et al. (2001). Implementing dual diagnosis services for clients with severe mental illness. *Psychiatric Services, 52*(4), 469–476.

Drake, R.E., Mueser, K.T., Brunette, M.F. & McHugo, G.J. (2004). A review of treatments for people with severe mental illness and co-occurring substance use disorders. *Psychiatric Rehabilitation Journal, 27*(4), 360–374.

Drake, R.E., Mueser, K.T. & McHugo, G.J. (1996). Clinical rating scales: Alcohol use scale (AUS), Drug use scale (DUS), and Substance abuse treatment scale (SATS). In L.I. Sederer and B. Dickey (Eds.), *Outcome Assessments in Clinical Practice* (pp. 113–116). Baltimore, MD: Williams & Wilkins.

Hasin, D., Trautman, K. & Endicott, J. (1998). Psychiatric research interview for substance and mental disorders: Phenomenologically based diagnosis in patients who abuse alcohol or drugs. *Psychopharmacology Bulletin, 34*(1), 3–8.

Hasin, D.S., Trautman, K.D., Miele, G.M., Samet, S., Smith, M. & Endicott, J. (1996). Psychiatric research interview for substance and mental disorders (PRISM). *American Journal of Psychiatry, 153*(9), 1195–1201.

Health Canada. (2002). *Best Practices: Concurrent Mental Health and Substance Use Disorders.* Ottawa: Minister of Public Works and Government Services Canada, Cat. #H39-599/2001-2E.

Hinkin, C.H., Castellon, S.A., Dickson-Furman, E., Daum, G., Jaffe, J. & Jarvik, L. (2001). Screening for drug and alcohol abuse among older adults using a modified version of the CAGE. *American Journal on Addictions, 10*(4), 319-326.

Kavanagh, D.J., Mueser, K.T. & Baker, A. (2003). Management of comorbidity. In M. Teesson & H. Proudfoot (Eds.), *Comorbid Mental Disorders and Substance Use Disorders* (pp. 78–120). Sydney, Australia: National Drug and Alcohol Research Centre, University of New South Wales.

Kranzler, H.R., Tennen, H., Babor, T.F., Kadden, R.M. & Rounsaville, B.J. (1997). Validity of the longitudinal, expert, all data procedure for psychiatric diagnosis in patients with psychoactive substance disorders. *Drug and Alcohol Dependence, 45*(1–2), 93–104.

Kush, F.R. & Sowers, W. (1996). Acute dually diagnosed inpatients: The use of self-report symptom severity instruments in persons with depressive disorders and cocaine dependence. *Journal of Substance Abuse Treatment, 14*(1), 61–66.

Margolese, H.C., Malchy, L., Negrete, J.C., Tempier, R. & Gill, K. (2004). Drug and alcohol use among patients with schizophrenia and schizoaffective disorder: Levels and consequences. *Schizophrenia Research, 67*(2–3), 157–166.

McIntyre, R., Kennedy, S., Bagby, M. & Bakish, D. (2002). Assessing full remission. *Journal of Psychiatry & Neuroscience, 27*(4), 235–239.

Mee-Lee, D. (2001). *ASAM PPC-2R: ASAM Patient Placement Criteria for the Treatment of Substance-Related Disorders* (2nd rev. ed.). Chevy Chase, MD: American Society of Addiction Medicine.

Minkoff, K. (2001). Developing standards of care for individuals with co-occurring psychiatric and substance use disorders. *Psychiatric Services, 52*(5), 597–599.

Mueser, K.T., Clark, R.E., Haines, M., Drake, R.E., McHugo, G.J., Bond, G.R. et al. (2004). The Hartford study of supported employment for persons with severe mental illness. *Journal of Consulting and Clinical Psychology, 72*(3), 479–490.

Mueser, K.T., Drake, R.E., Clark, R.E., McHugo, G.J., Mercer-McFadden, C. & Ackerson, T.H. (1995). A toolkit for evaluating substance abuse in persons with severe mental illness. Cambridge, MA: The Evaluation Center.

National Institute on Drug Abuse. (1994). *Mental Health Assessment and Diagnosis of Substance Abusers, Clinical Report Series* (NIH Publication No. 94-3846). Rockville MD: Author.

Negrete, J.C. (1993). The significance of psychiatric co-morbidity findings in substance abusers. In D. Riley (Ed.), *Dual Disorders* (pp. 23–31). Ottawa: Canadian Centre on Substance Abuse.

Pinard, L., Negrete, J.C., Annable, L. & Audet, N. (1996). Alexithymia in substance abusers: Persistence and correlates of variance. *American Journal on Addictions, 5*(1), 32–39.

Rosenberg, S.D., Drake, R.E., Wolford, G.L., Mueser, K.T., Oxman, T.E., Vidaver, R.M., et al. (1998). Dartmouth Assessment of Lifestyle Instrument (DALI): A substance use disorder screen for people with severe mental illness. *American Journal of Psychiatry, 155*(2), 232–237.

Sobell, L.C. & Sobell, M.B. (1996). *Timeline Followback User's Guide: A Calendar Method for Assessing Alcohol and Drug Use.* Toronto: Addiction Research Foundation.

Trainor, J., Pomeroy, E. & Pape, B. (2004). *A Framework for Support* (3rd Ed.). Toronto: Canadian Mental Health Association.

World Health Organization. (1992). *The ICD-10 Classification of Mental and Behavioural Disorders.* Geneva: Author.

Young, R.C., Biggs, T., Ziegler, E. & Meyer, D.A. (1978). A rating scale for mania: Reliability, validity and sensitivity. *British Journal of Psychiatry, 133*, 429-435.

Ziedonis, D.M. & Trudeau, K. (1997). Motivation to quit using substances among individuals with schizophrenia: Implications for a motivation-based treatment model. *Schizophrenia Bulletin, 23*(2), 229–238.

Chapter 2: Appendix 1
Screening and assessment tools

The collection of tools that can be used for screening for and assessing substance use and mental health problems is extensive and is growing rapidly. Some questions to consider when choosing from the list of alternatives:

- Will the instrument provide data that are relevant to your clients' treatment needs?
- Is the client form easy to use?
- Has it been tested and used with groups of people who are similar to the clients with whom you work (e.g., age, gender, cultural background)?
- How long does it take to administer and score?
- Is training required to administer the test and interpret the results?

This appendix contains brief descriptions of the instruments that are discussed in the chapter. The following resources provide more detailed information:

American Psychiatric Association. (2000). *Handbook of Psychiatric Measures.* Washington, DC: Author.

Koocher, G.P., Norcross, J.C. & Hill, S.S. (1998). *Psychologists' Desk Reference.* New York: Oxford University Press.

McCrady, B.S. & Epstein, E.E. (Eds.) (1999). *Addictions: A Comprehensive Guidebook.* New York: Oxford University Press.

Allen, J.P. & Wilson, V.B. (2003). *Assessing Alcohol Problems: A Guide for Clinicians and Researchers* (2nd ed.). Bethesda, MD: National Institute on Alcohol Abuse and Alcoholism (NIH Publication No. 03-3745). Available at: www.niaaa.nih.gov/publications.

Dawe, S., Loxton, N.J., Hides, L., Kavanagh, D.J. & Mattick, R.P. (2002). *Review of Diagnostic Screening Instruments for Alcohol and Other Drug Use and Other Psychiatric Disorders* (2nd ed.). Canberra: Australian Government Department of Health and Ageing. Monograph series No. 48. Available at: www.health.gov.au.

DEFINITIONS

Sensitivity is a measure of how well a tool detects the problem it is intended to detect. For example, a substance use screening tool with high sensitivity will identify most of the people who are subsequently diagnosed with a substance use disorder.

Specificity is a measure of how well a tool avoids giving a positive result when a problem doesn't exist.

Validity describes what the test measures and how well it does so. An instrument has good *content* validity if it measures all aspects of the particular condition. *Construct* validity requires that the instrument measure only those characteristics of the condition or construct it was designed to measure. *Concurrent* validity refers to the relationship between scores on the instrument of interest and another measure of the same construct or a diagnosis completed at the same time. *Predictive* validity, on the other hand, is the extent to which scores on a measure will accurately predict a person's future scores or behaviour.

Reliability refers to the instrument's ability to measure a construct consistently. *Test-retest* reliability is determined by administering the same instrument on two occasions and comparing the scores. *Inter-rater* reliability compares the conclusions of two or more trained observers.

A **structured interview** has rigid rules of administration. Questions are asked in the same way every time.

In a **semi-structured interview**, standard initial questions are provided but the interviewer may reword questions if necessary to clarify the meaning.

A **clinical interview** begins with a list of topics or general questions. Follow-up questions are determined by the information provided by the participant.

SCREENING: ALCOHOL

THE ALCOHOL USE DISORDERS IDENTIFICATION TEST (AUDIT)

(Saunders et al., 1993)

The AUDIT is composed of 10 separate items depicting evidence of alcohol misuse, including measures of quantity and frequency of drinking. These questions can be answered on a severity scale ranging from zero to four, for a possible total score of 40. Results of eight points or more are considered indicative of harmful drinking.

As it covers a wider spectrum of indicators, this screening instrument has been found to apply as well among female as in male respondents (Bradley et al., 1998) and among teenagers as in adults (Knight et al., 2003). But its sensitivity among older adult respondents was reported to be somewhat lower than the MAST-G's (Morton et al., 1996).

The AUDIT has been repeatedly used to screen for alcohol use disorders in psychiatric settings, and its psychometric properties with this particular population have been found to be fairly acceptable. However, as is the case with other self-report screeners, this instrument tends to yield a high proportion of false positives among people who have a mental illness—77 per cent, according to a recent study (Carey et al., 2003).

THE CAGE QUESTIONNAIRE

(Mayfield et al., 1974)

The CAGE is an effective set of four screening questions that can identify alcohol problems with a high degree of sensitivity. It performs better when administered to people in treatment for alcohol problems than as a screener in the community at large (Bisson et al., 1999). The specificity of the CAGE has been found to be weaker in older adults, and a modified version, which excludes the first question (i.e., "cut down"), has been suggested to decrease the rate of false positives in this population (Hinkin et al., 2001). With a sensitivity as low as 37 per cent among adolescents, the CAGE is not recommended for use with this age group (Knight et al., 2003).

In psychiatric populations the CAGE appears to perform as well as in the general population, particularly in lifetime occurrence of alcohol use disorders. But it seems to be less useful in detecting a currently active alcohol use disorder, a problem that may require a more pointed approach (Dyson et al., 1998).

THE MICHIGAN ALCOHOLISM SCREENING TEST (MAST)

(Selzer, 1971)

The 24-question MAST and its variants—the 13-item Short MAST (SMAST) and the 10-item Brief MAST (bMAST)—are self-report instruments with perhaps the longest and most widespread use.

The MAST questionnaire, which emphasizes the psychosocial consequences of problem alcohol use, was shown to possess a high sensitivity when it was validated in samples of people who were in treatment for problem alcohol use and who were contacted in addiction centres.

The rate of false negatives is considerably larger among people who may have an alcohol use disorder but who are not in treatment for this problem (Negrete & Alansari, 1987). Its ability to detect alcohol use disorders in older adults is also lower than the norm, so that modified geriatric versions (i.e., MAST-G and SMAST-G) have been proposed to improve sensitivity in this population (Moore et al., 2002; Morton et al., 1996). Similarly, the MASTs are not as sensitive with women's drinking problems as they are with their male counterparts (Bradley et al., 1998). As the MAST questionnaire was originally developed for adult responders, it is less useful as a screening tool for adolescents. Although there have been attempts at adapting it to this population, the modified form has not significantly improved on its performance (Snow et al., 2002).

Teitelbaum and Mullen (2000) concluded that, in psychiatric settings, the sensitivity of this instrument is better than its specificity. In other words, several of the questions tend to evoke a positive answer from people receiving psychiatric services who do not have an alcohol use disorder. A higher-than-recommended score should therefore be adopted as the indicator in this particular population.

T-ACE

(Sokol et al., 1989)

T-ACE is a four-item tool that substitutes a question on alcohol tolerance (How many drinks can you hold?) for the "guilt" item in the CAGE. The T-ACE has shown consistently higher sensitivity than the MAST or the CAGE when used to screen for alcohol problems in women who are pregnant (Chang et al., 1998).

THE TWEAK

(Russell et al., 1991)

TWEAK is an acronym for Tolerance (T-1: number of drinks to feel the effect; T-2: number of drinks one can hold), Worry (preoccupation with drinking), Eye-opener (morning drinking), Amnesia (alcoholic blackouts) and Cut down on drinking (C/K). Studies have shown that the TWEAK outperforms the CAGE and the MAST in screening for alcohol problems in women who are pregnant (Chang et al., 1999).

SCREENING: OTHER SUBSTANCES

THE DRUG ABUSE SCREENING TEST (DAST)

(Skinner, 1982)

The DAST, a 28-item questionnaire, and its shorter variant (DAST-10), were developed to detect all forms of problematic use of illicit substances and prescription drugs. Several trials of this instrument with samples of people with different types of mental illness (Carey et al., 2003; Cocco & Carey, 1998; Maisto et al., 2000; Staley & el-Guebaly, 1990) have reported satisfactory performance in discriminating between DSM diagnostic criteria for substance use disorders. The full-length version has proven sensitive at cut-off scores between six and 11 points. A cut-point of two has been recommended as appropriate when using the DAST-10 among persons with severe mental illness (Maisto et al., 2000). The high sensitivity value assures that very few cases of drug abuse will go undetected, but this comes at the expense of the instrument's low specificity; the DAST-10 yielded a high rate of false positives in a psychiatric hospital population (59 per cent).

The DAST-A, a 27-item version that has been modified for use with respondents in the 13 to 19 age range, includes questions on drug-related behaviours that are typical of adolescents. A trial with teenage psychiatric inpatients demonstrated that this variant of the DAST is capable of discriminating, in a psychiatric inpatient setting, between adolescents who have and do not have substance use disorders (Martino et al., 2000).

SCREENING: ALCOHOL AND OTHER DRUGS

THE CRAFFT

(Knight et al., 2002)

With only six items, the CRAFFT can be completed within two minutes. At a score of two as optimal cut-point, this questionnaire was able to identify cases of substance dependence 92 per cent of the time, but, like most short screeners, the specificity value is considerably lower (Knight et al., 2003). Preliminary results have indicated that the CRAFFT is an accurate screen for substance abuse disorder in adolescents (Knight et al., 2002). No specific information is available on the performance of this instrument in cases of concurrent disorders.

THE DARTMOUTH ASSESSMENT OF LIFESTYLE INSTRUMENT (DALI)

(Rosenberg et al., 1998)

The DALI was developed and validated with samples of people with severe mental illness who were contacted at mental health facilities, not in addiction treatment centres. It is an 18-item interviewer-administered scale that takes approximately six minutes to complete.

The first three questions deal with lifestyle issues and are meant to reduce respondent defensiveness; they do not count for the scoring. The remaining 15 questions have been drawn from six other widely used screening/assessment instruments: Reasons for Drug Use Screening Test, TWEAK, CAGE, DAST, ASI and Life-Style Risk Assessment Interview. The authors of the DALI selected these items because they were the ones most often endorsed by people with substance use disorders and severe mental illness when answering the original questionnaires. A validation trial with patients with severe mental illness showed the DALI to yield better sensitivity and specificity results than any of these tests (Rosenberg et al., 1998).

To date, the DALI is the only substance use disorder screening instrument specifically constructed for use with people with severe mental illness.

MACANDREW ALCOHOLISM SCALE—REVISED (MAC-R)

(Butcher et al., 1989)

The MAC-R consists of 49 items embedded within the 567 questions of the Minnesota Multiphasic Personality Inventory. Originally proposed to reveal a personality trait profile commonly present in people with alcohol abuse disorder, the MAC-R has also been found to detect proclivity toward problem substance use and pathological gambling (Smith & Hilsenroth, 2001). The MAC-R appears able to identify people with substance use disorder among samples of people diagnosed with borderline personality disorder (Smith & Hilsenroth, 2001).

THE SUBSTANCE ABUSE SUBTLE SCREENING INVENTORY (SASSI-3)
(Miller et al., 1997)

SASSI-3 is a 93-item questionnaire containing eight subscales. It must be administered by a clinician and takes at least 15 minutes to complete. It is intended to explore for evidence of substance use disorders while checking for the respondent's tendency to misrepresent.

Not surprisingly, this screener has been used with people who may have a vested interest in not disclosing their problem, such as young people with conduct disorder who are in conflict with the law (Rogers et al., 1997). It has also been tried in psychiatric populations, including samples of people with severe mental illness. In both cases it was found to show unacceptably low positive predictive values. In fact, it appears that the sections of the instrument most sensitive and specific to the problem of substance abuse are the ones that ask direct questions, rather than the "subtle" subscales. As a whole, when used with people who have concurrent disorders, the SASSI yields no better results than the much simpler CAGE (Clemens, 2002).

SCREENING: PSYCHIATRIC DISORDERS

BRIEF SYMPTOM INVENTORY
(Derogatis et al., 1983)

The BSI is a 53-item self-report questionnaire based on the SCL-90-R. It provides an overview of symptoms and their intensity. The BSI consists of nine scales: somatization, obsessive-compulsive, interpersonal sensitivity, depression, anxiety, hostility, phobic anxiety, paranoid ideation and psychoticism. The BSI also provides three global indices: overall psychological distress level, intensity of symptoms and number of self-reported symptoms.

These scales are highly sensitive to point-in-time "symptoms," and the scores tend to vary greatly, depending on the status (i.e., active use, withdrawal, sustained abstinence) of the respondent at the time of administration (Pinard et al., 1996).

CIDI-AUTO
(Andrews & Peters, 2000)

The Composite International Diagnostic Interview (CIDI) is a standardized interview schedule designed to provide DSM and ICD diagnoses.

The CIDI-AUTO is a computer-based version that can be administered by an interviewer or completed by the client. It takes between 20 to 90 minutes to complete, depending on the specific diagnoses selected. The reliability and validity of version 2.1 is currently under assessment, but earlier versions have been found to have acceptable to good inter-rater and test-retest reliability and acceptable validity, although the CIDI-Auto (like the CIDI) appears to be less sensitive than diagnoses made by clinicians.

There are no studies of the CIDI-Auto with people in substance abuse settings (Samet et al., 2004). Andrews and Peters (2000) report that clients tend to feel more comfortable completing the CIDI-AUTO than the interview version of the CIDI, and that the CIDI-AUTO allows them the opportunity to disclose information that has not been addressed in previous interviews.

GENERAL HEALTH QUESTIONNAIRE (GHQ)

(Goldberg & Williams, 1988)

The GHQ was designed to measure overall psychological health by looking at inability to carry out normal functions and symptoms of a distressing nature (Goldberg & Williams, 1988). There are several versions of the GHQ. One, the GHQ-28, has four subscales: somatic symptoms, anxiety and insomnia, social dysfunction and severe depression. These subscales do not necessarily correspond to specific diagnoses. It takes fewer than 10 minutes to complete. The GHQ-28 and its shorter version, the GHQ-12, were developed for use in community and non-psychiatric settings.

QUICK PSYCHODIAGNOSTICS (QPD) PANEL

(Shedler et al., 2000)

QPD screens for nine common disorders: major depression, dysthymic disorder, bipolar disorder, generalized anxiety disorder, panic disorder, obsessive-compulsive disorder (OCD), bulimia nervosa, alcohol or substance abuse, and somatization disorder.

This automated, self-administered procedure requires the patient to use a hand-held computer; it can be completed within 10 minutes. It has been validated in primary care settings and found to have acceptable levels of sensitivity and specificity for the target disorders (Shedler et al., 2000).

THE PRIMARY CARE EVALUATION OF MENTAL DISORDERS (PRIME-MD)

(Spitzer et al., 1994)

The PRIME-MD consists of a 26-item self-report, the Patient Health Questionnaire (PHQ), followed by a clinician's review of the answers and administration of a clinician-administered structured interview comprising five modules that correspond to the five classes of disorders covered by the procedure. Clinicians use only the modules that are indicated by the answers given in the PHQ. The PHQ questions explore the presence of currently active disorders only (e.g., depression in last two weeks, anxiety in last month).

Introduced in a pencil-and-paper version several years ago, the PHQ is now also available in a computerized interactive voice response format, which patients can access by phone (Kobak et al., 1997). This self-report part of the procedure has been found to be comparable to the complete PRIME-MD in sensitivity and specificity (Spitzer et al., 1999). Significant drawbacks are the limited range of disorders it explores (i.e., none of the psychoses nor drug dependence) and the relatively high level of cognitive function required of the respondent.

The PRIME-MD and its shorter component, the PHQ, have been found useful for psychiatric screening in primary care settings (Spitzer et al., 1999), but their performance with people with substance use disorders still needs a more specific study. Indeed, there were only a few cases of alcohol use disorder and no other substance use disorders among the 585 respondents who underwent a psychiatric diagnostic interview to test the psychometric properties of the PHQ.

THE PSYCHIATRIC DIAGNOSTIC SCREENING QUESTIONNAIRE (PDSQ)

(Zimmerman et al., 2004)

The PDSQ is a self-administered instrument that, in its most recent revision (Sheeran & Zimmerman, 2004), explores the current (in the last two weeks) occurrence of symptoms corresponding to 15 of the most prevalent Axis I disorders (dysthymia and anorexia are excluded).

Respondents answer highly sensitive stem questions. A positive answer leads to a list of questions designed to identify symptoms that indicate the presence of specific disorders. The length of the list varies from one disorder to the other, depending on the number of items contained in the DSM-IV diagnostic criteria for each of them.

A positive screen for a disorder is recorded when a minimum of positive answers (based on a specific cut-off figure for each disorder) has been scored. The occurrence of psychotic disorders is screened on the basis of six general questions rather than the specific symptom clusters; the instrument is thus not devised to identify this type of disorder in a diagnostic manner. Estimated average completion time of the self-administered portion is 15 to 20 minutes, after which a trained staff person must compute each scale and record the results.

The PDSQ has been extensively validated with people attending ambulatory psychiatric clinics, and its psychometric properties found quite satisfactory (Zimmerman et al., 2004). Indeed, the instrument's negative predictive values (NPV) in patients without substance use disorders range from 87 to 99 per cent, depending on the particular psychiatric diagnosis. The rate of false negatives is even lower among people who have substance use disorders (NPV range from .93 to 1.0).

However, as can be expected from all sensitive screeners, the specificity figures are considerably lower, particularly in people who are patients of mental health services and have concurrent substance use disorders, so that the positive predictive value of the PDSQ among this population ranges from merely .14 (obsessive-compulsive disorder) to .62 (depression). The demographic profile of the validation samples was rather narrow (high percentages of female and middle-aged participants, no public or uninsured patients), and the performance of this instrument has yet to be tested in more typical addiction programs populations.

SCHEDULE FOR CLINICAL ASSESSMENTS IN NEUROPSYCHIATRY (SCAN)
(Wing et al., 1990)

SCAN is a set of instruments that measures psychopathology and behaviour associated with psychiatric disorders. It consists of a structured clinical interview schedule (the Present State Examination), a glossary of differential definitions, the Item Group Checklist (IGC) and the Clinical History Schedule (CHS). It is only available to people who have completed specialized SCAN training.

Limited data are available on the reliability and validity of SCAN when it is used with clients with concurrent disorders (Samet et al., 2004).

SCID SCREEN PATIENT QUESTIONNAIRE (SSPQ)
(First et al., 1997)

The SSPQ is the computer-administered screening instrument based on the Structured Clinical Interview for *DSM-IV*™ (SCID). It covers the major areas of psychopathology: mood disorders, anxiety disorders, substance use disorders, psychotic symptoms, somatoform disorders and eating disorders.

Clients respond to questions on-screen. There are approximately 76 questions included in the basic SSPQ. However, fewer questions are usually administered. The average interview takes about 20 minutes to complete.

SYMPTOM DRIVEN DIAGNOSTIC SYSTEM FOR PRIMARY CARE (SDDS-PC)
(Weissman et al., 1998)

The SDDS-PC covers six non-psychotic disorders and has three components: a self-administered, 26-item screening questionnaire, a set of six diagnostic modules to be selectively applied by a clinical examiner to confirm the presence of the disorders that screened positive, and a longitudinal tracking form that allows the clinician to register changes from visit to visit (Leon et al., 1996). This instrument does not screen for the more severe psychiatric pathology. A computerized, quicker version of the self-assessment questionnaire is now available (Weissman et al., 1998).

COMPREHENSIVE ASSESSMENT

PSYCHIATRIC RESEARCH INTERVIEW FOR SUBSTANCE AND MENTAL DISORDERS (PRISM)
(Hasin et al., 1998; Hasin et al., 1996)

The PRISM was designed to help distinguish between the expected effects of intoxication and withdrawal, and substance-induced disorders and independent disorders

(Hasin et al., 1998; Hasin et al., 1996; Samet et al., 2004). The authors of this extensive and detailed instrument assert that its application significantly improves the test-retest reliability of psychiatric diagnoses, particularly that of major depression. But it has not been shown yet that it matches the validity of a clinical evaluation conducted after a period of abstinence. Even in the revised version, the PRISM interview can last more than 90 minutes. It must be administered by interviewers with a high degree of training in its use.

ASSESSMENT: SEVERITY OF ALCOHOL USE

THE ALCOHOL DEPENDENCE SCALE (ADS)

(Skinner & Allen, 1982)

The ADS is a 25-item paper-and-pencil self-administered questionnaire that inquires about the recent (last 12 months) occurrence of the most frequent and severe symptoms of alcohol use disorders. The respondent rates the severity of each symptom on a three-point scale. It is usually completed within five minutes. This instrument has been in use for more than 20 years; its psychometric properties are good, including among people with coexisting mental illness.

THE ALCOHOL USE SCALE (AUS)

(Drake et al., 1996)

The AUS, a five-point clinician-rated scale, uses information gathered over a minimum of six months and can only be meaningfully employed with people who have been in regular contact with the rater during that period. This scale has been specifically devised to measure the severity of alcohol problems in people with severe mental illness.

THE SEVERITY OF ALCOHOL DEPENDENCE QUESTIONNAIRE (SADQ)

(Stockwell et al., 1983)

The SADQ is a self-report questionnaire with 20 items grouped into five separate scales. It is usually completed within five minutes. Each scale contains four statements about a particular symptom of neuroadaptation (alcohol withdrawal or tolerance) in ascending order of severity. The respondent is asked to rate on a four-point scale how often he or she experiences the symptom described in each statement. A score of 30 or more, out of a possible 60 points, correlates with clinicians' ratings of severe dependence.

There are no reports on the performance of this instrument with people who have severe and persisting mental illness, but it has been widely used with people with alcohol use disorders and moderate mental illness.

ASSESSMENT: SEVERITY OF OTHER SUBSTANCE USE

COCAINE CRAVING SCALE (CCS)

(Weiss et al., 1997; Weiss et al., 2003)

The CCS is a three-item self-rating tool developed and used to predict the likelihood of continuing cocaine use in people who are being treated for that problem. In that sense, this instrument serves as an indication of the severity of cocaine dependence. As with the opioid questionnaires, the effects of coexisting psychiatric problems on the readings obtained with the cocaine scales do not appear to have been studied. However, it could be presumed, for instance, that the values should be influenced by factors such as anxiety or personality pathology (e.g., borderline personality disorder).

HALIKAS-CROSBY DRUG IMPAIRMENT RATING SCALE FOR COCAINE (HC-DIRS-C)

(Halikas & Crosby, 1991)

The severity of cocaine dependence has been quantified by rating the intensity of craving for the drug and by eliciting frequency/quantity of use figures. The HC-DIRS-C is a measure based on self-report information and examiner's ratings. It has been suggested as a valid procedure to establish quantitative parameters of point-in-time cocaine involvement, both as a baseline assessment profile and to gauge changes in the course of treatment.

THE MARIHUANA SCREENING INVENTORY (MSI-X)

(Alexander & Leung, 2004)

The MSI-X is a 31-item assessment tool developed recently to determine the presence of a marijuana problem. It is still in the pilot phase. It is actually meant to be used as a screener; but since it was found to be able to differentiate between cannabis abuse and dependence depending on the score obtained, it has the capability to grade the severity of the disorder (Alexander & Leung, 2004). The MSI-X has been piloted with adult subjects attending addiction treatment facilities. Initial results indicate good sensitivity and specificity (Weiss et al., 2003) at the recommended detection cut-off score of six points. No reports on performance with people with concurrent disorders are currently available.

MINNESOTA COCAINE CRAVING SCALE (MCCS)

(Halikas et al., 1991)

The MCCS is a self-rating questionnaire that assesses the intensity, frequency and duration of craving, three aspects that vary with the severity of cocaine dependence on a positive linear fashion.

THE SUBJECTIVE OPIATE WITHDRAWAL SCALE (SOWS)

(Handelsman et al., 1987)

The SOWS is a short paper-and-pencil questionnaire that can be easily self-administered by people with opioid use disorders when they are in withdrawal. It can also be completed based on previous experiences.

Examiners can rate the severity of the manifestations of opioid withdrawal they observe with the Objective Opiate Withdrawal Scale (OOWS) (Handelsman et al., 1987) or with the Clinical Institute Narcotic Assessment (CINA) (Peachey & Lei, 1988). These objective scales assign a quantitative value to such physiological symptoms as midriasis, piloroerection, sweating, lacrimation, rhinorrhea, yawning, tremors and psychomotor restlessness. Of course, the expression of some of these symptoms could be influenced by the effects of psychiatric medications on the autonomic nervous system. But the validation trials with these instruments have considered this particular factor as a co-variant.

ASSESSMENT: SEVERITY OF ALCOHOL AND OTHER SUBSTANCE USE

THE ADDICTION SEVERITY INDEX (ASI)

(McLellan et al., 1992)

The ASI is a semi-structured interview that must be conducted by an examiner trained in the method. It takes from 45 minutes to more than an hour to complete, and some 15 additional minutes are needed to score the results after completion. It yields quantitative scores of severity in seven separate problem areas: medical status, employment status, alcohol use, drug use, legal status, family/social relations and psychiatric status.

The instrument provides interviewer severity ratings and composite scores for each problem area. The latter involve only those items within each problem scale that are subject to change over time (i.e., occurrence in the last 30 days or during the follow-up period being monitored). The interviewer determines the severity of each problem—within a two- to three-point range—on a 10-point scale. The exercise also calls for an estimation of the need for intervention (i.e., counselling, treatment or referral) in each of the problem areas. The person being assessed must also give an estimate of the current importance of problems within each area and conclude on his or her specific need for treatment.

The ASI is probably the most widely used instrument of its kind; there are versions in several languages, and it has been adapted to local criteria in different countries (see Makela, 2004, for a recent review). The clinical and research utilization of this assessment procedure has often involved cases of concurrent disorders, and several research studies have tested its validity and reliability in psychiatric settings (Appleby et al., 1997; Carey et al., 1997; Hodgins & el-Guebaly, 1992; Zanis et al., 1997).

These trials generally support the use of the ASI with people with mental health problems, but the researchers also note some important limitations. There is quite a variance in the stability of the subjects' response; the test-retest reliability quotients are rather low. The validity of the alcohol and other drug use sections is acceptable, but the validity of family/social and employment subscales is weak. The administration of the psychiatric and medical problem scales has also yielded a mixed validity profile among people with severe mental illness.

Teitelbaum and Carey (Teitelbaum & Carey, 1997) have reviewed the difficulties particular to conducting the ASI interview with people who have mental illness. They conclude that the instrument is useful, but the administration must be adapted to facilitate more meaningful responses.

THE GLOBAL APPRAISAL OF INDIVIDUAL NEEDS (GAIN)

(Dennis, 1998)

The GAIN is a semi-structured assessment battery that was developed to support initial screenings, brief interventions and referrals, standardized biopsychosocial clinical assessments for diagnosis, placement and treatment planning, monitoring of changes in clinical status and service utilization.

It obtains and integrates data on the respondent's background and treatment arrangements, substance use, physical health, risk behaviours, mental health, environmental factors, legal/justice problems and vocational/occupational status. It is available in two versions: GAIN-I to conduct initial assessments and GAIN-M90, to measure changes on three-month follow-ups.

The mental health evaluation covers issues such as current psychiatric treatment and medication; some DSM-IV Axis I disorders according to diagnostic criteria (substance use, major depression, pathological gambling, generalized anxiety and attention-deficit/hyperactivity); and other psychiatric problems with screening questions only (mood/anxiety disorders, suicide risk, traumatic and posttraumatic distress, conduct and antisocial disorders, and borderline personality). The GAIN can be used with adults and adolescents who have substance use problems (Dennis et al., 2000) and some psychiatric comorbidity (Shane et al., 2003). There are no reports yet on the performance of this method with patients with severe mental illness.

THE MAUDSLEY ADDICTION PROFILE (MAP)

(Marsden et al., 1998)

The MAP is a multidimensional clinician-administered instrument that was developed and validated to measure the major problems presented by people with substance use disorders, including in the area of psychological health. The interview takes approximately 12 minutes to complete. The authors intended the MAP mainly for the purpose of treatment outcome research, but it also gives clinicians a well-structured schedule to measure the magnitude of substance use in other circumstances as well.

The MAP is an examiner-run procedure. It consists of an introductory section and 60 items covering substance use, health risk behaviour, physical and psychological health, and personal and social functioning. It covers the previous 30 days specifically, as do the ASI and the SDSS. Psychological health is explored with a 10-item scale that is derived from the anxiety and depression question clusters of the Brief Symptom Inventory (Derogatis et al., 1974). While not tested in people with psychotic impairment, the MAP has proven viable with respondents who experience active psychological distress (Marsden et al., 2000).

THE SUBSTANCE DEPENDENCE SEVERITY SCALE (SDSS)

(Miele et al., 2000)

The SDSS is a semi-structured clinical interview that can be used by trained examiners. The SDSS evaluates symptoms and use patterns for alcohol, cocaine, heroin, stimulants, licit opioids, sedatives, methadone, cannabis, hallucinogens and two "other drugs" categories (e.g., inhalants). The assessment covers substances used in the 30 days prior to the interview. Substance-specific scores are obtained by summing the ratings of *severity* of symptoms (on a six-point scale) and *frequency* of use (number of days of use in the previous 30 days).

This method has been tested for validity and reliability against DSM-IV and ICD-10 diagnostic criteria for substance use disorders. The trials—involving clients/patients in substance use centres and concurrent disorders treatment programs—found the SDSS to be useful for determining the severity of these disorders, except for cannabis abuse and dependence (Miele et al., 2001).

ASSESSMENT: RISK SITUATIONS

THE INVENTORY OF DRINKING SITUATIONS (IDS)

(Annis, 1982)

The IDS is a paper-and-pencil or computer self-administered questionnaire available in a long (IDS-100) or a short version (IDS-42). It lists eight categories of situations that can be associated with drinking: unpleasant emotions, physical discomfort, pleasant emotions, testing personal control, urges and temptations, conflict with others, social pressure to drink and pleasant times with others. The respondent is instructed to indicate on a four-point scale how often "heavy drinking" has occurred, in each of those situations, during the past year.

This instrument helps clients become more aware of the possible motivations that drive their excessive drinking, and gives the evaluator a mapping of the situations that represent a risk for each client. Although not specifically designed to explore such factors in people who drink heavily and have other psychiatric disorders, it can be reasonably assumed that the IDS would facilitate the progress of addiction therapy in people who experience emotional distress or interpersonal difficulties.

THE INVENTORY OF DRUG-TAKING SITUATIONS (IDTS)

(Annis et al., 1997)

Based on the IDS, the IDTS is a 50-item self-report questionnaire that profiles the situations in which a client has used alcohol or another drug over the past year. The questionnaire takes 10 minutes to complete.

Clients indicate their frequency of heavy drinking or other drug use in each of 50 situations, on a four-point scale, across eight types of high-risk situations: unpleasant emotions (10 items), physical discomfort (5), pleasant emotions (5), testing personal control (5), urges and temptations (5), conflict with others (10), social pressure to use (5) and pleasant times with others (5).

ASSESSMENT: READINESS TO CHANGE

STAGES OF CHANGE READINESS AND TREATMENT EAGERNESS SCALE (SOCRATES)

(Miller & Tonigan, 1996)

The SOCRATES is a 19-item scale with subscales that measure readiness, taking steps and ambivalence. It evaluates motivation for change in people with alcohol problems (version 5A) and other substance use problems (version 5D). The questionnaire items ask specifically about substance use behaviour, and can be completed in three minutes. SOCRATES has demonstrated good reliability and validity when used with people with severe mental illness (Carey et al., 2001).

THE SUBSTANCE ABUSE TREATMENT SCALE (SATS)

(McHugo et al., 1995)

The SATS is a clinician-rated scale that assesses the stage of substance use treatment involvement in patients with concurrent severe mental illness and substance use disorders. This instrument was designed to be consistent with a model of dual diagnosis treatment that recognizes eight stages: pre-engagement, engagement, early persuasion, late persuasion, early active treatment, late active treatment, relapse prevention, and remission or recovery.

The SATS provides criteria for each stage of treatment involvement, and clinicians produce a rating for the previous six months on the basis of all sources of information available to them. Data from community mental health centres have demonstrated adequate validity and reliability (Teesson et al., 2000).

UNIVERSITY OF RHODE ISLAND CHANGE ASSESSMENT SCALE (URICA)

(DiClemente & Hughes, 1990)

The URICA, a self-report, 28-item scale, yields four summary scores corresponding to the stages described by the authors in their "Transtheoretical Model" of the process of change: pre-contemplation, contemplation, action and maintenance. These scores can be added to give a "readiness to change" score. The questionnaire takes five to 10 minutes to complete.

ASSESSMENT: SEVERITY OF PSYCHIATRIC SYMPTOMS

BECK DEPRESSION (BDI) AND ANXIETY (BDA) INVENTORIES

(Beck et al., 1988; Beck et al., 1961)

The BDI and BDA Inventories are among the most widely used tools to measure the symptoms of depression and anxiety. The questionnaire takes from five to 10 minutes to complete when self-administered. The BDI and BDA yield quantitative values that are sensitive to changes in symptom severity over time. When these measurements are repeated at short intervals, they can help distinguish the rapidly improving subjective distress of a substance-induced depression from the more persisting one of an independent mood disorder (Kush & Sowers, 1996).

BRIEF PSYCHIATRIC RATING SCALE (BPRS) AND POSITIVE AND NEGATIVE SYNDROME SCALE (PANSS)

(Overall & Gorham, 1962; Kay et al., 1987)

The BPRS is an 18-item, clinician-administered scale. After a brief interview with the client, each item is rated on a seven-point scale. If the BPRS is administered by a clinician who has been trained to administer and score it, it has good reliability and validity (Flemenbach & Zimmerman, 1973).

The PANSS includes 30 items, which cover the three separate domains of the schizophrenic phenomenology: positive or productive symptoms (e.g., hallucinations, delusions); negative or deficit symptoms (e.g., affective blunting, social withdrawal), and general symptoms (e.g., anxiety, behavioural disorganization).

Both these instruments yield quantitative values and have been used to rate symptoms in people who have concurrent psychosis and substance use disorders (Margolese et al., 2004). However, as in the case of the less structured clinical diagnostic interviews, the validity and significance of these ratings can be heavily influenced by the psychological effects of intoxication or withdrawal. The same differential diagnostic caveats apply when drawing conclusions from both those approaches to the psychiatric assessment of people with substance use disorders. Moreover, clinicians need considerable training in mental status examination.

HAMILTON DEPRESSION RATING SCALES (HAM-D)

(Hamilton, 1960)

The longer (21 and 17 items) and the more recent and shorter (seven items) versions (McIntyre et al., 2002) of the HAM-D have long been the standard instruments to assess severity of depression. They are clinician-rated scales that measure the disorder in its cognitive, affective, somatic and vegetative symptoms. HAM-D severity values in people with alcohol use disorders have been observed to fall quickly after cessation of drinking (Negrete, 1993).

MONTGOMERY-ASBERG DEPRESSION RATING SCALE (MADRS)

(Montgomery & Asberg, 1979)

The MADRS is an examiner-administered instrument specifically designed to measure changes in depressive symptoms over time. This scale contains 10 items, which rate the biological, cognitive, affective and behavioural manifestations of depression.

REFERENCES

Alexander, D.E. & Leung, P. (2004). The Marijuana Screening Inventory (MSI-X): Reliability, factor structure, and scoring criteria with a clinical sample. *American Journal of Drug and Alcohol Abuse, 30*(2), 321–351.

Andrews, G. & Peters, L. (2000). *The CIDI-Auto: A Computerised Diagnostic Interview for Psychiatry*. Sydney, NSW: CRUFAD. Retrieved February 9, 2005, from: http://www.crufad.com/cru_index.htm

Annis, H.M. *Inventory of Drinking Situations.* (1982). Toronto: Addiction Research Foundation.

Annis, H.M., Turner, N.E. & Sklar, S.M. (1997). *Inventory of Drug-Taking Situations: User's Guide.* Toronto: Addiction Research Foundation, Centre for Addiction and Mental Health.

Appleby, L., Dyson, V., Altman, E., Luchins, D.J. (1997). Assessing substance use in multiproblem patients: Reliability and validity of the Addiction Severity Index in a mental hospital population. *Journal of Nervous and Mental Disease, 185*(3), 159–165.

Beck, A.T., Epstein, N., Brown, G. & Steer, R.A. (1988). An inventory for measuring clinical anxiety: Psychometric properties. *Journal of Consulting and Clinical Psychology, 56*, 893–897.

Beck, A.T., Ward, C.H., Mendelson, M., Mock, J. & Erbaugh, J. (1961). An inventory for measuring depression. *Archives of General Psychiatry, 4*, 561–571.

Bisson, J., Nadeau, L. & Demers, A. (1999). The validity of the CAGE scale to screen for heavy drinking and drinking problems in a general population survey. *Addiction, 94*(5), 715–722.

Bradley, K.A., Boydwickizer, J., Powell, S.H. & Burman, M.L. (1998). Alcohol screening questionnaires in women: A critical review. *Journal of the American Medical Association, 280*(2), 166–171.

Butcher, J., Dahlstrom, W., Graham, J., Tellegen, A. & Kraemmer, B. (1989). *Minnesota Multiphasic Personality Inventory (MMPI-2): Manual Administration and Scoring.* Minneapolis: University of Minnesota Press.

Carey, K.B., Carey, M.P. & Chandra, P.S. (2003). Psychometric evaluation of the Alcohol Use Disorders Identification Test and short Drug Abuse Screening Test with psychiatric patients in India. *Journal of Clinical Psychiatry, 64*(7), 767–774.

Carey K.B., Cocco, K.M. & Correia, C.J. (1997). Reliability and validity of the Addiction Severity Index among outpatients with severe mental illness. *Psychological Assessment, 9*(4), 422–428.

Carey, K.B., Purnine, D.M., Maisto, S.A. & Carey, M.P. (2001). Enhancing readiness-to-change substance abuse in persons with schizophrenia. A four-session motivation-based intervention. *Behavior Modification, 25*(3), 331–384.

Chang, G., Wilkins Haug, L., Berman, S. & Goetz, M.A. (1999). The TWEAK: Application in a prenatal setting. *Journal of Studies on Alcohol, 60*(3), 306–309.

Chang, G., Wilkins Haug, L., Berman, S., Goetz, M.A., Behr, H. & Hiley, A. (1998). Alcohol use and pregnancy: Improving identification. *Obstetrics and Gynecology, 91*(6), 892–898.

Clemens, R. (2002). Psychometric properties of the Substance Abuse Subtle Screening Inventory-3. *Journal of Substance Abuse Treatment, 23*, 419–423.

Cocco, K.M. & Carey, K.B. (1998). Psychiatric properties of the Drug Abuse Screening Test in psychiatric populations. *Psychological Assessment, 10*(4), 408–414.

Dennis, M.L. (1998). *Global Appraisal of Individual Needs (GAIN) Manual: Administration, Scoring and Interpretation.* Bloomington, IL: Lighthouse Institute Publications.

Dennis, M.L., Scott, C.K., Godley, M.D. & Funk, R. (2000). Predicting outcomes in adult and adolescent treatment with case mix vs. level of care: Findings from the Drug Outcome Monitoring Study (DOMS). *Journal of Drug and Alcohol Dependence, 60*(suppl. 1), s51.

Derogatis, L.R., Lipman, R.J. & Rickels, K. (1974). The Hopkins symptom checklist (HSCL-90), a self-report sympton inventory. *Behavioral Science, 19*, 1–15.

Derogatis, L.R. & Melisaratos, N. (1983). The Brief Symptom Inventory: An introductory report. *Psychological Medicine, 13*(3), 595–605.

DiClemente, C.C. & Hughes, S.O. (1990). Stages of change profiles in alcoholism treatment. *Journal of Substance Abuse, 2*(2), 217–235.

Drake, R.E., Mueser, K.T. & McHugo, G.J. (1996). Clinical rating scales: Alcohol Use Scale (AUS), Drug Use Scale (DUS), and Substance Abuse Treatment Scale (SATS). In L.I. Sederer & B. Dickey (Eds.), *Outcome Assessments in Clinical Practice* (pp. 113–116). Baltimore, MD: Williams & Wilkins.

Dyson, V., Appleby, L., Altman, E., Doot, M., Luchins, D.J. & Delehant, M. (1998). Efficiency and validity of commonly used substance abuse screening instruments in public psychiatric patients. *Journal of Addictive Diseases, 17*(2), 57–76.

First, M.B., Gibbon, M. & Williams, J.B.W. (1997). *SCID Screen Patient Questionnaire.* Washington, DC: American Psychiatric Press.

Flemenbach, A. & Zimmerman, R.L. (1973). Inter- and intra-rater reliability of the Brief Psychiatric Rating Scale. *Psychological Reports, 36*, 783–792.

Goldberg, D. & Williams, P. (1988). *A User's Guide to the General Health Questionnaire.* Windsor, England: NFER-NELSON Publishing Company.

Halikas, J.A. & Crosby, R.D. (1991). Measuring outcome in the treatment of cocaine abuse: The Drug Impairment Rating Scale for cocaine. *Journal of Addictive Diseases, 11*(2), 121–138.

Halikas, J.A., Kuhn, K.L., Crosby, R., Carlson, G. & Crea, F. (1991). The measurement of craving in cocaine patients using the Minnesota Cocaine Craving Scale. *Comprehensive Psychiatry, 32*(1), 22–27.

Hamilton, M. (1960). A rating scale for depression. *Journal of Neurology and Neurosurgical Psychiatry, 23*, 56–62.

Handelsman, L., Cochrane, K.J., Aronson, M.I., Ness, R., Rubinstein, K.J. & Kanof, P.D. (1987). Two rating scales for opiate withdrawal. *American Journal of Drug and Alcohol Abuse, 13*(3), 293–308.

Hasin, D., Trautman, K. & Endicott, J. (1998). Psychiatric research interview for substance and mental disorders: Phenomenologically based diagnosis in patients who abuse alcohol or drugs. *Psychopharmacology Bulletin, 34*(1), 3–8.

Hasin, D.S., Trautman, K.D., Miele, G.M., Samet, S., Smith, M. & Endicott, J. (1996). Psychiatric research interview for substance and mental disorders (PRISM). *American Journal of Psychiatry, 153*(9), 1195–1201.

Hinkin, C.H., Castellon, S.A., Dickson-Furman, E., Daum, G., Jaffe, J. & Jarvik, L. (2001). Screening for drug and alcohol abuse among older adults using a modified version of the CAGE. *American Journal on Addictions, 10*(4), 319–326.

Hodgins, D.C. & el-Guebaly, N. (1992). More data on the Addiction Severity Index; Reliability and validity with the mentally ill substance abuser. *Journal of Nervous and Mental Disease, 180*, 197–201.

Kay, S.R., Fiszbein, A. & Opler, L.A. (1987). The positive and negative syndrome scale (PANSS) for schizophrenia. *Schizophrenia Bulletin, 13*(2), 261–276.

Knight, J.R., Sherritt, L., Harris, S.K., Gates, E.C. & Chang, G. (2003). Validity of brief alcohol screening tests among adolescents: A comparison of the AUDIT, POSIT, CAGE and CRAFFT. *Alcoholism: Clinical and Experimental Research, 23*(1), 67–73.

Knight, J.R., Sherritt, L., Shrier, L.A., Harris, S.K. & Chang, G. (2002). Validity of the CRAFFT substance abuse screening test among general adolescent clinic patients. *Archives of Pediatric & Adolescent Medicine, 156*(6), 607–614.

Kobak, K.A., Taylor, L.H., Dottl, S.L., Greist, J.H., Jefferson, J.W., Burroughs, D. et al. (1997). A computer-administered telephone interview to identify mental disorders. *Journal of the American Medical Association, 278*(11), 905–910.

Kush, F.R. & Sowers, W. (1996). Acute dually diagnosed inpatients: The use of self-report symptom severity instruments in persons with depressive disorders and cocaine dependence. *Journal of Substance Abuse Treatment, 14*(1), 61–66.

Leon, A.C., Olfson, M., Weisman, M.M., Portera, L., Fireman, B.H., Blacklow, R.S. et al. (1996). Brief screens for mental disorders in primary care: A validation study. *Journal of General Internal Medicine, 11*(7), 426–430.

Maisto, S.A., Carey, M.P., Carey, K.B., Gordon, C.M. & Gleason, J.R. (2000). Use of the AUDIT and the DAST-10 to identify alcohol and drug use disorders among adults with severe and persisting mental illness. *Psychological Assessment, 12*(2), 186–192.

Makela, K. (2004). Studies of the reliability and validity of the Addiction Severity Index. *Addiction, 99*, 398–410.

Marsden, J., Gossop, M., Stewart, D., Best, D., Farrell, M., Lehmann, P. et al. (1998). The Maudsley Addiction Profile (MAP): A brief instrument for assessing treatment outcome. *Addiction, 93*(12), 1857–1858.

Marsden, J., Gossop, M., Stewart, D., Rolfe, A. & Farrell, M. (2000). Psychiatric symptoms among clients seeking treatment for drug dependence: Intake data from the National Treatment Outcome Research Study. *British Journal of Psychiatry, 176*, 285–289.

Margolese, H.C., Malchy, L., Negrete, J.C., Tempier, R. & Gill, K. (2004). Drug and alcohol use among patients with schizophrenia and schizoaffective disorder: Levels and consequences. *Schizophrenia Research, 67*(2–3), 157–166.

Martino, S., Grilo, C.M. & Fehon, D.C. (2000). Development of the Drug Abuse Screening Test for Adolescents (DAST-A). *Addictive Behaviors, 25*(1), 57–70.

Mayfield, D., McLeod, G. & Hall, P. (1974). The CAGE questionnaire: Validation of a new alcoholism instrument. *American Journal of Psychiatry, 131*(10), 1121–1123.

McHugo, G.J., Drake, R.E., Burton, H.L. & Ackerson, T.H. (1995). A scale for assessing the stage of substance abuse treatment in persons with severe mental illness. *Journal of Nervous and Mental Disease, 183*(12), 762–767.

McIntyre, R., Kennedy, S., Bagby, M. & Bakish, D. (2002). Assessing full remission. *Journal of Psychiatry & Neuroscience, 27*(4), 235–239.

McLellan, T.A., Kushner, H., Metzger, D., Peters, R., Smith, L., Grissom, G. et al. (1992). The fifth edition of the Addiction Severity Index. *Journal of Substance Abuse Treatment, 9*(3), 199–213.

Miele, G.M., Carpenter, K.M., Cockerham, M.S., Trautman, K.D., Blaine, J. & Hasin, D.S. (2000). Substance Dependence Severity Scale (SDSS): Reliability and validity of a clinician-administered interview for DSM-IV substance use disorders. *Drug and Alcohol Dependence, 59*(1), 63–75.

Miele, G.M., Carpenter, K.M., Cockerham, M.S., Trautman, K.D., Blaine, J. & Hasin, D.S. (2001). Substance Dependence Severity Scale: Reliability and validity for ICD-10 substance use disorders. *Addictive Behaviors, 26*(4), 603–612.

Miller, F.G., Roberts, J., Brooks, M.K. & Lazowski, L.E. (1997). *SASSI-3 User's Guide.* Bloomington, IN: Baugh Enterprises.

Miller, W.R. & Tonigan, J.S. (1996). Assessing drinkers' motivation for change: The Stages of Change Readiness and Treatment Eagerness Scale (SOCRATES). *Psychology of Addictive Behaviors, 10*, 81–89.

Montgomery, S.A. & Asberg, M. (1979). A new depression scale designed to be sensitive to change. *British Journal of Psychiatry, 134*, 382–389.

Moore, A.A., Seeman, T., Morgenstern, H., Beck, J.C. & Reuben, D.B. (2002). Are there differences between persons who screen positive on the CAGE questionnaire and the SMST-G? *Journal of the American Geriatrics Society, 50*(5), 858–862.

Morton, J., Jones, T.V. & Manganaro, M.A. (1996). Performance of alcoholism screening questionnaires in elderly veterans. *American Journal of Medicine, 101*(2), 153–159.

Negrete, J.C. (1993). The significance of psychiatric co-morbidity findings in substance abusers. In D. Riley (Ed.), *Dual Disorders* (pp. 23–31). Ottawa: Canadian Centre on Substance Abuse.

Negrete, J.C. & Alansari, E. (1987). Screening for alcohol abuse among general hospital patients: The reliability of self-administered instruments reconsidered. *Substance Abuse, 8*(2), 3–9.

Overall, J.E. & Gorham, D.R. (1962). The brief psychiatric rating scale. *Psychological Reports, 10,* 799–812.

Peachey, J.E. & Lei, H. (1988). Assessment of opioid dependence with Naloxone. *British Journal of Addiction, 83*(2), 193–201.

Pinard, L., Negrete, J.C., Annable, L. & Audet, N. (1996). Alexithymia in substance abusers: Persistence and correlates of variance. *American Journal of Addictions, 5*(1), 32–39.

Rogers, R., Cashel, M.L., Johansen, J., Sewell, K.W. & Gonzalez, C. (1997). Evaluation of adolescent offenders with substance abuse—Validation of the SASSI with conduct-disordered youth. *Criminal Justice and Behavior, 24*(1), 114–128.

Rosenberg, S.D., Drake, R.E., Wolford, G.L., Mueser, K.T., Oxman, T.E., Vidaver, R.M. et al. (1998). Dartmouth Assessment of Lifestyle Instrument (DALI): A substance use disorder screen for people with severe mental illness. *American Journal of Psychiatry, 155*(2), 232–237.

Russell, M., Martier, S.S., Sokol, R.J., Jacobson, S., Jacobson, J. & Bottoms, S. (1991). Screening for pregnancy risk drinking: TWEAKING the tests. *Alcoholism: Clinical and Experimental Research, 15*(2), 638.

Samet, S., Nunes, E.V. & Hasin, D. (2004). Diagnosing comorbidity: Concepts, criteria, and methods. *Acta Neuropsychiatrica, 16,* 9–18.

Saunders, J.B., Aasland, O.G., Babor, T.F., De la Fuente, J.R. & Grant, M. (1993). Development of the Alcohol Use Disorders Identification Test (AUDIT): WHO collaborative project on early detection of persons with harmful alcohol consumption. *Addiction, 88*(6), 791–804.

Selzer, M.L. (1971). The Michigan Alcoholism Screening Test: The quest for a new diagnostic instrument. *American Journal of Psychiatry, 127*(12), 1653–1658.

Shane, P.A., Jasiukaitis, P. & Green, R.S. (2003). Treatment outcomes among adolescents with substance abuse problems: The relationship between comorbidities and post-treatment substance involvement. *Evaluation and Program Planning, 26*(4), 393–402.

Shedler, J., Beck, A. & Bensen, S. (2000). Practical mental health assessment in primary care. Validity and utility of the Quick PsychoDiagnostics Panel. *The Journal of Family Practice, 49*(7), 614–621.

Sheeran, T. & Zimmerman, M. (2004). Factor structure of the Psychiatric Diagnostic Screening Questionnaire (PDSQ), a screening questionnaire for DSM-IV Axis I disorders. *Journal of Behavior Therapy and Experimental Psychiatry, 35*(1), 49–55.

Skinner, H.A. & Allen, B.A. (1982). Alcohol dependence syndrome: Measurement and validation. *Journal of Abnormal Psychology, 91*(3), 199–209.

Smith, S.R. & Hilsenroth, M.J. (2001). Discriminative validity of the MacAndrew Alcoholism Scale with cluster B personality disorders. *Journal of Clinical Psychology, 57*(6), 801–813.

Snow, M., Thurber, S. & Hodgson, J.M. (2002). An adolescent version of the Michigan Alcoholism Screening Test. *Adolescence, 37*(148), 835–840.

Sokol, R.J., Martier, S.S. & Ager, J.W. (1989). The T-ACE questions: Practical prenatal detection of risk drinking. *American Journal of Obstetrics and Gynecology, 160*(4), 863–868.

Spitzer, R.L., Kroenke, K. & Williams, J.B. (1999). Validation and utility of a self-report version of PRIME-MD: The PHQ primary care study. Primary Care Evaluation of Mental Disorders. Patient Health Questionnaire. *Journal of the American Medical Association, 282*(18), 1737–1744.

Spitzer, R.L., Williams, J.B., Kroenke, K., Linzer, M., deGruy, F.V. 3rd, Hahn, S.R. et al. (1994). Utility of a new procedure for diagnosing mental disorders in primary care. The PRIME-MD 1000 study. *Journal of the American Medical Association 272*(22), 1749–1756.

Staley, D. & el-Guebaly, N. (1990). Psychometric properties of the Drug Abuse Screening Test in a psychiatric patient population. *Addictive Behaviors, 15*(3), 257–264.

Stockwell, T., Murphy, D. & Hodgson, R. (1983). The Severity of Alcohol Dependence Questionnaire: Its use, reliability and validity. *British Journal of Addiction, 78*(2), 145–156.

Teesson, M., Clement, N., Copeland, J., Conroy, A. & Reid, A. (2000). *The Measurement of Outcome in Alcohol and Other Drug Treatment: A Review of Available Instruments.* Sydney: NDARC Technical Report No. 92.

Teitelbaum, L.M. & Carey, K.B. (1997). Tips on using the Addictions Severity Index in psychiatric settings. *The Behavior Therapist, 20*(2), 19–21.

Teitelbaum, L. & Mullen, B. (2000). The validity of the MAST in psychiatric settings: A meta-analytic integration. *Journal of Studies on Alcohol, 61*(2), 254–261.

Weiss, R.D., Griffin, M.L., Hufford, C., Muentz, I.R., Najavits, L.M., Jansson, S.B. et al. (1997). Early prediction of initiation of abstinence from cocaine: Use of a craving questionnaire. *American Journal on Addictions, 6*(3), 224–231.

Weiss, R.D., Griffin, M.L., Mazurick, C., Berkman, B., Gastfriend, D.R., Frank, A. et al. (2003). The relationship between cocaine craving, psychosocial treatment, and subsequent cocaine use. *American Journal of Psychiatry, 160*(7), 1320–1325.

Weissman, M.M., Broadhead, W.E., Olfson, M., Sheehan, D.V., Hoven, C., Conolly, P. et al. (1998). A diagnostic aid for detecting (DSM-IV) mental disorders in primary care. *General Hospital Psychiatry, 20*(1), 1–11.

Wing, J.K., Babor, T., Brugha, T., Burke, J., Cooper, J., Giel, R. et al. (1990). SCAN: Schedules for Clinical Assessment in Neuropsychiatry. *Archives of General Psychiatry, 47*, 589–593.

Zanis, D.A., McLellan, A.T. & Corse, S. (1997). Is the Addiction Severity Index a reliable and valid assessment instrument among clients with severe and persistent mental illness and substance abuse disorders? *Community Mental Health Journal, 33*(3), 213–227.

Zimmerman, M., Sheeran, T., Chelminski, I. & Young, D. (2004). Screening for psychiatric disorders in outpatients with DSM-IV substance use disorders. *Journal of Substance Abuse Treatment, 26*(3), 181–188.

Chapter 2: Appendix 2
Toxicology tests

TYPES OF TESTS

Blood screening

Screening for drugs in blood samples is not often used to detect substance use disorders. Such screening is cumbersome, invasive and impractical, because most drugs stay in blood at detectable levels for a short time only. However, blood or gastric content screening are the only options when the person is severely impaired (e.g., in a coma or very confused), and there is an urgent need to identify the intoxicating agent. Blood screening may also be required for legal purposes.

Breath analysis

Breath analysis is a relatively simple approach to front-line clinical screening for alcohol use, and it has been found helpful in hospital emergency rooms and trauma centres (Cherpitel, 1995; Seppa et al., 2004). It is also the method used by the police for roadside testing.

The concentration of alcohol in the breath is much smaller than in the blood, but the ratio between the two is constant (1:2,100). Therefore it is possible to assess how much alcohol is in the blood by taking a breath reading. The reading must be exact when using it as the base to estimate alcohol levels in blood, because any error will be multiplied by a factor of 2,100.

Three types of technology are behind all devices currently available for this screening:

- colorimetric chemical reaction
- infrared spectroscopy
- fuel-cell detectors (Swift, 2003).

All devices are calibrated to yield the blood alcohol figure corresponding to the concentration detected in breath. To provide an adequate air sample, the person being tested must blow as hard and as long as possible into the instrument's mouthpiece. An obvious source of error is the contamination of the sample by residual alcohol in the mouth. To avoid this problem, the breath sample must be taken after careful mouth rinsing. An underestimation might occur if the person is unable to exhale in full, such as in cases of severe chronic obstructive lung disease or bronchial narrowing.

Urine screening

Enzyme-mediated (EMIT) and radio immunoassays (RIA) of urine samples are the most widely used drug screening methods. Relatively simple and cost-efficient, they detect ethanol and most drugs of abuse, except for the more potent ones, such as Fentanyl and LSD, which are usually taken in such minute amounts that their concentration in urine is below the methods' detection levels.

Although sensitive, these popular screening methods are not specific enough to identify the individual members of a drug group. Thus, it is not possible, on the basis of an EMIT assay, to know exactly which individual benzodiazepine, amphetamine or opioid (except for methadone) is present. Injecting heroin or taking a common pain killer with codeine, for example, would both yield the same opioid-positive test. These tests may also indiscriminately cross-react with molecules that are only partially related to the targeted drugs; for example, a test may yield an amphetamine-positive screen when the person has taken a medicine containing a sympathomimetic decongestant.

The gas chromatography-mass spectrometry method (GC-MS) is a much more sensitive and specific assay. This technique is used to confirm the results of the more basic enzyme assays, particularly when they will be the object of legal disputes. This test requires a greater level of laboratory sophistication and is more expensive than the EMIT or RIA.

AVOIDING DETECTION

Savvy people who want to avoid detection of their drug use can find ways of manipulating the sample to interfere with the test capabilities. For instance, they can:

- drink large quantities of fluids, or add water to their sample, so that by diluting their urine they bring the drug concentration level below the detection limits (this kind of tampering can be detected by checking the concentration of creatinine in urine)
- add an alkaline substance, such as common soap, to the urine sample, which will interfere with the test's detection of acid drug metabolites (e.g., cannabinoids). But this manœuver can be unmasked by checking the pH value of the urine, which will be found less acid than normal.

Hair testing

Drugs that are circulating in blood penetrate the hair root through diffusion from the capillaries in the follicle. Most laboratories use only the lower three cm of a hair sample plucked with the follicle or cut at the level of the skin (three months' detection period), because the drug content is much diminished beyond that length. Thus, drug screening in hair samples is assumed to have a detection window much longer than the urine test, and to provide information on drug use over the previous 10 to 12 weeks.

Traces of drugs can be found in hair through environmental contamination (e.g., cannabis, freebase cocaine or heroin smoke), so a cleansing treatment is the first step in the process. Drugs can also be found in hair from contamination with sweat or oily secretions in the scalp. In such cases, a positive screen is valid evidence of drug use, but there can be no certainty as to when the drug use took place.

Most drugs of abuse can be screened in hair (Klein et al., 2000), including methadone and its metabolites (Goldberger et al., 1998), but the largest experience has been gained with cocaine, cannabinoids and opioids. Hair testing is not standard screening procedure yet, and the technology is available only in selected laboratories. It is also considerably more expensive than the urine screens and involves more demanding testing methods, such as GC-MS.

Saliva testing

To test saliva for evidence of alcohol use, a strip tipped with a reagent pad is inserted in the mouth and saturated with saliva. A specific enzymatic reaction takes place in the subsequent two minutes; this reaction oxidizes the alcohol and causes the pad to acquire different colours, depending on the alcohol concentration. The reading is done by matching the pad with an alcohol level colour chart.

Saliva testing for alcohol is a semi-quantitative method—it yields an approximate value only (i.e., within a given range).

Saliva alcohol screening can be very sensitive and highly specific (Pate et al., 1993; Schwartz et al., 1989), but it can be subject to procedural errors. The person being tested must not put anything in his or her mouth for at least 15 minutes prior to testing; special care should be taken that no alcoholic or non-alcoholic drinks, coffee, cigarettes, mouthwash, mouth sprays, breath mints, medications, cough syrup or foods are ingested in that period. The test reaction can also be affected by low environment temperatures, and it should not be performed outdoors.

Sweat testing

Drugs of abuse are excreted in body sweat, and can be detected in this fluid. The *sweat patch* is a device designed to collect the non-volatile components of human perspiration. Larger drug molecules remain trapped in an absorbent pad, which is removed for laboratory testing after one week. This is a non-invasive procedure, easily carried out and generally well accepted by the people being tested.

Sweat testing is usually used to monitor drug use on a continuous basis by reapplying the device week after week. It effectively ascertains that people who absolutely must abstain from drug use are indeed able to do so. Consequently, it is sometimes included in the return-to-work protocols proposed to people with substance use problems in sensitive occupations (e.g., airline pilots). It has also been successfully used as a monitoring tool in addiction treatment programs (Kintz et al., 1996; Taylor et al., 1998).

Safeguards prevent undue manipulation or deceit: the patch cannot be removed and reapplied, because the adhesive is formulated to work only once; and the patch cannot secretly be replaced by a fresh one, because each unit contains an identification number that is verified in the laboratory.

Environmental contamination must be especially avoided while manipulating the patch before application and after removal, and extreme care must be taken to cleanse the skin surface prior to placement. Cost is a major shortcoming, for this screening approach also requires the use of the more expensive GC-MS assay.

BIOLOGICAL MARKERS FOR ALCOHOL PROBLEMS

An alcohol use disorder can be initially detected, its severity measured and its course over time monitored by looking at laboratory data and measuring certain biological correlates. Not every person who drinks heavily presents this type of evidence, but the longer the drinking has been going on, the more likely the biological markers will be found.

Of course, many markers of recent alcohol ingestion can be found in blood and urine (Cook, 2003), and long-lasting exposure to high doses of alcohol results in measurable changes in a number of laboratory tests that are normally performed as part of general medical examinations (Sharpe, 2001). In fact, a computerized screening program (EDAC), which uses a routine test panel to perform a linear discriminant function analysis, has been tried and validated as a useful approach to identifying chronic excessive drinking (Harasymiw et al., 2004).

However, two particular laboratory results have emerged as valuable indicators of chronic alcohol abuse:

- an increased serum level of the liver enzyme gamma-glutamyltransferase (GGT)
- a larger than normal volume of the red blood cells (mean corpuscular volume, or MCV).

These two tests are included in the basic blood work that is performed in the course of regular medical examinations. As such, they are readily available to the practitioner and, if abnormal, they may represent the first objective evidence of an alcohol problem.

Another biochemical finding has been proven useful as a screening approach: an elevated plasma level of a variant of the glycoprotein transferrin, called carbohydrate-deficient transferrin (CDT). This is not a routine procedure, and it has no other clinical applications; it would have to be requested with the specific purpose of establishing whether the person drinks heavily.

GGT

Gamma-glutamyltransferase (GGT) is an enzyme produced predominantly in the liver. It is a sensitive marker of alcohol ingestion, especially when chronic alcohol liver disease results. But plasma elevations of GGT are not specific to alcohol damage, for GGT values are increased also by hepatotoxic drugs other than alcohol, by enzyme induction by some medications, in cases of non-alcoholic liver disease and in cases of congestive heart failure.

Normal plasma values for this enzyme range from seven to 50 units per litre, and levels are usually lower for women than for men. A sizable minority of people who have drinking problems will not show GGT elevation; the sensitivity of the test has been found to range from 42 to 80 per cent in studies of large samples (Anton et al., 2002; Reynaud et al., 2000). The test is more sensitive to heavy drinking in men than in women, and is more sensitive in people who drink regularly and are alcohol-dependent, rather than those whose alcohol problems are intermittent.

The specificity values elicited in the same studies are much higher, ranging between 76 per cent in a mixed-gender sample to 97 per cent in women who are heavy drinkers. Thus, although a high GGT level is less often found in women who have drinking problems, when present, it appears to be a more certain evidence of the problem than it is among men.

The interpretation of GGT findings in people with concurrent alcohol use and mental health disorders must consider the following:

- Psychiatric medications such as carbamazepine, valproic acid, olanzapine and quetiapine can act as enzyme inducers or cause some degree of hepatotoxic damage, with a resulting elevation of plasma GGT values.
- A similar problem may occur in people who are receiving disulfiram or naltrexone for treatment of problem drinking.

MCV

The mean corpuscular volume (MCV) is a measure of the size of red blood cells. Standard values for MCV range between 86 and 98 cubic micrograms for each cell. Figures of 100 micrograms or larger are considered excessive.

Alcohol and its metabolites have toxic effects on the production of hematologic precursor cells and on red cell morphology. Macrocytosis—enlarged erythrocytes—is found in people with chronic alcohol use disorders often enough to consider it as a biological marker of chronic excessive drinking. However, many people with alcohol use disorders do not present with high MCV; the sensitivity of this test is the lowest of all the laboratory indicators reviewed here (24 to 63 per cent).

As in the case of the GGT, the MCV is more sensitive to regular, heavy drinking behaviour than to intermittent bingeing. Some drug therapies (e.g., cytotoxic agents) can also cause red blood cell enlargement, as can some primary hematologic disorders, non-alcoholic liver diseases and folate deficiency (Savage et al., 2000). Except for the latter nutritional problem, these other causes of macrocytosis are infrequent enough that a high MCV figure is a very good marker of an alcohol use disorder. Indeed, an elevated MCV reveals the presence of an alcohol use disorder 96 per cent of the time (Reynaud et al., 2000); and the liver disease and heavy tobacco use that frequently accompany heavy drinking can also contribute to alter red cell volume (Aubin et al., 1998).

CDT

Transferrin is a glycoprotein synthesized and metabolized in the liver, whose main function is to ferry iron from sites of absorption and storage to sites of utilization. Modifications of this protein occur because of the addition of carbohydrate moieties containing sialic acid residues. Transferrin isoforms that are deficient in sialo-residues and/or carbohydrate moieties (i.e., carbohydrate-deficient transferrin, or CDT) have been found to be a marker of heavy and continuous alcohol intake (Golka & Wiese, 2004).

The appearance of CDT in the bloodstream is induced by the ingestion of 60 grams of alcohol (e.g., a 750 mL bottle of wine) daily for about seven days in a row. At low plasma levels, this marker reflects simply the regular use of alcohol. It is at blood concentrations of 60 mg/L or more that the finding is to be considered as an indicator of probable drinking problem (Reynaud et al., 1998). CDT is sensitive enough to detect relatively small changes in daily alcohol intake; and it is also an early indicator of relapse in people who are alcohol-dependent who return to drinking after a period of abstinence.

The sensitivity of this test in men who drink is fairly good: 67 per cent in cases of alcohol abuse and 85 per cent in alcohol dependence. Its specificity is even better: 97 per cent for both types of alcohol disorders (Reynaud et al., 2000). But its performance with women who drink is weaker, particularly in its sensitivity (41 per cent) (Anton et al., 2002). CDT is theorized to be less useful for women because its formation is related to hormonal and iron status. Its levels go up during pregnancy, menstruation and at the pre-menopausal phase, and down after menopause and when taking oral contraceptives.

CDT results also vary according to the different values obtained by the several types of assay used to determine them. Immunoassay technologies, for instance, suffer from specificity problems because the values they yield often include unintended isoforms of the protein. Although there has been a sustained effort to improve CDT reliability by perfecting procedures that could be universally adopted (Helander et al., 2001), this approach to biological screening still needs to be properly standardized.

Although the CDT test is not as widely available as the plasma GGT measurement, its superior performance as a gauge of recent heavy drinking makes it a very desirable tool, and sensitivity and specificity values are significantly improved when both those tests have been run in the same person (Anton et al., 2002; Reynaud et al., 2000).

Both GGT and CDT figures decrease promptly when the person stops drinking, but the latter does so more rapidly. It is also more able than GGT to pick up resumption of drinking, without delay.

The increase in blood CDT is particular to alcohol use; it does not happen when the liver is affected by non-alcoholic damage, nor is it the result of drug-inducement. Such high specificity should make the CDT test a more reliable biological marker when screening for alcohol abuse or dependence in people who are taking psychiatric medications.

REFERENCES

Anton, R.F., Lieber, C. & Tabakoff, B. (2002). Carbohydrate-deficient transferrin and gamma-glutamyltransferase for the detection and monitoring of alcohol use: Results from a multisite study. *Alcoholism, Clinical and Experimental Research, 26*(8), 1215–1222.

Aubin, H.J., Laureaux, C., Zerah, F., Tilikete, S., Vernier, F., Vallat, B. et al. (1998). Joint influence of alcohol, tobacco and coffee on biological markers of heavy drinking in alcoholics. *Biological Psychiatry, 44*(7), 638–643.

Cherpitel, C.J. (1995). Screening for alcohol problems in the emergency department. *Annals of Emergency Medicine, 26*(2), 158–166.

Cook, J.D. (2003). Biochemical markers of alcohol use in pregnant women. *Clinical Biochemistry, 36*(1), 9–19.

Goldberger, B.A., Darrai, A.G., Caplan, Y.H. & Cone, E.J. (1998). Detection of methadone, methadone metabolites and other illicit drugs of abuse in hair of methadone-treatment subjects. *Journal of Analytical Toxicology, 22*(6), 526–530.

Golka, K. & Wiese, A. (2004). Carbohydrate-deficient transferrin (CDT)—A biomarker for long-term alcohol consumption. *Journal of Toxicology and Environmental Health, Part B, Critical Reviews, 7*(4), 319–337.

Harasymiw, J., Seaberg, J. & Bean, P. (2004) Detection of alcohol misuse using a routine test panel: The early detection of alcohol consumption (EDAC) test. *Alcohol & Alcoholism, 39*(4), 329–335.

Helander, A., Fors, M. & Zakrisson, B. (2001). Study of axis-shield % CDT immunoassay for quantification of CDT in serum. *Alcohol and Alcoholism, 36*(5), 406–412.

Kintz, P., Tracqui, A., Mangin, P. & Edel, Y. (1996). Sweat testing in opioid users with a sweat patch. *Journal of Analytical Toxicology, 20*(6), 293–297.

Klein, J., Karaskov, T. & Koren G. (2000). Clinical applications of hair testing for drugs of abuse—The Canadian experience. *Forensic Science International, 107*(1–3), 281–288.

Pate, L.A., Hamilton, J.D., Park, R.S. & Strobel, R.M. (1993). Evaluation of a saliva alcohol test stick as a therapeutic adjunct in an alcoholism treatment program. *Journal of Studies on Alcohol, 54*(5), 520–521.

Reynaud, M., Hourcade, F., Planche, F., Albuisson, E., Meunier M.N. & Planche, R. (1998). Usefulness of carbohydrate-deficient transferrin in alcoholic patients with normal gamma-glutamyl transpeptidase. *Alcoholism, Clinical and Experimental Research, 22*(3), 615–618.

Reynaud, M., Schellenberg, F., Loisequx-Meunier, M.N., Schwan, R., Maradeix, B., Planche, B. et al. (2000). Objective diagnosis of alcohol abuse: Compared values of CDT, GGT and MCV. *Alcoholism, Clinical and Experimental Research, 24*(9), 1414–1419.

Savage, D.G., Ogundipe, A., Allen, R.H., Stabler, S.P. & Lindenbaum, J. (2000). Etiology and diagnostic evaluation of macrocytosis. *The American Journal of the Medical Sciences, 319*(6), 343–352.

Schwartz, R.H., O'Donnell, R.M., Thorne, M.M., Getson, P.R. & Hicks, J.M. (1989). Evaluation of a colorimetric dipstick test to detect alcohol in saliva: A pilot study. *Annals of Emergency Medicine, 18*(9), 1001–1003.

Seppa, K., Lahtinen, T., Antila, S. & Aalto, M. (2004). Alcohol drinking among emergency patients—Alcometer use and documentation. *Alcohol and Alcoholism, 39*(3), 262–265.

Sharpe, P.C. (2001). Biochemical detection and monitoring of alcohol abuse and abstinence. *Annals of Clinical Biochemistry, 38*(Pt 6), 652–664.

Swift, R. (2003). Direct measurement of alcohol and its metabolites. *Addiction, 98*(Suppl. 2), 73–80.

Taylor, J.R., Watson, I.D., Tames, F.J. & Lowe, D. (1998). Detection of drug use in a methadone maintenance clinic: Sweat patches versus urine testing. *Addiction, 93*(6), 847–853.

Chapter 3

Using motivational interviewing with clients who have concurrent disorders

LORNA SAGORSKY AND WAYNE SKINNER

Some clients enter therapy determined to change, and are able to express reasons for desiring change. However, many clients, particularly those with concurrent disorders, are not motivated to make changes, and may not even acknowledge that they have mental health and substance use problems (Martino et al., 2002; Smyth, 1996).

This low level of motivation is often the explanation for poor outcomes in treatment, because it leads to lack of engagement, adherence or completion of treatment (Daley & Zuckoff, 1998; Zeidonis et al., 1997). This has many adverse effects for the client, including an exacerbation of symptoms. In addition, lack of adherence to treatment affects the client's supportive relationships and contributes to frustration both in helping professionals and among family members (Daley & Zuckoff, 1998).

Motivational approaches are proving more effective than conventional methods of engaging clients with concurrent disorders. Such approaches are also useful in getting clients to identify goals they would like to work on, and in building hope and commitment to change and recovery (Graeber et al., 2000; Handmaker et al., 2002).

In this chapter, we describe the motivational interviewing (MI) approach, and explore the research findings supporting the use of MI in clients with concurrent disorders. This is followed by a summary of key MI techniques, which are demonstrated through a detailed case study.

In the second edition of their formative text on motivational interviewing, Miller and Rollnick note that over the 11 years since the first edition, they have placed less emphasis on techniques and given more focus to the spirit that provides the foundation for the work. They say that motivational interviewing is "a way of being with people . . . its underlying spirit lies in understanding and experiencing the human nature that gives rise to that way of being" (2002, p. 34). It aims to actively engage the client in the change process by drawing out the client's own motivation to change. It is a collaborative, empathic way of interaction that recognizes and supports the client's values and ability to make changes in his or her life. MI is an alternative to more customary confrontational ways of dealing with clients. As such, it invites counsellors to explore and challenge many of the ways in which they have previously understood and worked with clients with co-occurring substance use and mental health problems.

MI is a method of enhancing a client's own motivation to change. It is based on a blend of empirically validated principles used to improve client motivation (Martino et al., 2002; Smyth, 1996). MI was originally developed as a way of working with people with alcohol and other substance use problems. Once its effectiveness in this area became evident, the approach was applied to different client groups, including clients with bulimia, with hypertension, with diabetes and with concurrent disorders (Burke et al., 2002).

Miller and Rollnick (2002) describe the spirit of MI as consisting of three fundamental approaches:

- In an environment that is conducive to change, develop a collaborative partnership between the client and the counsellor that respects the client's expertise and perspective.
- Evoke resources and motivation for change, which are presumed to exist within the client, by drawing on the client's own perceptions, goals and values.
- Affirm the client's right to and capacity for self-direction.

Motivation is seen as the key to change, and it is elicited through interviewing—a much more collaborative, interactive and non-hierarchical process than is found in more standard treatment approaches. The MI way of being with clients can be seen as a true "*inter*-view": looking, learning and seeing together. Miller and Rollnick describe MI as "a directive, client-centred counselling style for eliciting behaviour change by helping clients to explore and resolve ambivalence around change" (2002, p. 25).

CHANGING BEHAVIOUR

The MI approach recognizes that the client finds behaviour change difficult because the benefits of changing are contradicted by an opposing set of benefits: those of staying the same. This ambivalence keeps the client from exploring constructive change. Using an empathic approach to resolve ambivalence is the main focus of MI. The desired effect is a tipping of the balance, so that the client recognizes that the benefits of change outweigh the losses that may result.

Originally, these strategies were focused on substance use problems, but their use has now extended to the broad domain of health behaviour change (Rollnick et al., 1999), with growing evidence of their value as an effective way of helping people with co-occurring mental health and substance use problems initiate and maintain healthier behaviours in any area in which the client has a goal (Mueser et al., 2003; Sciacca, 1997).

Decisional balance

In MI, the shift toward desiring change must come from the client, rather than being imposed externally by the therapist. The end goal of MI, like that of other therapies, is behavioural change. However, in MI the counsellor reaches this goal by evaluating with the client the advantages and disadvantages of change, instead of prescribing it. It is the client's role to talk about and resolve ambivalence to change. The counsellor accepts and expects resistance to change, and works with it, directing the conversation to elicit information about the client's resistance and supporting the client's belief in his or her ability to change (Miller & Rollnick, 2002). MI is thus client-centred, but counsellor-directed.

In MI, the process of identifying the pros and cons of making a change, and comparing them with the pros and cons of not changing, is known as a "decisional balance" exercise. Clients can work through the exercise on paper, using a four-cell grid.

Stages of change

The transtheoretical (or stages of change) model of change (Prochaska & DiClemente, 1984) provides a very potent complement to motivational theory and practice. Use of this model helps to determine the client's readiness to make a change, so that we can identify the most effective way of working with the client, based on his or her level of motivation. Prochaska and DiClemente (1984) identify six basic stages of change:

- precontemplation
- contemplation
- preparation
- action
- maintenance
- relapse.

These stages can be seen as taking place in a cycle, with entry usually being at the precontemplation stage and possible exit after a period of maintenance.

PRECONTEMPLATION

What standard models would call the denial stage is seen, in the transtheoretical model, as an important entry point to change. People in precontemplation do not see themselves as having a problem. They see no reason for change. When they present for therapy they may complain that they are being nagged or coerced into it. Their goal at this point is to remain the same and to get "them"—other people who are pressuring them to change—off their back. They also consider that generally accepted messages about harmful behaviours (such as that smoking is bad for one's health) do not apply to them.

This externalized view of the problem can sometimes be used as a motivating factor (e.g., "How can we work together to get your partner/parent/boss/probation officer off your back?" "What would have to happen for the people who want you to change to get off your back?" "What would need to happen for you to feel that this is something you need to give attention to?").

CONTEMPLATION

Most people can be of two minds about most behaviours, depending on the circumstance. Being intoxicated might be seen as great, but having spent all one's money or having withdrawal symptoms are usually considered less than great. Contemplation is the stage at which people begin to recognize that their behaviour is making them—and probably others—unhappy. They know they want to change, and can see the general direction of change, but are not yet ready to make firm plans.

PREPARATION

The preparation stage involves plans to act in the near future. However, ambivalence is not necessarily resolved at this point. The client may still procrastinate, worry and even argue with the counsellor against change. At this stage, "awareness is high and anticipation is palpable" (Prochaska et al., 1994).

ACTION

At this stage, behaviour is overtly modified: the client begins the process of giving up old behaviour patterns and replacing them with new ones. The action stage is a busy time, with plenty of visible change in evidence—but it is never the final stage of change. It is followed by a new and difficult stage: maintenance.

MAINTENANCE

In the maintenance stage, the temptation to revert to old, familiar ways is strong, as the client feels the losses, as well as the gains, that change has brought. Because the horizon in maintenance is open, the risks and challenges in achieving a sustained recovery are considerable.

During maintenance, the client-therapist relationship is still very important; indeed, its status as a supportive and collaborative relationship would be well-established by this time. Yet the frequency of contact will usually diminish, and the client will use the counsellor for booster sessions and follow-up contact. Sometimes, after the client has dealt with active issues related to addiction and mental illness, underlying issues related to past events or to future prospects may emerge. The client may want to make these issues the focus of another phase of treatment. They represent pressures that could lead to relapse.

RELAPSE

Relapse to substance use and to psychiatric symptoms is often seen as a totally negative experience, a sign that previous work has been a waste of time or that the client is deficient in some way. In the transtheoretical model, building on the formative work of Marlatt and Gordon (1985) in this area, relapse is reframed as a common, even worthwhile, component of lasting change. A relapse can be a valuable opportunity to help the client understand what situations might make him or her vulnerable to future relapses, and to be better equipped to avoid or minimize their impact in the future.

SUMMARY OF THE TRANSTHEORETICAL MODEL

The transtheoretical model complements the motivational approach in several ways. MI is often targeted particularly at clients who are ambivalent and in the precontemplation stage, but it is useful at all the stages of change. Having identified the stage at which a client is situated, the counsellor can use MI techniques appropriate to that stage to move the client further along.

All MI skills can be employed during each stage, though there are particular tasks for the client and counsellor at each point:

- Precontemplation is a useful time to increase the client's awareness and to open a discussion of the benefits and drawbacks of making a change.
- Contemplation often involves "tipping the balance" away from ambivalence and in the direction of change.
- Action is a time for practical advice and for affirming the client's hard work in getting this far.
- Relapses should be seen as opportunities for learning, and for reinforcing motivation, so that hard-won changes "stick" the next time around.

Stages of change and stages of treatment

The stages of change model provides a template that describes the process of intentional behaviour change. Research into the treatment of people with severe mental health and substance use problems has resulted in the development of a complementary step-wise model of stages of treatment. This model describes four major stages in the process of recovery:

- engagement
- persuasion
- active treatment
- relapse prevention (McHugo et al., 1995).

The step-wise treatment schema breaks down each of these four stages into two subphases, with each phase being defined operationally.

Note the similarity between the language used here and the vocabulary of motivational interviewing. Only one term—"persuasion"—carries connotations that offend the collaborative and client-centred principles so important in MI. For that reason, we suggest using the word "planning" instead. "Planning" refers to the process of identifying the client's goals and needs, and looking at the barriers and challenges to achieving these goals.

By bringing together these two complementary models of change and treatment, it becomes possible to map out the motivational principles and strategies relevant to particular stages in the process of change, treatment and recovery, as we see in Table 3-1: Principles and Strategies for Stages of Change and Treatment.

TABLE 3-1

Principles and strategies for

STAGE OF CHANGE	STAGE OF TREATMENT	TASKS AND MOTIVATIONAL STRATEGIES	STAGE OF CHANGE
PRE-CONTEMPLATION	Pre-engagement	Outreach to establish contact with client. Listen reflectively. Affirm.	Client has no contact with mental health or substance use worker.
	Engagement	Give practical help for client's immediate concerns. Model open, honest communication. Express empathy.	Client has assigned worker but no regular contact.
CONTEMPLATION	Early planning	Align with client's struggle with mental health and substance use problems. Explore client's goals. Support client's desire to change.	Client has regular contact but no reduction in substance use.
PREPARATION	Late planning	Explore client's concerns about mental health and substance use. Develop discrepancies between the client's goals and his or her current behaviours. Identify options and help client decide on a course of action. Plan social supports.	Client discusses substance use in regular contact, and shows reduction in use for at least 30 days.

(continued on next page)

STAGE OF CHANGE	STAGE OF TREATMENT	TASKS AND MOTIVATIONAL STRATEGIES	STAGE OF CHANGE
ACTION	Early active treatment	Start action plan. Elicit change talk. Reward progess. Use slips as learning opportunities. Involve social supports. Develop specific action steps to work on target behaviours. Encourage self-efficacy.	Client is engaged in treatment with the goal of abstinence or reduction, though he or she may still be using substances.
	Late active treatment	Continue to elicit change talk. Review and reinforce actions that are producing behaviour change. Review and identify new goals as client continues with change. Emphasize health alternatives. Identify examples of self-efficacy. Nurture and sustain social supports.	The client is engaged, and has achieved clear goals for changing his or her substance use for less than six months.
MAINTENANCE	Relapse prevention	Keep focus on client's goals. Reinforce link between change behaviour and accomplishment of client's goals. Identify continuing high-risk situations Develop relapse prevention plans. Reinforce self-efficacy.	The client is engaged, and has achieved clear goals for changing his or her substance use for at least six months (occasional lapses allowed).

(continued on next page)

STAGE OF CHANGE	STAGE OF TREATMENT	TASKS AND MOTIVATIONAL STRATEGIES	STAGE OF CHANGE
MAINTENANCE (CONTINUED)	Recovery	Focus attention on client's gains. Review for new areas of risk. Identify other goal areas. Support continued social engagement for mutual aid, leisure, spirituality, learning and volunteering.	The client has had no problems with substance use for at least one year, and is no longer in substance use treatment (but may continue with aftercare and/or mutual aid/peer support).

stages of change and treatment

CONCURRENT DISORDERS CLIENTS AND CHANGE

Many experts who work with clients with concurrent disorders stress the importance of developing strategies to increase the client's engagement and motivation (e.g., Martino et al., 2002). Clients with concurrent disorders are more likely than others to have experienced failed attempts to change (Zeidonis & Trudeau, 1997). The interactions of their substance use and mental health problems may have compounded problems with adherence to treatment plans and compromised the success of previous therapies, and may also make it difficult to match clients with suitable care (Handmaker et al., 2002). These clients are more likely than other clients to feel demoralized and discouraged about the prospects of improving their situation, because of their symptoms, past failure in treatment or poor functional adjustment (Martino et al., 2002). Clients may feel that their substance use gives them relief from other symptoms and from the distress they feel in their lives, and so they may be ambivalent about changing behaviours that they see as helping them cope.

Motivational interviewing and concurrent disorders

Many therapists in the concurrent disorders field find motivational interviewing an appealing approach, because of its emphasis on building a client's motivation to change and on developing strategies for handling resistance to the change process in a collaborative and flexible way (Martino et al., 2002). MI provides the tools to enable the therapist and client to work together productively to address habits that—at least in some key ways—the client values. Because it is a non-confrontational approach, it is well suited for clients with mental health problems—particularly people with schizophrenia, who are less likely to benefit from confrontational approaches (Van Horn & Bux, 2001).

MI's focus on enhancing the client's self-esteem and self-efficacy is important, as these qualities tend to be undermined by the many social and developmental disappointments that clients may have experienced (Carey, 1996). MI can be used from the first contact with a client at an assessment or screening interview, and throughout the treatment process. As a result, over time, clients see the impact of their behaviour choices on their functioning (Carey, 1996).

MI may be used to achieve a number of objectives for clients with concurrent disorders. The client and therapist may discuss focusing on multiple changes, such as adherence to attending appointments, taking prescribed medication and reducing substance use (Handmaker et al., 2002). Alternatively, MI can be used to focus on one behaviour change at a time. MI can therefore be organized into a hierarchy of treatment goals, with the client choosing how to proceed (Handmaker et al., 2002).

Setting goals and building hope

While the therapist has an active role in MI, the method is profoundly client-centred. The therapist starts with the client's goals. This means accepting that some clients will not want to change their substance use, or will want to stop using only one drug while continuing to use another. It means that the client may not want to stay on prescribed medications or to take them as often as advised.

Acknowledging a client's goals does not necessarily mean agreeing with the client's perspectives and lifestyle. It does require assuming that the client is ambivalent both about change and about the behaviours that he or she is attached to. The therapist's objective is to help clients see the discrepancy between their current situation and their goal. Even more than that, the therapist wants the client to feel more hopeful about the prospects of change. Building hope for the future is one of the key tasks of MI.

Clients' goals may include:

- getting an apartment
- upgrading skills
- continuing their schooling
- finding satisfying recreational activities
- being in a relationship with someone they care for
- working for pay
- reconnecting with their family
- being more physically fit or losing weight.

Clients often have very practical and immediate goals. Even when their goal appears too lofty, it is usually possible to identify immediate steps that are required if the goal is to pursued. By listening to, affirming and respecting the client as someone with hopes and goals, the therapist seeks to activate the process of change.

The therapist becomes an advocate of change. This includes considering the full needs of the client, and ensuring that plans are followed through and barriers identified and overcome. It may also involve helping the client to get practical help, including housing, financial entitlements, medical care, and family and peer support. It does not mean that the therapist is shackled with these tasks as responsibilities; rather that in mobilizing the clients to resolve the discrepancies between where they are and where they want to be, the work often moves to very practical considerations and requires a very pragmatic therapeutic mindset.

Relapse

In the motivational approach, relapse—a normal part of the journey to recovery according to the transtheoretical model—is expected and is used in a positive way. MI practitioners accept that change is not always unidirectional, but may often reverse. The key for the therapist is to be continuously aware of the client's current state, and to work with the client as he or she is in the present moment.

Benefits of using motivational interviewing

There are numerous advantages to using the MI approach with clients who have concurrent disorders:

- First, MI is client-centred at heart, and therefore can be tailored to the complex interactions between clients' mental health and their substance use problems.
- Further, the motivational approach does not initially require that clients admit they have a problem, and it allows goals to be matched to the client's needs and abilities, as well as allowing for affirmation of the most subtle accomplishments.
- MI offers short-term goals as part of a long-term relationship. Because the motivational approach is not based on the pursuit of set goals, there is always something to do in sessions, even when it appears that an impasse has been reached.
- MI values incremental change (e.g., a client's accepting that there is a downside to using street drugs to alleviate mood problems) as well as categorical change (e.g., quitting street drugs altogether).
- A further, related benefit for clients with concurrent disorders is the relationship-building dimension of MI. Studies have shown that such clients tend to require long-term treatment. Indeed, length of treatment is shown by many studies to be the most important variable in predicting outcome.
- In contrast to the intense, often brief and sometimes explosive interventions of standard substance use treatment, MI goals and strategies are flexible and will alter with time. This aids the development of a lasting client–therapist relationship. MI is thus

suited to a variety of long-term settings such as day programs, outpatient units and supportive continuing care (Health Canada, 2002).

MOTIVATIONAL INTERVIEWING PRINCIPLES

MI practice is often referred to as an interpersonal "style" rather than a series of rules. It is commonly broken down into four therapeutic principles:
- Express empathy.
- Develop discrepancy.
- Roll with resistance.
- Support self-efficacy.

Express empathy

MI is characterized by a client-centred and empathic counselling style that reflects and clarifies the client's experiences and meanings without the addition of any material from the counsellor. By listening to, affirming and respecting the client as someone with hopes and goals, the counsellor seeks to activate the process of change.

The counsellor's role is non-judgmental acceptance of the client. However, acceptance does not necessarily include agreement, and you may often have to explain this subtle distinction. Empathic acceptance reduces the likelihood that the client will become defensive if he or she "fails" to progress as desired. Interestingly, when clients perceive empathy in their counsellor, they often also become more receptive to gentle challenges and observations. Research has shown that empathy from the counsellor is a significant determinant of the client's response to treatment (Miller & Rollnick, 2002).

Develop discrepancy

The concept of discrepancies in MI is a departure from pure client-centred counselling. The aim of developing discrepancy is to create and then amplify the client's sense of the gulf between the client's present behaviour and his or her broader goals and values. The importance of change emerges as a natural result of acknowledging discrepancies; how to effect this change is dealt with at a later stage.

Roll with resistance

Counselling interviews are not about winning and losing. Resistance to change is normal, and in fact useful, because it reveals the client's views and further defines his or her problem areas. Resistance in the form of anger, silence or disagreement need not indicate a lack of motivation on the client's part. Resistance can be reframed to create further momentum for change.

Support self-efficacy

The client's self-efficacy—the belief in his or her ability to succeed—is essential in order for change to occur. Although it is understood in MI sessions that change is made by the client, the counsellor's support, encouragement and positive expectations are essential in moving the process along. Referring to the client's past achievements or other clients' success stories is a useful affirmatory tool. Reminding the client that there is no single correct way to make change—that he or she may have creative and useful ideas to try—is another useful strategy.

MOTIVATIONAL INTERVIEWING TECHNIQUES

MI relies on four basic techniques:
- open-ended questions
- affirmations
- reflective listening
- summaries.

Open-ended questions

Open-ended questions are questions that cannot be answered by a simple "yes" or "no" or by just a few words. Instead, these questions invite the client to talk about his or her life and concerns. Typical opening questions are "What brings you here today?" (for a first meeting) or "Could you tell me what has happened since we met last week?" Open-ended questions are intended to create momentum and to help the client explore his or her situation and the possibility of change (Miller & Rollnick, 2002).

Affirmations

Affirmations are statements by the counsellor that acknowledge the client's strengths. People with substance use problems have probably had failures, and may doubt their ability to make things better. Pointing out strengths can instil much-needed confidence (Miller & Rollnick, 2002).

Reflective listening

Reflective listening involves listening attentively and then responding to what the client has said. Reflective responses are the counsellor's best guess at what the client means. Reflection is not intended to question the client's meaning, but to demonstrate understanding and acceptance. Therefore the reflective listener gives this meaning back in the form of a statement, not a question; the intonation of a reflective listening statement goes down at the end, not up as it would with a question (Miller & Rollnick, 2002).

Summaries

Summaries are a special form of reflective listening in which the counsellor reflects back what the client has been saying over a longer period. Summaries communicate the counsellor's interest and build rapport. Summaries can focus on important parts of the interview, make links, or change the direction of the interaction. This technique is particularly useful when the counsellor wants to move on from an interaction that is not productive (Miller & Rollnick, 2002).

ADAPTING MOTIVATIONAL INTERVIEWING FOR CONCURRENT DISORDERS

While MI is well established as a technique for addressing motivational issues in clients with concurrent disorders, it is only recently that therapists and researchers have started to adapt it to target issues specific to groups within the concurrent disorders population. For example, dual diagnosis motivational interviewing (DDMI) is an application of MI designed to be used with clients who have concurrent psychotic disorders and substance use problems (Martino et al., 2002).

DDMI adds two guidelines to the four principles of MI. First, the therapist should adopt an integrated concurrent disorders interview approach that targets more than just substance use. This can be done by asking clients open-ended questions about the interaction of their substance use and their mental health. DDMI also recommends that the therapist focus on increasing the client's motivation to follow a treatment plan and to follow medication schedules, as well as changing substance use behaviours.

Second, the therapist should accommodate the client's cognitive impairments, in particular, problems with attention and concentration, short-term memory, the organization of information and mental flexibility. This can be done by using more repetition, using concrete language and visual aids, and providing more breaks within sessions. It is often necessary to put more emphasis on strategically guiding the conversation, since unstructured conversations that probe belief systems may exacerbate psychotic behaviours.

DDMI also recommends modifying MI techniques such as open-ended questions, reflection and affirmation:

- **open-ended questions:** Use plain language. Each question should deal with one idea. Simplify the decisional balance exercise so that the client is asked to evaluate only the benefits and costs of changing his or her behaviour, rather than also considering the pros and cons of not changing.
- **reflection:** Pause to reflect more often, use metaphors, put less emphasis on negative life events, use summaries to organize the client's thoughts and give clients more time to respond.
- **affirmation:** Account for the effects of the "double stigma" faced by clients with serious mental health and substance use problems. Remember that clients with concurrent disorders are often made to feel that they are "system misfits," and that they may need a great deal of assurance that they can change.

RESEARCH STUDIES WITH CONCURRENT DISORDERS CLIENTS

Recent research in MI shows its effectiveness in engaging and retaining clients with concurrent disorders, along with a positive effect on medication compliance and on treatment outcomes. However, empirical evidence is modest as to its longer-term impact on client health.

In small sample groups, MI has been shown to increase the likelihood of clients attending follow-up visits after a period in hospital:

- Daley and Zuckoff (1998) studied psychiatric inpatients with a concurrent addiction problem, and found that a motivational interview prior to discharge nearly doubled the rate of adherence with the first outpatient session from 35 per cent to 67 per cent.
- Daley et al. (1998) reinforced these findings with similar results from a more specific client population: those with concurrent major depressive disorder and cocaine dependence.
- Swanson et al. (1999) studied the effect of MI on aftercare attendance among 121 inpatients (77 per cent of whom had a concurrent substance abuse disorder). Similarly to the previous two studies, they demonstrated that two MI sessions more than doubled the rate of adherence with an initial outpatient session after discharge, from 16 per cent to 42 per cent.

MI techniques have also been shown to increase client commitment to treatment:

- In a pilot study, Martino et al. (2000) showed that of a sample of clients who were due to attend an outpatient day program, those who received a 40- to 60-minute motivational interview showed better attendance patterns than those who received the standard pre-admission interview.
- In another pilot study, Graeber et al. (2000) compared three 60-minute MI sessions with three educational treatment sessions for clients with concurrent alcohol depen-

dency and schizophrenia. Although both groups reduced their alcohol consumption, the group that received the motivational sessions had far fewer drinking days than the other clients. In addition, their attendance in the treatment program and continuous sobriety during the first 30 days were significantly higher. This study is the first to show that MI in addition to outpatient treatment improves short-term alcohol drinking outcomes with clients who have severe, chronic mental disorders.

- A U.K. study (Kemp et al., 1996) looked at the differences in medication compliance in 47 inpatients who received either "compliance therapy" (a modified version of MI) or routine supportive counselling. At six-month follow-up, the clients who had received the MI-type intervention had 23 per cent higher rates of compliance than the control group. A subsequent study (Kemp et al., 1998) randomly assigned 74 clients to MI-type or other therapies, and found 18 months later that those in the former group had better "global assessment of functioning," higher rates of retention in treatment, better insight, better compliance and lower rates of rehospitalization than the others.

In all the above studies, sample sizes were relatively low and the effectiveness of treatment was measured according to very limited criteria. Larger studies, with a wider scope, are needed to shed further light on the benefits of the motivational approach.

COMBINING MOTIVATIONAL INTERVIEWING WITH OTHER APPROACHES

MI does not involve training clients in behavioural coping skills, since it is assumed that the principal obstacle to overcome in eliciting change is the client's ambivalence. Nonetheless, the teaching of useful skills to complement the client's new, more motivated state may take place in other therapeutic settings. MI is a therapeutic approach that can usefully and easily be integrated with other, more didactic approaches, with other psychotherapies such as cognitive-behavioural therapy, and with pharmacotherapy.

MOTIVATIONAL INTERVIEWING IN ACTION: MARCUS'S STORY

The following case study is taken from our recent experience. Although certain details have been changed to preserve confidentiality, we have used the client's own words as far as possible and have narrated his change experience in rich detail in order to illustrate the tenets of motivational work. Marcus's story is divided here into several phases, which correspond to the stages of change as set out by Prochaska and colleagues (1994). The description of each stage is followed by our commentary.

Introduction

Marcus was born in Canada, of Caribbean parents. He is in his mid-30s. Since completing high school he has worked intermittently, mainly for brief periods. His housing and relationships have also been unstable. As he puts it, "I still haven't put down roots." He has been involved with the criminal justice system off and on for 15 years. Increasingly this has included crimes of violence, often committed under the influence of drugs.

Marcus has been treated by the mental health system on occasion, but there too his connections are usually short-lived and episodic. He has been diagnosed with schizoaffective disorder with paranoid features, with co-occurring substance dependence (alcohol, cocaine and marijuana). He has been effectively treated by small amounts of antipsychotic medication for the delusional thinking that tends to trigger his bouts of aggressive behaviour. Currently, Marcus has been directed by the courts to seek treatment for both his mental health and substance use problems, as a condition of probation.

Marcus's precontemplation stage

Marcus is angry and hostile when he presents for his initial appointment. He argues that he has been taking the medication that was prescribed for him during his forensic assessment. He further claims that he has stopped using cocaine, which he sees as the cause of all his problems. He has agreed to curtail his occasional drinking, but is adamant that he should be allowed to continue to use marijuana.

He thinks he is doing what is reasonable to expect of him, based on what he calls "the dumb situation that I'm caught in." When asked to explain, he says that he got into an argument with some people, including a woman he thought he liked, at a bar. They started saying some nasty things to him, and when he couldn't handle it any longer, he struck back. Unfortunately, the woman got hurt. He adds that he has already apologized to her for throwing his glass at her. She hadn't been seriously injured, and there isn't much else that he can do about it.

Marcus says that he does want to get a handle on cocaine and has not used it in three months. He feels that alcohol is part of life, though he can take it or leave it. He knows that his probation will be more hassle-free if he doesn't drink, so has agreed to that. What he doesn't agree to is the expectation that he not smoke marijuana. He says he is very interested in the Rastafarian religion and accepts its claim that marijuana has spiritual significance: "That's my experience, man. When I'm smoking marijuana, I'm much more calm, much more spiritual, more at peace. If it was available, do you think I'd be doing any of these other drugs?" Marcus then states that he has already had one urine screen come back positive for the drug and that, because of his record, if it happens again he's likely to be busted and sent back to jail. He is receiving social assistance and living in supported housing.

At this point, the therapist summarizes what Marcus has said and highlights his accomplishments, including his convincing the court that he could handle a probationary sentence. The therapist points out that Marcus has already stopped using cocaine, he isn't drinking, and he is getting settled in the community after being in detention and then in hospital for almost three months. The therapist asks how important it is for Marcus to stay out of jail and in the community, to which Marcus replies, "Man, I don't want to go back!" The therapist sympathizes, and then observes that other than the marijuana use, there is nothing threatening Marcus's goal to stay in the community.

The therapist then asks the client what the good things are about using marijuana. The client talks about the benefits that he experiences, including being less anxious and paranoid, more able to enjoy the moment, and even to do some drawing, adding that he would like to become an artist. The therapist summarizes these positives and then asks what is not so good about using the drug. The client thinks for a moment and then says, "To tell you the truth, nothing. There is nothing bad about marijuana use." He goes on to say that this has been a part of the life of his community and of the men in his family for as far back as he knows. His father and grandfather smoked marijuana. Again the therapist summarizes the client's comments and concludes, "So on the inside—how the drug makes you feel, and what it means for you—there are some really positive things to say, but when it comes to negatives, nothing stands out. From where you sit, this isn't a problem—in fact, it's a good thing."

The client responds, "You got it!"

Therapist: Yet you have a problem here. Even though this is not a problem for you, your probation officer says that if it continues to show in your urine screens, he will breach your probation. How do you feel about that?

Client: It pisses me off, is how I feel about it—I don't think it's fair.

T: Have you tried to talk to him about it?

C: Yes, and the more I do, the more I feel that he'll bust me!

T: So where does that leave you?

C: It leaves me feeling really angry and ripped off.

T: So while you feel there's nothing wrong with your smoking, it could be the cause of you going back to jail. How important is not going back to jail?

C: Man, it's the most important thing. I feel that I'm finally close to getting some good things to happen in my life. My housing therapist is also connecting me with some art lessons.

T: How important is it to keep smoking pot?

C: It's how I chill, man, plus most of my buddies are into it.

T: If you had other ways of chilling, would that matter?

C: If you mean for me to be taking more of your drugs, man, I'm not into it. Have you ever tried any of that stuff?

T: No, I wasn't thinking of just that, although sometimes medication can play a helping role.

C: Well, if you have good ideas, I could use them, because otherwise, I'm at a standoff with them, and if it stays that way, I lose and they win.

T: Well, let's see if we can find a way of working on this where nobody has to lose. It sounds like you want to stay in the community more than anything, but if you have to stop marijuana use to accomplish that, it's going to be hard, because for a number of reasons, smoking is something you rely on.

C: That just about says it all, man. I don't want to go back.

COMMENTARY

- Marcus starts this session in a precontemplative state about his marijuana use. He does, however, express a commitment to change his cocaine use as well as to stop drinking. In these two areas, he is at the contemplative stage.
- Marcus is taking action—but it is important to note that this need not mean that he stops being ambivalent. He is in fact angry at being in this situation.
- Rather than confronting or challenging Marcus, the therapist takes a respectful interest in his concerns and his goals. By taking a non-judgmental stance, the therapist is not telling Marcus what to do, but making him aware that he has choices.
- The client is ambivalent about change, but he acknowledges a discrepancy between

his views about marijuana and the requirements he has to meet to stay on probation. That is the motivation for change that the therapist can tap into at this time.

- In terms of his marijuana use, Marcus is now in the position to do the work of the contemplation stage of change: looking at and weighing the pros and cons.

Marcus's contemplation stage

When Marcus returns to meet with the therapist, the therapist asks him about the areas in which he has already made change, checking and complimenting his continuing progress. At the same time, the therapist keeps the conversation about marijuana open, trying to move the decisional balance toward change. In order to make this decision, the client needs to perceive the pain of change as being less than the pain of staying the same.

Marcus informs the therapist that he has been to see his probation officer, who has informed him that a second drug screen has come back positive for marijuana.

C: And, you know, he told me he was going to have to send in a report for me, saying I was non-compliant with my probation order. He even admits that I'm cool regarding the other stuff I'm supposed to do, but that isn't good enough. I have to stop smoking pot too.

T: So, in light of your progress in other areas, you think he is making too much of this other issue? Have you asked him why he's sticking to the rules?

C: When I tell him coke and crack have been what screwed me up, he says he's not so sure, since the last time I got in trouble I was drinking and had just smoked a joint. But I told him he just doesn't get it—that was a total exception.

T: So he's not so sure that marijuana is as trouble-free a drug as you see it to be. And you are admitting that the last episode didn't involve cocaine, but alcohol and pot. So, even if you don't blame it on the pot, it looks like it wasn't able to protect you by keeping you cool in a situation that became very hot.

C: You know, I thought it would keep me cool, but it didn't that time. I really did lose it.

T: You're in a tough spot, Marcus. On the one hand, you're pretty reliant on marijuana; but on the other hand, if you continue, you could be sent back to jail. Have you thought of your options?

C: Sometimes I want to take a stand, you know. Tell them to do what they've got to do and become like a political prisoner or something. I know that I can get all the pot I want in jail. But then I realize that as right as that might make me feel, I'd be wasting away in there, wasting my life and wasting my time. I'm headed for 40, man, and I want to get my life back.

T: So, are you saying that you could keeping smoking pot and probably go to jail, but that if you want to get your life back, you'll have to stop smoking?

C: Sure seems like that to me, unless you got any other ideas.

T: No, I wish I did, but I don't—you're in a tough spot and you've got tough decisions to make. But let me ask you: Is it that you don't want to stop or that you don't believe you can?

C: It's mainly that I don't really want to, but even if I decided to, it wouldn't be the easiest thing to do.

T: Well, that's a good sign. The hardest part here is accepting that you'll need to stop smoking pot to ensure that you don't go back to jail. The fact that you realize that it won't be easy is just as important. How about if we talk about the challenges you'd have to face if you were to decide that getting your life back is the most important priority to you right now. That would give us an idea of some of things that you'd have to tackle if this is going to work for you. You're saying the key to ensuring that is stopping the pot.

C: OK, I really don't want this to get in the way of where I need to go right now. But it gives me a really queasy feeling to think about doing this.

COMMENTARY

- Marcus has entered the contemplation stage of change, and understandably has "queasy" feelings about the challenges ahead.
- By strengthening the client's perception of the disadvantages of not changing and the advantages of making a change, the therapist is helping "tip the balance."
- The therapist avoids being prescriptive or alarmist. Instead, he listens to the client empathically and develops the discrepancies in Marcus's situation in order to place his dilemma in sharper relief.
- By asking the client to imagine some of the challenges he would have to face to make change, the therapist hopes to build Marcus's sense of self-efficacy at the same time as identifying the practical tasks of change.

Marcus's action and maintenance phases

Marcus has been able to abstain from marijuana for some time now. He had to be patient, because it takes weeks for the drug to be cleared from the body. It was only in his second month of non-use that Marcus's urine screens came back negative for the drug. He has worked with his therapist to avoid high-risk situations, and to explore and introduce alternative behaviour in his life.

For example, he has returned to playing recreational sports and now rides a bike to get around the city. He has had one relapse to marijuana use, but the therapist was able to meet with Marcus and his probation officer to review the situation. The probation officer agreed that it was more of a learning experience than a fatal rule violation.

COMMENTARY

- Marcus's motivation to enter the action phase has been internally generated. His reasons for wishing to stay away from the drug are uniquely his own, and therefore he does not feel coerced or "talked into" abstinence.
- His decision involved considerable personal sacrifice, yet he felt that the rewards of change were greater than the rewards of staying the same.
- His one slippage back into marijuana use was, in this instance, not framed as a "relapse" but as an acceptable part of his difficult maintenance period.

Onwards around the wheel

Marcus is once again going through a rough spot. It has been nine months since he made the decision to stop smoking marijuana. His probation still has more than 18 months to go.

Now the issue is medication compliance. Marcus is unhappy with some of the side-effects, and since its action is more to dampen his tendency toward paranoid delusions than to induce a positive state of well-being, he is feeling down and demoralized. His progress has plateaued and he feels that the medication is producing more problems than benefits.

C: I don't think I need the medication any more. I don't like the way it dries me out, and I expected I would lose more weight than I have since I became more physically active. I've been cutting back.

T: Have you spoken with your doctor about this?

C: Yes, but he says I should stay on it. He doesn't seem to get it that the meds are really starting to bug me. I tried to tell him, but he told me to hang in there, that everything is working well.

T: So, you're not so sure if the meds are of any benefit any more, but you are sure that there are other effects that you're aren't so happy about. What did you like about them, if anything, when you started?

C: Well, they helped me keep my head from going offside with crazy thoughts that get me into trouble. They might have helped a bit when I first stopped smoking pot. But now I don't know, I just know about the downside to being on this stuff.

T: So, it was easier to see that the medication was having some benefit at the beginning, but now that you are in a better space it's harder to know if you're getting any benefit from it. What would be the worst thing that could happen as a result of stopping it or cutting back on your own?

C: I could get all those paranoid thoughts back and, if I really lost it again in terms of my getting angry easily, I could end up in trouble with the law. I sure don't want to be arrested and jailed again.

T: What's the worst thing about continuing?

C: The way it makes me feel physically—plus for someone who believes in smoking pot, I don't believe in taking drugs a lot.

T: Sounds like the risks of having those paranoid thoughts come back do concern you, although you don't feel you're getting any benefit from the meds right now. And you don't like the way they are making you feel.

C: You got it. I'm starting to wonder why I am working on this stuff anyway. I'm feeling stuck and it's getting to me.

T: Sometimes change is an uneven process, with some rough spots. Maybe now's a good time to review how much progress you've made and the next goals you want to set. I'd suggest we involve the doctor and the others who are working with you, including the probation officer. I'm going to make sure they realize the important changes you've made already. But first, how about if you and I go over your progress to date, and also what's frustrating you, to make sure we give them the right understanding of that as well?

C: That's sounds like what we should do, but let's do it quick—I don't want to have to wait forever for a meeting.

T: Agreed, and let's talk about what we can be doing in the meantime to make things work better for you.

COMMENTARY

- One of the major challenges in the maintenance stage of change is non-compliance with medication. Understanding this and the risk of relapse to substance use are the two key factors in preventing these problems.
- Rather than contesting or arguing with the client, the therapist listens and reflects back to the client that he understands the client's concern.
- The therapist then explores the discrepancy between the earlier time, when the client was more inclined to use the medication, and now, when he is complaining about it. This allows the client to identify some of the benefits to date.
- By answering questions about worst-case scenarios of stopping or continuing the medication, the client himself articulates the high stakes for him if paranoid delusions return to his thinking process.
- The therapist nonetheless does not discount the client's concern and growing frustration, suggesting that these be the focus of a review that will highlight how the client has done to date.
- Marcus's new difficulties suggest that relapse is a real danger at this point. But, older and wiser and with a strong relationship with his therapist on his side, he is more powerfully equipped to re-enter the wheel of change should relapse occur.

SUMMARY

When we work with clients using the motivational paradigm, they will often report that this is the first time they have been able to talk about the often confusing, contradictory and uniquely personal elements of their conflict. They have noted that the interactional experience was "different" and that they are now seeing things differently from before. They are surprised that we have taken a respectful interest in the positive aspects of their substance use, and to the ambivalence they sometimes have about prescribed psychotropic medications, without subjecting them to gratuitous advice and direction.

We have observed that a new atmosphere of choice, appraisal, reflection and responsibility emerges, based more on the pragmatics of the clients' current situation and their longer-term goals than on idealized formulations that originate with the counsellor. Instead, clients ideally find someone who is compassionately joined to their dilemma—they have difficult decisions to make, but the counsellor is willing to work with them every step of the way, one step at a time.

The motivational approach, to return to Miller and Rollnick's (2002) core premise, is "a way of being with people." As such, it is more than a set of techniques or manoeuvres. MI does not attempt to displace the needs for other elements in the process of treatment, change and recovery, such as pharmacotherapy and psychosocial rehabilitation resources, or behavioural skills training. But what it asserts is a fundamental belief about the human experience of working with people who have problems and who are usually ambivalent and demoralized about their prospects for constructive change. It is a way of joining with the client who intends to start and to continue a process of constructive action that is profoundly person-centered and passionately committed to a collaborative journey of change.

REFERENCES

Burke, B.L., Arkowitz, H. & Dunn, C. (2002). The efficacy of motivational interviewing. In W.R. Miller & S. Rollnick (Eds.), *Motivational Interviewing: Preparing People for Change* (2nd ed.), pp. 217–250. New York: Guilford Press.

Carey, K.B. (1996). Substance use reduction in the context of outpatient psychiatric treatment: A collaborative, motivational harm reduction approach. *Community Mental Health Journal, 32*, 291–306.

Daley, D.C., Salloum, I.M., Zuckoff, A., Kirisci, L. & Thase, M.E. (1998). Increasing treatment adherence among outpatients with depression and cocaine dependence: Results of a pilot study. *American Journal of Psychiatry, 155*, 1611–1613.

Daley, D.C., & Zuckoff, A. (1998). Improving compliance with the initial outpatient session among discharged inpatient dual diagnosis clients. *Social Work, 43*, 470–473.

Dunn, C., Deroo, L. & Rivara, F.P. (2001). The use of brief interventions adapted from motivational interviewing across behavioral domains: A systematic review. *Addiction, 96*(12), 1725–1742.

Graeber, D., Moyers, T., Griffiths, G., Guajardo, E. & Tonigan, S. (2000). *Comparison of motivational interviewing and educational intervention in patients with schizophrenia and alcoholism.* Paper presented at the scientific meeting of the Research Society on Alcoholism, Denver, CO.

Handmaker, N., Packard, M. & Conforti, K. (2002). Motivational interviewing in the treatment of dual disorders. In W.R. Miller & S. Rollnick (Eds.), *Motivational Interviewing: Preparing People for Change* (2nd ed.), pp. 363-376. New York: Guilford Press.

Health Canada (2002). *Best Practices: Concurrent Mental Health and Substance Use Disorders.* Ottawa: Minister of Public Works and Government Services Canada, Cat. #H39-599/2001-2E.

Kemp, R., David, A. & Hayward, P. (1996). Compliance therapy: An intervention targeting insight and treatment adherence in psychotic patients. *Behavioural and Cognitive Psychotherapy, 24,* 331–350.

Kemp, R., Kirov, G., Everitt, B., Hayward, P. & David, A. (1998). Randomised controlled trial of compliance therapy: 18 month follow-up. *British Journal of Psychiatry, 172,* 413–419.

Marlatt, G.A. & Gordon, J.R. (Eds.). (1985). *Relapse Prevention: Maintenance Strategies in the Treatment of Addictive Behaviors.* New York: Guilford Press.

Martino, S., Carroll, K.M., O'Malley, S.S. & Rounsaville, B.J. (2000). Motivational interviewing with psychiatrically ill substance abusing patients. *American Journal on Addictions, 9,* 88–91.

Martino, S., Carroll, K., Kostas, D., Perkins, J. & Rounsaville, B. (2002). Dual diagnosis motivational interviewing: A modification of motivational interviewing for substance-abusing patients with psychotic disorders. *Journal of Substance Abuse Treatment, 23,* 297–308.

McHugo, G.J., Drake, R.E., Burton, H.L. & Ackerson, T.H. (1995). A scale for assessing the stage of substance abuse treatment in persons with severe mental illness. *Journal of Nervous and Mental Disease, 183*(12), 762–767.

Miller, W.R. & Rollnick, S. (2002). *Motivational Interviewing: Preparing People for Change.* New York: Guilford Press.

Mueser, K.T., Noordsy, D.l., Drake, R.E. & Fox, L. (2003). *Integrated Treatment for Dual Diagnosis: A Guide to Effective Practice.* New York: Guilford.

Prochaska, J. & DiClemente, C. (1984). *The Trans-Theoretical Model: Crossing the Traditional Boundaries of Therapy.* Malabar, FL: Krieger.

Prochaska, J.O., Norcross, J.C. & DiClemente, C.C. (1994). *Changing for Good.* New York: Avon Books.

Rollnick, S., Mason, P. & Butler, C. (1999*). Health Behavior Change: A Guide for Practitioners.* London: Churchill Livingstone.

Sciacca, K. (1997). Removing barriers: Dual diagnosis and motivational interviewing. *Professional Counselor, 12*(1), 41–46.

Smyth, N.J., (1996). Motivating persons with dual disorders: A stage approach. *Families in Society: The Journal of Contemporary Human Services, 77,* 605–614.

Swanson, A.J., Pantalon, M.V. & Cohen, K.R. (1999). Motivational interviewing and treatment adherence among psychiatric and dually-diagnosed patients. *Journal of Nervous and Mental Disease, 187,* 630–635.

Van Horn, D.H.A. & Bux, D.A. (2001). A pilot test of motivational interviewing groups for dually diagnosed inpatients. *Journal of Substance Abuse Treatment, 20,* 191–195.

Zeidonis, D.M. & Trudeau, K. (1997). Motivation to quit using substances among individuals

Part II

Practical Applications

Chapter 4

A program model for integrated treatment: The Concurrent Disorders Service

ANDREA TSANOS

When we move beyond the general concept of integrated treatment and begin to talk about treatment approaches tailored for specific combinations of substance use and mental health problems, we find that the evidence becomes more sparse. Much of what is discussed in the following chapters is based on our clinical experience, and is influenced by the way our program developed and the clients we serve. This chapter outlines the program model of the Concurrent Disorders Service (CDS), and describes the referral, screening and assessment process, as well as the program ingredients and overall structure of this integrated treatment program.

The CDS evolved out of a substance use treatment service at the Addiction Research Foundation (ARF; one of the founding partners of the Centre for Addiction and Mental Health). This service offered a full range of treatment interventions, including health promotion, prevention, early intervention, brief outpatient treatment, and intensive day and residential treatment. In the early days of the CDS, most of the clients had mild to moderate mental health problems—anxiety and mood disorders were the most commonly diagnosed.

We began by customizing the approaches we had been using in our work with clients with substance use problems, to meet the needs of people who also had mental health problems. As we got more experience working with clients with concurrent disorders, and as more research into concurrent disorders treatment approaches became available, we developed groups and programs to meet the specialized needs that had become apparent. These are discussed in the chapters that follow.

WHAT THE CONCURRENT DISORDERS SERVICE OFFERS

The CDS offers specialized outpatient treatment to clients with substance use problems accompanied by mental health issues. Services include:

- comprehensive psychiatric assessment
- treatment planning and group preparation
- group therapy
- focused individual therapy
- case management
- pharmacotherapy
- access to medical and non-medical withdrawal management, if needed.

Rather than having rigid exclusion criteria, we accept clients in referral for consultation, which may or may not lead to treatment services being offered. If a client is not a suitable match for the services available through the CDS, staff will provide the referral source with treatment recommendations.

DIAGNOSTIC PROFILE OF CLIENTS AT THE CONCURRENT DISORDERS SERVICE

Because the majority of clients arrive at the CDS via the Addictions Program Intake Assessment, it is not surprising that the addiction problem is usually of greater concern and urgency to the client. Alcohol-related problems are the most common, followed by cannabis, cocaine and opioids (Table 4-1). About half of the clients in the CDS have more than one substance use diagnosis that meets the criteria of the American Psychiatric Association's *Diagnostic and Statistical Manual of Mental Disorders* (DSM-IV) (CAMH, 2000).

TABLE 4-1

Substance use among CDS clients, 2000

SUBSTANCE	% OF CLIENTS MEETING CRITERIA FOR ABUSE OR DEPENDENCE	# OF CLIENTS MEETING CRITERIA FOR ABUSE	# OF CLIENTS MEETING CRITERIA FOR DEPENDENCE
Alcohol	61%	75	228
Cocaine	27%	37	96
Opioids (heroin, prescription drugs, over-the-counter [OTC] preparations)	19%	16	77
Cannabis	30%	81	69

Mood disorders are the most prevalent concurrent mental health problems, followed by the anxiety disorders.

TABLE 4-2

Mental Health Axis I Disorders among CDS clients, 2000

DSM-IV (AXIS I) DIAGNOSTIC CATEGORY	# OF CLIENTS MEETING CRITERIA	% OF CLIENTS MEETING CRITERIA
Any DSM-IV diagnosis	**663**	**84.4**
All Mood Disorders	**452**	**60.3**
Major Depressive Disorder	157	20.9
Dysthymic Disorder	59	7.9
Bipolar Disorder	40	5.3
Cyclothymia	2	0.3
Substance-induced Mood Disorder	84	11.2
Unclear whether substance-induced	110	14.7
All Anxiety Disorders	**202**	**26.9**
Social Phobia	47	6.3
Panic Disorder	54	7.2
Generalized Anxiety Disorder	15	2.0
PTSD	25	3.3
Substance-induced Anxiety Disorder	20	2.7
OCD	15	2.0
Unclear whether substance-induced	26	3.5
All Psychotic Disorders	**101**	**13.5**
Schizophrenia	42	5.6
Schizoaffective Disorder	15	2.0
Schizophreniform Disorder	3	0.4
Substance-induced Psychosis	15	2.0
Unclear whether substance-induced	21	2.8
Other Axis I Disorders	**38**	**5.1**
Adjustment Disorder	12	1.6
Eating Disorders	11	1.5
ADHD	6	0.8
Dissociative Disorder	2	0.3

Note that it is often difficult to isolate substance use disorders and mental health disorders, particularly early in the assessment process; hence the category of "unclear whether substance-induced" was created.

TABLE 4-3

Axis II Disorders among CDS clients, 2000

DSM-IV (AXIS II) DIAGNOSES	# OF CLIENTS MEETING CRITERIA	% OF CLIENTS MEETING CRITERIA
Personality Disorders	**179**	**23.9**
Borderline	46	6.1
Antisocial	34	4.5
Mixed	27	3.6
Avoidant	18	2.4
Narcissistic	12	1.6
Paranoid	11	1.5
Dependent	9	1.2
Obsessive-Compulsive	8	1.1
Histrionic	7	0.9
Schizotypal	5	0.7
Schizoid	1	0.1
NOS	1	0.1

Note that many clients assessed were found to have Axis II "traits." However, clients meeting subthreshold criteria for personality disorders are not included in this data.

ACCESSING THE CONCURRENT DISORDERS SERVICE

For most clients, access to CDS programs is a three-tiered process:

1. an intake assessment
2. a Psychiatric Diagnostic Interview or therapist interview
3. Assessment of Group Suitability and Group Preparation.

The client can self-refer, or a clinician can call on the client's behalf. The referral procedure is identical regardless of whether the referral comes from an external program or a CAMH program.

Clients can be referred to the CDS in general, or directly to the Dialectical Behaviour Therapy (DBT) Clinic. The DBT clinic is also the only CDS program that accepts clients who do not have substance use problems.

Intake assessment

The CDS is a treatment service within a larger program at CAMH known as the Addictions Program. All of the addiction treatment services within the broader

Addictions Program share a common intake assessment. This preliminary assessment lasts approximately two hours, and consists of:

1. a semi-structured interview that includes administration of a core assessment tools package
2. outcome measures
3. a screen for mental health problems. This screener will determine if a client will be referred to the CDS.

The information gathered in the intake assessment enables us to recommend the best kind of treatment for the person's needs.

SEMI-STRUCTURED INTERVIEW

The semi-structured interview explores the nature of the person's substance use, and identifies his or her needs and strengths. It collects information about the client, such as:

- referral source and psychosocial situation (such as legal problems, living situation, etc.)
- substances used, by administering the Psychoactive Drug History Questionnaire, which collects information about frequency, quantity, patterns of use (e.g., alone or with friends), whether family or friends misuse substances, family history of substance use problem, substances of concern and substance use goal(s)
- treatment history for addiction and mental health problems, and medication status
- substance use problems, by administering the Adverse Consequences of Substance Use questionnaire, which collects information about, for example, health problems, blackouts, mood changes, relationship problems, verbal/physical abuse, school/work problems, legal problems and financial problems
- risk behaviours, such as injection drug use, unprotected sexual encounters
- anger issues
- risk of harm to self or others
- withdrawal symptoms
- history of physical, sexual or emotional trauma
- health-related conditions, such as pregnancy or developmental disabilities
- obstacles to treatment
- readiness to change.

OUTCOME MEASURES

Three measures provide baseline indicators of functioning. These measures are administered every three months while the client is in treatment, and when the client is discharged:

- Basis 32
- Resident Assessment Instrument (RAI), which is a set of substance use and gambling questions
- Global Assessment of Functioning (GAF), in which the assessment therapist provides an overall rating of the client.

MENTAL HEALTH SCREENING

As part of the intake assessment, the client completes a computerized screen for psychiatric and substance use problems. If a client screens positive for a current (active in the past month) mood, anxiety or eating disorder or lifetime history of a psychotic disorder (i.e., a disorder in the schizophrenia spectrum, or mania), the client is automatically referred to the Concurrent Disorders Service for a more comprehensive interview. Clients who do not screen positive are given options for referrals to other addiction treatments within our broader Addictions Program (e.g., Structured Relapse Prevention Group or Cocaine Coping Skills Group), or are given an external referral.

In the past, first appointments in CDS were always with a psychiatrist or psychologist for diagnostic assessment. However, this system created a bottleneck in that these appointments resulted in a nine-week wait between intake assessment and the first CDS appointment. To address this problem, we revised the referral procedure. Now, appointments are still made with a CDS psychiatrist directly from the Assessment Service, provided there is a need for the consultation. This would be determined by the presence of:

1. medication issue or potential need for medication
2. need for diagnostic clarification
3. need for recommendations about whether mental health problems might render a client unsuitable for a particular service in the broader Addictions Program (e.g., Women's Service, etc.).

The major change to the referral procedure is that assessment therapists can also make referrals directly to one of the CDS therapists for assessment for the particular group that matches the client's needs. With this new referral procedure, the appointment with the CDS therapist is made available within one to two weeks. To help in making a referral, assessment therapists have been provided with a description of the groups in CDS that are actively accepting referrals, along with clear inclusion/exclusion criteria (see Appendix: Concurrent Disorders Service: Inclusion and Exclusion Criteria).

For example, if a client who has a mood problem and a substance use problem reports difficulty with interpersonal functioning, the client would be referred to one of the therapists on the team who facilitates the Interpersonal Group (provided the client meets the criteria). If there is no need to see a psychiatrist, the client bypasses that appointment, and can be swiftly assessed for suitability for the group. This cuts down on wait time to get connected in the CDS, and also saves the client from having to repeat his or her "story" unnecessarily to yet another clinician who may not be the one who ultimately offers clinical service to the client. We find that this process also allows for better engagement and retention.

By the time the client reaches the CDS, there is a comprehensive description of the substance use problems and a strong indication of a mental health problem in one or more areas.

Psychiatric Diagnostic Interview

The Psychiatric Diagnostic Interview (PDI) is a semi-structured interview based on DSM-IV criteria and guidelines for differential diagnosis. The interview is typically one hour long, although subsequent appointments may be required to complete the interview.

At the end of the PDI process, the assessor arrives at provisional substance use and mental health diagnoses. These diagnoses are often revised based on ongoing assessment, particularly after periods of abstinence that can help clarify the diagnosis. We believe that three to four weeks of abstinence will generally allow for a more reliable diagnostic formulation for mood and anxiety disorders, as Schuckit and Monteiro (1988) have found. Another study, which followed people with alcohol use disorders and concurrent psychiatric symptoms, found the following symptom resolution times: four to six weeks for psychotic symptoms, three to six months for anxiety and depressive symptoms, and one to two years for personality disorder behaviours (Vaillant, 1983). These timelines can be a helpful guideline.

The information from the PDI is used for diagnostic formulation and treatment recommendation and planning, both within and outside the CDS. Recommendations based on the PDI are discussed with the client at the end of the PDI, or in a subsequent session after the case has been discussed in the team's Case Rounds meeting.

Occasionally, a client screens positive for a mental health problem but then, after undergoing the PDI, is not found to meet criteria for an Axis I or Axis II DSM-IV psychiatric disorder. In such cases, the client does not meet the definition for concurrent disorders, and thus would be referred to a more suitable treatment program.

Case Rounds

Case Rounds is a forum for presenting new cases and discussing diagnostic formulation and appropriate treatment planning. The case is presented by the psychiatrist or psychologist who assessed the client, after which the client is assigned to a group and a therapist. Once clients are assessed, the team decides on which treatment program will best suit each client.

A comprehensive document—listing the inclusion and exclusion criteria for each clinical group—serves as the guideline for determining whether or not a client is a suitable match for the services offered in the program (see Appendix: Concurrent Disorders Service: Inclusion and Exclusion Criteria). This determination is not based on diagnosis alone, but is a composite determination based on the client's situation and associated needs. The team discusses clients on a case-by-case basis, so that the inclusion/exclusion criteria might not be strictly adhered to, in the best interest of determining program suitability for the particular client.

CDS CLINICAL PROGRAMS

There are four specialty clinics within the CDS:
- the Integrative Group Psychotherapies (IGP) Clinic
- the Dialectical Behaviour Therapy (DBT) Clinic
- the Eating Disorders and Addiction Clinic
- the Anger and Addiction Clinic.

Integrative Group Psychotherapies Clinic

INTERPERSONAL GROUP

In the Interpersonal Group, members work on the primary goal of getting their substance use under control and are helped to explore and identify their interpersonal communication style and its impact on others. Part of the group focus is on trying to understand interpersonal issues in their historical contexts and familial backgrounds. Members explore how problematic and self-defeating relational patterns contribute to, or manifest in, mental health symptoms and substance use problems. Part of the group process involves work in the here-and-now, which includes observing and discussing interactions between group members and giving each other feedback. Clients attend a group once weekly, for a 90-minute session. In addition to attending group once weekly, many clients also receive supplemental individual therapy.

CONCURRENT DISORDERS PSYCHO-EDUCATION GROUP

The Concurrent Disorders Psycho-education Group is designed to give clients knowledge and strategies for coping with concurrent mental health and addiction issues. It consists of 12 weekly topic-based sessions, with each session running 1 1/2 hours. The emphasis is on uncovering clients' capacity to assume responsibility for their own recovery, with increased hope and commitment to change, self-awareness, compassion and perseverance.

THE ADDICTION GROUP FOR PSYCHIATRIC SURVIVORS

The Addiction Group for Psychiatric Survivors is for clients with active addiction problems and chronic, severe mental health disorders, such as schizophrenia. The group relies on a variety of therapy approaches, including relapse prevention, motivationally based and supportive strategies to facilitate change. This ongoing group meets weekly for an hour.

CONCURRENT DISORDERS TRAUMA GROUP

The Concurrent Disorders Trauma Group is for male and female clients who have a substance use problem and who have experienced serious childhood trauma (i.e., sexual, physical, emotional abuse, neglect, or other trauma) that is causing interference in their lives. This group meets once weekly for two-hour group sessions.

INTEGRATIVE GROUP THERAPY FOR CLIENTS WITH CONCURRENT ANXIETY AND SUBSTANCE USE DISORDERS

Integrative Group Therapy for Clients with Concurrent Anxiety and Substance Use Disorders is a four-month (16-session) group targeting goals related to substance use and anxiety symptom management, while also addressing the more global areas of functioning, such as self-care, affect regulation, self-esteem and personal responsibility. The group approach is an integrative one, involving cognitive explorations, behavioural approaches and the use of a psychodynamic framework.

Dialectical Behaviour Therapy Clinic (for clients with borderline personality disorder)

The Dialectical Behaviour Therapy (DBT) Clinic is an outpatient treatment program specifically designed for people who meet criteria for borderline personality disorder. The program is tailored to people who may also have multiple concurrent mental health problems or addiction problems. Treatment is comprehensive and involves a combination of weekly individual therapy, group skills training and after-hours telephone consultation. A psychoeducation group for family and friends is also available. Treatment focuses on helping people manage emotions, deal with problems, improve their relationships and lead a more balanced lifestyle.

Eating Disorders and Addiction Clinic

Treatment in the Eating Disorders and Addiction Clinic involves a combination of individual and group psychotherapy, both for female and male clients who have concurrent substance use and eating disorders. The treatment approach involves a combination of weekly two-hour group therapy sessions that are gender-specific (involving both experiential therapy and coping skills training), weekly one-hour individual psychotherapy sessions, and meetings with a physician, nurse and dietitian, as needed.

Anger and Addiction Clinic

The Anger and Addiction Clinic combines individual and group psychotherapy for male and female clients who have concurrent substance use and anger-related problems. Therapy is conducted by a treatment team, and involves weekly two-hour skills-training groups, and individual therapy as appropriate.

PHILOSOPHY OF CARE WITHIN THE CDS

In the CDS, substance use and mental health problems are both treated as primary problems. Group treatment approaches span both problem areas, and consider the impact of one on the other.

Mood and anxiety disorders

The majority of CDS clients have concurrent substance use and mood and/or anxiety disorders. With these clients, our first emphasis is to attempt to stabilize the client's substance use—this may involve helping the client to abstain from, or at least to cut down on, the substance use.

The body of evidence on treatment of these problems is still quite small. However, the available evidence supports treating the substance use first within an integrated treatment plan (Health Canada, 2002). We agree with this approach, for the following reasons:

- If the client is presenting to an addiction treatment centre, the substance use problem is usually of greater concern and higher urgency.
- Working toward abstinence will assist with a more reliable diagnosis for cases that have unclear etiologies (e.g., substance-induced anxiety/depression or not) (Verheul et al., 2000), because abstinence may cause the mental health problem to improve or even remit.
- Problematic substance use compromises the client's attention and resources for addressing the mental health problem. It is difficult to treat anxiety or depressive symptoms while substance use is excessive or out of control.
- Abstinence or reduced substance use should help to improve other life domains as well (e.g., return to work, interpersonal relationships). Social support and encouragement can promote further and sustained changes.
- Progress on the substance use problem has immediate beneficial effects on self-esteem, mood, etc. Efficacy with this problem can, it is hoped, be applied to other areas of concern for the client.

Other mental health disorders

It is important to note that, while the above recommendations are for mood and anxiety disorders, they do not apply to the anxiety disorder posttraumatic stress disorder (PTSD) or to psychotic disorders, eating disorders or personality disorders.

In people who have concurrent PTSD and a substance use disorder, targeting the substance problem without attending to the PTSD symptoms may cause the client's psychological functioning to worsen; conversely, if the PTSD symptoms are targeted without addressing the substance use, the client may feel at risk of using substances to cope. For PTSD, a careful integrated approach is the recommended treatment plan (Brown et al., 1998; Evans & Sullivan, 1995; Najavits et al., 1997).

Concurrent treatment of substance use and mental health problems is also recommended for clients with eating disorders, severe mental illnesses and borderline personality disorders. Integrated treatment approaches for these disorders are discussed in subsequent chapters.

The team approach

We think of all clients as clients of the CDS as a whole. However, each client has both a therapist and a psychiatrist attached to his or her case. The team members discuss their shared cases in the weekly Case Rounds meeting, and both are also available for ad-hoc consultation with other colleagues on the team.

ROLE OF THE PSYCHIATRIST

The psychiatrist who conducts the first psychiatric assessment becomes the client's physician-of-record and will provide psychiatric follow-up for care such as pharmacotherapy (if needed), if the client is accepted for treatment at the CDS. If the client has a long-standing, pre-existing relationship with an outside psychiatrist, it often makes sense to preserve this relationship (shared care) instead of assigning a CDS psychiatrist.

ROLE OF THE THERAPIST

In most cases, the therapist leads the group the client attends, and meets in one-on-one sessions with the client, when appropriate. The therapist is also the client's case manager, responding to needs and crises that may arise during treatment. In a few cases, the psychiatrist will co-lead the therapy group, see the client for individual therapy, and prescribe and monitor medication.

Some clinicians feel that the group therapist should deal with the group, while the individual therapist should deal with the issues pertaining only to the individual therapy. Others feel that such a model is too fragmented and that clients often reveal material in individual therapy that they may not ever bring into the group therapy, thus compromising the depth of exploration in the group. There are other advantages to having the same clinician responsible for both group and individual therapy:

- The clinician can get to know the client on an individual level, which assists with the depth of the clinical alliance.
- The clinician has the opportunity to see the client interact in a group setting with the client's peers.
- Such a model promotes continuity between the individual and group sessions.
- Fewer clinicians are involved in the client's care plan.

As with many clinical issues, there is no clear-cut answer to this question. The CDS uses both models, depending on the clinic.

CONFIDENTIALITY

Occasionally, the team approach can present its challenges to clients. For example, clients may share a disclosure with the therapist in an individual session and then ask that it not be discussed with anyone else, such as their psychiatrist on the team. Certainly, not all information that is discussed in therapy needs to be relayed to the psychiatrist. Disclosure to the team is typically motivated by a concern for the welfare of the client.

For example, if the client reports either discontinuing medication or using substances without the knowledge of the prescribing psychiatrist, the therapist may need to discuss this behaviour with the rest of the team for their awareness and/or for input into management of the issues.

If information must be shared with the team, we begin by exploring the client's discomfort around the other caregiver's being aware of this information. We need to balance this discussion by trying to empathize with the client's anxiety about the issue. We review the rationale for the team approach with the client, as a gentle reminder that this was explained when treatment began. It is often useful to address the client's fears and fantasies about what may occur should the information be shared.

One way to reduce the client's discomfort is to offer choice as to how this information will be relayed. For example, the client may wish to disclose the information directly, rather than have it be disclosed on his or her behalf.

Case management

There is no universal definition or model of clinical case management. Our definition of case management may differ from others in the literature.

Anyone who has worked with clients of concurrent disorders services knows that this is a vulnerable population with multiple needs. It is our goal to see that clients receive services that are matched to their needs and that occur in the right sequence and in a timely fashion.

While it is sometimes necessary to refer the client to services in the community, it is better to treat a client in one facility. Clients who receive care at more than one location are often exposed to multiple models of care. This may confuse a client early in recovery. Within our treatment setting, the client's therapist is expected to respond to all his or her needs.

THE THERAPIST AS CASE MANAGER

There are several functions inherent in the role of case manager.

Co-ordination and accountability

In the CDS, the case manager co-ordinates the client's services in the following ways. He or she:

- is the point of responsibility when multiple caregivers and service components are involved

- knows what is going on with the client throughout all stages of the client's participation in the group
- collaborates and consults with the psychiatrist on the team who is also involved in the client's care
- helps develop, implement and monitor the treatment plan with the client's psychiatrist
- includes the client's additional caregivers in our treatment planning
- *with the clients' consent*:
  - contacts community workers who meet with clients in their natural settings as well as other counsellors or community psychiatrists
  - liaises with other allied service providers and professionals the client may be linked to (e.g., a family physician) for collateral information
  - supports and consults with the client's family members
- links the client with needed services and resources, such as by:
  - making referrals to community partners to provide outreach and practical assistance around basic needs such as transportation, housing, money management, occupational therapy or support
  - liaising with community agencies, such as Probation and Parole, The Children's Aid Society and other social and financial programs
  - making contact with family members or others who are able to provide support.

Clinical role

CDS case managers may also play a clinical role, acting as the client's group therapist and providing any supplemental individual counselling that may be required. Case managers:
- are contacted by the client, should crises arise between therapy appointments (although we are not a 24-hour service)
- maintain documentation in the client's file of all relevant clinical contacts
- facilitate termination and discharge when required.

Bridging the treatment service gap: Outpatient and residential

Occasionally, it is apparent that our outpatient intervention is not sufficient or intensive enough to produce the desired results in clients. For example, some clients require withdrawal management or residential addiction treatment. There is often a six-week wait until an opening is available for these more intensive interventions.

These limitations can be very difficult, even for clients who are willing to follow through with treatment, as these clients are usually in an acute/crisis phase that has precipitated the need for more intensive intervention. The only option is to continue to work with the client as an outpatient until appropriate services are available. Clients' motivation can shift rapidly, even from day to day—we try to keep clients engaged to ensure they do not become discouraged while they are waiting.

Even in cases where the client is not willing to follow through with a residential program, our overriding goal is still to keep the client engaged in treatment.

Research indicates that retention in treatment alone is associated with better outcomes (Institute of Medicine, 1990). At times, we need to recommend to the client, "you should . . . ," but, more typically, we elect to work collaboratively according to the stage of motivation that the client is at. This helps to maintain the relationship with the client and the many important gains that have already been made.

When clients will not consider residential treatment, frequent, brief contact can be a useful alternative approach. This strategy allows the client to stay with the outpatient service where there is already a strong alliance and history. Brief and frequent support focuses on problem solving and more intensive emotional support, and consists of strategies such as:

- offering more flexible time slots
- offering to have daily brief telephone contact (e.g., 10 minutes per call)
- letting the client know that he or she may feel free to leave a voicemail message after hours (Clients report that this resource is often helpful in that it is calming and reassuring to know their therapist will pick up the message in the morning and be apprised of what is occurring.)
- arranging a session involving the client, the therapist, the psychiatrist attached to the client's case and, possibly, the client's other caregivers (This is useful during times of crisis. Regular meetings can also make case co-ordination and planning more effective.)
- offering support via e-mail, although many therapists are not comfortable with e-mail as a clinical medium.

Our goal is to work on the client's motivation to change within an outpatient framework, on a negotiated basis, to try to help the client to move to a more stable period. If unsuccessful, we may then attempt to motivate the client to re-consider his or her initial reluctance to move to a more intensive step of treatment intervention, such as residential treatment.

While integrated services for concurrent disorders are still uncommon in many communities, they are growing. Treatment providers are making great gains in this area, in that they are increasingly aware of the importance of screening clients for concurrent disorders and, where identified, linking clients to integrated treatment if possible. We hope that our description of the program model used in the Concurrent Disorders Service offers some examples of how the integrated treatment approach can be implemented, as well as providing context for the chapters that follow.

REFERENCES

American Psychiatric Association. (1994). *Diagnostic and Statistical Manual of Mental Disorders* (4th ed.). Washington, DC: Author.

Brown, P.J., Stout, R.L. & Gannon-Rowley, J. (1998). Substance use disorders–PTSD comorbidity: Patients' perceptions of symptom interplay and treatment issues. *Journal of Substance Abuse Treatment, 14*, 1–4.

Centre for Addiction and Mental Health (2000). [Diagnostic profile of clients at the Concurrent Disorders Service]. Unpublished raw data.

Evans, K. & Sullivan, J.M. (1995). *Treating Addicted Survivors of Trauma.* New York: The Guilford Press.

Health Canada. (2002). *Best Practices: Concurrent Mental Health and Substance Use Disorders.* Ottawa: Minister of Public Works and Government Services Canada, Cat. #H39-599/2001-2E.

Institute of Medicine. (1990). *Broadening the Base of Treatment for Alcohol Problems.* National Academy Press: Washington.

Najavits, L.M., Weiss, R.D. & Shaw, S.R. (1997). The link between substance abuse and posttraumatic stress disorder in women: A research review. *American Journal on Addictions,* 6(4), 273–283.

Schuckit, M.A. & Monteiro, M.S. (1988). Alcoholism, anxiety and depression. *British Journal of Addiction, 83,* 1373–1380.

Vaillant, G. (1983). *The Natural History of Alcoholism.* Cambridge, MA: Harvard University Press.

Verheul, R., Kranzler, H.R., Poling, J., Tennen, H., Ball, S. & Rounsaville, B.J. (2000). Axis I and Axis II disorders in alcoholics and drug addicts: Fact or artifact? *Journal of Studies on Alcohol, 61*(1), 101–110.

Chapter 4: Appendix

Concurrent Disorders Service: Inclusion and exclusion criteria

I. INTEGRATIVE GROUP PSYCHOTHERAPIES (IGP) CLINIC

Concurrent Disorders Psycho-education Group

DESCRIPTION OF GROUP

This group is designed to provide clients with knowledge and strategies for coping with concurrent mental health and addiction issues. It consists of 12 weekly topic-based sessions, with each session running 1 1/2 hours. Key topics include understanding personal patterns and links between substance use and mental health symptoms, coping with urges to use substances, managing thoughts and emotions in healthy ways, self-care, nutrition, and developing supportive relationships. The emphasis is on uncovering clients' capacity to assume responsibility for their own recovery with increased hope and commitment to change, self-awareness, compassion and perseverance.

This group may be used as a "first step" prior to entering an Interpersonal Group, or concurrently with an Interpersonal Group.

DESCRIPTION OF GROUP COMPOSITION

- Group is open to adult males and females.
- Members may be somewhat lower functioning than, or similar functioning to, Interpersonal Group members. They tend to be higher functioning than members in the Addiction Group for Psychiatric Survivors.
- This group may be used for clients who are functioning at the level of Interpersonal Group clients, but who are not suitable for, or are not ready to work in, an interpersonal format (as in the Interpersonal Group).

INCLUSION CRITERIA

- clients who identify problems with mood and/or anxiety and concurrent substance use issues
- current goal of abstinence or reduction of substance use
- desire to actively learn about mental health and addiction issues in a group setting
- ability to read and write English, in order to participate in homework assignments

- ability to speak personally about their own problems and goals, and to utilize abstract thinking
- commitment of the full 12 weeks (weekly daytime group sessions are 1.5 hours long)
- optimal that members also have additional therapy in place while in this group (e.g., continuing therapy with the referring therapist, Interpersonal Group, ongoing psychiatric follow-up)

EXCLUSION CRITERIA

- significant suicidality/self-harm in the last six months
- currently in crisis
- antisocial personality disorder or traits
- inability to regulate anger or rage
- behaviours that would be disruptive to other group members or the group process (e.g., hostility)
- substance use pattern (quantity/frequency) that suggests an inability to refrain from use on the day of the group or that suggests that a more intensive form of substance use intervention is warranted before being eligible for this group (e.g., withdrawal management or residential program)
- inability to abide by group ground rules (e.g., listen to and respect others, refrain from extra-group socializing)

Interpersonal Group (for alcohol recovery with abstinence as a goal)

DESCRIPTION OF GROUP

The group is designed for clients who are new to the program and in the early stages of recovery from an alcohol use disorder specifically. Clients attend a 90-minute session once a week. Focusing on the here-and-now, members work on the primary goal of getting their alcohol use under control and managing related mental health issues. The duration of this group is six months, with possible extension. In addition to attending group once weekly, many clients also receive supplemental individual therapy.

DESCRIPTION OF GROUP COMPOSITION

- up to a maximum of 10 adult males and females
- most members having a diagnosis of depression and/or anxiety
- meets weekly Wednesday 10:00 a.m. to 11:30 a.m.
- interpersonal group therapy model

INCLUSION CRITERIA

- diagnosis of alcohol abuse/dependence in last year
- current goal of abstinence
- psychologically minded (good verbal and self-reflective capacity)
- concerns about self-esteem, relationships
- ability to tolerate feedback

EXCLUSION CRITERIA

- other substance abuse/dependence diagnosis within last six months
- psychotic disorders
- bipolar I disorder (manic episode within two years)
- antisocial personality disorder or traits
- inability to regulate anger or rage
- significant suicidality
- self-harm in the last six months
- substance use pattern (quantity/frequency) that suggests an inability to refrain from use on the day of the group, or that suggests that a more intensive form of substance use intervention is warranted before being eligible for this group (e.g., withdrawal management or residential program)
- inability to commit for a minimum of six months
- inability to attend regularly

Interpersonal Group (flexible goal choice)

DESCRIPTION OF GROUP AND COMPOSITION

This ongoing long-term group is for people who experience concurrent mental health difficulties (such as depression, anxiety, personality disorders) and addiction (alcohol and other drugs, but other addictive behaviours may be considered, too).

Clients are helped to explore and identify their interpersonal communication style and its impact on others. Part of the group focus is on making efforts to understand interpersonal issues in their historical contexts and particular familial backgrounds. In this group, members explore how problematic and self-defeating relational patterns contribute to or manifest in mental health symptoms as well as addictions. Part of the group process involves work in the here-and-now, which includes observing and discussing interactions between group members and providing each other with feedback.

The group is for men and women, with no more than nine to 10 clients. Currently, the group has a slight predominance of women, and group members range in age from mid-20s to mid-50s.

The group is unstructured, in the sense that therapists work with themes, issues and relational patterns that come up spontaneously in each group. This can mean that, in some group sessions, only relational issues are addressed; in others, the entire focus is on addictions, or the discussion can centre on group members' interactions in the moment.

Most group members are abstinent; some still use substances problematically, but infrequently enough to allow exploration of relational issues. When the group has had clients who are using substances heavily, there have typically been problems around reliability and affective containment, and that has had a disruptive effect upon the entire group; premature termination is the norm in these cases.

Many clients in this group identify relationship issues as central. Some are dealing with the breakup of spousal relationships, current dissatisfactions and their ambivalence about staying in their relationships. Others are at a stage where they identify entering and maintaining new relationships as their primary difficulty.

INCLUSION CRITERIA

- Clients have had a substance abuse/dependence diagnosis in last year.
- Clients have concurrent addiction and mental health concerns.
- Clients can tolerate strong affect without resorting to self-harm, relapsing, or experiencing other disruptive behaviours associated with high emotional instability.
- Clients can appreciate interpersonal process and be receptive to viewing problems through the interpersonal lens.
- Clients are psychologically minded to the extent that they can think in psychological terms, and appreciate concepts such as psychological motivation, levels of awareness and denial, and can interpret meaning of observed behaviours, including expression of emotions.
- Clients should not require additional case management or individual therapy from a group therapist, as we do not see clients individually outside of group preparation sessions. This being said, we do strongly recommend that group clients engage in combined individual psychotherapy to address and help contain their reactions to the group process and that they seek support during challenging or confrontational stages of the group process, among other benefits.

EXCLUSION CRITERIA

- not meeting inclusion criteria
- heavy daily substance use, especially if client is unable abstain on the day of the group
- psychotic disorders
- prominent antisocial traits
- unable to commit to at least six months of regular attendance
- unable to abide by the group ground rules
- unwillingness to enter group, or exhibition of very high levels of anxiety, related to entering the group, that cannot be sufficiently contained within the regular group preparation protocol (especially if client had previous negative group experience)
- being in need of an approach that is more intensive in helping client to actively and planfully build resources to reduce addictive behaviours and increase tolerance for unpleasant experiences
- being in crisis

The Addiction Group for Psychiatric Survivors

DESCRIPTION OF GROUP COMPOSITION

- Members are male and female.
- Age range is from late 20s to late 50s.

- Based on level of functioning, most have a history of psychosis; common diagnoses include schizophrenia, psychotic disorder, bipolar disorder, depression.
- Most members are on medication and are followed by a psychiatrist.
- Some have case managers in the community; some do not.
- Clients are at all stages of change with regard to their substance use.
- Some members are concrete in their thinking, have flat/restricted affect, do not spontaneously interact.
- Some members have difficulty focusing.
- Some members communicate effectively and are psychologically minded (good verbal and self-reflective capacity).
- Most members receive financial assistance through the Ontario Disability Support Program (OSDP) or some other form of social assistance.
- Several members have been or are on probation and are required to attend addiction treatment.

INCLUSION CRITERIA

- diagnosis of a severe mental illness (e.g., schizophrenia, schizoaffective disorder, bipolar disorder) or would generally be described as low functioning in comparison to other CDS groups (most have a history of psychosis)
- also a diagnosis of a substance use disorder
- willingness to work on a substance use goal (e.g., abstinence, substance reduction or at minimum, monitoring/exploring their use)
- willingness to join a group
- willingness to make an initial commitment of six months
- willingness to try to attend regularly
- inpatient clients also accepted, if eligible to attend

EXCLUSION CRITERIA

- acute psychotic episode that is not yet stabilized
- psychotic features (e.g., paranoia) that would be activated/worsened by group interaction
- substance use pattern (quantity/frequency) that suggests an inability to refrain from use on the day of the group, or that suggests that a more intensive form of substance use intervention is warranted before being eligible for this group

Concurrent Disorders Trauma Group

DESCRIPTION OF GROUP AND COMPOSITION

This group is for male and female clients with a substance use disorder, who have suffered from serious childhood trauma (i.e., sexual, physical, emotional abuse, neglect or other trauma) that is causing interference in their lives. This group meets once weekly for two-hour group sessions. The group commitment is one year.

INCLUSION CRITERIA

- experience of significant childhood trauma
- concurrent substance use and mental health concerns
- current goal of harm reduction
- ability to tolerate strong affect without resorting to self-harm, relapsing or experiencing other disruptive behaviours associated with high emotional instability
- being involved in individual therapy
- being psychologically minded (good verbal and self-reflective capacity)
- ability to tolerate feedback within a group structure

EXCLUSION CRITERIA

- meeting criteria for an active psychotic disorder (e.g., schizophrenia, schizoaffective disorder or bipolar I disorder)
- inability to commit for a minimum of one year
- antisocial personality disorder or traits
- significant suicidality
- self-harm in the last six months
- substance use pattern (quantity/frequency) that suggests an inability to refrain from use on the day of the group, or that suggests that a more intensive form of substance use intervention is warranted before being eligible for this group (e.g., withdrawal management or residential program)
- inability to attend regularly
- inability to regulate anger or rage

Integrative Group Therapy for Clients with Concurrent Anxiety and Substance Use Disorders

DESCRIPTION OF GROUP AND COMPOSITION

This is a four-month (16-session) group targeting goals for substance use as well as anxiety symptom management, while also addressing more global areas of functioning: self-care, affect regulation, self-esteem and personal responsibility. The group approach is an integrative one involving cognitive explorations and behavioural approaches, within a psychodynamic framework addressing concurrent issues throughout.

II. DIALECTICAL BEHAVIOUR THERAPY (DBT) CLINIC (FOR CLIENTS WITH BORDERLINE PERSONALITY DISORDER)

DESCRIPTION OF GROUP AND COMPOSITION

This is an outpatient treatment program specifically designed for people who meet criteria for borderline personality disorder. The program is tailored to individuals who also have multiple concurrent mental health problems, which may include addiction problems.

Treatment is comprehensive and involves a combination of weekly individual therapy, group skills training and after-hours telephone consultation. A psycho-educational group for family and friends is also available. Treatment focuses on helping people manage emotions, deal with problems, improve their relationships and lead a more balanced lifestyle. Treatment entails a team approach and requires a minimum one-year commitment.

EXCLUSION CRITERIA

- clients who meet criteria for an active psychotic disorder (e.g., schizophrenia, schizoaffective disorder or bipolar disorder)

III. EATING DISORDERS AND ADDICTION CLINIC

DESCRIPTION OF GROUP AND COMPOSITION

Treatment in this clinic involves a combination of individual and group psychotherapy for female and male clients with concurrent substance use and eating disorders.

The treatment approach involves a combination of:

- weekly two-hour group therapy sessions that are gender-specific (involving both experiential therapy and coping skills training)
- weekly one-hour individual psychotherapy sessions
- meetings with a physician, nurse and dietitian, as needed.

This therapy focuses on helping individuals to decrease problematic eating and substance use behaviours, and increase healthy relationships, sense of self, ability to manage emotions and cope with stress. This therapy program has a one-year commitment.

INCLUSION CRITERIA

- Clients must be over 18 years of age for this treatment.
- Clients must have a diagnosis of eating disorder and a substance use disorder.
- The client has to be willing to participate in a skills group.

EXCLUSION CRITERIA

- clients who meet criteria for an active psychotic disorder (e.g., schizophrenia, schizoaffective disorder or bipolar disorder)
- clients who have engaged in self-harm behaviour in the past six months
- clients who are in a weight loss program
- clients who are in therapy for an eating disorder or substance use problem

IV. ANGER AND ADDICTION CLINIC

DESCRIPTION OF GROUP AND COMPOSITION

Therapy in this clinic involves a combination of individual and group psychotherapy for male and female clients with concurrent substance use and anger-related problems.

Therapy is conducted by a treatment team, and involves weekly two-hour skills-training groups, and individual therapy as appropriate. Therapy focuses on reducing anger and aggressive behaviour, eliminating substance use, enhancing mindfulness and regulation of emotions, and improving distress tolerance and interpersonal effectiveness.

MAIN GOALS OF ASSESSMENT

The main goal of assessment in the Anger and Addiction Clinic is to determine if anger is a principal causing agent that disrupts personal or work relationships. This is a skills-based treatment that targets emotion dysregulation. If the goals of the client are not to decrease anger and not to decrease substance use, then this program is not the appropriate treatment for the client (these issues are attended to in the clinic's standard orientation to the treatment). However, as part of the "orientation and commitment pre-treatment phase" of this Clinic, significant emphasis is placed on engaging and motivating clients to address their anger and substance use.

INCLUSION CRITERIA

- Clients have to be willing to work on reducing their anger and addiction problems.
- A minimum level of literacy is necessary.
- The client has to be willing to participate in a skills group.

EXCLUSION CRITERIA

- Clients who score high on psychopathy will be screened out of this treatment.
- If clients have any outstanding criminal charges, they would be excluded from acceptance into the program; however, clients on probation and parole, and court-mandated clients, are welcome.
- Clients who are in a primary individual therapy elsewhere are also not eligible for this treatment.

Chapter 5

Integrated group psychotherapy for clients with concurrent disorders

ANDREA TSANOS, SUZANNE MORROW AND VICKI MYERS

INTRODUCTION

Clients with concurrent disorders are a challenging treatment population, with rates of relapse in both substance use and psychiatric problems that are higher than with clients with a single disorder alone. The Integrative Group Psychotherapies (IGP) Clinic was designed to provide integrated treatment to clients whose addiction and mental health problems have, in the past, been treated separately. The main focus of our treatment program is group psychotherapy. Both problems are treated within a single setting by a team of clinicians trained in both disorders. In this chapter, we share the story of our group work, highlighting the groups designed for specific populations within concurrent disorders.

Group therapy for concurrent disorders

The addiction and mental health literature supports group therapy as being beneficial, and many studies have evaluated various group therapy approaches:

- cognitive-behavioural therapy (CBT) for concurrent posttraumatic stress disorder and substance use (Najavits et al., 1996)
- CBT for concurrent bipolar and substance use disorders (Weiss et al., 2000)
- CBT for panic disorder with agoraphobic and concurrent alcohol use disorders (Bowen et al., 2000)

- relapse prevention for concurrent bipolar and substance use disorders (Weiss et al., 2002, 1999)
- motivational interviewing for concurrent schizophrenia and substance use disorder (Barrowclough et al., 2001; Van Horn & Bux, 2001)
- interpersonal group therapy (Malat et al., 1999).

Individual therapy for concurrent disorders

However, in addition to the value of group therapy, we believe that a program should have the capacity to offer individual therapy, because some people with concurrent disorders are not suited to, nor best treated in, a group format. Clinical examples of this could include:

- severe social phobia
- severe paranoia
- traumatic experiences such as sexual abuse that the client might not feel safe discussing in group.

While we aim to be client-centred and flexible with our treatment programming, we refrain from simply giving clients a choice between individual and group, as most people would opt for individual therapy, because it feels more private and comfortable. We explain the many benefits of group therapy and the advantages it can offer over individual therapy, and then determine if supplemental individual therapy is required. A program that offers options and collaborates on the treatment plan with the client will prevent the client from feeling forced into treatment options that may be unsuitable. We believe this collaboration enhances treatment retention and ultimately outcome.

The Integrative Group Psychotherapy Clinic

The IGP Clinic is made up of a team of clinicians who use techniques of group psychotherapy to provide treatment to clients with concurrent mental health and substance use problems. Under the leadership of a clinic head, who is a psychiatrist, therapists working in the IGP Clinic help clients develop self-awareness and skills that help them reduce their substance use, address mental health concerns, improve their relationships and self-esteem, cope better with emotions and lead a healthier and more balanced lifestyle.

We offer the following specialized treatment groups:

- concurrent disorders psychoeducational groups
- interpersonal/action groups (groups for individuals who have abstinence as a goal, and groups that have mixed goal choice)
- maintenance groups (for concurrent mental health and substance use problems).

The latter two groups are generally offered to clients with substance use problems who also have a broad range of concurrent psychiatric problems, such as mood disorders

TABLE 5-1

Individual and group therapy

	ADVANTAGES	DISADVANTAGES
INDIVIDUAL THERAPY	• an opportunity to customize treatment to unique needs • privacy • more flexible pace, frequency, and duration • opportunity for a deepened relationship, which can allow for exploration that may not be possible in group • can be a useful step leading up to eventual group preparation and readiness	• missed opportunity for the benefits of group, including feedback from more than one person • may be too intense for some to handle
GROUP THERAPY	• decreased isolation; decreased stigma • making goals "public" in the group enhances motivation • if client has poor internal self-control, group's eyes act as external control • helps client identify with others • client gains experience in helping and supporting others • offers sharing of information and resources • gives client hope and optimism for change; opportunity to see others further along in recovery as role models • diluted: not as potentially demanding as individual therapy	• might not offer enough individual attention • certain issues might be too uncomfortable/unsafe to disclose in group (e.g., sexual abuse, conflicts related to sexual identity, deviant behaviours) • confidentiality concerns (more risk than with individual) • for clients with assertiveness or self-disclosure difficulties, group can allow them to blend into the background, potentially creating less gain in therapy

and anxiety disorders, but who also identify themselves as having challenges in interpersonal functioning. Such challenges might include:

- having problematic patterns of relating with others, creating impasses or destructive interactions
- being too domineering or unassertive and having difficulty getting needs met by others
- feeling isolated by others
- having poor affect tolerance, leading to attempts to manage painful affects through substance use.

ASSESSMENT, TREATMENT PLANNING AND GROUP PREPARATION FOR THE IGP CLINIC

Assessment

After intake and referral to the Concurrent Disorders Service (CDS; see Chapter 4), the CDS streams any suitable clients to the IGP Clinic, where a therapist is assigned to them. This therapist will be the client's main link throughout treatment. Once the client is linked to a therapist on the IGP Clinic team, the therapist conducts a further assessment. This assessment concentrates on psychosocial issues. It also prepares the client for group entry (medication issues may be noted, but clients resolve such issues with their physician).

Some of the topics covered in this phase of assessment include:

- beginning of establishment of a therapeutic alliance
- assessment of client's background, including personal and family history
- assessment of client's current stability:
  - living arrangement
  - level of social support
  - financial situation
  - legal situation (if any)
  - severity of substance use
  - severity of mental health symptoms.

The therapist then suggests strategies for stabilization (if required). Finally, the therapist conducts a functional analysis of the client's substance use as it relates to his or her mental health and solidifies the client's goals for addressing identified problems.

Treatment planning

Although treatment planning begins at the time of the client's initial assessment, we revisit the plan throughout treatment. The group setting allows us to observe the client's strengths and interpersonal difficulties. Often, the client's mental health issues become more evident in the group setting.

After the client has participated in the group for two to three sessions, the group therapist and the client meet in an individual session to explore the client's experience in group and discuss any concerns. At this point, the client and therapist agree on the frequency of individual contact for case management, support and counselling. These sessions may be scheduled regularly or as needed.

TABLE 5-2

Sample referral-to-CDS and IGP Clinic flow chart

TREATMENT PROCESS	TIMELINES
1. intake assessment	The wait for this appointment is typically two weeks.
2. PDI with psychiatrist (e.g., to uncover concurrent dysthymia and alcohol dependence)	This typically occurs two weeks after the intake assessment.
3. discussion of case in CDS Case Rounds meeting; referral to a therapist on the CDS team	This occurs the same week or week after the PDI.
4. assessment with therapist for determination of group suitability	This occurs the following week.
5. if suitable for the IGP Clinic, individual session(s) for group preparation	This occurs the following week, as needed.
6. client joins interpersonal group	Group meets once/week, for 1.5-hour sessions (minimum commitment: six months).
7. client followed by a CDS psychiatrist for initiation on medication and ongoing medication monitoring	Follow-up appointments are every six weeks.
8. client recieves supplemental individual sessions with the group therapist	These occur every other week.
9. administration of "treatment outcome measures" by therapist	These tools are administered six months after the intake assessment, every six months thereafter for the duration of treatment, and again at discharge.

The following is an example of the type of treatment goals that clients with concurrent disorders work on.

Case example: Goal setting

A client has problems with panic disorder and alcohol dependence. His goals are:

- to learn strategies for coping with panic and anxiety
- to learn strategies to achieve abstinence from substance use
- to reduce/eliminate the frequency and intensity of panic attacks and other distressing anxiety symptoms
- to reduce avoidance behaviour related to anxiety
- to reduce or come off the use of anxiolytic medication as he achieves mastery of psychological ways of coping

- to increase tolerance for negative affects
- to draw on social and professional supports
- to increase self-care behaviour
- to increase his sense of self-efficacy and overall self-esteem
- to increase his overall level of functioning and quality of life.

Group members are encouraged to set their own substance use goals (often with helpful input from other group members), such as:

- abstinence
- reduced/controlled substance use
- self-monitoring/exploring substance use.

In contrast to many treatment and self-help settings, the CDS does not require abstinence as a treatment goal. While we feel that abstinence is certainly the preferable goal for people with mental health problems, we have found that we need to be more flexible in our treatment interventions. We aim to meet clients "where they are at," without imposing our own goals and biases. This approach helps us engage those clients who might otherwise feel too threatened to commit to treatment. We would rather have the opportunity to work with ambivalent clients than see them go without any treatment contact at all.

Some of our clients enter treatment believing that abstinence is too daunting or that it is simply undesirable. These clients often hope that they can become social or recreational users. We seek to validate their feelings of resistance and fear regarding change, and address the loss they expect to feel if they were to lose the substance altogether. After some exploration of the pros and cons of substance use at the current or reduced levels, we agree on a realistic short-term goal. Often, we frame this as a collaborative experiment, with the client in control of the outcome.

Clients who are free to explore their capabilities on their own terms are more likely to stay engaged in treatment. We have found that clients who have experimented with a goal of controlled use often find it difficult to attain. After this experience, they often become ready to consider abstinence.

While we continue to work from a harm-reduction philosophy, we have found that many clients at the IGP Clinic eventually learn that abstinence is the only goal that works for them. Some have reported liking the simplicity of the abstinence goal. Knowing that they will not have to make a series of decisions—about when they can use or how much they can use—helps to keep their goal clearly defined. Abstinence goals also coincide with the philosophy of self-help groups (e.g., Alcoholics Anonymous). Many of our clients look to these groups for additional support during recovery.

Group preparation

ASSESSMENT OF GROUP SUITABILITY

The following criteria may mean that a group is not the best fit for the client at a particular time:

- significant suicidality/self-harm behaviour
- antisocial personality disorder diagnosis
- inability to regulate anger or rage
- behaviours that would be disruptive to other group members or the group process (e.g., intolerance of others, hostility)
- substance use pattern (quantity/frequency) that suggests an inability to refrain from use on the day of the group, or that suggests a more intensive form of substance use intervention is warranted (e.g., withdrawal management or residential addiction treatment program)
- high levels of anxiety about entering the group, which cannot be sufficiently contained within the regular group preparation protocol (especially if the client had previous negative group experience)
- unwillingness to enter group
- inability to abide by group ground rules
- inability to commit for a minimum of six months
- inability to attend regularly.

EXPLAINING THE BENEFITS OF GROUP THERAPY

If group therapy is appropriate, the next step is to explain the rationale and benefits of group therapy, followed by a thorough discussion of group guidelines and related issues. This preparation can often be covered in one session, in which the therapist and client discuss:

- what group therapy is and how it works
- the therapeutic aspects of a group
- stages of group development
- group norms and guidelines:
  - the importance of commitment and the consequences of premature termination from the group
  - impact of irregular attendance on the group
  - substance use goal choice
  - impact and consequences of arriving to the group under the influence
  - coping with the challenges of group therapy
  - attitude toward socializing with group members outside of the group
  - the possibility that trainees may come to observe the group, given we are a teaching hospital.

Following this discussion, clients are given a document that covers these topics. They are encouraged to discuss their thoughts and concerns with their therapist. We have found that the time and effort spent in group preparation results in increased client retention in treatment.

EXPLAINING INTERPERSONAL THERAPY

(For more detailed information about interpersonal therapy, please see Chapter 12, "Interpersonal Group Therapy for Concurrent Alcohol Dependence and Interpersonal Problems.")

Clients will gain an understanding of interpersonal group process from experiencing the group. However, before deciding whether this is the type of group they wish to join, clients need information about the therapy approach used in the group.

Group is a social microcosm

We describe the group as a social microcosm—interactions, dynamics and relationships that take place in the group often are representative of what goes on in the outside world. The hope is that examining these interpersonal patterns within the boundary and safety of the group setting will allow a safe place for exploration and growth, which can then be applied to the outside world.

Group is a process of exploration

The group is also described as a place where honest, spontaneous, personal and interpersonal exploration is encouraged. We explain that interpersonal therapy is an exploratory approach; one that encourages self-reflection and curiosity. We are careful to frame group as a process, so that clients realize that this therapy is by no means a quick fix.

Clients are responsible for their treatment

We emphasize that clients bear responsibility for their treatment. The more they put into the group, the more they will ultimately benefit from the group. While self-disclosure is an important part of the therapy, we reassure clients that what to disclose, and when to disclose it, is their decision.

Group is a place to give and receive feedback

An important part of interpersonal therapy is the giving and receiving of feedback in the group. During group preparation, we teach the client that, to be effective, the feedback process:

- needs to be clear and immediate
- should contain an emotional component
- should be non-blaming and non-judgmental.

We explain that feedback is information about the *relationship between the sender and receiver.* We find it helpful for the therapist to model and demonstrate an actual example of interpersonal feedback to the client in the pre-group individual sessions.

Group is sometimes stressful

Finally, we prepare clients to expect some degree of stress and puzzlement with the group at times (especially initially). We normalize this as a natural part of the therapy process. A discussion of this general model and framework provides a foundation and a more realistic expectation that clients can bring with them to the group experience.

COMMON CLIENT CONCERNS ABOUT GROUP

We find that there are several common issues that clients express in the protest of group. Most clients, if given the choice between group therapy and individual therapy, would choose individual therapy. It is usually easier to form trust and an alliance with one person than with a group of strangers.

Feeling unready

Some clients are concerned about group readiness, and additional individual sessions may be required. These sessions help to address and normalize many common concerns, such as:

- fear of confrontation
- fear of contagion of negative emotions
- fear of rejection
- anxieties about confidentiality
- fear of forced disclosure.

Through this discussion, a primary objective is to begin to establish a therapeutic working alliance.

Other concerns

- Some clients speculate that we offer groups to save money—group is a way of seeing 10 clients in one hour rather than 10 hours. We acknowledge that group therapy is more cost-effective but follow this with a discussion about the effectiveness of group therapy, and its relevance to the client's issues. This discussion often clarifies clients' assumptions.
- Some believe that as one member in a group of 10, they will only get nine minutes of personal attention in each 90-minute session. They conclude that this is poorer quality care than a full hour of individual therapy.
- Some clients object to group because they feel that their issues are unique, and they will not have anything in common with the other group members.
- Some have reservations that are based on past negative group experiences. In such cases, the therapist needs to explore these experiences, and to discuss the client's expectations, misconceptions, interpersonal fears and fantasies. The therapist can then predict potential difficulties in the client's engagement or participation in the group, and the therapist and client can discuss ways of dealing with these, while reviewing the procedure for discontinuing the group before the treatment contract is completed.

THE GROUPS OF THE IGP CLINIC

Treatment approaches

Our IGP Clinic groups employ a number of treatment approaches. We believe that having a menu of interventions is most helpful (if not necessary) in working with this often challenging population. The freedom to approach our group work with such diversity allows us to achieve flexibility and much-needed creativity in working with our clients.

The most predominant approach is process-oriented groups, working in the "here-and-now" within an interpersonal framework. This theoretical approach is based on the work of Malat, Leszcz and Negrete (1999) and Leszcz (1992), which derives from the work of:

- Yalom (1995) on interpersonal group therapy
- Kiesler (1996) on interpersonal theory
- Khantzian (1997) with his modified psychodynamic group psychotherapy approach developed for the addiction population.

Khantzian's approach centres on four areas in the context of process-oriented group psychotherapy. These include improving:

1. self-care
2. affect regulation
3. interpersonal functioning
4. self-esteem.

We also incorporate:

- motivational interviewing (Miller & Rollnick, 2002)
- cognitive-behavioural therapy (Beck et al., 1993)
- relapse prevention (Marlatt & Gordon, 1985).

Goals of treatment: Stages of change

The primary goal of our group facilitation is to help clients move through the stages of change (Prochaska et al., 1992). These are:

- precontemplation (not thinking about change)
- contemplation (thinking about change)
- preparation (preparing for change)
- action (making the change)
- maintenance (maintaining the change)
- relapse (slipping into unwanted behaviour).

Treatment groups include clients at various stages of the change process. Having some representatives of the contemplation stage mixed in with clients at the action stage, for example, helps to move clients from one stage of change to the next; clients at the action and maintenance stages act as role models and provide hope and inspiration to those at the contemplation stage. Group members who have met their substance use goals are often able to provide useful concrete strategies to members who are at earlier stages of change.

Having mixed stages of change in the groups can be challenging for the group facilitators. We attempt to shape our interventions in the group largely by considering the overall stage of change that is characteristic of the group at that moment; however, occasionally the group needs to focus on an individual's stage of change.

For example, if the majority of members in the group appear to be stuck in the contemplation stage, the group as a whole might engage in the "decisional balance exercise," drawing from motivational interviewing. In this exercise, participants discuss the pros and cons of changing and not changing their substance use. Any members who are well into the action stage would be invited to help lead this discussion. They might talk about the time that they struggled with ambivalence, or share some of the reasons that motivated them to change. Actively engaging the member(s) in the action stage in this manner serves to recognize and reinforce their progress, while ensuring that they find the discussion meaningful.

As another example, perhaps a member has reverted to the relapse stage, and requires careful attention to process this occurrence to get back on track. In this scenario, clients in the action and maintenance phases can vicariously process this occurrence, from the safety of their vantage point as fellow group members. Processing this occurrence with the group as a whole allows each group member to learn from this experience.

Thus, experiences of clients in the early stages of change remind clients in the later stages of where they have been and all that they have attained along the process of recovery.

Types of groups

As mentioned above, the IGP Clinic offers groups for:

- concurrent disorders psychoeducation
- interpersonal/action (groups for individuals who have abstinence as a goal, and mixed-goal groups)
- maintenance (for concurrent mental health and substance use problems).

CONCURRENT DISORDERS PSYCHO-EDUCATION GROUP

The Concurrent Disorders (CD) Psycho-education Group was designed to fill a gap in service. Before this group was developed, CDS clients who could benefit from psychoeducation were referred to the Structured Relapse Prevention or Coping Skills Groups in our broader Addictions Program. However, CDS clients felt that their concurrent (and often perceived-to-be underlying) mental health issues were not being addressed in these groups.

Recognizing the importance of psychoeducation as a foundation of treatment—particularly for clients who were new to recovery and had never been exposed to this content before—we developed this group program. Because integrated treatment is central to our treatment philosophy, we needed to not only ensure that there was both addiction and mental health content in the psychoeducational curriculum, but also that the content would address the interrelationship between the concurrent disorders (e.g., understanding personal patterns and links between substance use and mental health symptoms).

The CD Psycho-education Group is appropriate for clients who want knowledge about, and practical strategies for coping with, their concurrent mental health and substance use issues. For example, "I want to learn ways to be able to manage my depression better, and to understand what role my drinking plays." This is often the first group that clients new to treatment attend within the CDS.

- Because this group has a shorter commitment (three months, instead of six months or a year as with the other groups in the CDS), it is often easier for clients hesitant about treatment to make a commitment.
- Because this group is highly structured (without time afforded for disclosure and interpersonal processing), it can represent a safe option for clients in early recovery who are not ready for a more interpersonal-based group.

Clients who complete the CD Psycho-education Group often go on to join an Action/Interpersonal Group.

Structure of group sessions

The group is time-limited, and consists of 12 weekly sessions. The sessions are topic-based and co-facilitated, with each session running 90 minutes. The groups run on a closed basis, because the early sessions serve as prerequisite material for the subsequent sessions.

Content

Table 5-3: Concurrent Disorders Psycho-educational Group Topics, below, illustrates key discussion topics and activities that deal with both substance use and mental health issues in the CD Psycho-education Group. The emphasis is on uncovering clients' capacity to assume responsibility for their own recovery, with increased hope and commitment to change, self-awareness, compassion and perseverance.

ACTION/INTERPERSONAL GROUP

The most common treatment subprogram within the CDS is the Action/Interpersonal Group, which uses an interpersonal group psychotherapy approach. Members attend a weekly 90-minute session. The group focuses on the "here-and-now," with the primary goal of getting substance use under control while also managing related mental health issues. There are two options for clients joining an Action/Interpersonal Group:

- One is a more homogeneous group in that it is designed for clients with an identified alcohol problem who share abstinence as the treatment goal.
- The other is a group composed of clients with mixed substance representation and mixed substance use goals.

TABLE 5-3

Concurrent Disorders Psycho-educational Group topics

SESSION #	PSYCHO-EDUCATIONAL GROUP SESSION TOPICS
SESSION 1	• introduction to treatment • increasing motivation and hope about recovery from addiction and mental health problems • developing commitment to change
SESSION 2	• identifying the relationship between mental health and substance use • capacity of certain drugs to trigger problems with mental health • effects of substance use on medication • withdrawal and withdrawal management information
SESSION 3	• identifying the factors (thoughts, feelings, situations, physical sensations) that lead to use • naming the consequences of use • developing coping strategies to deal with high-risk situations without substance use
SESSION 4	• using greater awareness of self-sabotaging thoughts (e.g., negative self-messages, distortions, rationalizations for using drugs, minimization of risk) that lead to substance use to learn specific ways to help yourself safely
SESSION 5	• identifying, accepting and dealing effectively with emotions
SESSION 6	Perseverance: • dealing with lapses (learning to stop early before it does even more damage to your relationships, health, finances and self-esteem) • turning destructive self-criticism into constructive self-evaluation that increases self-esteem and helps you move on
SESSION 7	Self-care: • respecting yourself and your body • living in accordance with your values • keeping yourself safe from emotional vulnerability • sleep and relaxation
SESSION 8	Self-care (continued) • nutrition
SESSION 9	• developing healthy and supportive relationships • getting support
SESSION 10	• balancing recovery with the rest of your life • adding pleasurable activities to life to help you avoid alcohol and other drugs

(continued on next page)

SESSION #	PSYCHO-EDUCATIONAL GROUP SESSION TOPICS
SESSION 11	Spiritual dimensions of recovery: • ways to address spiritual needs relevant to recovery from substance use and psychological problems
SESSION 12	Termination session: Taking the group with you: • guidelines for continuing recovery successfully after completing the group

The client commits to the group for six months. Clients move at different paces of change, so the ultimate length of involvement in the group is assessed over time. Because the problems faced by people with concurrent disorders are often complex, many clients extend the treatment contract beyond the initial six months.

MAINTENANCE GROUP

The Maintenance Group was designed to recognize that substance use and mental health problems often involve episodes of relapse. The hope with the Maintenance Group is that attention to issues above and beyond the initial half-year of abstinence (attained in the Action/Interpersonal Group) will serve to maintain gains and further prevent relapse.

The Maintenance Group is open to clients who have completed the action phase of the recovery process and are ready to participate in a more psychodynamically oriented group focusing on relapse prevention and interpersonal goals. This group builds on the positive changes of the Action/Interpersonal Group and shifts the primary focus to other life issues that can enhance self-esteem and provide greater value to the client's recovery experience, which then serves as greater motivation to maintain substance use and mental health progress. Other life issues include, for example:

- developing/rebuilding relationships with peers or with a social group
- enhancing self-esteem and sense of purpose by finding work or meaningful activity (such as volunteering)
- reconnecting with estranged family members.

This group meets once weekly for a 90-minute session, for six months.

Group structure

LEADERSHIP

We use a co-therapy model, in which groups are led by two facilitators. Co-led groups are more resource-intensive but are advantageous with this client population for the following reasons:

- safety: Group members can arrive acutely psychotic, suicidal, intoxicated or acting out. In this case, one therapist may have to intervene with the person directly, outside of the group, while the other therapist carries on with the group session.

- avoidance of burnout: Running a long-term group for clients with complex needs can be emotionally draining. Two therapists can share the clinical caseload, support each other, plan for the group and manage challenging clinical group issues together.
- more diverse therapeutic backgrounds offered: Having two co-therapists brings a richer and more varied perspective to the group. Often the therapists have had different training, orientations and professional backgrounds, spanning psychology, social work, psychiatry and other disciplines.
- professional development: Co-therapists can prepare for the group before the session and de-brief together after the session is over. This stimulates analysis of group developments. Exposure to each other's insights can enhance professional development and skills, and allows for peer support.
- sharing of other responsibilities: Co-facilitators can share administrative requirements such as entering visits into the patient database, writing the clinical group notes, setting up the group room and preparing refreshments.
- student supervision/clinical training: There is value in having one seasoned, experienced therapist running a group along with a less experienced clinician or graduate student. This can be an important learning experience and an opportunity for close supervision.

Despite these advantages of the co-therapy model, it is worth noting that there can also be challenges. For example, long-term psychotherapy groups can reveal differences in the therapists' personal and therapeutic styles that may need to be addressed. We find that differences can be worked through in most cases, and believe that co-therapists who openly and actively work on their relationship enhance their effectiveness within the group.

COMPOSITION

The IGP Clinic groups are inclusive, and are therefore heterogeneous. We have found that exposure to diversity teaches clients to become more accepting of differences.

Substance use

Some group members have problems with alcohol, while others in the same group may have problems with cocaine or cannabis, or be dependent on more than one substance or are concerned about being dependent on prescription medications. Some group members have had a pattern of using every day, while others in the group have binge patterns. Some members may already be abstinent, while others may still be actively using or may have a goal of controlled or reduced substance use. In any of our groups, some group members will have been in previous addiction treatment many times; for others, this may be their first treatment experience or their first time in group therapy.

Mental health

Some group members have been struggling with their symptoms for many years, while others have recently experienced their first onset of symptoms. Some have trouble with one mental health issue, such as depression, while others may have not only mood problems but also other issues, such as anxiety, or personality disorders. In any of our groups, some members are on psychoactive medication, while others are not.

TABLE 5-4

Group composition

	ADVANTAGES	CHALLENGES
HOMOGENEOUS GROUPS	• Interventions are easier to tailor to target problems. • Common problems may help to foster a sense of group belonging.	• Group membership is not representative of the range of people and issues that members will "face on the outside." • Working with a number of people with similar issues may increase potential for clinician burnout. • Treatment for some clients could be delayed—in some settings, it can take a significant amount of time to assemble a critical mass of clients.
HETEROGENEOUS GROUPS	• Clients are encouraged to become accepting of differences. • Group members are encouraged to look for common elements among mental health problems. • Diversity is characteristic of the real world and can offer more variety and perspective within the group.	• Interventions lose specificity.

Similarities

All of our group members have both a substance use problem and a mental health issue. We find that clients are grateful for being in a place where concurrent disorders are recognized and validated. They often describe a sense of finally feeling understood and accepted, and where they feel they can readily relate to the experiences of the other group members. They say that, regardless of what the particular substance of abuse is or what the particular psychiatric diagnosis is, the common denominator is the function that the substance use is serving and how it has affected their mental health and other aspects of their life.

BENEFITS OF OPEN GROUP

If there is space in the group, new members can join at any time. A group typically has a capacity of 10 members. There are both pros and cons to the open concept (see

Table 5-5: Open versus Closed Groups). Each individual member cycles into a group for a six-month commitment, but the group is ongoing.

CHALLENGES OF THE IGP CLINIC

HANDLING RELAPSE

Relapse is often a part of recovery from mental health and substance use problems. Clients are encouraged to view lapses and relapse as temporary setbacks.

Relapse of substance use

With relapse to substance use, we are careful to correct the interpretation that relapse means failure in recovery. Instead, we try to use such experiences in therapy, as an opportunity for learning and problem solving. Relapse is also an opportunity for clients to reaffirm their substance use goal.

The work of Marlatt and Gordon (1985) is very helpful for addiction treatment. We try to create an environment where clients feel comfortable disclosing a relapse, without fearing that they will be asked to withdraw from the program. Clients are encouraged to feel free to disclose slips to the group, rather than trying to ignore or hide it, if the lapse is already over. It is helpful for clients to explore the trigger(s) that led to the slip, and then discuss more adaptive coping responses.

The permission to be honest about relapse in the treatment process helps to normalize this as an occurrence, and helps to prevent the client from feeling he or she cannot be genuine in therapy.

On an emotional level, often, the perception that "relapse equals failure" creates such a significant experience of shame, pessimism about the ability to change, and sometimes self-loathing from repeating old patterns. In settings where relapse is not normalized, clients have reported dropping out of the group prematurely, because they could not imagine returning and facing the group.

Relapse of mental health problem

Relapse is also a common occurrence with mental health problems, such as depression and psychosis. However, we find that clients do not have the same sense of guilt and shame associated with their relapse to substances. The underlying belief for many clients seems to be that the use of substances is expressly their fault, but a relapse to psychiatric symptoms is largely beyond their control.

However, psychiatric relapse often carries with it a sense of disappointment, learned helplessness, and profound demoralization that the psychiatric condition will need to be struggled through quite likely for a lifetime. This is a common reaction in clients with chronic depression or bipolar disorder.

TABLE 5-5

Open versus closed groups

	ADVANTAGES	CHALLENGES
OPEN GROUP	• Because new members can join at any time, the group feels accessible. • This availability capitalizes on clients' motivation to change. • There is no undue delay for the group to develop a critical mass and start—such delays can often be weeks or months in closed groups. • The changing composition as new members join or leave reflects the real world that is full of change: this is an opportunity for learning. • New members provide new perspective and offer novel input and added insight. • Open concept allows members to process endings and loss when members terminate from the group.	• Because new members are joining when there is space and others are graduating, this changing composition can create an atmosphere of disruption, unreliability or instability in the group. • New members often need extensive coaching to handle their anxiety about joining an already established group. • An adjustment period, both for new and old members, often causes a delay in group development.
CLOSED GROUP	• All group members can start together, so there is a shared history in the group. • Members can go through the group's developmental stages (beginning, middle and end phases) together. • Structured groups with a set curriculum require a closed concept (e.g., Psycho-education Group).	• Missed opportunity for the benefits of an open group, listed above.

To better empower clients in fostering a more helpful mindset about managing relapses, first and foremost we normalize the idea that relapses occur in both domains. We then attempt to help clients identify early warning signs that mental health is deteriorating.

Such signs in, for example, depression might include sensing the tendency to withdraw socially, beginning to lose interest in activities usually enjoyed and experiencing an increase in negative thinking. Once the client becomes aware of these early warning signs, or "red flags," we encourage the client to develop strategies for coping and intervening early on in the cycle. These interventions might include relaying symptoms to a caregiver and implementing personal coping strategies, with the overall goal of circumventing a full relapse from occurring.

NO-SHOWS

Clients are encouraged to contact their therapist when they must be absent from the group. When a client is absent for the first time, without calling to cancel, therapists generally follow up by phone. By so doing, the therapist hopes to convey the message that the client's absence was felt by the therapists and by the group. Reaching out in this way helps the client to reconnect with the group as soon as possible.

Clients with concurrent disorders tend to have complex issues that prevent them from being responsible at all times, or from putting themselves first at all times. We recognize that this client population can destabilize from time to time—relapse of substance use or psychological symptoms and/or psychosocial stressors can create more immediate concerns than attending the therapy session. We try to find a balance between showing concern by reaching out, and giving clients an opportunity to take responsibility for their absence and for making the effort to reconnect.

Clients who feel truly cared about by their therapist, who receive an empathic, hopeful, non-judgmental attitude from their therapist, are more likely to re-connect following a relapse or period of disconnect (Minkoff, 2001). We subscribe to the treatment philosophy that "the most significant predictor of treatment success is an empathic, hopeful, continuous treatment relationship, in which integrated treatment and co-ordination of care can take place through multiple treatment episodes" (Minkoff, 2001).

TRIGGERS

Occasionally, a group member reports feeling triggered as a result of the group session. Because the word "triggered" connotes many different things, as a first step, the group therapist should explore what the client means by this.

Exposure

Clients at our clinic, for example, have said they felt triggered in that they feel at risk or more vulnerable to the use of substances than when they first entered the group session. One possible reason for this is that a great deal of exposure occurs in group: discussions about substance use, other members talking about their relapses, or members talking about dealing with a high-risk situation that is strongly associated with using. This kind of verbal and emotional exposure can be as challenging as physical or environmental triggers for substance use. When a client interprets these triggers as an effect of having attended the group, we explain that exposure that occurs in a safe context (such as the group setting) is an opportunity to experience these challenging feelings and apply adaptive strategies for coping.

Emotional vulnerability

Other group members have described feeling triggered in the emotional sense—they feel more emotionally precarious at the end of the group session than when they first came into the session.

Clinical example: Triggers—Sense of loss

One member in the Action/Interpersonal Group often cried quietly at the end of a session. When this was observed and gently inquired about, the group member responded that he found himself feeling a profound sense of loss every time the group session was over. He elaborated that the group is only 1 1/2 hours out of his week, and the prospect of the group being over, and facing the remaining six days of the week on his own, without the group's support, was daunting.

This clinical example points to the importance of continually attending to the needs of clients in the group. We must ensure that they have adequate support outside of the group, offering a supplemental individual session when necessary for added support, and attempting to help clients build other supports and activities into their lives—so that they do not run the risk of overvaluing the group at the expense of finding other meaning in life.

Clinical example: Triggers—Emotional responses

In another case, one of the group members had voiced his plan and intent around committing suicide. This naturally became a primary concern in the group session, which the therapists handled effectively.

The subsequent week, two other members failed to return to the group, and, after following up with them, it emerged that they felt too emotionally vulnerable to attend. After encouraging them to return to the group, and in processing their feelings within the group session, these two members described a similar experience of feeling overwhelmed at the emotional intensity of the first member's suicidal feelings.

One reported feeling such concern that he experienced constant rumination and worry throughout the week after that session, with thoughts and fears around the possibility that his fellow group member may, in fact, take his own life, and not knowing how he would cope, were that to happen.

The other described feeling triggered in that he identified all too intensely with his fellow group member's experience of feeling suicidal. He recalled how he felt in the past, when he himself was suicidal, and that this recollection was distressing, which caused him to feel too emotionally fragile. His fear that the subsequent group session would be a continuation of this discussion was too threatening and was the reason for his subsequent absence.

When a client feels at risk with a distressing emotional state, the person's first inclination is often to quell this distress with the use of a substance, to take away such discomfort. The risks of this occurring should be monitored by the group facilitators, although the group itself can also be of assistance, as the group is often keenly intuitive and sensitive at picking up on warning signs in fellow group members.

Avoiding end-of-session disclosure

Often, clients disclose feelings of emotional vulnerability, and being at risk of relapse, at the end of the session. This leaves very little time for processing and safeguarding.

To prevent this, the group leaders can periodically ask the group how they are feeling, especially when there has been a particularly difficult group session. When one member discloses that he or she feels triggered, leaders can explore that it is likely that others feel the same way, and encourage them to talk about how they are feeling. Encouraging clients to scan themselves for how they are feeling emotionally, both during a session and as a result of a session, is important self-care.

VIOLATIONS OF GROUP NORMS

Norms are generally established to provide structure, safety and a framework for boundaries. The group contract is helpful to refer to when it has been observed that there has been a deviation from the group norms. In our experience, it is not always easy to tell whether some group issues should be processed as potential violations of norms or not.

While we recognize that individuals can make their own choices about whether or not to spend time with other group members outside of the group, our group facilitators discourage socializing outside of the group for various reasons (see examples below) that may affect or jeopardize the therapy.

The IGP Clinic groups are different from self-help groups such as Alcoholics Anonymous, where contact with sponsors and other group members is encouraged. In our clinic, events that take place outside of group can have a profound effect on one's group involvement. In group psychotherapy, if a group member forms a special relationship with another group member, that relationship tends to get in the way of group development. Secrets may develop, and certain issues may not get addressed in the group because of the friendship that has developed.

If group members choose to have outside contact with group members, the group facilitators emphasize that this needs to be discussed (in the group optimally, but if this is not possible, then with the group facilitator in an individual session), so that the effect on the group can then be considered. During group preparation, group members are asked for their commitment to share, within the group, such out-of-group contacts, should they occur.

Clinical examples: Extra-group socializing
Group members are well aware of the norm that discourages socializing outside of group.

1. In one of our Maintenance Groups, it emerged that one of the male group members had offered to drive a female fellow group member to an AA meeting once per week. The member accepting the ride had been insecure about attending AA meetings alone, and because of her fear, she avoided going. When the other group member graciously offered to take her, this succeeded in giving her the courage to be able to go, and it also made her feel cared about by the other group member.

While this gesture was certainly well intentioned, the group therapists saw the potential for consequences, and perceived this as a violation of the group norms. This was a special arrangement that two of the group members had formed, and something distinct from, and outside of, the rest of the group as a whole.

Both of the members involved divulged this arrangement in an individual session. Each was encouraged to bring it back to the group for transparency and for discussion. The female group member did so, and reported the advantages of this arrangement in allowing her to get this added support. The response of the group was positive, and moreover, the larger group did not appear to see any issue with it at all.

The group therapist's goal was to have one of the group members disclose this arrangement, and then observe what this evoked in the members. It was also of interest to the group to learn about the motives of the group member who took it upon himself to offer this arrangement, and what need it served in the group member who was receptive to this arrangement.

2. Two members made a bet with each other outside the group. The client who lost the bet did not return to the group for three weeks. When this was followed up, the client divulged that he felt he could not return to the group because he did not have the money to pay back his fellow group member.

3. One of our group members mysteriously disconnected from the group. When the therapist followed up, she learned that the client had begun a clandestine intimate relationship with a fellow group member. When the other group member eventually broke off the relationship, the original client felt too emotionally fragile to return to the same group that her ex-partner was in, and therefore, thought her only recourse was to drop out.

INTERFACE OF SELF-HELP / MUTUAL AID WITH GROUP THERAPY

12-STEP APPROACH

Many clients of our group have attended Alcoholics Anonymous, Cocaine Anonymous and Narcotics Anonymous meetings. Some clients have found it helpful, reporting benefits such as help in maintaining abstinence and in decreasing social isolation.

However, there is often a conflict between the philosophical approach of traditional self-help groups and the client's treatment goals:

- Most groups are abstinence based, although some are acknowledging that harm reduction is an alternative for some people.
- Some groups strongly recommend abstinence from all psychotropic medications. This can lead members to discontinue medication without telling their physician, leading to a relapse of mental illness symptoms, which may then lead to relapse of substance use.

Clients who have concurrent disorders have often reported feeling stigmatized at 12-step meetings because of their mental health problem (i.e., their psychotic symptoms or side-effects from their medication). If clients are already attending, or are considering attending 12-step meetings, therapists may need to prepare them for possible contradictions.

In recognizing the prevalent concurrent disorders population, mutual aid groups have been developed to meet the unique needs of people with concurrent disorders (Hamilton & Samples, 1995). Such mutual aid groups include "Double Trouble in Recovery" (Vogel, 1999) and even a web-based mutual aid group, "Dual Recovery Anonymous" (www.dualrecovery.org), for those who have computer skills and Internet access.

Concurrent disorders–focused mutual aid groups can be a useful complement to treatment and support from addiction and mental health professionals:

- There is no charge for affiliation, so money is not a barrier.
- Members can attend as often as needed, for as long as desired.
- There is a social network of welcoming people who share common goals.
- A sponsor system is available for 24-hour support.
- Such meetings can also help to fill up one's time, to reduce boredom, provide more structure and minimize the risk of relapse.

In our groups, we discuss the potential benefits of these groups and encourage attendance, but clients are free to make their own decision about this involvement.

CONCLUSION

Growing awareness of the concurrent disorders philosophy of care and the essential components of integrated treatment is encouraging. The menu of treatment approaches available today, and the growing evidence base for their effectiveness, are allowing clinicians to be more flexible in customizing treatment for each client.

This chapter illustrates how group work with clients who have concurrent disorders differs from therapy with clients of services that are addictions-only or mental-health–only. We hope that we have inspired clinicians to continue to develop their knowledge of group work, individual therapy and individualized case management, as these are important components of comprehensive, co-ordinated and longitudinal concurrent disorders treatment.

REFERENCES

Barrowclough, C., Haddock, G., Tarrier, N., Lewis, S.W., Moring, J., O'Brien, R. et al. (2001). Randomized controlled trial of motivational interviewing, cognitive behavior therapy, and family intervention for patients with comorbid schizophrenia and substance use disorders. *American Journal of Psychiatry, 158*(10), 1706–1713.

Beck, A.T., Wright, F.D., Newman, C.F. & Liese, B.S. (1993). *Cognitive Therapy of Substance Abuse.* New York: Guilford.

Bowen, R.C., D'Arcy, C., Keegan, D. & Senthiselvan, A. (2000). A controlled trial of cognitive behavioral treatment of panic in alcohol inpatients with comorbid panic disorder. *Addictive Behaviors, 25,* 593–597.

Hamilton, T. & Samples, P. (1995). *The 12 Steps and Dual Disorders.* Center City, MN: Hazelden.

Khantzian, E.J. (1997). The self-medication hypothesis of substance use disorders: A reconsideration and recent applications. *Harvard Review of Psychiatry, 4,* 231–244.

Kiesler, D.J. (1996). *Contemporary Interpersonal Theory and Research: Personality, Psychopathology, and Psychotherapy.* New York: John Wiley & Sons Inc.

Leszcz, M. (1992). The interpersonal approach to group psychotherapy. *International Journal of Group Psychotherapy, 43,* 37–62.

Malat, J., Leszcz, M. & Negrete, J.C. (1999). [A randomized controlled pilot study of interpersonal group therapy]. Unpublished raw data.

Marlatt, G.A. & Gordon, J. (Eds.). (1985). *Relapse Prevention.* New York: Guilford.

Miller, W.R. & Rollnick, S. (Eds.) (2002). *Motivational Interviewing: Preparing People to Change* (2nd ed.). New York: Guilford.

Minkoff, K. (2001). *Dual Diagnosis: An Integrated Model for the Treatment of People with Co-occurring Psychiatric and Substance Disorders: A Lecture by Kenneth Minkoff* [Video]. The Mental Illness Education Project Lecture Series. Brookline Village, MA: The Mental Illness Education Project.

Najavits, L.M., Weiss, R.D. & Liese, B.S. (1996). Group cognitive behavioral therapy for women with PTSD and substance use disorder. *Journal of Substance Use Treatment, 13,* 13–22.

Prochaska, J.O., DiClemente, C.C. & Norcross, J.C. (1992). In search of how people change: Applications to addictive behavior. *American Psychologist, 47,* 1102–1114.

Van Horn, D.H.A. & Bux, D.A., Jr. (2001). A pilot test of motivational interviewing groups for dually diagnosed patients. *Journal of Substance Abuse Treatment, 20,* 191–195.

Vogel, H. (1999). *Double Trouble in Recovery (DTR): How to Start and Run a DTR Group.* Albany: New York Office of Mental Hygiene, Mental Health Empowerment Project.

Weiss, R.D., Greenfield, S.F. & O'Leary, G. (2002). Relapse prevention for patients with bipolar and substance use disorders. In H.L. Graham, A. Copello, M.J. Birchwood & K.T. Mueser (Eds.), *Substance Misuse in Psychosis: A Handbook of Approaches to Treatment and Service Delivery* (pp. 207–226). Chichester, England: John Wiley & Sons.

Weiss, R.D., Griffin, M.L., Greenfield, S.F., Najavits, L.M., Wyner, D., Soto, J.A. et al. (2000). Group therapy for patients with bipolar disorder and substance dependence: Results of a pilot study. *Journal of Clinical Psychiatry, 61*(5), 361–367.

Weiss, R.D., Najavits, L.M. & Greenfield, S.F. (1999). A relapse prevention group for patients with bipolar and substance use disorders. *Journal of Substance Abuse Treatment, 16,* 47–54.

Yalom, I.D. (1995). *The Theory and Practice of Group Psychotherapy* (4th ed.). New York: Basic Books.

Chapter 6

Group therapy for severe mental illness and concurrent substance use disorders

ANDREA TSANOS, VICKI MYERS AND SUZANNE MORROW

INTRODUCTION

The need for a specialized group

The history of treatment for clients with concurrent severe mental health problems and substance use problems begins in the early 1980s, when clinicians began to add 12-step model substance use interventions to traditional mental health programs. By the late 1980s, clinicians in the United States had started to develop more comprehensive programs and to identify some of the core components of integrated treatment for these co-occurring problems. Dual diagnosis treatment programs that used multidisciplinary teams became more common during the 1990s. By the mid-1990s the results of controlled studies of treatment programs were beginning to appear, and specific interventions were being developed and tested (Drake et al., 2004).

At the Centre for Addiction and Mental Health (CAMH), treatment for clients with concurrent severe mental illness and substance use problems evolved out of an addiction program (in contrast to the American experience, where dual diagnosis treatment started in mental health programs). So, while much of the growing dual diagnosis evidence base was applicable to our work, and our development followed the same process of modifying approaches that had been used successfully in our programs, some of the features of the CAMH program reflect its different origins.

When our Concurrent Disorders Service first offered treatment in the early 1990s, it was the only program in Ontario to offer treatment to people who had concurrent substance use and mental health problems. At first, any client who met the criteria for a substance use disorder in combination with an Axis I or Axis II mental health disorder was eligible to join one of our groups.

It soon became apparent, however, that some clients were having trouble with the pace and intensity of the group. Because of behaviours related to their mental health problems (and the reaction of other group members to these behaviours), clients with severe mental illnesses were often isolated from the rest of the group. Many of these problems in group stemmed from the clients':

- cognitive difficulties (thought disorder, hallucinations or delusions)
- affective deficits (reduced emotional affect or reduced range of affect)
- interpersonal deficits (incongruence between thoughts, emotion and facial expression).

These symptoms can affect concentration and make self-examination, self-observation, introspection and insight more difficult.

Many clients with severe mental illness were also separated from the rest of the group because of differences in lifestyle—education, employment, income level and housing. Occasionally, some group members expressed a fear of being stigmatized by their association with the group members who had psychotic illnesses.

Some clients have had negative experiences with substance use and addiction treatment. They report that they have been stigmatized by mental health and addiction professionals. Because many of these clients are prone to having a relapse of substance use or acute psychotic or manic episodes, some clinicians view them as "treatment failures" or have simply characterized them as "unmotivated." Clients of emergency departments and withdrawal management centres who become known as "repeat customers" can exhaust and frustrate the staff.

We designed the Addiction Group for Psychiatric Survivors to meet the specific treatment needs of clients with severe mental illness and to offer them a safe place to address issues that are unique to their situation.

Substance use and severe mental illness

SELF-MEDICATION

Many clinicians believe that people who have severe mental health problems use substances (e.g., cannabis) to relieve psychotic symptoms or side-effects of medication. However, researchers have not been able to find a link between specific symptoms and use of a specific substance (Dixon et al., 1991). Availability (rather than effect) is the primary determinant of which specific substances are used (Mueser et al., 1992).

Dixon et al. (1991) found a difference between clients' and clinicians' perceptions of why clients use substances. According to this study, only a few people with schizophrenia were using substances to relieve negative side-effects of medication or to relieve positive psychotic symptoms, such as auditory hallucinations and delusions.

The following were the most common reasons given for using substances:

- 75 per cent of subjects stated it was for euphoria (i.e., "to get high," "to relax").
- 50 per cent used substances to relieve depression or increase pleasure, energy or emotions.
- 50 per cent used substances to increase social contacts or social relationships or to go along with the group.

Therefore, this research suggests that most clients are not using substances to relieve positive symptoms.

SUPERSENSITIVITY

Researchers have argued that people with severe mental illness are more sensitive to the effects of alcohol and other drugs—an increased biological vulnerability to mental health problems may lower people's threshold for experiencing negative consequences from substance use (Mueser et al., 1998).

For example, cannabis use may precipitate schizophrenia in people who are vulnerable, or it may exacerbate psychotic symptoms. The supersensitivity model argues that the quantity of the substance use is less important than the consequences. Even mild or moderate cannabis use by a person with psychosis may lead to consequences such as:

- failing to pay rent
- losing housing
- failing to show up for appointments
- neglecting to take psychotropic medications
- relapsing to psychotic symptoms
- having reduced motivation
- having a dramatically increased risk of more severe substance use.

Treating concurrent substance use and severe mental health problems

According to best practice recommendations (Health Canada, 2002), treatment for co-occurring substance use and severe mental health problems starts with a foundation of mental health services for the client, including:

- medical management (includes pharmacotherapy)
- family support and education
- supported employment
- training in psychiatric self-management
- crisis response services
- housing
- inpatient psychiatric stay, when needed.

These services should be complemented by specialized concurrent disorders treatment:

- a concurrent disorders assessment
- clinical case management

- motivational interviewing, within a harm reduction approach
- CBT for substance use change
- concurrent disorders group intervention
- social skills training
- self-help liaison
- psychoeducation with families (Health Canada, 2002).

Traditional mental health and substance use interventions need to be modified for clients with concurrent substance use and severe mental illness (so that the addiction issue is not addressed separately or not at all) and combined in a single, seamless strategy that considers the interrelationship between the two problems. How this is achieved is explained later in the chapter.

THE ADDICTION GROUP FOR PSYCHIATRIC SURVIVORS

Role of group therapy

Clients participate in our Addiction Group for Psychiatric Survivors as part of an overall treatment plan that usually also includes individual therapy and pharmacotherapy. Participation in the group experience can be helpful in enhancing insight into mental illness and addictive behaviour and improving social skills, while also fostering a sense of belonging.

One of the important benefits to the integrated group for this client population is that the isolation and stigma appear to be decreased when members discover others with similar difficulties. It is a powerful experience when members are able to talk openly about the stigma they have suffered and to now feel accepted in the group. Throughout the group process, members learn through different ways that they are not alone. They give and receive support and feedback. As their strengths are recognized, they are able to see themselves as "more than a diagnosis," which is how some clients have felt treated. The group provides them with a place where they can:

- feel welcomed and cared about
- talk and feel listened to
- find meaning and hope
- increase self-care
- learn new skills and coping strategies
- gain confidence in developing relationships in the community
- enhance their overall self-esteem.

Group composition

MENTAL HEALTH DIAGNOSES

Clients in the Addiction Group for Psychiatric Survivors have a serious and chronic mental illness (e.g., schizophrenia, schizoaffective disorder or bipolar disorder), and most have a history of psychosis.

Co-occurring problems such as substance use further complicate diagnosis, as intoxication or withdrawal can mimic or mask psychiatric symptoms, and this is especially true for people with severe mental illness. Because of the complexity of these concurrent disorders, we often need to make provisional diagnoses, which may be modified over time. Regardless of the provisional nature of the diagnosis, the symptoms (whether related to substance use or mental health problems, or both) need attention and intervention, so the group can still be an appropriate setting for these clients.

SUBSTANCE USE DIAGNOSES

The most common substance use disorders among current clients in our groups are:

- alcohol (62 per cent of clients seen meet DSM criteria for abuse or dependence)
- over-the-counter (OTC) preparations such as codeine (Tylenol 1®) or Sudafed® (38.2 per cent)
- marijuana (21 per cent)
- crack cocaine (15 per cent).

This prevalence profile closely matches both that of the broader CDS population as well as that of the general population, with the exception of the prevalence of OTC substances, which are much more common in people with severe mental illness.

According to the client population attending our groups, 65 per cent have a single substance use disorder, while 35 per cent have two or more substance use disorders. We recognize that these data reflect a treatment-engaged sample, and one that is group appropriate. We suspect that the complexity and severity of the substance use profile may be even greater among those people who are not connected to treatment.

It should be noted that 74 per cent of our current clients in this subpopulation are dependent on nicotine, but these data are not reflected here as the identified substance use disorder. During treatment, we have targeted smoking in our groups, and have encouraged clients to consider reducing or stopping their tobacco use. We have found that many of them have been motivated to do so, and several have attended CAMH's Nicotine Dependence Clinic, which is available on-site, and have made successful efforts to cut back.

LEVEL OF FUNCTIONING

While a broad range of functioning is represented in the group, most clients are unemployed and on some form of social assistance. As a result, many struggle with a lack of structure and meaningful activities. Some clients talk about feeling ashamed of being dependent on social assistance. Low income often forces them to share accommodations in neighbourhoods that pose a high risk of substance availability.

Clients in our group are often socially isolated and have poor interpersonal functioning, which may be related to their illnesses. Many clients who had good social functioning before the onset of their illness have described the pain of feeling shunned by peers. As a result, they have experienced loss of self-esteem, loss of confidence, depression, anxiety and demoralization. Some of their coping behaviours include spending time and energy concealing the illness, withdrawing or avoiding social interaction altogether.

Clients in the group tend to be more concrete in their thinking, with a limited ability for abstract thought. In terms of insight, most clients in the group are aware and accepting of their psychiatric illness; however, some clients do not see their substance use as problematic.

Group structure and setting

The Addiction Group for Psychiatric Survivors is an open-group format. New members are added into the group when space becomes available. The ideal size for the group is eight to 10 members. Usually there is a core group of members who attend regularly. However, many clients with severe mental illness tend to cycle in and out of treatment. To have eight to 10 clients at each group meeting, we need to recruit up to 15 members per group.

ATTENDANCE

We encourage regular attendance. However, many of these clients lead chaotic lives at times, and some may tend to disconnect as part of their mental illness or addiction, so we offer more flexibility than with other groups. We believe that a stricter attendance policy would mean that we would lose many clients who are well-invested in our program.

Rather than being rigid and punitive, we try to be accommodating when responding to absences. If clients know in advance that they need to miss a group, they are asked to contact the facilitators. Absences are reported to the group as a method of encouraging clients to be responsible for their attendance and to show them that their presence is important. Members are often curious and concerned about other group members who are absent. This is evidence that group cohesion occurs, even though attendance can be sporadic.

As a general rule, clients with severe mental illness need more intensive outreach. Some members reconnect when they are ready, while others require prompting and encouragement. The therapist may need to invite the client in for an individual session, or to have more frequent telephone contact during the week before the next group session. With the agreement of the client, the therapist may contact people in the client's support system when individual appointments or group sessions are missed.

DURATION OF GROUP SESSION

The meeting time of the Addiction Group for Psychiatric Survivors is generally determined via discussion with the group members. Most of the groups meet weekly for one hour. The group sessions tend to be shorter than other CDS groups, because this client population has a slightly shorter attention span, and restlessness is often a side-effect of antipsychotic medication.

> *Example*
> At one time, group members felt that a one-hour group was not long enough, so the group was extended to 1 1/2 hours. However, in the longer session, therapists noted that clients had difficulties in concentration and a tendency to shift to social conversation in the latter portion of the group. The time frame was discussed with the group members directly, and the group members' feedback was that they preferred a shorter session. After a pilot period, it became evident that 1 1/4 hours was optimal.

The group accommodates members who need to take occasional breaks, or occasionally need to leave before the end of the session because of overstimulation, agitation or restlessness that may be symptoms of the mental health problem or side-effects of medication.

PHYSICAL SPACE OF GROUP

The physical space occupied by the group is an important consideration in all groups, but it seems to be even more so with this client group, particularly with clients who are experiencing paranoid ideation. We believe that high priority should be given to having a consistent location that is quiet, comfortable and private. Members need to feel that this is a consistent place where they can give and receive help, and feel oriented and connected.

How the group room is set up is also important. For example, we have noted that clients appear to be more comfortable when the lights are dimmed, the chairs are arranged in a circle around a low round table with refreshments, and members have room to move their chairs closer or farther apart as they wish.

The observation mirror in the group room can evoke paranoia or evaluation anxiety in some members. The chairs should be arranged so that the backs are facing toward the observation mirror in the group room. Having the blinds closed on the observation mirror also helps to disguise the mirror. The mirror is not used with this client group—these clients prefer that the trainees physically sit in on the group session and not sit behind the mirror.

ENGAGING AND WORKING WITH CLIENTS IN THE GROUP

Start with a collaborative approach

Clinicians need to be able to see things from the client's point of view. Kenneth Minkoff (2001) gives some examples of how advice from counsellors might sound to a client:

> Abstain from all substance use (even though it is the only thing that helps me feel good).
>
> Take antipsychotic medication—sometimes multiple medications, and some of which might need to be by injection!
>
> Take these medications even though they give me horrible side-effects like serious weight gain, sedation and sexual dysfunction.
>
> Go on disability, since I can't work.
>
> Live in a group home with other mentally ill people, with a mentally ill roommate, under the watchful eye of caring staff 24 hours a day. We can take turns with the household chores, such as washing the dishes and cleaning the toilets.
>
> Get to have a case manager who will make me an "individualized treatment plan" that lists all my defects in black and white, just for me.
>
> And have a Payee (since I can't manage my money myself).

Minkoff's parody highlights the accommodations and adjustments that clients are expected to make when they are taken into care. When clients resist this type of advice, we see this as positive and natural behaviour, rather than seeing it as non-compliance or denial.

Connecting with these clients is particularly challenging because of the complex nature of their difficulties. Addressing immediate practical concerns, such as transportation, housing and money management, helps to reassure them that changes in substance use behaviour is not the only item on the agenda.

Because these clients tend to have a high rate of missed appointments, outreach techniques—such as making follow-up calls, sending follow-up letters and, if consent has been obtained, contacting people in the client's support system (e.g., parents)—are crucial. Contact with community workers (e.g., assertive community treatment

[ACT] workers, who meet with clients in their natural settings, and community psychiatrists) can also be helpful.

Goal setting

SUBSTANCE USE GOALS

The initial contact with a client is also an opportunity to discuss and collaborate on short- and long-term goals. Many clients in the Addiction Group for Psychiatric Survivors lack the skills and/or motivation to change their substance use. Substance use is often the only activity that allows these otherwise isolated clients to have any social contact. Similar to how most other people use substances, many clients with severe mental illness also use substances to regulate unpleasant states.

For example, some clients with schizophrenia use crack cocaine for stimulation, or alcohol to escape boredom. Treatment planning needs to be flexible enough to work with a variety of people at varying stages of motivation and insight. We tend to look at three main options for substance use goals:

- abstinence
- controlled substance use
- no change, but monitoring and discussing substance use.

Abstinence

Our preferred and recommended substance use goal is abstinence. Although many clinicians believe that abstinence is not a realistic and attainable goal for most clients with severe mental illness, we must recognize that, while a reduction goal within a harm reduction framework may be of greater applicability with this population, in our experience, many of these clients have successfully attained and maintained abstinence. This has been surprising at times, but certainly encouraging.

Controlled substance use

Controlled use can be harder for clients with severe mental illness than for those with less severe mental health problems. Clients with severe mental illness tend to use substances impulsively and often lack the impulse control to achieve the narrowly defined limits of controlled use. In addition, many clients at our clinic have their main problems with marijuana and crack cocaine, and limits of these substances become more difficult to quantify. However, in many cases we have seen clients make important reductions in their substance use, followed by positive changes to other behaviours that often accompany more frequent or heavy substance use, such as less engagement in theft or assault.

No change, but monitoring and discussing substance use

A final option is a no-change goal that includes, at least, an agreement to monitor and discuss substance use. Clients who have limited insight into their illness, or who are forced into treatment by the courts, often find this goal appealing. The group process can be very powerful with such clients at this stage; remember that goals are not static, and neither is motivation. This short-term goal sometimes changes as treatment progresses.

MENTAL HEALTH GOALS

Mental health goals can include:
- learning to manage psychotic symptoms
- following through with medication
- learning to manage/tolerate unpleasant side-effects of medication
- finding skills for improving social contact
- managing depression.

OTHER LIFE GOALS

Broader quality-of-life goals include:
- finding meaningful employment or activity
- being able to live more independently
- becoming more responsible with money management (being able to spend money on things the client needs, such as a stereo, instead of substances).

It is helpful to repeat linkages between, and reminders about, the interrelationship of goals, so that the client understands and recognizes how achieving the substance use goal will also help to achieve mental health goals and vice versa.

Assessment of group suitability

At assessment, the client's goals are explored and concretized, and a functional analysis of the relationship between substance use and mental health is conducted. We generally do not exclude clients on the basis of their:
- outstanding legal involvement
- history of violence
- lack of verbal ability
- personality disorder diagnosis
- inpatient status.

Clients should not be actively psychotic at the time of joining the group; however, after joining, clients may develop hallucinations or paranoid ideation, which requires appropriate attention and intervention.

Factors that may require that a client be excluded from the group include:
- unwillingness to be seen by a psychiatrist
- unwillingness to accept medication to stabilize severe psychiatric symptoms.

To benefit from the group, members need to be capable of appropriate communication and conduct. In cases where a group member has decompensated, the therapist and psychiatrist work with the client to stabilize the client's mental status. Stabilization may require some weeks for an adjustment in pharmacotherapy to become fully effective; in other cases, it may require a brief hospitalization.

Once stability is achieved, the client can return to the group. Some clients are permitted to attend the group during periods of hospitalization, which promotes continuity of care. Although the group is part of an outpatient program, some of its members are in long-term inpatient care, such as in mental health units for patients with schizophrenia or forensic units. For these clients, an additional benefit of the group is a change of environment from the hospital ward.

Group preparation

Group preparation is an important phase for successful engagement and appraisal of readiness to change. The client begins the group after completing further assessment and preparation with one of the group's co-therapists. Group guidelines and norms are similar to those discussed in the previous chapter.

With this client population, group preparation usually requires more than one session. As in any therapy, building rapport and establishing an alliance of trust is the critical initial task. In this initial phase of preparation for the group, we find that clients with concurrent severe mental illness and substance use problems often need help with very practical concerns, such as housing and income support. We recognize that some clinicians hold pessimistic attitudes about the prognosis for clients with such complex concurrent issues. However, in our experience, we have seen the importance of continually instilling hope in clients, along with belief in the possibility that they can change. This kind of optimism seems to enhance clients' sense of self-efficacy.

APPROACHES TO GROUP TREATMENT

Our goal is to offer clients group treatment in which they can work to stabilize their substance use and work on avoiding relapse, while focusing on managing various aspects related to their mental illness and addictive behaviours. Throughout the group process, clients are helped to increase their life satisfaction and their ability to live in the community.

The Addiction Group for Psychiatric Survivors uses various therapeutic approaches, including:

- stages of change theory and motivational interviewing
- psychoeducation
- relapse prevention
- cognitive-behavioural therapy (CBT)
- interactive/interpersonal group therapy and Modified Dynamic Group Therapy
- social skills training.

Stages of change theory and motivational interviewing

An important study by Martino et al. (2002) highlights the barriers to using traditional motivational interviewing (MI) with this client population. These include clients' difficulties in:

- cognitive functioning
- reflecting on past behaviours
- abstract reasoning
- following through on planned intentions
- anhedonia (the inability to feel pleasure or enjoyment).

In addition, given that active psychotic symptoms, medication non-compliance and social stigma also make MI more difficult with this population, Martino et al. (2002) suggest modifying traditional MI with an integrated approach that addresses more than just substance use. This modified approach is called Dual Diagnosis Motivational Interviewing (DDMI). It:

- focuses consistently on enhancing motivation for changing three targeted behaviours: substance use, treatment compliance (program attendance and commitment to participate) and medication compliance. A metaphor of a three-legged stool is used to help clients understand the importance of each component in recovery.
- looks at the interaction between the one behaviour (e.g., substance use) and how it affects the others (e.g., psychotic symptoms)
- makes accommodations for cognitive deficits, such as concentration or memory problems, and disordered thinking, such as tangentiality, by using repetition, keeping strategies brief, using simple concrete and verbal materials, and providing frequent breaks within sessions.

TECHNIQUES FOR MODIFYING MOTIVATIONAL INTERVIEWING TO OVERCOME BARRIERS

There are three important modifications to the traditional techniques to adapt the MI micro–skill set for working with this population:

- modifications of open-ended questions: simplifying by asking about one topic at a time and avoiding compound questions
- modification of reflections: reflecting one area at a time (e.g., feelings, behaviour or an event), reflecting often, keeping reflections concise, reflecting only the positive, logically organized material and giving enough time for a response (Martino et al., 2002)
- modifications of affirmations: heightening emphasis on affirmations by always affirming anything that can be related to the three targeted behaviours—substance use (e.g., "good for you that you were able to say no to the dealer"), treatment compliance (e.g., "it is so good that you are here today") or medication compliance (e.g., "it is really positive that you are taking your medication"). Affirmations of client's personal qualities are exceptionally important for this population, because such affirmations tend to inspire initial change efforts and help to establish the therapeutic relationship.

Psychoeducation

Psychoeducation is provided on an as-needed basis both by the facilitators and by members of the group.

Psychoeducation topics covered in the group include:
- the supersensitivity model
- the importance of taking or staying on medication
- the importance of taking medication even when members have used substances
- the relationship between their substance use and mental health symptoms
- the merits of good self-care
- the importance of developing relationships with peers who do not use substances.

Clients with severe mental illness need to learn that the two most significant risk factors for psychotic relapse are:
- poor adherence with session attendance or medication
- use of substances.

These are related, in that substance use can lead people to stop taking their medication (some clients believe that substance use will interfere with their medication), or they may simply forget to take medication when under the influence. Cannabis is even more harmful in people with severe mental illness who are not on medications.

Psychoeducation can be therapist-directed, or clients can learn from their peers.

THERAPIST-DIRECTED

Sometimes, therapists offer direct education. For example, group members are helped to identify links between their substance use and mental illness. They are taught that their psychiatric symptoms may increase due to substances altering their brain chemistry and that substances cause a decrease in the effectiveness of antipsychotic medication. Clients discuss their experiences of their judgment having been impaired. They reflect on times that they have chosen not to take their medication, or to use more substances or to use for a longer period of time than intended. Clients learn about the supersensitivity hypothesis in terms they are able to understand.

If a specific educational topic has been identified by a number of members, a group session is planned to focus on the issue (e.g., diet and substance use; mood and food). More often, education is provided as needed within a session, and co-facilitators involve group members in the process.

LEARNING FROM PEERS

We believe that clients learn primarily from each other and secondarily from the co-therapists. Therefore, members are encouraged to provide education to one another. For example, our group highlights the importance of finding enjoyable social and leisure activities that do not involve substance use. Clients are encouraged to help one another generate ideas about enriching this area of their lives. Group members encourage each other and offer suggestions for community activities and resources.

Example
When members identified a common concern with negative thinking and ruminating thoughts, the group generated a list of more than 20 coping strategies. The co-facilitators then suggested that group members identify one or two of the strategies to try during the upcoming week and, in the next session, tell the group how the strategies had worked. This was so helpful that some members kept the list of strategies in their pocket, to refer to when necessary.

Relapse prevention

Relapse prevention techniques help clients identify warning signs of relapse, analyse episodes of use and identify future solutions.

Overcoming Addictions: Skills Training for People with Schizophrenia (Roberts et al., 1999) has been helpful in our group work with this client population. It describes an integrated approach that combines cognitive-behavioural therapy and relapse prevention techniques, modified for use with clients with schizophrenia and substance use problems. It recommends the following phased approach to treatment:

- Psychiatric symptoms are brought under control.
- Clients receive basic training (for the pre-contemplation & contemplation stages). Basic training consists of eight 45-minute educational sessions that educate and motivate, while teaching basic relapse prevention techniques. In this phase, the sessions use discussion, without role-play. Topics include:
  - damage control
  - creation of an emergency card
  - habits and craving control
  - knowing how to identify and cope with high-risk situations
  - recognizing warning signs of relapse
  - healthy pleasures and healthy habits
  - reviewing reasons for quitting substance use
  - money management.
- Clients receive skills training (for action stage of change), in which they practise nine specific skills. The emphasis in these sessions is on learning skills through role-play, as (the authors feel that) talk therapy is not enough to produce behaviour change. The nine skills include:
  - quitting after a slip
  - reporting a slip
  - refusing drugs offered by a dealer
  - refusing drugs offered by a relative or friend
  - getting an appointment with a busy person
  - getting a support person
  - reporting symptoms and side-effects to a doctor
  - asking someone to join you in a healthy pleasure
  - negotiating with a Public Trustee representative payee.

In addition, clients can attend practice sessions at all stages of treatment (including clients receiving basic training or those who have completed skills training). Practice sessions focus on applying to real-life situations the concepts learned in basic training and the skills learned in skills training.

The group forum allows clients to share their struggles with triggers, such as drinking when smoking cigarettes, in a safe context. Discussion typically involves working on problem solving, in order to handle triggers and high-risk situations more effectively the next time. The group helps the client to anticipate substance use triggers for the coming week and identify and commit to a plan of action.

Members often find it difficult to admit to relapse, as they may feel ashamed or guilty. However, we encourage clients to return to the group, despite these feelings, and not assume that a relapse means they no longer belong. We frame relapses as opportunities for learning, reviewing the treatment plans and re-affirming their commitment to change. In our work with clients, relapse prevention goals include:

- having slips less often
- having shorter-lasting slips when they do occur
- using less of the problem substance (when used at all)
- having fewer negative consequences associated with the substance use.

The group is also a place to celebrate occasions when the client was able to succeed. Abstinent clients serve as role models to those still struggling with ongoing use.

Cognitive-behavioural therapy (CBT)

Twenty-five to 50 per cent of people with schizophrenia continue to experience positive and negative symptoms, even while adhering to optimal pharmacotherapy (Harrow et al., 1985). This has highlighted a need to develop interventions that target these persistent symptoms, which often cause distress and disrupt social and occupational functioning.

Cognitive-behavioural therapy (CBT) approaches have recently been adapted for use with clients who have concurrent substance use and severe mental health problems. *Cognitive-Behavioral Integrated Treatment: A Treatment Manual for Substance Misuse in People with Severe Mental Health Problems* (C-BIT, Graham et al., 2003) describes interventions that are appropriate to the client's stages of change in dealing with these concurrent disorders. Based on cognitive therapies developed by Beck (1976), Padesky and Greenberger (1995) and Salkovskis (1996), the C-BIT approach integrates strategies for treating substance use problems and psychosis in a way that appears to the client to be seamless.

The C-BIT approach has three main goals:

1. It helps clients identify the unhelpful, unrealistic beliefs they hold about their substance use. Clients then learn to challenge and replace these beliefs with ones that will serve to strengthen commitment to behaviour change. For example, a client may believe, "cannabis stops my voices" (substance-related belief). The therapist then uses a three-question technique:

- "What is the evidence for that belief?"
- "Are there times when that is not the case?"
- "If so, what does that mean?"

The outcome is that the original belief might be modified to become more accurate and realistic; the client may say, "I guess after one or two joints, they do seem to stop for awhile, but if I smoke any more, it makes the voices worse."

2. It helps clients develop an understanding of the relationship between their mental illness and substance use.
3. It teaches clients skills for:
   - managing and controlling their substance use
   - identifying early warning signs of psychosis that their substance use may trigger or make worse
   - developing the social supports that will promote and sustain a healthier lifestyle.

The C-BIT approach has four stages that correspond to the stages of treatment (engagement, persuasion, active treatment and relapse prevention). Incorporating techniques of motivational interviewing and relapse prevention, it encourages clinicians to adopt a motivational/educational role. While the C-BIT is a structured and systematic approach, it is also flexible in that it allows clinicians to offer the intervention in whatever time they have available with the client for the sessions, and over whatever time period works for the client.

Interactive/Interpersonal group therapy and Modified Dynamic Group Therapy

We have found that an interactional, interpersonal approach (Yalom, 1995) is useful, as is Modified Dynamic Group Therapy (Khantzian et al., 1990). Clients of the Addiction Group for Psychiatric Survivors can be capable of staying in the here-and-now and of providing constructive feedback to other group members. However, facilitators must pay careful attention to the group members' ability to tolerate the intensity of intervention (i.e., when interpersonal feedback or confrontation occurs in the group).

Example

One of the group members talked about his unsuccessful attempts to find a girlfriend. Group members gave him feedback about why the direct approach that he had described—of walking up to strangers on the street and directly asking them to go for coffee—was not effective.

They posed that his difficulty might not necessarily be about personal rejection, but perhaps was a consequence of a lack of social skills about more appropriately initiating conversation with women. They then offered suggestions as to how he might find ways to effectively meet women, such as by joining an interest group, taking a course or spending time at one of the known recreational clubs where substance use is not permitted. The members gave the client gentle feedback when commenting on an assumption that he had often made in the group: that he seemed to expect that "getting a girlfriend" is something that occurs instantly. Instead, they offered their understanding that relationships typically develop only after getting to know someone over time. They went on to suggest that he refrain from asking women out in the first conversation, and defer this until there is a connection and comfort established.

This kind of caring and practical support appeared to help the client address this particular social skills difficulty.

Social skills training

Many people with psychotic disorders have difficulties with:
• social perception (e.g., reading others' affect)
• problem solving
• communication (i.e., having effective behavioural skills).

Surprisingly, people with psychotic disorders who use substances tend to have slightly better social functioning (Bellack et al., 1997; Mueser, 1998; Mueser & Bellack, 1998). This may be because people using substances need to have at least the minimal social skills to be able to seek substance availability and interact with drug dealers. Many people with severe mental illness use substances with other people, so they need to use minimal social skills, at least, to be able to interact. Clients with concurrent substance use problems and severe mental illness struggle with making new friends and so often use substances as a means of joining or gaining acceptance with peers. In fact, many of these people rely on substance use as the only opportunity for social contact in their lives.

Social skills training can help clients deal with peer pressure, develop strategies to refuse substances, and establish relationships with other people who do not use substances. Training may also include helping clients to express their emotions. Assertiveness training helps clients learn how to make requests or refuse unreasonable requests. For example, clients in our group often describe being asked repeatedly for money or cigarettes by others living in their building; consequently, they give away what little they have, finding it too hard to say no. Techniques such as role-playing, rehearsal, modelling, support and feedback both from leaders and members are also useful.

Appropriate social behaviour is emphasized and supported in the group. For example, when a member comes to the group looking brighter, cleaner, well-groomed or is generally more socially appropriate, co-facilitators and group members alike offer complimentary feedback to reinforce these efforts.

Direct social skills training can be used in the group to target both verbal behaviour (e.g., learning to use an appropriate loudness of voice) and non-verbal behaviour (e.g., learning how close to stand to another person). Practice is important if skills are to be generalized to real-life situations.

Example
A group member was hypomanic and concerned about the difficulties she had in making friends. Group members suggested that she try listening to others, as many people like to talk about themselves. The co-facilitators then suggested that the member practise the skill of listening by choosing a group member and role-playing asking the other member some questions about himself. She was able to complete this task with coaching, support and feedback from other members. In these and other ways, the group offers an in-vivo opportunity for social skills enhancement and interpersonal feedback.

Natural opportunities for learning can also occur outside the group session.

Example
One of the group members with schizophrenia had a routine of dropping by his group therapist's office unexpectedly at various points in the week. He would bang repeatedly on her door, using a very loud and repetitive knocking, while simultaneously yelling out her name, asking if she was inside. The therapist addressed this area for social skills development with the client in an individual session. She explained about what is appropriate social etiquette when knocking on someone's door, particularly in a public setting.

This client made some improvements, but often forgot that the original behaviour was inappropriate and reverted to it occasionally.

We find that, once the behaviour is addressed directly with the client, it is easier to address the next time it occurs. Repetition of information is usually required to produce lasting and consistent new behaviours with clients in our group.

INTEGRATING THE APPROACHES

The approaches described above are integrated throughout the lifespan of the group. We have no set agenda for the group sessions, and the topics vary from week to week as group members raise issues for discussion. There is no formal check-in process, but if a client has been absent from the group and then returns, or has been quiet for the duration of the session, a member of the group or the therapist will acknowledge this and ask how the client is doing. The group focuses on helping members problem-solve whatever issues they may be facing.

The following examples illustrate the different topics or approaches we may cover:

- We may use psychoeducation to show the impact of substance use on mental health. To do this, we may use very specific examples, such as exploring the impact of drinking on degree of paranoia and delusional thinking.
- Behavioural skills training is a useful way to address identified high-risk situations, such as: "I go by the bar on the way home when I have nothing else to do." Suggestions for therapeutic responses include helping the client to:
  - modify the environment where possible (e.g., identify safer places to socialize)
  - brainstorm and problem-solve to find new responses (e.g., find new routes, to avoid drug dealers or bars that the client was previously lured in by)
  - engage in activity scheduling to provide structure and prevent boredom.
- Clients practise assertiveness training and behavioural rehearsal (role-play) within a social skills training approach to practise refusing an offer of drugs from a persistent drug dealer (e.g., "everyone in my building smokes crack, and there are always dealers knocking on my door").
- If relapses occur, we provide a forum for learning; we always praise the client's honesty and reinforce the steps taken to get back on track.
- We adopt a longitudinal and realistic approach, expecting small steps toward change.

COMMON GROUP THERAPY CHALLENGES

Dealing with different levels of functioning within the group

The functioning of the group can vary from one session to the next, depending on the mental health of those in attendance and on the issues being discussed. Leaders need to be able to provide the level of support or structure that is necessary.

For example, before admitting a new member with a particularly low level of functioning, the co-facilitators talked with the group to explain some of the difficulties that the new member was having. The group members recognized the importance of this client's getting help for his substance use. Therefore, they agreed to do what they could to encourage him to participate and to help him to feel a connection with the group. Higher-functioning members of the group benefitted from being able to share their knowledge and experience with others, thus enhancing their self-esteem.

Dealing with symptoms such as paranoia

Sometimes, members having paranoid thoughts are able to test the reality of their concern by asking other group members whether they have similar beliefs. Group members can offer support by saying that they have had similar experiences, but they can also challenge the irrational beliefs. Challenges coming from fellow group members are much more helpful than interventions from the leaders. The group can often sense when a member is too vulnerable to accept feedback; in such cases, the group may choose to remain silent.

> *Example*
> When a distressed member expressed paranoid ideas, the co-therapist stated that she had never seen the client so agitated and wondered if the client was feeling all right. This supportive comment helped the client calm down, and members were then able to express concern and provide helpful suggestions.

Dealing with concrete thinking

Members of the Addiction Group for Psychiatric Survivors are often good at giving concrete suggestions to others. As with any group, members feel better about themselves when helping others. However, at times their advice can come across as too directive. In these instances, the leaders need to point out that people are unique and that what works for one person may not work for another. When doing so, leaders always try to support the member giving the suggestion by acknowledging his or her attempt to be helpful.

After various suggestions have been offered, the leader may ask the receiving member, "What has it been like to get all these suggestions? Are you able to pick one of these suggestions to use within the next week? Do you have a different strategy of your own that you would like to try?"

A NOTE ON CANNABIS

While cannabis can tend to get normalized or viewed as not carrying the same liabilities as other substances, we believe it deserves careful consideration. Therapists must be aware of how cannabis can affect the etiology, course and prognosis of severe mental illness.

Research indicates that people who use cannabis show higher rates of relapse to psychosis than with other substances. In those having a first episode of psychosis, cannabis has been found to be the primary substance used. An important study by Linszen et al. (1994) looked at three groups of people with schizophrenia; those who:

- never used cannabis
- were "light" cannabis users
- were "heavy" users.

They found that people who used cannabis heavily were more likely to have more psychotic relapses and rehospitalizations.

While there is not support for a causal relationship between cannabis and psychotic disorders, Mueser and Glynn (1995) describe a stress-vulnerability model, in which people vulnerable to schizophrenia have a "sensitive brain," which is particularly sensitive to stress (environmental or chemical, as in substance use). Given that cannabis use is one of the only factors that is amenable to change (that is associated with poor outcome in schizophrenia), we recognize the importance of, at minimum, monitoring clients' cannabis use and of using motivational strategies to promote desired change.

INTERFACE OF MUTUAL AID SELF-HELP WITH GROUP THERAPY

A review article by Noordsy et al. (1996) explores the role of self-help groups for people with concurrent severe mental illness and substance use disorders. They found that, in this population, clinician-led groups are better attended than self-help groups. Only a minority of people in this population can connect with self-help groups and attend consistently over time. The article concludes that:

- Psychiatric diagnosis appears to play a role in a person's ability to affiliate. People with mood disorders are more likely to attend self-help groups than are those with schizophrenia. However, people with severe mental illness who tried the self-help approach found that it made it easier to live with their disabilities.
- People with better social skills possibly find it easier to participate in self-help groups (Samson et al., 1988).
- Barriers to linkage to self-help included psychiatric symptoms:
  - Medication use and related side-effects often make these clients feel different from others.
  - Some clients avoid attendance because of anxiety (i.e., discomfort with large crowds), suspiciousness or paranoia.
  - The religious themes and discussion of spiritual recovery can become associated with their delusions.
- People also found it difficult to continue attending for other reasons, such as:
  - They found it hard to sit still, but felt uncomfortable about leaving the meeting.
  - They felt triggered to use by the stories told by other group members.
  - They were unable to relate to the losses described in the stories, as they didn't have a job, car or spouse to lose.

These findings coincide with the observations we have made in our work with this client population. Some of the clients of the Addiction Group for Psychiatric Survivors have tried Alcoholics Anonymous (AA), Cocaine Anonymous (CA) and Narcotics Anonymous (NA). Some clients have reported benefits such as added support in maintaining abstinence, decreased social isolation and a structure to fill up their time. However, most have not fully connected with this model of support. Many clients resist going to 12-step meetings, or attend one meeting and are not interested in returning.

Concurrent disorders–focused mutual aid groups are not yet as available as traditional AA/NA/CA meetings. However, several mutual aid groups have been developed to address some of these problems; these include:

- Double Trouble in Recovery (DTR) (Vogel, 1999)

- Double Trouble Groups (Hamilton & Samples, 1995; Hendrickson et al., 1994)
- Dual Recovery Anonymous (DRA) (www.dualrecovery.org)—an online concurrent disorders–focused mutual aid group. Unfortunately, most clients with severe mental illness do not have computer access or skills, so this is not useful for most clients with concurrent substance use and severe mental health problems.

Mutual aid self-help programs are most helpful when they are chosen voluntarily, and the program philosophy is consistent with the client's own models of understanding (Noordsy et al., 1996). If clients are already attending, or are considering attending 12-step mutual aid groups, they may face contradictions with their treatment plan, particularly if they are in a treatment program with a philosophy of harm reduction, rather than abstinence. In such cases, the therapist may need to help prepare the client for the alternative philosophy, and help clients reconcile any confusing differences that may arise during involvement in both groups.

CONCLUSION

Growing awareness of the treatment approaches described above allows clinicians more flexibility in building a "toolkit" to respond to the multiple needs of clients who have concurrent substance use problems and severe mental illnesses. We share the philosophy articulated by Bellack and Gearon (1998), who write that:

> treatment must be conceptualized as an ongoing process in which motivation to reduce substance use waxes and wanes. They [clients with severe mental illness and substance use problems] need the ongoing support provided by programs that extend over time and are tolerant of patients dropping in and out, sometimes trying to quit, and sometimes not, abstaining for awhile only to relapse. (page 750)

While group work is an integral component in the care plan, the package of supports recommended in *Best Practices: Concurrent Mental Health and Substance Use Disorders* (Health Canada, 2002) is critical to working effectively with this unique client population. Given the heterogeneity, severity and chronicity of the multiple issues surrounding these clients, Minkoff has aptly described the helpful ingredients for ensuring a more successful outcome: "an empathic, hopeful, continuous treatment relationship in which integrated treatment and co-ordination of care can take place through multiple treatment episodes" (Minkoff, 2001).

When we embarked on this project of offering addiction support groups for clients with severe mental illnesses, some colleagues who knew the population doubted that group work would be effective. Our experience suggests that, if the principles we have discussed here are followed, and clients are supported to join these groups, many attend and become engaged, loyal and committed members. Clients credit the group with giving them a sense of social acceptance and caring; they report benefiting from feeling accountable to a peer group struggling with similar issues. Far from being something that they feel they are required to attend, the group is seen by its members as an important part of their weekly structure, and they demonstrate a high level of cohesion to one another and come to rely on it as a vital resource.

What was one group is now three, and other programs, both within and outside CAMH, have asked for assistance and training in setting up similar groups. Creating a safe environment where clients can talk about substance use issues in a peer group has a role in the broad set of biopsychosocial strategies we can employ to help clients with severe mental illness and substance use problems.

REFERENCES

Beck, A.T. (1976). *Cognitive Therapy and the Emotional Disorders.* New York: International Universities Press.

Bellack, A. & Gearon, J.S. (1998). Substance abuse treatment for people with schizophrenia. *Addictive Behaviours, 23*(6), 749–766.

Bellack, A.S., Mueser, K.T., Gingerich, S. & Agresta, J. (1997). *Social Skills Training for Schizophrenia: A Step-by-Step Guide.* New York: Guilford.

Dixon, L., Haas, G., Weiden, P.J., Sweeney, J. & Frances, A.J. (1991). Drug abuse in schizophrenic patients: Clinical correlates and reasons for use. *American Journal of Psychiatry, 148*, 224–230.

Drake, R.E., Mueser, K.T., Brunette, M.F. & McHugo, G.J. (2004). A review of treatments for people with severe mental illnesses and co-occurring substance use disorders. *Psychiatric Rehabilitation Journal, 27*(4), 360–374.

Early Psychosis Prevention and Intervention Centre. (2001). *Case Management in Early Psychosis: A Handbook.* Melbourne: Author.

Graham, H.L., Copello, A., Birchwood, M., Mueser, K.T., Orford, J., McGovern, D. et al. (2003). *Cognitive-Behavioural Integrated Treatment: A Treatment Manual for Substance Misuse in People with Severe Mental Health Problems.* Chichester: John Wiley & Sons.

Hamilton, T. & Samples, P. (1995). *The 12 Steps and Dual Disorders.* Center City, MN: Hazelden.

Harrow, M., Carone, B.J. & Westermeyer, J. (1985). The course of psychosis in early phases of schizophrenia. *American Journal of Psychiatry, 142*, 702–707.

Health Canada. (2002). *Best Practices: Concurrent Mental Health and Substance Use Disorders.*

Ottawa: Minister of Public Works and Government Services Canada, Cat. #H39-599/2001-2E.

Hendrickson, E., Schmal, M., Albert, N. & Massaro, J. (1994). Dual disorder treatment: perspectives on the state of the art. *TIE-Lines, XI*, 1–15.

Khantzian, E.J., Halliday, K.S. & McAuliffe, W.E. (1990). *Addiction and the Vulnerable Self.* New York: Guilford Press.

Linszen, D.H., Dingemans, P.M. & Lenior, M.E. (1994). Cannabis use and the course of recent-onset schizophrenic disorders. *Archives of General Psychiatry, 51*, 273–279.

Martino, S., Carroll, K., Kostas, D., Perkins, J. & Rounsaville, B. (2002). Dual diagnosis motivational interviewing: A modification of motivational interviewing for substance-abusing patients with psychotic disorders. *Journal of Substance Abuse Treatment, 23*(4), 297–308.

Minkoff, K. (2001). *Dual Diagnosis: An Integrated Model for the Treatment of People with Co-occurring Psychiatric and Substance Disorders: A Lecture by Kenneth Minkoff* [Video]. The Mental Illness Education Project Lecture Series. Brookline Village, MA: The Mental Illness Education Project.

Mueser, K.T. (1998). Social skill and problem solving. In A.S. Bellack & M. Hersen (Eds.), *Comprehensive Clinical Psychology: Vol. 6* (pp. 183–201). New York: Pergamon.

Mueser, K.T. & Bellack, A.S. (1998). Social skills and social functioning. In K.T. Mueser & N. Tarier (Eds.), *Handbook of Social Functioning in Schizophrenia* (pp. 79–96). Needham Heights, MA: Allyn & Bacon.

Mueser, K.T., Drake, R.E. & Wallach, M.A. (1998). Dual diagnosis: A review of etiological theories. *Addictive Behaviours, 23*(6), 717–734.

Mueser, K.T. & Glynn, S. (1995). *Behavioral Family Therapy for Psychiatric Disorders.* New York: Allyn & Bacon.

Mueser, K.T., Yarnold, P.R. & Bellack, A.S. (1992). Diagnostic and demographic correlates of substance abuse in schizophrenia and major affective disorder. *Acta Psychiatrica Scandinavica, 85*, 48–55.

Noordsy, D., Schwab, B., Fox, L. & Drake, R. (1996). The role of self-help programs in the rehabilitation of persons with severe mental illness and substance use disorders. *Community Mental Health Journal, 32*(1), 71–81.

Padesky, C. & Greenberger, D. (1995). *Mind Over Mood: Change How You Feel by Changing the Way You Think.* New York: The Guilford Press.

Roberts, L.J., Shaner, A. & Eckman, T.A. (1999). *Overcoming Addictions: Skills Training for People with Schizophrenia.* New York: WW Norton.

Salkovskis, P. (1996). *Frontiers of Cognitive Therapy.* New York: The Guilford Press.

Samson, J.A., Simpson, J.C. & Tsuang, M.T. (1988). Outcome studies of schizoaffective disorders. *Schizophrenia Bulletin, 14*, 543–554.

Vogel, H. (1999). *Double Trouble in Recovery (DTR): How to Start and Run a DTR Group.* Albany: New York Office of Mental Hygiene, Mental Health Empowerment Project.

Yalom, I.D. (1995). *The Theory and Practice of Group Psychotherapy* (4th ed.). New York: Basic Books.

Chapter 7

Adapting dialectical behaviour therapy to the treatment of concurrent substance use and mental health disorders

SHELLEY MCMAIN

Dialectical behaviour therapy (DBT) was developed by Marsha Linehan in the 1980s and 1990s to treat people with borderline personality disorder (BPD) who are chronically suicidal (Linehan, 1993). In her early work, Linehan had studied the efficacy of cognitive-behavioural therapy (CBT) for such clients. She soon realized that the emphasis on change inherent in CBT was highly aversive to people with BPD. For example, when clients were taught interpersonal skills, they often responded with anger and argued that the therapist didn't understand their situation. These negative reactions often interfered with the recovery process.

Linehan recognized that the heightened sensitivity of these clients required the therapist to pay greater attention to conveying an attitude of acceptance. The DBT model that she subsequently developed integrates acceptance-based strategies—informed by Zen philosophy and client-centred principles—with conventional CBT interventions, to create a structured approach that explicitly targets clients' maladaptive behaviour.

The DBT treatment process is facilitated by the therapist, who focuses on acceptance while simultaneously pushing for change. Dialectical philosophy provides a framework for this integration of apparently opposing strategies, and also informs treatment goals and processes. According to dialectical philosophy, all objects and processes are composed of naturally occurring opposites. For example, breathing involves the inhalation of oxygen and the exhalation of carbon dioxide. Change is achieved by the continual synthesis of natural tensions, through the gradual reconciliation of opposites. The overarching goal of DBT treatment is to help clients reduce their problematic behaviours through finding balance.

In the Concurrent Disorders Service at the Centre for Addiction and Mental Health (CAMH), DBT was first used as a treatment for clients with concurrent BPD and substance use problems. Treating people with BPD had caused significant challenges for clinicians, and there was considerable interest in developing a specialized program for these clients. We were aware that Linehan was using DBT with clients with similar problems, and early reports suggested that this approach was yielding positive results.

After training with Linehan at the University of Washington in Seattle, we ran our own pilot study. Early observations and later research findings (McMain et al., 2004) confirmed that clients of our service were responding well. Equally importantly, clinicians reported feeling more enthusiastic about their work. This was critical because it had been difficult for us to enlist therapists into this field of work.

There were also a growing number of reports in the literature about the utility of using DBT to help a wide range of clients with multiple mental health and addiction disorders. For example, Telch et al. (2001) reported success in using DBT to treat binge eating, and others described DBT's effectiveness in the treatment of anger problems (Fruzzetti & Levensky, 2000). The common theme was that DBT was being successfully adapted and used with clients who exhibited significant behavioural dyscontrol and who were not responding well to standard treatments. The DBT approach appeared to be particularly helpful to people diagnosed with multiple substance use and/or mental health problems.

These positive results, and Linehan's commitment to evaluating treatment outcomes by comparing DBT with standard treatments, helped DBT gain immediate recognition in the field. A number of studies show that DBT is superior to standard community treatment in reducing the frequency and medical severity of parasuicidal behaviours, and in reducing hospitalization days for people with BPD (Koons et al., 1998; Linehan et al., 1991; Linehan et al., 1993; Linehan et al., 1999; Stanley et al., 1998). In the initial study of DBT for people with BPD and substance use disorders, DBT was found to be better than a standard treatment in retaining clients in treatment, decreasing days of substance use, and improving social and global functioning as measured at the end of the one-year treatment and at 16-month follow-up (Linehan et al., 1999).

From its origins as a treatment for BPD, DBT has been successfully adapted to treat a broad range of issues, including concurrent substance use and mental health problems. Because Linehan's approach was developed specifically for clients with BPD and multiple mental health disorders who had predominant behavioural dysregulation problems, it lends itself to the treatment of clients with other difficulties that have a similar source.

In addition, the successful adaptation of DBT can be attributed to the fact that it shares a theoretical base with ideas that have been used to explain other behavioural problems, such as substance use problems. For example, the fundamental premise of DBT is that disordered behaviour is the consequence of an underlying dysfunction in emotional regulation (Linehan, 1993). High rates of substance use among people with BPD—as well as other impulsive behaviours such as suicidal gestures, angry outbursts and interpersonal difficulties—are conceptualized as by-products of emotional dysregulation or as attempts to resolve problematic emotions.

The following three chapters provide an overview of the application of DBT to specific groups of clients with concurrent disorders. The first of these describes the application of DBT for concurrent borderline personality and substance use disorders, introduces the structure and strategies of DBT, and describes the assessment and treatment process. The next two chapters describe adaptations of DBT for clients with concurrent anger and substance use disorders and clients with substance use and eating disorders.

REFERENCES

Fruzzetti, A.E. & Levensky, E.R. (2000). Dialectical behavior therapy for domestic violence: Rationale and Procedures. *Cognitive & Behavioral Practice, 7,* 435–447.

Koons, C.R., Robins, C.J., Bishop, G.K., Morse, J.Q., Tweed, J.L., Lynch, T.R. et al. (1998, November). *Efficacy of dialectical behavior therapy with borderline women veterans: A randomized controlled trial.* Paper presented at the 32nd Annual Meeting of the Association for the Advancement of Behavior Therapy, Washington, DC.

Linehan, M.M. (1993). *Cognitive Behavioral Treatment of Borderline Personality Disorder.* New York: Guilford Press.

Linehan, M.M., Armstrong, H.E., Suarez, A., Allmon, D. & Heard, H.L. (1991). Cognitive-behavioral treatment of chronically parasuicidal borderline patients. *Archives of General Psychiatry, 48*(12), 1060–1064.

Linehan, M.M., Heard, H.L. & Armstrong, H.E. (1993). Naturalistic follow up of a behavioral treatment for chronically parasuicidal borderline patients. *Archives of General Psychiatry, 50*(12), 971–974.

Linehan, M.M., Schmidt, H. 3rd, Dimeff, L.A., Craft, J.C., Kanter, J. & Comtois, K.A. (1999). Dialectical behavior therapy for patients with borderline personality disorder and drug-dependence. *American Journal on Addictions, 8*(4), 279–292.

McMain, S., Korman, L., Blak, T., Dimeff, L., Collis, R. & Beadnell, B. (November, 2004). *Dialectical behaviour therapy for substance users with borderline personality disorder: A randomized controlled trial in Canada.* Paper presented at the Association for the Advancement of Behavior Therapy Annual Meeting, New Orleans.

Stanley, B., Ivanoff, A., Brodsky, B., Oppenheim, S. & Mann, J. (November, 1998). *Comparison of DBT and "treatment as usual" in suicidal and self-mutilating behavior.* Paper presented at the 32nd Annual Meeting of the Association for the Advancement of Behavior Therapy, Washington, DC.

Telch, C.F., Agras, W.S. & Linehan, M.M. (2001). Dialectical behavior therapy for binge eating disorder. *Journal of Consulting and Clinical Psychology, 69*(6), 1061–1065.

Chapter 8

Dialectical behaviour therapy for people with concurrent borderline personality and substance use disorders

SHELLEY MCMAIN, SHIRA GREEN, LAUREN DIXON AND HARRIET WEAVER

The need for specialized treatment for people with concurrent borderline personality disorder (BPD) and substance use problems derives from the high degree of overlap between these disorders, and from the unique challenges they pose to treatment. This chapter describes an integrated dialectical behaviour therapy (DBT) approach to the treatment of people with these concurrent disorders. DBT was originally developed by Linehan (Linehan, 1993a; Linehan, 1993c) to treat people with BPD who are chronically suicidal, and was subsequently adapted to the treatment of concurrent BPD and substance use problems (Linehan & Dimeff, 1995). See these original sources for a more thorough presentation of DBT and DBT for substance use disorders (DBT–SUD).

DIAGNOSIS AND DESCRIPTION

Prevalence

The prevalence of BPD in the general population is estimated at about two per cent (U.S. National Institute of Mental Health, 1998), accounting for about six million people in North America. Studies of BPD and substance abuse reveal high, though varying, rates of overlap, with reported rates of co-occurrence ranging from 21 per cent to 84 per cent

(Dulit et al., 1990; Inman et al., 1985; Johnson et al., 1995; Koenigsberg et al., 1985; Kosten et al., 1989; Krudelbach et al., 1993; Nace et al., 1983; Skodol et al., 1999; Tousignant & Kovess, 1989; Vaglum & Vaglum, 1985; Zanarini et al., 1989).

Symptoms

BPD is characterized by a pervasive pattern of dysregulation of:
- emotions
- behaviours
- interpersonal relations
- cognitions
- identity.

To meet DSM-IV criteria for BPD, a person must have at least five of the following symptoms:
1. affective instability
2. inappropriate anger
3. chronic suicidal behaviour
4. impulsivity in two areas of functioning
5. chronic feelings of emptiness
6. identity disturbance characterized by uncertainty
7. unstable and chaotic relationships
8. frantic efforts to avoid abandonment
9. transient stress-related paranoid ideation or severe dissociative symptoms (American Psychiatric Association, 1994).

These behaviours must begin by early adulthood and occur in a variety of contexts.

Impulsivity is a hallmark feature of BPD. An estimated 75 per cent of people with BPD have a history of parasuicidal behaviour, and approximately 10 per cent will eventually die by suicide.

The clinical features of BPD—with or without the presence of concurrent substance use problems—are often serious enough to interfere with productive functioning occupationally, socially and in other important areas of a person's life. Problematic interpersonal relationships are common. Relationships tend to be characterized by interpersonal sensitivity and fears of rejection or abandonment. People with BPD often vacillate between feelings of love and anger toward others. They often have difficulty empathizing with others and are vulnerable to frequent mood shifts, which makes it hard for them to develop stable relationships. Such instability can impair the person's relationships, contributing to loneliness and the absence of a social support network. Interpersonal problems and mood lability can also make it difficult for people with BPD to secure and maintain employment. If a person also has substance use problems, this can exacerbate existing problematic personality traits, and intensify impulsivity and mood lability.

Self-destructive behaviour is often the primary reason why people with BPD seek treatment. Given the high rates of parasuicidal behaviours (i.e., self-harming behaviour with or without the intent to die) in this population, it is not surprising that the use of emergency services, crisis services and inpatient admissions is high. Clients with BPD often have difficulty accessing standard substance use treatment, since people who engage in self-harm behaviours may find themselves excluded from traditional substance use services.

Implications of co-occurring BPD and substance use disorders

For people with BPD, the risk of developing substance use disorders is three times greater than it is for the general population (Verheul et al., 1995). Symptoms of BPD and substance use problems often overlap. This complicates assessment and treatment, since each problem exacerbates or intensifies the characteristics of the other.

A diagnosis of BPD rarely exists in isolation. People with concurrent BPD and substance use problems typically have multiple difficulties and meet criteria for numerous other psychiatric and/or substance use disorders (SUD):

- In a chart review of psychiatric inpatients, Fyer et al. (1998) observed that the majority of those diagnosed with BPD had multiple additional diagnoses, including a large number who met diagnostic criteria for SUD.
- People with concurrent BPD and SUD are more likely to attempt suicide, to have unsatisfactory and disturbed interpersonal relationships, and to have concurrent depressive or other psychiatric disorders (Inman et al., 1985; Kosten et al., 1989; Nace et al., 1983; Nace et al., 1986).

Those with concurrent BPD and substance use problems have greater dysfunction than people with substance use problems alone, including:

- poorer school performance, lower levels of education and higher rates of unemployment (Links, Heslegrave et al., 1995; Links, Mitton et al., 1995; Thomas et al., 1999)
- more legal problems (Cacciola et al., 1996)
- poorer impulse control and more vulnerability to seeking a "quick fix" to a problem through the use of drugs (Khantzian & Treece, 1985)
- likelihood of having a more severe substance use profile and a range of increased risk-taking behaviours (e.g., risky needle use, sexual promiscuity) (Darke et al., 2003)
- increased likelihood of having a history of polysubstance use, to continue drug use and to have higher rates of relapse (Nace et al., 1991; Pettinati, 1990).

Given the complicated clinical presentation of people with co-occuring SUD and BPD, treatments for this population require modifications to address their unique needs.

Treatment prognosis

BPD is difficult to treat, and the additional presence of substance use problems complicates treatment and reduces the likelihood that it will be successful. While intensive treatment is often indicated for people with concurrent BPD and substance use problems, a number of factors impede treatment. It is notoriously hard to engage such clients in treatment—typically much harder than for people with either BPD or a SUD alone (Blume, 1989; Inman et al., 1985). Treatment dropout and failure rates are higher than those for clients with a SUD alone (Croughan et al., 1982; Kosten et al., 1989; Nace & Davis, 1993; Nace et al., 1983; Reich & Green, 1991; Woody et al., 1985).

Further, treating people with concurrent BPD and substance use problems is often stressful for therapists because of the clients' high-risk—and potentially lethal—behaviours. The incidence of suicide attempts is higher for people with BPD who have a coexisting SUD than for those without substance use problems (Nace et al., 1983; Inman et al., 1985; Stone, 1990; van den Bosch et al., 2001). The behaviour of these clients typically engenders feelings of anger, discouragement and rejection in therapists and causes stress that can lead to burnout. Inman et al. (1985) suggest that "for substance abuse treatment staff, work with borderline disordered individuals requires a special awareness of patient needs and behaviours as well as preparation to deal with the stress arising from the treatment of these individuals" (p. 230).

CONCURRENT BPD AND SUBSTANCE USE DISORDERS: A DBT CONCEPTUALIZATION

According to Linehan's (1993a) biosocial theory, BPD involves a pervasive dysfunction of the emotion regulation system. Emotion dysregulation is characterized by increased vulnerability to emotional experiences and an inability to modulate emotional states. Emotional vulnerability can be thought of as a "difficult" temperament and is assumed to be biologically based. According to DBT's biosocial theory, BPD develops through the transaction over time between the person's temperament and environmental interactions that predominantly involve invalidating experiences.

The high overlap between BPD and SUD is likely due to an interplay between specific biological and environmental factors:

- Trait impulsivity is associated with higher rates of concurrent SUD (Trull et al., 2000). People with BPD and SUD appear to have higher levels of impulsivity (e.g., Krudelbach et al., 1993; Morgenstern et al., 1997), suggesting there is a genetic predisposition to misuse substances.
- Further, adverse family experiences and delinquent peer groups, which are common among people with BPD, likely play an important role in the development and maintenance of addictive behaviour (Herman et al., 1989).

- Underlying emotion dysregulation is at the core of BPD and increases the risk of SUD (Linehan, 1993b; Marziali et al., 1999). According to DBT's biosocial theory, psychoactive substances perform a function similar to that of other dysfunctional behaviours associated with BPD; they are a means to alter negative mood states.

The following example illustrates how biological and environmental factors can contribute to the development of BPD and concurrent substance use problems.

> Linda, a woman in her 30s, sought treatment for cocaine dependence, cannabis abuse and chronic suicidal behaviours. In Linda's case, numerous biological and genetic factors may have contributed to her emotional sensitivity, including a family history of BPD, depression and substance dependence, in addition to her mother's drug use during pregnancy. Linda recounted numerous invalidating experiences during her childhood, including separation from her birth mother at age three, a highly critical adoptive mother and sexual abuse by her adoptive father. Linda's vulnerable temperament may have been exacerbated over time by other, repeated traumatic childhood experiences including the discounting of her experience, lack of support and lack of nurturance from others.
>
> The consequence of these experiences was that Linda developed a highly self-critical style. She tended to dismiss, discount and inhibit her emotional reactions, and she failed to develop effective coping strategies to tolerate intense negative affect. Additionally, she learned through repeated experiences that others would respond to her only if she reacted in an extreme manner (e.g., a suicide threat or drug use). She depended on illicit substances such as crack and marijuana to help numb herself to overwhelming and negative emotional states. At times she resorted to drug use as a means of communicating anger toward others. Fights with her parents were often followed by the urge to use drugs, and the thought that "I'll show them."

In the DBT model, Linda's chronic suicidality, anger and substance use are viewed as maladaptive coping strategies. These behaviours serve to regulate emotions or are the by-product of dysregulated emotions (Linehan, 1993a). Dysfunctional behaviours such as substance use and self-harm are difficult to change because they are often highly effective, in the short run, in modulating dysregulated affect. For example, crack use can be a powerful method of altering depressed mood. The implication of DBT's biosocial theory is that the primary goal of treatment is to help clients develop more effective strategies to regulate their emotions. A central component of DBT treatment involves teaching clients skills (e.g., tolerance of distress) to help them cope with their emotions more adaptively.

DBT outcome studies for concurrent BPD and substance use problems

A few recent studies examine the effectiveness of DBT treatment for concurrent BPD and substance use problems. They include four randomized controlled trials targeting people with concurrent BPD and SUD.

1. In the first study by Linehan et al. (1999), the efficacy of DBT for people with BPD and substance dependence was compared to community-based treatment-as-usual. Twenty-eight women diagnosed with BPD and substance dependence were randomly assigned to either of the treatments. The results indicated that the retention of participants in the DBT group was significantly better (64 per cent compared to 27 per cent in treatment-as-usual). In addition, participants in the DBT group had fewer days of substance use and better social and global adjustment, both after one year of treatment and at 16-month follow-up.
2. In the second study, looking at a similar population (Linehan et al., 2002), DBT was compared to the major acceptance-based component of DBT—comprehensive validation therapy (CVT)—plus participation in a 12-step program. Results indicated that both treatments were effective in reducing opioid use. However, participants in the DBT-only group maintained reductions in opioid use over the 12 months of treatment, while those assigned to CVT plus a 12-step program increased opioid use in the last four months of treatment. The CVT group achieved a 100 per cent retention rate compared to only 64 per cent in the DBT group.
3. In the third study (Verheul et al., 2003), DBT was compared to treatment-as-usual for women with BPD, both with and without concurrent SUD. Results indicated that significantly more participants in the DBT condition remained in treatment, and that those treated with DBT showed greater reductions in self-mutilating and self-damaging impulsive behaviours than those in the treatment-as-usual condition.
4. In our own study (McMain et al., 2004), DBT was compared to treatment-as-usual for women with concurrent BPD and SUD. Subjects in the DBT condition engaged in fewer self-harm behaviours and had greater reductions in alcohol consumption than those in the treatment-as-usual condition. There were no differences between conditions in treatment retention or the severity of drug use. The cumulative evidence of these studies demonstrates that DBT may be effective in the treatment of concurrent BPD and substance use problems.

DIAGNOSTIC ASSESSMENT

Reliable and valid assessment of concurrent BPD and substance use problems is complicated by the fact that the symptoms overlap. Symptoms associated with BPD—such as unstable relationships, impulsivity, affective instability, identity disturbance, inappropriate anger and, less commonly, irresponsibility and criminality—may also be characteristics of people with substance use problems (Nurnberg et al., 1993; Rounsaville et al., 1998).

For example, people with cocaine use problems commonly exhibit emotional lability, aggressive behaviour, chaotic interpersonal relations and lifestyle, and impulsivity (e.g., sexual promiscuity, shoplifting). Similarly, symptoms of problematic substance use may mask underlying BPD. Distinguishing deliberate parasuicidal behaviour from the actions commonly associated with substance use can be complicated. For example, heavy substance use, overdoses and risky use of dirty syringes may be forms of deliberate self-harm.

A comprehensive and structured assessment of mental health and substance use problems can increase the validity of diagnoses. Structured diagnostic interviews, such as the Structured Clinical Interview for the DSM-IV Axis II Personality Disorders (SCID II, First et al., 1995) and the International Personality Disorder Exam (IPDE, Loranger, 1995), can enhance the reliability of diagnoses. Careful attention to the time of onset of symptoms, periods of abstinence from substance use or an absence of BPD symptoms will help determine whether BPD exists independently of substance use problems.

A comprehensive assessment should also include a detailed description of the client's specific problematic behaviours. This provides a basis for defining target behaviours, which is critical to evaluating treatment progress. Behaviours should be described in terms of:

- specific characteristics
- time of onset
- severity and frequency.

To illustrate, in Linda's case, her marijuana use was defined as follows:

> Linda used marijuana weekly from age 16 until age 20, at which point she began using daily. Over the past four years she has smoked marijuana daily. During the past three months she has used eight to 10 joints a day, on average. She typically starts her day with a ritual of drinking coffee and smoking a joint. She has had no periods of abstinence since age 16.

Since BPD rarely exists in isolation, a comprehensive assessment of coexisting mental health problems is recommended. Failure to identify the presence of other mental health or substance use problems can impede appropriate treatment planning. Again, a structured or unstructured diagnostic assessment is advisable, along with taking a comprehensive social history. Apart from thoroughly assessing the range of mental health and substance use problems, assessments of people with concurrent BPD and substance use problems should:

- evaluate the client's suicide risk
- assess obstacles to treatment
- identify the client's social support
- evaluate the need for ancillary treatments.

Suicide risk assessment

People with concurrent BPD and substance use problems are at high risk for suicide, and so a detailed assessment of suicidal and self-harm behaviours should be conducted prior to beginning treatment. Detailed information should be obtained on the client's history of self-harm and suicidal behaviours, including frequency, methods and the lethality of the chosen methods. In addition, the precipitants and consequences of the person's suicidal behaviours should be evaluated.

Current suicide risk should always be assessed in an initial interview. A number of tools are available to help the therapist assess suicidal and self-harm behaviours. The Parasuicidal History Interview (Linehan et al., 1990) can be used to assess the methods, intent, medical severity and context of parasuicidal behaviours. In addition, the Lifetime Parasuicide Count (Linehan & Comtois, 1996) can be used to assess parasuicidal behaviour across the client's lifetime. Both these instruments are useful for charting methods and intent of suicidal behaviours, and for determining risk.

Identifying obstacles to treatment

An important part of developing a treatment plan is anticipating and identifying potential barriers to engagement in treatment. Examples of such barriers include inadequate housing, a chaotic lifestyle, insufficient money, agoraphobia or child care problems. A detailed history of the client's experiences in past treatments can help to identify potential obstacles to engagement in treatment. To return to Linda's example:

> Linda informed her therapist at the outset of treatment that she typically dropped out of treatment after four or five sessions, usually because she felt angry with her therapist. It was important for her therapist to recognize that this anger might emerge again and might lead Linda to end the treatment.
>
> The therapist planned with Linda in advance how to identify Linda's anger, and tried to help Linda communicate her feelings more directly.

Linehan and Dimeff (1995) outline a number of strategies to increase clients' attachment to treatment. As an initial step, clients should be oriented to the attachment problem so that potential obstacles can be identified and solutions generated. Additional attachment strategies include:

- increasing contact with the client in the initial phase of treatment
- using the telephone and voice mail to increase contact and to interrupt avoidance
- holding sessions in the client's environment
- shortening or lengthening sessions
- actively pursuing clients when they fail to attend sessions.

Assessing social support

Community and social supports can play an important role in easing the client's transition to a life outside the mental health system. Some evidence suggests that people with BPD who lack a supportive social network have a poorer treatment prognosis (Linehan & Dimeff, 1995). At the outset of treatment, it is therefore critical to identify the client's level of social support. Clients who lack supportive networks should be helped to develop social supports, since friends and family members can play a vital role in treatment.

It can be hard to locate clients who are avoiding treatment or who have relapsed. Thus a social network map, which includes names, addresses and phone numbers of people in the client's life, should be developed at the outset of therapy (Linehan & Dimeff, 1995). If a client leaves treatment, the therapist can use this information to locate the client.

Support groups for family and friends can also strengthen the effectiveness of treatment. In our experience, the lack of support from family and friends is often a primary factor contributing to clients' leaving treatment. The psychoeducational group offered in our clinic is a means of providing support to members of the client's social network. The group includes sessions on understanding BPD, using validation to enhance communication, and handling crises.

Consideration of ancillary treatments

Clients should be assessed by a psychiatrist at the outset of treatment to evaluate the possible need for medication (e.g., antidepressants, methadone). A case manager may be necessary for clients who require help with basic needs such as money and shelter. People who are unemployed may benefit from employee adjustment programs, or retraining programs, to help them to return to the workforce.

TREATMENT

Overview

BPD is a heterogeneous disorder, and people with the same diagnosis can have different types and severity of problems. Standard DBT was developed as an intensive outpatient approach. It assumes that new behaviours are best learned if they are applied within the client's natural environment, rather than in atypical contexts, such as residential programs or hospital settings, from which behavioural change is not readily transferable.

Like other cognitive and behavioural approaches, DBT treatment is highly structured and active, and emphasizes a focus on the here-and-now. The primary goal of therapy is to help clients increase contentment in their lives. Specific therapeutic goals are defined in terms of concrete behaviours to be increased or decreased. The treatment includes two stages, and its focus varies according to the client's level of functioning.

In Stage I of DBT, the focus is on reducing out-of-control behaviour—including substance use, suicidal behaviours and treatment non-compliance—and increasing functional behaviours. Accordingly, in the case of Linda, the goals of treatment were to decrease crack and marijuana use, suicidal behaviours and all behaviour that interfered with treatment engagement (e.g., missing sessions, attending appointments while intoxicated).

In Stage II, the focus shifts to the resolution of posttraumatic stress symptoms or the enhancement of emotional experiencing. Progress to Stage II is advisable only after clients demonstrate control over their behaviours. Typically, this necessitates a four-month period in which the client abstains completely from all out-of-control behaviours.

Standard DBT treatment includes four modes:

- individual therapy
- skills group
- telephone coaching
- therapist consultation team.

The function of each treatment mode is described in Table 8-1: Description of Standard Treatment Modes and Functions, below.

TABLE 8-1

Description of standard treatment modes and functions

TREATMENT MODE	FUNCTION	FREQUENCY
Individual therapy	To increase client's motivation to change and address personal crises	1 hour weekly
Skills group	To develop specific skills, including interpersonal effectiveness, emotion regulation, distress tolerance and mindfulness	2 hours weekly
Telephone coaching	To help clients cope with crises that arise between scheduled sessions and to ensure that new learning is generalized into the client's environment.	After hours, available as needed
Therapist consultation team	To support therapists in order to reduce burnout and enhance effectiveness	1–2 hours weekly

DBT was originally developed within the context of suicidal clients with BPD and was later extended to address the needs of people with concurrent BPD and SUD. DBT for BPD and SUD is very similar to the standard DBT protocol and involves all treatment modes (i.e., individual therapy, skills group, telephone coaching, therapist consultation team). However, it also incorporates new elements relevant to the treatment of SUD, including:

- a more detailed treatment hierarchy, which includes a focus on substance use disorders
- the concept of dialectical abstinence
- attachment strategies
- new skills to address problems associated with urges and cravings.

Socialization to treatment

ORIENTATION AND COMMITMENT TO TREATMENT

Prior to beginning treatment, the client should be oriented to treatment and should make a clear commitment to engage in treatment for a minimum of one year. The client should be told about his or her diagnosis and be given written information about BPD and the specific substances with which he or she has problems. Linehan's biosocial conceptualization of BPD, described earlier, can be used to help clients understand their problems. The orientation to treatment should also involve explaining the treatment approach and structure. Clients should have an opportunity to discuss what is expected of them and what they can expect from the therapist. It is useful to review the potential obstacles to treatment engagement, including those that may interfere with the client's ability to attend sessions or do the homework regularly.

Clients are informed that they are considered to have dropped out of treatment if they miss four consecutive weeks of either group or individual sessions. Clients cannot re-engage in treatment until their one-year treatment contract has expired. Linehan (1993a, 1993c) established this rule to help clients clarify when they are in and when they are out of treatment. In our experience, this arbitrary dropout rule enhances clients' engagement in treatment.

ESTABLISHING TREATMENT GOALS

Setting treatment goals is important with all clients, but especially so with clients who have BPD, who typically present with multiple severe problems. Once a client has been assessed and the range of current and past problems identified, an individualized treatment plan can be developed. In the orientation phase, the therapist's task is to motivate the client to pursue specific goals. A number of specific commitment strategies are used in DBT, many of which (e.g., evaluating pros and cons, or a "devil's advocate" approach) are similar to the techniques employed in motivational interviewing. To build and strengthen the therapeutic alliance, therapists must treat only the problems that the client agrees to change. However, clients must make a few basic commitments in order to gain acceptance to DBT treatment. Minimally, clients must agree to eliminate suicidal and life-threatening behaviours, and to engage fully in the treatment (e.g., attend all sessions, do the homework and commit to one year of treatment).

Linehan and Dimeff (1995) use the concept of "dialectical abstinence" to describe a DBT approach to establishing and achieving substance abuse goals. "Dialectical abstinence" is an attempt to synthesize abstinence and harm reduction philosophies of addiction treatment. Abstinence is considered the most appropriate treatment goal for clients with BPD, because most substance use is viewed as a means to regulate affect; as such, it typically interferes with the development of more effective coping strategies. During the pre-treatment phase, therapists ask clients to commit to abstinence from all problematic substances for a period of at least one year. Commitment strategies are emphasized in an effort to increase a client's motivation to abstain.

Because not all clients agree to abstain from substance use, abstinence is not a prerequisite to entering into DBT. Nonetheless, during the commitment phase, the therapist pushes the client to abstain from the most problematic substances. While the client may not initially commit to abstain from all substances, substance use goals may shift over the course of treatment and can be re-visited periodically. If the client agrees to abstain from a specific substance, the primary goal is to help the client not use that substance. It is often difficult for clients to envision a life free of substance use, so they are encouraged to think of taking small steps toward abstinence, in other words, to focus on "one day at a time." The therapist balances this stance with helping the client to accept relapses as understandable slips.

PRIORITIZING TREATMENT TARGETS

One of the difficulties in treating clients with multiple problems is deciding which problems to address first. In DBT, individual sessions are structured according to the information provided on the client's weekly diary card. On this card, the client records information including:

- urges to self-harm, commit suicide or use substances
- intensity of emotions rated on a scale of subjective units of distress
- acts of self-harm and substance use.

Clients are expected to complete this card daily and present it to the therapist at the start of each session. After reviewing the card, the therapist and client collaboratively set an agenda for the session, guided by the DBT hierarchy of targets. This targeting system helps the therapist and client remain focused on the most important problems, rather than getting overwhelmed and distracted by the immediate crisis and thereby failing to help the client make progress on goals. Problematic behaviours are addressed in the following order of importance:

1. life-threatening behaviours (e.g., suicidal threats or acts, self-harming behaviour)
2. treatment-interfering behaviours on the part of the client (e.g., missing sessions, coming to sessions intoxicated or being hostile in group) or the therapist (e.g., not returning calls or coming late to sessions)
3. behaviours that interfere with quality of life (e.g., substance use, binge eating, depression or angry outbursts).

In DBT for people with concurrent BPD and substance use disorders, drug-specific behaviours are targeted before any other quality-of-life-interfering behaviour. Drug-specific behaviours, however, are ranked below life-threatening and therapy-interfering behaviours. For example, if a client has self-harmed, missed a group session and used cocaine, the cocaine use will be lower in priority than the self-harm and treatment-interfering behaviours.

The drug-specific behaviours are also prioritized according to a hierarchy of behavioural targets (Linehan & Dimeff, 1995). These behaviours, in order of importance, include:

1. decreasing substance use
2. decreasing physical discomfort associated with abstinence and/or withdrawal
3. decreasing urges, cravings and temptations to use substances
4. decreasing "apparently irrelevant behaviours" or behaviours that the client deems unimportant but may potentially lead to substance use (e.g., socializing with people who use substances)
5. decreasing the option to use substances (e.g., keeping alcohol or other drugs at home).

Core techniques and strategies

DBT draws on a broad array of cognitive-behavioural and acceptance-based interventions. DBT's four treatment modes, identified earlier, provide a comprehensive approach.

CHANGE STRATEGIES

DBT incorporates a number of change strategies, including:

- behavioural monitoring
- behaviour analysis
- solution analysis
- contingency management
- skills training
- cognitive modification
- exposure procedures.

Behavioural analysis involves the identification of specific antecedents and consequences of target behaviours and is one of the main strategies in individual therapy. This, in turn, allows for potential solutions to be examined to promote more functional behaviour. The process of analyzing and solving problems is illustrated by the following example.

> Linda's crack use was a significant concern and was analyzed in a number of sessions. In one session, Linda reported that she had used crack on two days in the previous week. In addition, she had failed to attend group because she was intoxicated.

> Analysis of the factors precipitating her crack use and her failure to attend group revealed a typical chain of events. Linda had had a fight with her boyfriend prior to using crack. Her boyfriend had criticized her and told her that she wasn't going to amount to anything. Criticism from others tended to evoke intense and overwhelming feelings of shame and anger, which she had difficulty tolerating and expressing directly. Her anger toward others was typically communicated passively, often through self-defeating behaviours. She recalled that on this occasion her urge to use crack had been precipitated by the thought, "I'll show him." Her decision not to attend group was related not only to her intoxicated state but also to her belief that there was no point in trying to change if people didn't recognize her accomplishments. The therapist focused on helping her to increase her ability to tolerate shame and to communicate more directly with others.

ACCEPTANCE STRATEGIES

In DBT, strategies for communicating the therapist's acceptance of the client are balanced with strategies for change. The core acceptance strategy is validation. Validation entails confirming the wisdom, or the kernel of truth, in the client's experience. It is often difficult for therapists to recognize functional or valid behaviours in the midst of numerous dysfunctional behaviours. Yet Linehan (1993a) maintains that there is always a "grain of wisdom," in other words, some aspect in the client's behaviour that makes sense. For example, in the case of Linda, the therapist may validate the client's desire to communicate her frustration to her boyfriend or her desire to escape painful feelings of shame.

ATTACHMENT STRATEGIES

DBT's attachment strategies were developed to aid clinicians working with clients who have BPD and SUD, who are difficult to engage in treatment. These clients are referred to as "butterflies," meaning they "fly in and out of their therapist's hands" (Linehan, 1993a). For example, a client may miss two weeks of group and individual therapy, during which time he or she fails to return phone calls, and reappears on week three. The client with BPD and SUD typically leads a chaotic lifestyle. The lack of routine, financial instability and physical and psychological effects associated with regular substance use are some of the factors that contribute to a client's poor attendance in treatment.

Attachment strategies are first used during the orientation phase described earlier. From the outset of treatment, the therapist and client discuss potential obstacles to treatment and develop a plan for dealing with these barriers should they arise. In addition, a written "crisis plan" is completed during the orientation phase, which provides information including emergency contacts and friends, relatives or treatment providers, whose help can be elicited to re-engage the client in treatment, should he or she go missing. Moreover, therapists should increase contact by scheduling extra sessions, lengthening sessions and calling the client to provide additional support.

The benefits of increased contact with the client during the early stages of treatment are twofold. It will help clients reduce the chaos in their lives, and it enhances the client's relationship with the therapist (McMain et al., 2004).

If a client misses several sessions without contacting the therapist, the DBT team mobilizes in active pursuit of the client. For example, the therapist may send a card with an encouraging message, visit the client in his or her environment, or send a thoughtful gift (e.g., flowers, balloons, pizza).

In our clinic, the implementation of attachment strategies has resulted in greater treatment engagement with clients who have BPD and SUD. When these strategies were used, clients were more likely to commit to the treatment, attend regularly and graduate from the program.

SKILLS TRAINING

In addition to individual therapy, DBT treatment involves a weekly psychoeducational skills group. The group focuses on enhancing clients' capacities by teaching skills in four core areas, including:

- emotion regulation
- mindfulness
- interpersonal effectiveness
- distress tolerance.

Clients are pushed to replace their problematic behaviours with more functional means of coping with problems. New skills were incorporated into DBT–SUD to address people with substance use disorders (McMain et al., in press). For example, "urge surfing" is a mindfulness skill that involves teaching clients to observe urges and cravings in a non-attached manner. The emphasis is on helping people learn to wait out the urges, rather than respond with fear of anticipation of failure. "Burning bridges" is a distress tolerance skill that involves teaching people to cut off all options to use substances. It may involve having clients discard all drug paraphernalia or destroy phone numbers of dealers.

These skills are generalized outside therapy through homework practice and telephone coaching after hours, which also gives the therapist the opportunity to manage crisis behaviours within a well-formulated treatment plan developed in collaboration with the client.

MANAGING STAFF BURNOUT

Because staff burnout is often a central problem in working with clients with concurrent BPD and substance use problems, support for therapists is essential. In standard DBT, a weekly team meeting helps enhance therapists' motivation and their ability to provide effective treatment, and helps prevent burnout. In addition, to reduce the likelihood of staff forming polarized factions, the team is encouraged to embrace open expression and to strive to synthesize diverse perspectives.

TREATMENT TERMINATION

In our clinic, a review of treatment progress and re-contracting occurs at the end of the first year of treatment. Clients are generally ready to enter Stage II treatment once their behaviours have been under control for three to four months. In our experience, many clients with concurrent BPD and SUD may not be ready for Stage II work until they have completed 18 months to two years of intensive DBT treatment.

Many clients with BPD have difficulty ending treatment relationships, and so their dysfunctional behaviour may be inadvertently reinforced by the promise of extending treatment if they remain "ill." Therefore, extension of treatment contracts beyond the first year should be based on the client's progress, rather than solely on the continued existence of problematic behaviours. Additionally, clients in our clinic have demonstrated a higher propensity for gains in treatment when a clear contract end date is determined at the outset.

Termination should be raised on a regular basis with the client throughout treatment. This provides the client the opportunity to process his or her feelings about ending and prevents avoidance of these emotions. Given the interpersonal difficulties experienced by people with BPD and SUD, negotiating a healthy goodbye is an important life skill. The therapeutic relationship offers an opportunity to practise this skill.

Ending intensive therapy abruptly may be less desirable than phasing out treatment with more widely spaced sessions. Clients in our clinic develop a tapering schedule in collaboration with their individual therapists. Clients often terminate from the skills group before tapering individual sessions. In the final sessions, client and therapist should focus solely on ending treatment. Topics that should be raised include previous goodbyes, a review of the client's progress and troubleshooting potential future setbacks. Given the anxiety associated with ending treatment, anticipating termination sometimes leads to a resurgence of symptoms in clients with BPD. It is important to recognize that this does not necessarily mean that the client is not ready to terminate. The therapist should discuss the impact of termination with the client and normalize the client's fear and anxiety about ending.

In our clinic, clients who terminate treatment (without dropping out prematurely) are considered to have graduated from the program. Upon finishing the treatment, "certificates of completion" are presented to the client by his or her primary therapist. Graduation from the skills group is marked by a group celebration. The graduation process is a way to reinforce the gains made in treatment and to promote a healthy transition. As a result, clients leave the program with a sense of mastery and accomplishment. A formal graduation also provides an opportunity to model the ending of treatment, which can benefit the other clients.

SUMMARY

DBT–SUD is a comprehensive treatment developed for people who have BPD and SUD. Studies have shown that DBT–SUD is effective in reducing substance use and enhancing adaptive functioning in this population. The basic tenet of DBT–SUD is that pervasive problems with emotion regulation underlie BPD and contribute to substance use problems. Consequently, treatment focuses on helping people eliminate problematic substance use by developing more effective strategies to regulate emotions. Therapy is a structured approach and involves a blend of diverse strategies, including acceptance, change and dialectical techniques.

REFERENCES

American Psychiatric Association. (1994). *Diagnostic and Statistical Manual of Mental Disorders* (4th ed.) Washington, DC: Author.

Blume, S.B. (1989). Dual diagnosis: Psychoactive substance dependence and the personality disorder. *Journal of Psychoactive Drugs, 21*(2), 139–144.

Cacciola, J.S., Rutherford, M.J., Alterman, A.I., McKay, J.R. & Snider, E.C. (1996). Personality disorders and treatment outcome in methadone maintenance patients. *The Journal of Nervous and Mental Disease, 184*(4), 234–239.

Croughan, J.L., Miller, J.P., Matar, A. & Whitman, B.Y. (1982). Psychiatric diagnosis and prediction of drug and alcohol dependence. *Journal of Clinical Psychiatry, 43*(9), 353–356.

Darke, S., Williamson, A., Ross, J., Teesson, M. & Lynskey, M. (2003). Borderline personality disorder, antisocial personality disorder and risk-taking among heroin users: Findings from the Australian Treatment Outcome Study (ATOS). *Drug & Alcohol Dependence, 74*(1), 77–83.

Dulit, R.A., Fyer, M.R., Hans, G.L., Sullivan, T. & Frances, A.J. (1990). Substance use in borderline personality disorder. *American Journal of Psychiatry, 147*(8), 1002–1007.

First, M.B., Spitzer, R.L., Gibbon, M. & Williams, J.B.W. (1995). *Structured Clinical Interview for Axis I DSM-IV Disorders—Patient Edition (SCID-I/P).* New York: Biometrics Research Department, NY State Psychiatric Institute.

Fyer, M.R., Frances, A.J., Sullivan, T., Hurt, S.W. & Clarkin, J. (1988). Comorbidity of borderline personality disorder. *Archives of General Psychiatry, 45*(4), 348–352.

Herman, J.L., Perry, J.C. & van der Kolk, B.A. (1989). Childhood trauma in borderline personality disorder. *American Journal of Psychiatry, 146*(4), 490–495.

Inman, D.J., Bascue, L.O. & Skoloda, T. (1985). Identification of borderline personality disorder among substance abuse inpatients. *Journal of Substance Abuse Treatment, 2*(4), 229–232.

Johnson, J.G., Hyler, S.E., Skodol, A.E., Bornstein, R.F. & Sherman, M.F. (1995). Personality disorder symptomatology associated with adolescent depression and substance abuse. *Journal of Personality Disorders, 9*, 318–329.

Khantzian, E.J. & Treece, C. (1985). DSM-III psychiatric diagnosis of narcotic addicts: Recent findings. *Archives of General Psychiatry, 42*(11), 1067–1071.

Koenigsberg, H., Kaplan, R., Gilmore, M. & Cooper, A.E. (1985). The relationship between syndrome and personality disorder in DSM-III: Experience with 2,462 patients. *American Journal of Psychiatry, 142*(2), 207–212.

Kosten, R.A., Kosten, T.R. & Rounsaville, B.J. (1989). Personality disorders in opiate addicts show prognostic specificity. *Journal of Substance Abuse Treatment, 6*(3), 163–168.

Krudelbach, N., McCormick, R.A., Schulz, S.C. & Gruneich, R. (1993). Impulsivity, coping styles and triggers for craving in substance abusers with borderline personality disorder. *Journal of Personality Disorders, 7*, 214–222.

Linehan, M.M. (1993a). *Cognitive-Behavioral Treatment of Borderline Personality Disorder.* New York: Guilford Press.

Linehan, M.M. (1993b). DBT for treatment of BPD: Implications for the treatment of substance abuse. In L. Onken, J. Blaine & J. Boren (Eds.), *Behavioral Treatments for Drug Abuse and Dependence, NIDA Research Monograph 137* (pp. 201–217). Rockville, MD: U.S. Department of Health and Human Services, National Institute on Drug Abuse.

Linehan, M.M. (1993c). *The Skills Training Manual for Treating Borderline Personality Disorder.* New York: Guilford Press.

Linehan, M.M. & Comtois, K.A. (1996). *Lifetime Parasuicide Count.* Seattle, WA: University of Washington.

Linehan, M.M. & Dimeff, L.A. (1995). *Extension of Standard Dialectical Behavior Therapy (DBT) to Treatment of Substance Abusers with Borderline Personality Disorder.* Unpublished manual. (Available by request at the University of Washington).

Linehan, M.M. & Dimeff, L. (1997). *Dialectical Behavior Therapy Manual of Treatment Interventions for Drug Abusers with Borderline Personality Disorder.* Seattle: University of Washington.

Linehan, M.M., Dimeff, L.A., Reynolds, S.K., Comtois, K.A., Welch, S.S., Heagerty, P. et al. (2002). Dialectical behavior therapy versus comprehensive validation therapy plus 12-step for the treatment of opioid dependent women meeting criteria for borderline personality disorder. *Drug & Alcohol Dependence, 67*(1), 13–26.

Linehan, M.M., Heard, H.L., Brown, M. & Wagner, A.W. (1990). *Parasuicidal History Interview (PHI)*. Seattle, WA: University of Washington.

Linehan, M.M., Schmidt, H., Dimeff, L.A., Craft, J.C., Kanter, J. & Comtois, K.A. (1999). Dialectical behavior therapy for patients with borderline personality disorder and drug-dependence. *American Journal on Addictions, 8*(4), 279–292.

Links, P.S., Heslegrave, R.J., Mitton, J.E., van Reekum, R. & Patrick, J. (1995). Borderline personality disorder and substance abuse: Consequences of comorbidity. *Canadian Journal of Psychiatry, 40*(1), 9–14.

Links, P.S., Mitton, J.E. & Patrick, J. (1995). Borderline personality disorder and the family environment. *Canadian Journal of Psychiatry, 40*(4), 218–219.

Loranger, A.W. (1995). International Personality Disorder Examination (IPDE) Manual. White Plains, NY: Cornell Medical Center.

Marziali, E., Munroe-Blum, H. & McCleary, L. (1999). The effects of the therapeutic alliance on the outcomes of individual and group psychotherapy with borderline personality disorder. *Psychotherapy Research, 9*(4), 424–436.

McMain, S., Dimeff, L., Sayrs, J. & Linehan, M.M. (in press). Dialectical behavior therapy for substance abusing individuals with borderline personality disorder. In L. Dimeff & K. Koerner (Eds.), *Dialectical Behavior Therapy Adaptations*. New York: Guilford Press.

McMain, S., Korman, L., Dimeff, L.A., Blak, T. & Beadnell, B. (2004). *Dialectical Behavior for Substance Users with Borderline Personality Disorders: A Randomized Controlled Trial in Canada*. Unpublished manuscript.

Morgenstern, J., Langenbucher, J., Labouvie, E. & Miller, K.J. (1997). The comorbidity of alcoholism and personality disorders in a clinical population: Prevalence rates and relation to alcohol typology variables. *Journal of Abnormal Psychology, 106*(1), 74–84.

Nace, E.P. & Davis, C.W. (1993). Treatment outcome in substance-abusing patients with a personality disorder. *The American Journal on Addictions, 2*, 26–33.

Nace, E.P., Davis, C.W. & Gaspari, J.P. (1991). Axis II comorbidity in substance abusers. *American Journal of Psychiatry, 148*(1), 118–120.

Nace, E.P., Saxon, J.J. & Shore, N. (1983). A comparison of borderline and nonborderline alcoholic patients. *Archives of General Psychiatry, 40*(1), 54–56.

Nace, E.P., Saxon, J.J. & Shore, N. (1986). Borderline personality disorder and alcoholism treatment: A one-year follow-up study. *Journal of Studies on Alcohol, 47*(3), 196–200.

Nurnberg, H.G., Rifkin, A. & Doddi, S. (1993). A systematic assessment of the comorbidity of DSM-III-R personality disorders in alcoholic outpatients. *Comprehensive Psychiatry, 34*(6), 447–454.

Pettinati, H. (1990). Diagnosing personality disorders in substance abusers. In *Problems of Drug Dependence 1990: Proceeding of the 52nd Annual Scientific Meeting, NIDA Research Monograph 105* (pp. 236–242). Retrieved February 10, 2005 from: http://www.drugabuse.gov/pdf/monographs/download105.html

Reich, J.H. & Green, A.I. (1991). Effect of personality disorders on outcome of treatment. *Journal of Nervous and Mental Disease, 179*(2), 77–82.

Rounsaville, B.J., Kranzler, H.R., Ball, S., Tennen, H., Poling, J. & Triffleman, E. (1998). Personality disorders in substance abusers: Relation to substance use. *Journal of Nervous and Mental Disease, 186*(2), 87–95.

Skodol, A.E., Oldham, J.M. & Gallaher, P.E. (1999). Axis II comorbidity of substance use disorders among patients for treatment of personality disorders. *American Journal of Psychiatry, 156*(5), 733–738.

Stone, M.H. (1990). Treatment of borderline patients: A pragmatic approach. *The Psychiatric Clinics of North America, 13*(2), 265–285.

Thomas, V.H., Melchert, T.P. & Banken, J.A. (1999). Substance dependence and personality disorders: Comorbidity and treatment outcome in an inpatient treatment population. *Journal of Studies on Alcohol, 60*(2), 271–277.

Tousignant, M. & Kovess, V. (1989). Borderline traits among community alcoholics and problem-drinkers: Rural-urban differences. *The Canadian Journal of Psychiatry, 34*(8), 796–799.

Trull, T.J., Sher, K.J., Minks-Brown, C., Durbin, J. & Burr, R. (2000). Borderline personality disorder and substance use disorders: A review and integration. *Clinical Psychology Review, 20*(2), 235–253.

U.S. National Institute of Mental Health. (1998). *Priorities for Prevention Research at NIMH: A Report by the National Advisory Mental Health Council Workgroup on Mental Disorders Prevention Research.* Retrieved February 10, 2005, from: http://www.nimh.nih.gov/publicat/nimhpriorrpt.pdf

Vaglum, S. & Vaglum, P. (1985). Borderline and other mental disorders in alcoholic female psychiatric patients: A case control study. *Journal of Psychopathology and Behavioral Assessment, 18*(1), 50–60.

van den Bosch, L.M.C., Verheul, R. & van den Brink, W. (2001). Substance abuse in borderline personality disorder: Clinical and etiological correlates. *Journal of Personality Disorders, 15*(5), 416–424.

Verheul, R., van den Bosch, L.M.C., Koeter, M.W.J., de Ridder, M.A.J., Stijnen, T. & van den Brink, W. (2003). Dialectical behaviour therapy for women with borderline personality disorder: 12-month, randomised clinical trial in The Netherlands. *British Journal of Psychiatry, 182*, 135–140.

Verheul, R., van den Brink, W. & Hartgers, C. (1995). Prevalence of personality disorders among alcoholics and drug addicts: An overview. *European Addiction Research, 1*, 166–177.

Woody, M.E., McLellan, T., Luborsky, L. & O'Brien, C.P. (1985). Sociopathy and psychotherapy outcome. *Archives of General Psychiatry, 42*(11), 1081–1086.

Zanarini, M.C., Gunderson, J.G., & Frankenburg, F.R. (1989). Axis I Phenomenology of borderline personality disorder. *Comprehensive Psychiatry, 30*(2), 149–156.

Chapter 9

Concurrent anger and addiction treatment

LORNE M. KORMAN

Few areas of the behavioural sciences have as much of an imbalance between epidemiological research and treatment as the study of concurrent anger and addiction. Though there is a fairly large literature on the epidemiology of concurrent substance use, anger and violence, very little is known about how to treat these problems concurrently.

Substance use is frequently a concurrent problem (and an exclusion criterion) of clients seeking anger management, and anger is a common problem for individuals seeking addiction treatment. At the Centre for Addiction and Mental Health (CAMH), for example, more than one-third of clients seeking treatment for addiction also report problems with anger. Yet few publications have addressed the treatment of concurrent anger and addiction. Fewer still have evaluated treatment outcomes.

This chapter discusses some of the limitations of current treatments for and research on concurrent anger and substance use problems, describes the treatment of concurrent anger and addiction at CAMH, and identifies some of the assessment and treatment challenges associated with these problems.

WHAT IS ANGER?

Anger is one of a number of innate or basic primary human emotions. Basic emotions, such as anger, fear and sadness, are highly adaptive and have characteristic facial expressions and attendant physiological and psychological action tendencies (Frijda,

1986). Anger mobilizes us physically and/or emotionally to attack or repel others in reaction to the appraisal or interpretation of violation or intended harm (Arnold, 1960; Ekman, 1984; Ekman & Friesen, 1975; Frijda, 1986; Izard, 1977; Matsumoto et al., 1988). In this way, anger is a hardwired, adaptive emotion that orients us to violations by others, and mobilizes us to attack, repel or redress the perceived violation (Korman & Greenberg, 1996).

Though anger is often adaptive, problems related to the maladaptive expression of anger are common among people seeking treatment. Probably the most compelling problem associated with maladaptive anger is that it is often associated with aggression and violence. Self-reports of anger are correlated positively with aggression (Baron, 1972; Gentry, 1970; Rule & Hewitt, 1971) and individuals who report that they control their anger tend to be less aggressive across a variety of situations than those who do not (Megargee et al., 1967).

THE RELATIONSHIP BETWEEN ANGER AND AGGRESSION

The relationship between anger and aggression has received some attention in the scientific literature. Eckhardt and Deffenbacher (1995) defined aggression as overt verbal or physical behaviour that does or could bring harm to another person, object or system. Berkowitz (1993) asserted that anger, as an experience, "does not directly instigate aggression but usually only accompanies the inclination to attack a target" (p. 20).

The terms "anger" and "aggression" are often used interchangeably, but they are not the same construct. Not all anger is accompanied by aggression, and similarly, instrumental aggression can occur in the absence of anger—for example, quite disparate aggressive behaviours, such as checking an ice hockey opponent, violently robbing another individual, or dropping bombs from an airplane, can occur in the absence of anger.

While anger and aggression are not the same construct, they often co-occur (Kassinove & Sukhodolsky, 1995). Averill (1993) likened anger to an architect's blueprint: "The availability of a blueprint does not cause a building to be constructed, but it does make construction easier. In fact, without a blueprint, there might not be any construction at all . . . " (p. 188). In this way, anger makes the expression of aggressive behaviours much more likely. Anger orients the person's attention to the subject or the instigator of the perceived violation and mobilizes the person psychologically and physiologically for aggressive behaviours.

In practice, clinicians working with clients with anger problems typically must treat a holistic dysfunction of cognition, behaviour and dysregulated affect involving both anger and aggressive action.

SUBSTANCE USE, ANGER AND AGGRESSION

Anger problems and aggressive behaviours are more prevalent among people who have substance use problems than among the general population (Miczek, 1987). People with alcohol use disorders commit more assaults than the general population (Berglund & Tunving, 1985; Greenwald et al., 1994).

Alcohol is a significant factor in many homicides and suicides. It has also been implicated in domestic violence and child abuse (World Health Organization, 1996). The co-occurrence of domestic violence and alcohol use is an area that has received considerable attention, with a number of studies indicating much higher rates of alcohol use and alcoholism among men who batter than among those who do not (e.g., Fitch & Papantonio, 1983; Stith et al., 1991). Rates of domestic violence are much higher among men seeking treatment for alcohol use (Chermack et al., 2000; O'Farrell & Murphy, 1995). Men who batter also tend to drink more heavily than men who do not batter (see Tolman & Bennett, 1990), and the risk of severe male-to-female violence has been found to be more than 11 times higher on days during which men drink than on days of no drinking (Fals-Stewart, 2003). Frieze and Noble (1980) found that 50 per cent of a sample of wives who had been assaulted reported that their husbands had been drinking at the time of the abuse.

The association between violence and substance use is not limited to domestic violence. Pernanen et al. (2002) conducted a study of people entering Canadian federal penitentiaries as inmates between 1993 and 1995. More than half of all respondents reported that they had been under the effects of psychoactive substances when they committed the most serious crime associated with their current sentence.

The study found that, among respondents convicted of homicide:

- Thirty-four per cent reported that they were under the influence of alcohol during the homicide for which they were convicted.
- Seven per cent said they were under the influence of illicit substances.
- Twenty-four per cent reported they were under the influence both of alcohol and of illicit substances.

Among respondents whose most serious crime was assault:

- Thirty-nine per cent reported they were under the influence of alcohol.
- Nine per cent reported they were under the influence of illicit drugs.
- Twenty-four per cent reported they were under the influence of both alcohol and other drugs.

An earlier summary of similar studies by Roizen (1993) estimated that people convicted of violent offences had consumed alcohol before 28 to 86 per cent of homicides, 24 to 37 per cent of assaults and seven to 72 per cent of robberies.

Illicit drug use generally has been found to correlate less strongly with violence than alcohol. While illicit drug use probably plays a more significant role in non-violent "gainful" crimes than it does in violent crimes (Pernanen et al., 2002), illicit drug use is nevertheless associated to some degree with violence.

For example, the prevalence of violence is much higher among people who use cocaine than the general population. In a study of 625,000 people who used cocaine regularly, 40 per cent were found to have been involved in violent criminal behaviour (Gfroerer & Brodsky, 1993).

In the Canadian federal penitentiary study (Pernanen et al., 2002), cocaine and cannabis were the illicit drugs most often mentioned by people who were incarcerated. Twelve per cent of respondents reported being under the influence of cocaine when they committed their most serious crime. Seven per cent reported being under the influence of cannabis.

Other aggression and substance use

Recent use of cocaine and heroin has been associated with physical aggression (Tardiff et al., 1997). Even many benzodiazepines, such as diazepam, more commonly thought to have anti-aggressive properties, may be associated with increases in aggressive behaviours (e.g., Bond & Lader, 1979; Salzman et al., 1974; Wilkinson, 1985).

Anger and aggression among people seeking treatment for substance use

People seeking treatment for substance use problems have also been shown to score significantly higher than non-substance users on measures of aggression and hostility (McCormick & Smith, 1995).

Data collected at one program of the Centre for Addiction and Mental Health underscore the high prevalence of anger problems among people with substance use problems. Of the 5,071 people seeking treatment for substance use problems over an 18-month period beginning in June 1997:

- 35.6 per cent reported having anger problems at intake.
- More than 19 per cent reported having committed acts of physical aggression that were related to substance use.
- 9.7 per cent admitted that they had been physically aggressive in the 90 days prior to seeking treatment.

Uncertainties in the relationship between substance use, anger and aggression

Although a substantial research base indicates a strong correlation between violence and substance use (particularly alcohol), the exact nature of this relationship is not yet well understood—it may be neither causal nor direct.

For example, batterers who stop heavy use of alcohol and other drugs may continue to be violent (see Sonkin et al., 1985). Personality, attitudes favouring violence and discrimination, socio-demographic variables, developmental history and other factors may mediate the relationship between substance use and violence in men who batter their partners and in other populations.

The inherent complexity in this field of study, as well as methodological limitations in the existing research, including the preponderance of self-reports and the reliance on correlational data, make it difficult to draw firm conclusions about the role of alcohol and other substance use in causing anger, aggression and violence (Lipsey et al., 1997; Murdoch et al., 1990).

TREATMENT RESEARCH

Given the seriousness and prevalence of problem anger, empirical studies of treatment outcomes with clinical populations are surprisingly limited. This deficiency may be due, in part, to a lack of clear conceptualizations about problem anger (Tafrate, 1995), a function perhaps of the inherent complexity of problem anger and of shortcomings in the areas of measurement and diagnosis.

A most obvious deficiency in anger treatment research is the paucity of controlled studies with ecologically valid populations. In a review of the anger treatment outcome research between 1974 and 1994, Tafrate (1995) cited only 17 controlled, multi-session studies specifically targeting anger in adults.

However, a more serious shortcoming of the empirical literature on problem anger concerns the external validity of anger treatment outcome studies. For example, of the 17 controlled studies of anger treatment cited by Tafrate, only six involved clinical populations. The rest involved student populations consisting mostly of undergraduates and nursing students, some of whom reported anger problems. Streiner (2002) and others have argued that this type of research shows the efficacy of the treatments evaluated rather than their effectiveness or external validity. That is, the generalizability of these findings—actual treatment-seeking and mandated problem anger clients typically presenting with comorbid Axis I and Axis II disorders and other problems—arguably is questionable. Not surprisingly, while most of the 17 studies in Tafrate's meta-analysis yielded strong treatment effects, these effects tended to be weaker in studies of clinical populations.

Despite the high prevalence of co-occurring anger, aggression and substance use, virtually no treatment interventions have been developed. Fewer still have been suggested to treat these concurrent problems (Awalt et al., 1997).

Our own search of the social science and psychiatry literature yielded less than a handful of articles addressing these issues comorbidly. Fewer still suggested interventions targeting the anger and substance use problems concurrently.

Clients with concurrent anger and substance use problems routinely fall through the cracks of mental health and addiction systems. Most anger management programs in the Province of Ontario, for example, screen out people who have substance use problems. Substance use services are often reluctant to treat clients who are potentially violent (Awalt et al., 1997). Difficulties associated with treating clients with anger and substance use problems are compounded further by the increased probability of substance use relapse associated with angry states (Marlatt & Gordon, 1980), and by the fact that consumption of alcohol and other substances is associated with increases in aggressive behaviours (c.f., Bond et al., 1997).

ASSESSMENT FOR ANGER AND ADDICTIONS

The Anger and Addiction Clinic was created at the Centre for Addiction and Mental Health in 2001 to address the needs of the relatively high number of adults seeking treatment for substance use problems who also have problems with anger and aggression. Many of these clients have experienced significant social, vocational, legal and health consequences directly related to anger and addiction problems. Some of them have been ordered to seek treatment by the courts. Others have come to therapy with court orders regulating their relationships with family members. Many have other concurrent Axis I and Axis II mental health problems. People with thought disorders, who rate high on indices of psychopathy, or who have pending criminal charges or sentencing, are excluded from treatment in the clinic.

Clients entering the clinic undergo a comprehensive pre-treatment assessment. This consists of a diagnostic evaluation and objective assessments of anger and addiction severity. The initial assessment attempts to identify the nature of the relationship between each client's substance use and problem anger and aggressive angry behaviours.

IDENTIFYING THE RELATIONSHIPS BETWEEN ANGER AND SUBSTANCE USE

Skinner's (2003) model of concurrent disorders informs this assessment. Adapted for use in the Anger and Addiction Clinic, the model delineates four different types of relationships between anger and addictive behaviours:

- problem anger engendered or exacerbated by substance use
- substance use that serves to modify or regulate anger
- substance use and problem anger that occur independently and are not functionally related
- problem anger and substance use that are both related to a third factor or trait (e.g., impulsivity).

IDENTIFYING THE PROCESSES BEHIND THE BEHAVIOURS

In addition to determining the relationships between clients' substance use and problem anger behaviours, the initial assessment also attempts to identify the idiopathic cognitive, behavioural and affective processes contributing to each client's aggressive and problem anger behaviours. That is, rather than viewing problem anger as having a consistent cause or set of causes, the assessment looks at a number of qualitatively different but interdependent processes or paths as leading to aggressive behaviour related to problem anger. These processes include:

- the presence of maladaptive beliefs or attitudes engendering anger and/or violence
- an inability to symbolize, tolerate and/or express painful primary affect and a tendency to express secondary anger
- the presence of environmental and/or covert contingencies reinforcing problem anger behaviours
- deficits in interpersonal skills
- classically conditioned ultra-sensitivity to anger, loss, shame and fear-related cues
- an angry ruminative or obsessive style
- difficulties tolerating frustration and anger
- the inability to forgive; the inability to accept and resolve prior experiences of violation, hurt and loss; angry acting and/or thinking styles; and a rigid, humourless cognitive style.

TREATMENT PLANNING

Effective treatments for concurrent anger and substance use must efficiently target the complex, client-specific processes underlying these problems.

For example, while two different people may both exhibit anger and substance use problems, their behaviours may be the by-products of different processes. For example, Client A drinks to regulate or soothe his under-regulated anger, which he often expresses in reaction to primary feelings of hurt and shame associated with sensitivity to perceived rejection and criticism. Alcohol also reduces his inhibitions, causing him to act on aggressive impulses associated with his anger.

Treatment for this client may require:

- training in affect awareness and regulation skills, increasing the client's motivation to experience painful primary affect
- exposure to criticism, increasing his ability to tolerate distress
- behavioural and motivational strategies to encourage abstinence from alcohol.

Client B, on the other hand, over-regulates his anger. He is unassertive interpersonally, believing it is impolite to "rock the boat" with close friends and family members. He drinks "to blow off steam" when he feels exploited. When Client B drinks, his inhibitions related to his over-regulated anger are reduced, resulting in aggressive behaviour.

Treatment for Client B may require:

- learning, practising and generalizing assertiveness skills
- modifying dysfunctional beliefs about intimate relationships and anger
- teaching behavioural strategies to support his abstinence from alcohol.

THE VIOLENCE AND ANGER HISTORY INTERVIEW INSTRUMENT

The importance of identifying both the unique relationships between clients' anger and substance use and the idiopathic processes that lead to problem anger led to the design of an instrument for these purposes.

The Violence and Anger History Interview (VAHI) instrument (Korman & Collins, Appendix: Violence and Anger History Interview) is a structured interview developed to elicit information from clients about their problem anger and violent behaviours.

The VAHI was inspired in part by Linehan's (1996) Parasuicide History Interview (PHI-2), a structured interview targeting intentional self-injurious behaviours. Like the PHI-2, the VAHI consists of two parts:

- The first is a core section attempting to establish an overview of the frequency and nature of clients' violent and angry behaviours.
- The second asks questions about specific, selected violent and angry events.

The VAHI seeks to identify prompting events, situational factors (including substance use), actions and consequences associated with specific instances of violent and aggressive behaviours that have led to serious consequences to the client and to others.

From a behavioural perspective, the VAHI aims to identify the prompting events and potentially reinforcing contingencies of serious violent and angry events. The VAHI is also designed to make an initial assessment of the relationship, if any, between clients' substance use and their violent and aggressive behaviours. It also asks specifically about the idiopathic anger processes mentioned earlier in this section.

TREATMENT FOR ANGER AND ADDICTION

The Anger and Addiction Clinic employs an integrative outpatient protocol. In the absence of other established treatments for concurrent anger and addictions, we chose dialectical behaviour therapy (DBT) as the treatment platform at our clinic for several reasons:

- DBT provides a practical, adaptable and integrative framework for treating multiple behavioural problems.
- DBT targets emotion dysregulation, which is a common underlying problem in disorders of anger and addiction.
- DBT has shown some effectiveness as a treatment for borderline personality disorder. Anecdotally, 60 to 75 per cent of clients entering the Anger and Addiction Clinic have been diagnosed with a cluster B personality disorder. There is also some evidence that DBT is effective in reducing substance use (Linehan et al., 1999) and anger (Linehan et al., 1993) concurrently with other behavioural targets in people with borderline personality, a disorder characterized by impulsivity and anger.
- DBT helps prevent therapist burnout, which is a common problem associated with treating this population.

Our clinic uses the standard DBT treatment modes (i.e., individual therapy, skills group, consultation-supervision team and after-hours pager contact). The treatment, however, has been modified to address anger and addiction problems specifically. These modifications include:

- changes to the course content
- a change in emphasis in the weekly skills groups
- a change in the hierarchy of targets addressed in individual therapy
- an increased emphasis on insight
- when necessary, an immediate focus on getting clients' anger under control enough to allow them to participate in skills groups.

Anger awareness skills training

The weekly skills group teaches the four modules covered in the standard DBT treatment for borderline personality disorder (mindfulness, interpersonal effectiveness, emotion regulation and distress tolerance). These modules have been abbreviated, and a fifth module on anger awareness has been added. In addition, a number of skills have been integrated from Linehan and Dimeff's (1997) DBT adaptation for substance use disorders.

The anger awareness module teaches clients to identify violent, menacing, intimidating, abandoning and other types of aggressive behaviours. The groups also explore how aggressive behaviours have diminished the quality of clients' lives. This is important, because many clients are ambivalent or unhappy about working to moderate the energizing and distracting function of anger in the face of underlying primary pain, shame, fear, loss and despair. While being careful to avoid the pitfalls of process-oriented therapy in the groups with emotionally dysregulated clients, it has been especially useful to have participants briefly share how their anger has hurt them.

In addition, adopting aspects of a milieu-based approach, we try to include one or two veteran clients in our groups to model adaptive behaviours and to influence their cohorts. This is facilitated by running "open" groups, in which new clients are integrated into groups with clients who are more committed to working on their anger, and more experienced and able to model the skills being taught in this treatment. Throughout the training, the clinic protocol emphasizes that the aim of the treatment is not to give up anger but to increase mindfulness and skilful responding.

In the anger awareness module, we also modified other interventions, from other major theories of therapy and anger treatment, into skills that are taught in the weekly skills-training group. These include:

- primary emotion check
- evaluation of actual damage
- anger interpretation check
- other anger management skills.

PRIMARY EMOTION CHECK

Clients are taught to recognize the difference between primary and secondary emotional expression (Greenberg & Safran, 1987; Korman & Greenberg, 1996), a skill termed "primary emotion check."

Primary emotions are initial adaptive responses that orient the person, provide information about the personal significance of events and ready the person for adaptive action (e.g., flight from perceived threat).

Secondary emotions are reactions to underlying primary emotions (e.g., secondary anger at primary sadness and loss) and typically are problematic. When people commit acts of domestic violence, for example, primary emotions of fear or shame may precede the rage and violence associated with secondary anger (Dutton, 1995).

Treatment in the Anger and Addiction Clinic emphasizes helping clients to increase their awareness of their primary emotions (and of the adaptive information these emotions provide) and to decrease the expression of their secondary emotions. Clients are taught about core relational themes (Lazarus, 1991), which link generic categories of emotion-related themes or interpretations (e.g., loss) to basic (innate) adaptive emotional responses (e.g., sadness). If a client is angry because his girlfriend is leaving him, for example, the theme or interpretation is one of loss. The client's expression of anger likely is secondary to a primary emotion of sadness.

EVALUATION OF ACTUAL DAMAGE

"Evaluation of actual damage" is a skill adapted from the rational-emotive-behavioural therapy model (Dryden & Ellis, 1988; Ellis & Tafrate, 1999). Clients are asked to compare the intensity of their anger to the actual damage caused by the perceived violation committed by the object of their anger. If the intensity of the emotional response is disproportionate to the client's perception of the actual consequences of a perceived violation (e.g., rage and yelling in reaction to the discomfort of having to wait for a partner who is late for a movie), clients are asked to assess the pros and cons of:

- expressing their emotion
- using skills from the mindfulness and/or distress tolerance modules to accept and self-soothe painful emotions
- using change-focused DBT skills from the emotion regulation and/or interpersonal effectiveness modules to change the emotion and/or address relational priorities.

ANGER INTERPRETATION CHECK

"Anger interpretation check" is a skill adapted from cognitive therapy's approaches to emotions (Beck, 1976; Beck et al., 1979) and cognitive approaches to the treatment of anger (Novaco, 1975, 1976). This skill involves identifying and evaluating the accuracy of (often tacit) interpretations associated with the generation of anger. The treatment also helps clients identify the types of cognitive distortions (Deffenbacher & McKay, 2000) and irrational beliefs (Ellis & Tafrate, 1999) associated with the generation of anger, as well as common cognitive errors associated with fundamental attribution error (Ross, 1977).

OTHER ANGER MANAGEMENT SKILLS

In addition, our clinic also teaches other anger management skills, such as:

- stress inoculation training (Meichenbaum, 1985; Novaco, 1975, 1976)

- non-deprecating "silly" humour (Deffenbacher, 1995)
- relaxation training (Bernstein et al., 2000)
- stimulus control (avoiding angry cues or situations)
- "time outs" (temporarily and non-aggressively removing themselves from an anger-prompting situation when clients expect that they will not be able to effectively manage their anger).

Note that both stimulus control and time outs involve cue avoidance. These skills are taught early in the treatment.

Over the longer term, however, a major treatment goal is to re-expose clients to anger-provoking cues (similar to working with substance use), allowing clients to shape, practise and generalize new adaptive behaviours and, when necessary, to extinguish maladaptive responses. In addition to the anger awareness training, anger management and awareness skills are integrated in other modules. The module on mindfulness, for example, covers observing and describing anger and adopting a non-judgmental stance.

Individual sessions

Agendas for individual sessions, as in standard DBT, are established based on clients' reported behaviours on diary cards. These diary cards serve as weekly logs, in which clients track:

- the occurrence of relevant target behaviours (e.g., violence and anger, substance use)
- the intensity of their emotional experience
- their use of skills.

Clients bring these diary cards with them to weekly individual sessions. If a client has not completed his or her card before the session, the client is asked to complete one before the session begins.

An important aspect of treatment involves identifying and targeting both overt and covert angry and aggressive behaviours. Covert aggressive behaviours, such as angry ruminating, often precede and foment overt aggressive acts and can easily go undetected. Identifying and tracking covert angry behaviours increases clients' awareness of these behaviours and makes the behaviours available for targeting in session.

Diary cards in the Anger and Addiction Clinic prompt clients to record such covert aggressive behaviours as vengeful fantasies, scanning the environment for "things to be angry about," angry ruminating and "injustice collecting."

A behavioural target hierarchy determines the focus of behavioural targeting in each session. Each session targets problem behaviours, which are ranked in the following hierarchy, in decreasing importance:

- behaviours that are life-threatening to the client or to others and aggressive behaviours that are linked to life-threatening behaviours
- behaviours that interfere with therapy
- substance use and problem anger
- other behaviours that interfere with the client's quality of life.

When substance use precedes or precipitates life-threatening aggressive behaviours, this behaviour is targeted as life-threatening and takes higher precedence.

This hierarchy has been modified from the standard DBT structure to address the particular problems of this population and to reflect similar modifications by other DBT programs treating problem anger and violent behaviours (e.g., Fruzzetti & Levensky, 2000; McCann et al., 2000).

Behavioural analyses of target behaviours in individual sessions help determine the relationship (if any) between clients' substance use and aggressive behaviours. They also help identify the idiopathic cognitive, behavioural and affective processes contributing to each client's anger and aggressive behaviours.

As in standard DBT treatment for borderline personality disorder, the Anger and Addiction Clinic team meets weekly to enhance therapists' ability and motivation to treat their clients, to prevent burnout and to share information. In addition, the team consults such issues as victim and child safety.

TREATMENT CHALLENGES

Adapting DBT for people with substance use and anger problems has presented a number of unique challenges.

Reporting to the justice system

A core guiding principle of DBT is that therapists avoid intervening in clients' environments. This includes not speaking for clients, whenever possible. Therapists coach clients to act as their own effective agents in the world. They avoid treating clients as helpless or fragile or reinforcing clients' passivity. This principle also prevents therapists from shielding clients from the natural consequences of their behaviours (including jail time and revocation of parole).

At the Anger and Addiction Clinic, however, some clients must report to the justice system. Clients in the clinic often ask therapists to report on their progress to the clients' probation and parole officers. It has been hard at times to adhere to this DBT principle in the face of demands by clients and the courts that therapists verify clients' status and progress in treatment.

One solution has been to provide a standard form on which clients can monitor their own progress in treatment. The form serves as a "report card" of clients':

- attendance and punctuality in individual and group sessions
- completion of homework assignments
- attention to and engagement in sessions.

Once completed by clients, the form can be initialled as "verification" (if accurate) by individual and skills group therapists on a session-by-session basis.

Not perceiving anger as a problem

Another challenge relates to the nature of anger. Unlike most other problematic emotions that can prompt people to come to therapy (e.g., sadness/grief, shame, fear/anxiety), anger often is not experienced as aversive, painful, or unpleasant. Instead, clients with anger problems often present in therapy because of the consequences of aggressive behaviours generated by their problem anger (e.g., relationship loss, dismissal from work, criminal charges).

Thus, a unique problem with anger is that, unlike feelings of sadness or anxiety, people are sometimes loath to give it up. In part, this may also be because, when the expression of secondary anger is blocked, attention is more likely to be redirected to painful primary emotions. In these cases, successful resolution of problem secondary anger usually requires clients to be both motivated and able to tolerate pain affect.

Standard DBT skills, though sometimes helpful, are at other times insufficient to engage clients' motivation to reduce anger-related behaviours over the long term.

Case example: Claude

One client, Claude, arrived in therapy with a history of sarcastic and verbally abusive behaviours, typically levelled in anger. Consequences associated with these behaviours included dismissal from his previous job and loss of his last girlfriend, both of which he regretted. Claude also had a history of regularly medicating both his anger—and shame associated with his anger—by using cannabis. He drank alcohol to deal with feelings of loss and disappointment related to memories of a physically and emotionally abusive father. He also occasionally used alcohol as a means of "fortifying" himself to assert his needs with others.

Though Claude learned and integrated many of the mindfulness, emotion regulation, interpersonal effectiveness and distress tolerance skills in therapy, his problematic anger and his aggressive, caustic and alienating behaviours continued through the first few months of therapy, both in and out of sessions. Initial behavioural analyses revealed distorted anger-engendering cognitions and appraisals (e.g., blaming and judging, mistakenly attributing pernicious motives to others) prior to Claude's angry outbursts.

In individual therapy, cognitive restructuring and behavioural rehearsal of adaptive coping strategies only partially diminished his chronic feelings of anger. Subsequent behavioural analyses indicated that unrecognized or unsymbolized fleeting feelings of hurt, helplessness and impotence tended to precede his angry outbursts—his anger thus was reinforced by attentional shifts away from, and reduction in these painful feelings.

Therapy for these problems involved the use of the mindfulness strategies to help Claude recognize bodily referents (e.g., teariness, choked-up throat, pit in stomach, sagging posture) associated with the experience of hurt and powerlessness. It also involved validating Claude's vulnerability, teaching him to validate his own feelings and offering psychoeducation about the function of painful feelings.

In individual therapy, Claude also learned to soothe his distress to lessen the risk of substance use relapse. By end of the six-month treatment, Claude had achieved abstinence from alcohol and other drugs, was better able to tolerate pain and frustration, and reported less anger and improved quality of life.

Problems associated with treating clients like Claude reflect the challenges of adapting and integrating treatment strategies to concurrent anger and substance use problems, and the importance of careful and continuous assessment of the relationship between clients' anger and their substance use.

CONCLUSION

Despite the large body of research indicating the extremely high prevalence of comorbid substance use, anger and aggression, few treatment options exist for people with these concurrent problems. The Anger and Addiction Clinic at CAMH is unique in its mandate to develop, evaluate and provide assessment and treatment services specifically for concurrent anger and addictions. New efforts across the fields of addiction and mental health are needed to develop and empirically evaluate treatment strategies addressing concurrent anger and substance use problems.

REFERENCES

Arnold, M. (1960). *Emotion and Personality.* New York: Columbia University Press.

Averill, J.R. (1993). Illusions of anger. In R.B. Felson & T.T. Tedeschi (Eds.), *Aggression and Violence: Social Interactionist Perspectives* (pp. 171–192). Washington, DC: American Psychological Association.

Awalt, R.M., Reilly, P.M. & Shopshire, M.S. (1997). The angry patient: An intervention for managing anger in substance abuse treatment. *Journal of Psychoactive Drugs, 29*(4), 353–358.

Baron, R.A. (1972). Aggression as a function of ambient temperature and prior anger arousal. *Journal of Personality and Social Psychology, 21*, 183–189.

Beck, A.T. (1976). *Cognitive Therapy and the Emotional Disorders.* New York: Meridian.

Beck, A.T., Rush, A.J., Shaw, B.F. & Emery, G. (1979). *Cognitive Therapy of Depression.* New York: Guilford.

Bennett, L.W., Tolman, R., Rogalski, C.J. & Srinivasaraghavan, J. (1994). Domestic abuse by male alcohol and drug addicts. *Violence and Victims, 9*, 359–368.

Berglund, M. & Tunving, K. (1985). Assaultive alcoholics 20 years later. *Acta Psychiatrica Scandinavia, 71*, 141–147.

Bernstein, D.A., Borkovec, T.D. & Hazlett-Stevens, H. (2000). *New Directions in Progressive Relaxation Training: A Guidebook for Helping Professionals.* Westport, CT: Praeger.

Berkowitz, L. (1993) *Aggression: Its Causes, Consequences, and Control.* New York: McGraw-Hill.

Bond, A.J., Lader, M.H. & da Silveira, J.C.C. (1997). *Aggression: Individual Differences, Alcohol, and Benzodiazepines (Maudsley Monograph 39).* New York: Psychology Press.

Bond, A.J. & Lader, M.H. (1979). Benzodiazepines and aggression. In M. Sandler (Ed.), *Psychopharmacology of Aggression* (pp. 173–182). New York: Raven Press.

Brochu, S. (1995). *Estimating the costs of drug-related crime.* Paper presented at the Second International Symposium on Estimating the Social and Economic Costs of Substance Abuse, Montebello, Quebec.

Chermack, S.T., Fuller, B.E. & Blow, F.C. (2000). Predictors of expressed partner and non-partner violence among patients in substance abuse treatment. *Drug & Alcohol Dependence, 58*, 43–54.

Deffenbacher J.L. (1995). Ideal treatment package for adults with anger disorders. In H. Kassinove (Ed.), *Anger Disorders: Definition, Diagnosis and Treatment* (pp. 151–172). Washington DC: Taylor & Francis.

Deffenbacher, J.L. & McKay, M. (2000). *Overcoming Situational Anger and General Anger: A Protocol for the Treatment of Anger Based on Relaxation, Cognitive Restructuring, and Coping Skills Training. Client Manual.* Oakland, CA: New Harbinger Publications.

Dryden, W. & Ellis, A. (1988). Rational-emotive therapy. In K.S. Dobson (Ed.), *Handbook of Cognitive-Behavioral Therapies* (pp. 214–272). New York: Guilford.

Dutton, D.G. & Golant, S.K. (1995). *The Batterer: A Psychological Profile.* New York: HarperCollins.

Eckhardt, C. & Deffenbacher, J.L. (1995). Diagnosis of anger disorders. In H. Kassinove (Ed.), *Anger Disorders: Definition, Diagnosis, and Treatment* (pp. 27–47). Washington, DC: Taylor & Francis.

Ekman, P. (1984). Expression and the nature of emotion. In K.S. Scherer & P. Ekman (Eds.), *Approaches to Emotion* (pp. 319–343). Hillsdale, NJ: Erlbaum.

Ekman, P. & Friesen, W.V. (1975). *Unmasking the Face.* Englewood Cliffs, NJ: Prentice-Hall.

Ellis, A. & Tafrate, C. (1999). *How to Control Your Anger Before It Controls You.* Secaucus, NJ: Citadel Press.

Fals-Stewart, W. (2003). The occurrence of partner physical aggression on days of alcohol consumption: A longitudinal diary study. *Journal of Consulting & Clinical Psychology, 71*(1), 41–52.

Fitch, F.J. & Papantonio, A. (1983). Men who batter: Some pertinent characteristics. *Journal of Nervous & Mental Disease. 171*(3), 190–192.

Frieze, I.H. & Noble, J. (1980). The effects of alcohol on marital violence. Paper presented to the American Psychological Association, Montreal, Canada.

Frijda, N.H. (1986). *The Emotions.* Cambridge: Cambridge University Press.

Fruzzetti, A.E. & Levensky, E.R. (2000). Dialectical behavior therapy for domestic violence: Rationale and procedures. *Cognitive & Behavioral Practice, 7*(4), 435–447.

Gentry, W.D. (1970). Effects of frustration, attack and prior aggressive training on overt aggression and vascular processes. *Journal of Personality and Social Psychology, 16*, 718–725.

Gfroerer, J.C. & Brodsky, M.D. (1993). Frequent cocaine users and their use of treatment. *American Journal of Public Health, 83*(8), 1149–1154.

Greenberg, L.S. & Safran, J.D. (1987). *Emotion in Psychotherapy: Affect, Cognition and the Process of Change.* New York: Guilford.

Greenwald, D.J., Reznikoff, M. & Plutchik, R. (1994). Suicide risk and violence in alcoholics. *Journal of Nervous and Mental Disorders, 182*, 3–8.

Izard, E.E. (1977). *Human Emotions.* New York: Plenum Press.

Kassinove, H. & Sukhodolsky, D.G. (1995). Anger disorders: Basic science and practice issues. In H. Kassinove (Ed.), *Anger Disorders: Definition, Diagnosis, and Treatment* (pp. 1–26). Washington, DC: Taylor & Francis.

Korman, L.M. & Greenberg, L.S. (1996). Emotion and therapeutic change. In J. Panksepp (Ed.), *Advances in Biological Psychiatry, Vol. II.* (pp. 1–22). Greenwich, CT: JAI Press.

Lazarus, R.S. (1991). *Emotion and Adaptation.* New York & Oxford: Oxford University Press.

Linehan, M. (1993). *Cognitive Behavioral Treatment of Borderline Personality Disorder.* New York: Guilford.

Linehan, M.M. (1996). *Parasuicide History Interview (PHI-2).* Unpublished manuscript. University of Washington, Behavioral Research & Therapy Clinics.

Linehan, M.M., Armstrong, H.E, Suarez, A., Allmon, D. & Heard, H.L. (1991). Cognitive-behavioral treatment of chronically parasuicidal borderline patients. *Archives of General Psychiatry, 48*, 1060–1064.

Linehan, M.M. & Dimeff, L.A. (1997). *Dialectical Behavior Therapy for Substance Abuse Treatment Manual.* Seattle: University of Washington.

Linehan, M.M., Heard, H.L. & Armstrong, H.E. (1993). Naturalistic follow-up of a behavioral treatment for chronically parasuicidal borderline patients. *Archives of General Psychiatry, 50*, 971–974.

Linehan, M.M., Schmidt, H., Dimeff, L.A., Craft, J.C., Kanter, J. & Comtois, K.A. (1999). Dialectical behavior therapy for patients with borderline personality disorder and drug-dependence. *The American Journal on Addictions, 8*, 279–292.

Lipsey, M.W., Wilson, D.B., Cohen, M.A. & Derzon, J.H. (1997). Is there a causal relationship between alcohol use and violence? A synthesis of evidence. In M. Galanter (Ed.), *Recent Developments in Alcoholism, Vol. 13* (pp. 245–282). New York: Plenum Press.

Marlatt, G.A. & Gorden, J.R. (1980). Determinants of relapse: Implications for the maintenance of behavior change. In P.O. Davidson & S.M. Davidson (Eds.), *Behavioral Medicine: Changing Health Lifestyles* (pp. 410–452). New York: Brunner-Mazel.

Matsumoto, D., Kudoh, T., Scherer, K. & Wallbott, H. (1988). Antecedents of and reactions to emotions in the U.S. and Japan. *Journal of Cross-Cultural Psychology, 19*(3), 267–286.

McCann, R.A., Ball, E.M. & Ivanoff, A. (2000). DBT with an inpatient forensic population: The CMHIP forensic model. *Cognitive & Behavioral Practice, 7*(4), 447–456.

McCormick, R. & Smith, M. (1995). Aggression and hostility in substance abusers: The relationship to abuse patterns, coping style, and relapse triggers. *Addictive Behaviors, 20*(5), 555–562.

Megargee, E.E., Cook., P.E. & Mendelsohn, G.A. (1967). Development and evaluation of an MMPI scale of assaultiveness in overcontrolled individuals. *Journal of Abnormal Psychology, 72*, 519–528.

Meichenbaum, D. (1985). *Stress Inoculation Training.* New York: Pergamon Press.

Miczek, K.A. (1987). The psychopharmacology of aggression. In L.L. Iversen, S.D. Iversen & S.H. Snyder (Eds.), *Handbook of Psychopharmacology* (pp. 183–328). New York: Plenum Press.

Murdoch, D., Pihl, R.O. & Ross, D. (1990). Alcohol and crimes of violence: Present issues. *The International Journal of Addictions, 25*(9), 1065–1081.

Novaco, R.W. (1975). *Anger Control: The Development and Evolution of an Experimental Treatment.* Lexington, MA: D.C. Heath.

Novaco, R.W. (1976). Treatment of chronic anger through cognitive and relaxation controls. *Journal of Consulting and Clinical Psychology, 4*, 681.

O'Farrell, T. & Murphy, C.M. (1995). Marital violence before and after alcoholism treatment. *Journal of Consulting & Clinical Psychology, 63*(2), 256–262.

Pernanen, K., Cousineau, M.M., Brochu, S. & Sun, F. (2002). *Proportions of Crimes Associated with Alcohol and Other Drugs in Canada.* Ottawa: Canadian Centre on Substance Abuse.

Roizen, J. (1993). Issues in the epidemiology of alcohol and violence. In S.E. Martin (Ed.), *Alcohol and Interpersonal Violence: Fostering Multidisciplinary Perspectives* (Research Monograph No. 24) (pp. 3–36). Washington, DC: National Institute on Alcohol Abuse and Alcoholism.

Ross, L. (1977). The intuitive psychologist and his shortcomings. In L. Berkowitz (Ed.), *Advances in Experimental Social Psychology* (Vol. 10) (pp. 173–220). New York: Academic.

Rule, B.G. & Hewitt, L.S. (1971). Effects of thwarting on cardiac response and physical aggression. *Journal of Personality and Social Psychology, 19*, 181–187.

Salzman, C., Kochansky, G.E., Shader, R.I., Porrino, L.J., Harmatz, J.S. & Swett, C.P. (1974). Chlordiazepoxide-induced hostility in a small group setting. *Archives of General Psychiatry, 31*, 401–405.

Skinner, W. (2003). *Best clinical practices in concurrent disorders.* Paper presented at the Coming of Age Conference, Alcohol and Drug Recovery Association of Ontario, Toronto.

Sonkin, D., Martin, D. & Walker, L. (1985). *The Male Batterer: A Treatment Approach.* New York: Springer.

Stith, M., Crossman, R.K. & Bischof, G.P. (1991). Alcoholism and marital violence: A comparative study of men in alcohol treatment programs and batterer treatment programs. *Alcoholism Treatment Quarterly, 8*(2), 3–20.

Streiner, D.L. (2002). The 2 "Es" of research: Efficacy and effectiveness trials. *Canadian Journal of Psychiatry, 47*, 552–556.

Tafrate, R.C. (1995). Evaluation of treatment strategies for adult anger disorders. In H. Kassinove (Ed.), *Anger Disorders: Definition, Diagnosis, and Treatment* (pp. 109–129). Washington, DC: Taylor & Francis.

Tardiff, K., Marzuk, P.M., Leon, A.C. & Portera, L. (1997). A prospective study of violence by psychiatric patients after hospital discharge. *Psychiatric Services, 48*(5), 678–681.

Tolman, R.W. & Bennett, L.W. (1990). A review of quantitative research on men who batter. *Journal of Interpersonal Violence, 5*(1), 87–118.

Walker, L.E. (1984). *The Battered Woman Syndrome.* New York: Springer.

Wilkinson, C.J. (1985). Effects of diazepam (Valium) and trait anxiety on human physical aggression and emotional state. *Journal of Behavioral Medicine, 8*, 101–114.

World Health Organization (1996). *Fact Sheet, 127.* Geneva: Author.

Chapter 9: Appendix

Violence and anger history interview

Violence and Anger History Interview Subject ID: ________________ Date: ____________________

Core Questions

C1. INTERVIEWER: Ask Subject:

"Has your anger or violent behaviour ever caused relationship, work or other consequences to YOU or SOMEONE ELSE?"

☐ yes ☐ no

If YES, INTERVIEWER: Ask Subject:

	Enter # of times
"How many times total in **the past 3 months** has your anger or violent behaviour caused problems for YOU?"	______
"How many times total in **the past year** has your anger or violent behaviour caused problems for YOU?"	______
"How many times total in **your lifetime** has your anger or violent behaviour caused problems for YOU?"	______
"How many times total in **the past 3 months** has your anger or violent behaviour caused problems for SOMEONE ELSE?".	______
"How many times total in **the past year** has your anger or violent behaviour caused problems for SOMEONE ELSE?".	______
"How many times total in **your lifetime** has your anger or violent behaviour caused problems for SOMEONE ELSE?".	______
"How old were you the first time your angry or violent behaviour caused problems for YOU?"	______
"How old were you the first time your angry or violent behaviour caused problems for SOMEONE ELSE?".	______

C2. INTERVIEWER: Ask Subject:

"What are the worst things that have happened to YOU as a consequence of your anger or violent behaviour in (**your lifetime before the last 3 months**) OR (**last 3 months**) OR (**since last assessment**)?

INTERVIEWER: Circle the time period(s) covered in this assessment, ask lifetime questions if this is the first assessment.

a) Lifetime (before the last 3 months): ______________________________

____

____

____

Violence and Anger History Interview Subject ID: ______________ Date: ______________

b) Last 3 months/since last assessment: ______________

____

____

____

C3. INTERVIEWER: Ask Subject:

"What are the worst things that have happened to **SOMEONE ELSE** as a consequence of your anger or violent behaviour in (**your lifetime before the last 3 months**) OR (**last 3 months**) OR (**since last assessment**)?

INTERVIEWER: Circle the time period(s) covered in this assessment, ask lifetime questions if this is the first assessment.

a) Lifetime (before the last 3 months): ______________

____

____

____

b) Last 3 months/since last assessment: ______________

____

____

____

C4. INTERVIEWER: Ask Subject:

"There are many kinds of aggressive or violent behaviours. I'm going to ask you about specific aggressive or violent behaviours. Have you ever done any of the following?"

INTERVIEWER: Circle and/or specify behaviour(s) below as applicable.

	Yes	No	# times last **3** months	On a scale from **0** (not at all angry) to **5** (extremely), how angry were you the last time you____?
1. Shouted, yelled, screamed, swore at someone or called someone names?				
2. Grabbed, pushed or shoved someone?				
3. Hit, punched, kicked, slapped or choked someone?				
4. Thrown, punched, hit, smashed, kicked SOMETHING in anger? (damaged property)				
5. Threatened someone?				
6. Followed or stalked someone?				
7. Used an object or weapon against someone? SPECIFY:				
8. Forced someone to do something against his or her will? SPECIFY:				
9. Done something else violent against someone or something? SPECIFY:				

Violence and Anger History Interview Subject ID: ________ Date: ________

INTERVIEWER: If any items 2 through 9 above are endorsed, Ask Subject:

"Were any of the aggressive/violent behaviours you described above directed toward a boyfriend, girlfriend, partner/spouse, child or other family member?

If yes, check all that apply:

☐ boyfriend ☐ girlfriend ☐ partner/spouse

☐ child* ☐ other family member (specify who): ________

*If any violence occurred ask about the age of the victim. If violence involved minors, check here ☐ (Note: if minors are involved, refer to your provincial/state child protective service reporting guidelines)

"During the last 3 months on how many different occasions were you violent?" ________

INTERVIEWER: Specify total number of anger/violent events you have selected for event interviews.

Consequences to self ________ Consequences to other ________

Anger/Violence Event Questions

Complete for Each Selected Event

INTERVIEWER: Indicate when the selected anger/violent event occurred:

Time frame of selected EVENT:

☐ lifetime ☐ since the last assessment

☐ last 3 months ☐ other (specify): ________

INTERVIEWER: Indicate the type of anger/violent event occurred:

Type of event:

☐ anger—serious consequence to self ☐ anger—serious consequence to other

☐ other (specify event): ________

INTERVIEWER: Instruct Subject:

"I'm going to ask you questions about the event you told me had the most serious consequence to (yourself/someone else/other event). I'll start by asking you for a brief general description of what happened and then I'll ask questions about specific details about what happened before, during and after you were angry or violent."

Angry/Violent Event Summary

INTERVIEWER: Ask Subject:

"Please briefly describe what made you angry or violent, what you did when you were angry or violent, and what happened after."

____

____

____

____

____

____

____

Violence and Anger History Interview Subject ID: ________________ Date: ____________________

BEFORE the Violence/Anger

INTERVIEWER: Instruct Subject:

"The next series of questions will focus on specific details about what happened BEFORE you were angry or violent."

B1. INTERVIEWER: Ask Subject:

"Did you drink alcohol before you were angry or violent?"

☐ yes ☐ no

If YES, INTERVIEWER: Ask Subject:

"What did you drink?" ____________________

"How much did you drink?" (in standard drinks) ____________________

B2. INTERVIEWER: Ask Subject:

"Did you take any other drugs or substances before you were angry or violent, such as prescription medications, over-the-counter drugs or illicit drugs?"

☐ yes ☐ no

If YES, INTERVIEWER: Ask Subject:

"What type of substance(s)?" (check all that apply)

☐ prescription medications ☐ illicit drugs
☐ over-the-counter meds ☐ tobacco

List substances and route of administration: ____________________

____

"How much did you use?" Specify substance(s) and amount of each: ____________________

____

____

B3. INTERVIEWER: Ask Subject:

"Did you gamble before you were angry or violent?"

☐ yes ☐ no

If YES, INTERVIEWER: Ask Subject:

"What type of gambling?" (check all that apply)

☐ slots ☐ VLTs ☐ bingo ☐ lottery tickets
☐ pull tab instant win ☐ scratch & win ☐ cards ☐ horses
☐ sports ☐ Internet ☐ casino games
☐ other (specify): ____________________

"Were you angry and/or violent because you gambled?"

☐ yes ☐ no

"Were you angry and/or violent because someone confronted you about your gambling?"

☐ yes ☐ no

"Did you lose?"

☐ yes ☐ no

If YES, INTERVIEWER: Ask Subject:

"How much money did you lose?" $ ____________________

"Were you angry and/or violent because you lost money gambling?"

☐ yes ☐ no

Violence and Anger History Interview Subject ID: ______________ Date: ______________

B4. INTERVIEWER: Ask Subject:

"Before acting angry or violent, did you threaten to act angrily or violently?"

☐ yes ☐ no

If YES, INTERVIEWER: Ask Subject:

"How much time passed between your threat and your angry or violent action?"

_____ seconds _____ minutes _____ hours _____ days _____ months

Record exact answer: ______________________________

____

____

B5. INTERVIEWER: Ask Subject:

"Before acting angry or violent, did you think about or plan to act angry or violent?"

☐ yes ☐ no

If YES, INTERVIEWER: Ask Subject:

"How long did you think about or plan to act angrily or violently before actually doing so?"

_____ seconds _____ minutes _____ hours _____ days _____ months

Record exact answer: ______________________________

____

____

B6. INTERVIEWER: Ask Subject:

"Before you acted violently or angrily, did you say, or communicate to anyone, that you were thinking of hurting someone or that you wanted bad things to happen to someone?"

☐ yes ☐ no

INTERVIEWER: Prompt for details; record exact answer: ______________________________

____

____

____

B7. INTERVIEWER: Ask Subject:

"Before you acted angrily or violently, did you say, or communicate, or do anything that might have given any hint that you were going to act angrily or violently?"

☐ yes ☐ no

INTERVIEWER: Prompt for details; record exact answer: ______________________________

____

____

____

____

____

____

____

Violence and Anger History Interview Subject ID: ________________ Date: ____________________

B8. INTERVIEWER: Hand card to Subject

"Before you acted angrily or violently were you feeling any of the following?"

INTERVIEWER: Have client rate each feeling. **0**=Not at all, **5**=Extremely

Record each client's rating for each feeling in the table below.

Rating 0–5	Feeling	Rating 0–5	Feeling	Rating 0–5	Feeling
	1. Ashamed		11. Used/Exploited		21. Guilty
	2. Uneasy/Uncomfortable		12. Helpless		22. Numb
	3. Hurt		13. Angry		23. Hopeless
	4. Humiliated		14. Dismissed		24. Antagonized/Goaded
	5. Criticized		15. Panic		25. Suicidal
	6. Abandoned		16. Mocked/Ridiculed		26. Indignant
	7. Frustrated		17. Sad		27. Unimportant
	8. Afraid		18. Controlled/ Manipulated		28. Neglected/Uncared for
	9. Disrespected		19. Excited		29. Other (specify):
	10. Embarrassed		20. Furious/Enraged		30: Other (specify):

B9. INTERVIEWER: Ask Subject:

"Do you think that any of these feelings played a role or led to your anger or violence?"

☐ yes ☐ no

If YES, INTERVIEWER: Ask Subject:

"Which feelings?"

Record exact answer: ____

____

____

INTERVIEWER: if subject states more than one feeling, Ask Subject:

"Which of the feelings you mentioned played the biggest role in setting off your anger or violence?"

Record exact answer: ____

____

____

B10. INTERVIEWER: Ask Subject:

"What were you thinking just before you were angry and/or violent?"

Record exact answer: ____

____

____

Violence and Anger History Interview Subject ID: ______________ Date: ________________

B11. INTERVIEWER: Ask Subject:

"Do you think your thoughts at the time contributed to your anger or violence?"

☐ yes ☐ no

Record exact answer: ____

____

____

B12. INTERVIEWER: Ask Subject:

"Do you think it was something about the situation at the time that contributed or led to your anger or violence?"

☐ yes ☐ no

If YES, INTERVIEWER: Ask Subject:

"What was it about the situation that contributed or led to your anger or violence?"

Record exact answer: ____

____

____

B13. INTERVIEWER: Ask Subject:

"Do you think anything you did contributed or led to your anger or violence?"

☐ yes ☐ no

Record exact answer: ____

____

____

End of BEFORE event section
Next section: DURING event

Violence and Anger History Interview Subject ID: ______________ Date: ________________

DURING the Violence/Anger

INTERVIEWER: Instruct Subject:

"The next series of questions will focus on specific details about what happened DURING your anger or violence."

D1. INTERVIEWER: Hand card to Subject

INTERVIEWER: Ask Subject:

"I'm going to ask you about specific aggressive or violent behaviours. For each behaviour tell me if you did this while you were angry/violent and on a scale from **0** (not at all angry) to **5** (extremely angry) how angry were you when you did the behaviour?"

INTERVIEWER: Circle and/or specify behaviour(s) below as applicable.

"While you were angry or violent, did you . . ."

	Yes	No	On a scale from **0** (not at all angry) to **5** (extremely), how angry were you?
1. Shout, yell, scream, swear at someone or call someone names?			
2. Grab, push, or shove someone?			
3. Hit, punch, kick, slap or choke someone?			
4. Throw, punch, hit, smash or kick SOMETHING in anger? (damage property)			
5. Threaten someone?			
6. Follow or stalk someone?			
7. Use an object or weapon against someone? Specify:			
8. Force someone to do something against his or her will? Specify:			
9. Do anything else violent against someone or something? Specify:			

INTERVIEWER: ASK QUESTION D2 *ONLY* IF ANY OF ITEMS 2–9 IN ABOVE LIST WERE ENDORSED

D2. INTERVIEWER: Ask Subject:

"Were any of the aggressive/violent behaviours you described above directed toward a boyfriend, girlfriend, partner/spouse, child or other family member?"

☐ yes ☐ no

If YES, check all that apply:

☐ boyfriend ☐ girlfriend ☐ partner/spouse

☐ child* ☐ other family member (specify who): ______________________

*If any violence occurred, ask about the age of the victim. If violence involved minors, check here ☐ (Note: if minors are involved, refer to your provincial/state child protective service reporting guidelines)

Violence and Anger History Interview Subject ID: ______________ Date: ________________

INTERVIEWER: ASK QUESTIONS D3–D4 *ONLY* IF EVENT INVOLVED VIOLENCE

D3. INTERVIEWER: Ask Subject:

"Did you intend to make physical contact?"

☐ yes ☐ no ☐ unsure

D4. INTERVIEWER: Ask Subject:

"Did you intend to cause injury?"

☐ yes ☐ no ☐ unsure

D5. INTERVIEWER: Hand card to subject. Ask Subject:

"I am going to read a list of feelings and I would like to know if you felt any of these feelings during your anger and/or violence. Please rate how intensely you felt each of these feelings, on a scale of **0** to **5**, with **0** meaning you didn't feel the feeling at all, **3** meaning you felt the feeling moderately, and **5** meaning you felt the feeling very intensely."

INTERVIEWER: Record subject's rating for each feeling in the table below.

Rating 0–5	**Feeling**	**Rating 0–5**	**Feeling**	**Rating 0–5**	**Feeling**
	1. Ashamed		11. Used/Exploited		21. Guilty
	2. Uneasy/Uncomfortable		12. Helpless		22. Numb
	3. Hurt		13. Angry		23. Hopeless
	4. Humiliated		14. Dismissed		24. Antagonized/Goaded
	5. Criticized		15. Panic		25. Suicidal
	6. Abandoned		16. Mocked/Ridiculed		26. Indignant
	7. Frustrated		17. Sad		27. Unimportant
	8. Afraid		18. Controlled/ Manipulated		28. Neglected/Uncared for
	9. Disrespected		19. Excited		29. Other (specify):
	10. Embarrassed		20. Furious/Enraged		30: Other (specify):

D6. INTERVIEWER: Ask Subject:

"Were you feeling unreal, dissociative, or like you were in a movie happening to someone else when you were angry or violent?"

☐ yes ☐ no ☐ unsure

If YES, INTERVIEWER: Ask Subject:

"Did these feelings of unrealness, being in a movie, or dissociation begin before or at the same time you were acting angrily or violently?"

☐ before ☐ same time ☐ unsure

D7. INTERVIEWER: Ask Subject:

"Did your anger and/or violence occur while you were 'blacked out' or during a 'grey out'?"

☐ yes ☐ no ☐ unsure

End of DURING event section

Next section: AFTER event

Violence and Anger History Interview Subject ID: ________________ Date: ____________________

AFTER the Anger/Violence

INTERVIEWER: Instruct Subject:

"The next series of questions will focus on specific details about what happened AFTER you were angry or violent."

A1. INTERVIEWER: Hand card to Subject; Ask Subject:

"I am going to read a list of feelings again, and I would like to know if you felt any of these feelings AFTER your anger and/or violence. Please rate how intensely you felt each of these feelings, on a scale of **0** to **5**, with **0** meaning you didn't feel the feeling at all, and **5** meaning you felt the feeling very intensely."

INTERVIEWER: Record subject's rating for each feeling in the table below:

Rating 0–5	Feeling	Rating 0–5	Feeling	Rating 0–5	Feeling
	1. Ashamed		11. Used/Exploited		21. Guilty
	2. Uneasy/Uncomfortable		12. Helpless		22. Numb
	3. Hurt		13. Angry		23. Hopeless
	4. Humiliated		14. Dismissed		24. Antagonized/Goaded
	5. Criticized		15. Panic		25. Suicidal
	6. Abandoned		16. Mocked/Ridiculed		26. Indignant
	7. Frustrated		17. Sad		27. Unimportant
	8. Afraid		18. Controlled/ Manipulated		28. Neglected/Uncared for
	9. Disrespected		19. Excited		29. Other (specify):
	10. Embarrassed		20. Furious/Enraged		30: Other (specify):

A2. INTERVIEWER: Ask Subject:

"Did you drink alcohol after you were angry or violent?"

☐ yes ☐ no

If YES, INTERVIEWER: Ask Subject:

"What did you drink?" ____________________

"How much did you drink?" (in standard drinks) ____________________

"Did your anger increase, decrease or stay the same after you drank?"

☐ increased ☐ decreased ☐ stayed the same

"Did you drink to try to decrease or change your anger?"

☐ yes ☐ no ☐ unsure

A3. INTERVIEWER: Ask Subject:

"Did you take any drugs or substances after you were angry or violent, such as prescription medications, over-the-counter drugs, illicit drugs, or tobacco?"

☐ yes ☐ no

If YES, INTERVIEWER: Ask Subject:

"What type of substance(s)?" ☐ prescription medications ☐ illicit drugs

(check all that apply) ☐ over-the-counter meds ☐ tobacco

Violence and Anger History Interview Subject ID: ______________ Date: ______________

List substances and route of administration: ______________________________

____

____

"How much did you use?" Specify substance(s) and amount of each: ______________

____

____

"Did your anger increase, decrease or stay the same after you used drugs or substances?"
☐ increased ☐ decreased ☐ stayed the same

"Did you use drugs or other substances to try to decrease or change your anger?"
☐ yes ☐ no ☐ unsure

A4. INTERVIEWER: Ask Subject:

"Did you gamble after you were angry or violent?"
☐ yes ☐ no

If YES, INTERVIEWER: Ask Subject:

"What type of gambling?" (check all that apply)

☐ slots ☐ VLTs ☐ bingo ☐ lottery tickets
☐ pull tab instant win ☐ scratch & win ☐ cards ☐ horses
☐ sports ☐ Internet ☐ casino games
☐ other (specify): ______________________________

"Did your anger increase, decrease or stay the same after you gambled?"
☐ increased ☐ decreased ☐ stayed the same

"Did you gamble to try to decrease or change your anger?"
☐ yes ☐ no ☐ unsure

INTERVIEWER: ASK A5 AND A6 *ONLY* IF THE EVENT INVOLVED VIOLENCE

A5. INTERVIEWER: Ask Subject:

"What was the physical condition of your victim after you were violent?"

Details: ____

____

A6. INTERVIEWER: Ask Subject:

"Did your victim go to the hospital after you were violent?"
☐ yes ☐ no ☐ unsure

Details: ____

____

INTERVIEWER: Rate the physical condition of the victim(s) after the incident (if multiple victims, rate most severe injury).

☐ no physical injury ☐ slightly injured ☐ moderately injured
☐ severely injured ☐ killed

A7. INTERVIEWER: Ask Subject:

"Were the police involved after you were violent and/or angry?"
☐ yes ☐ no

Details: ____

____

Violence and Anger History Interview Subject ID: ______________ Date: ________________

A8. INTERVIEWER: Ask Subject:

"Were you charged after you were violent or angry?"

☐ yes ☐ no

If YES, "Are charges pending?"

☐ yes ☐ no

If NOT pending, "Were you convicted?"

☐ yes ☐ no time served: ______________

"Are you court mandated to attend an anger or addiction program?"

☐ yes ☐ no

"Are there any court orders related to this event?"

☐ yes ☐ no

"Are you currently on probation or parole related to this event?"

☐ yes probation ☐ yes parole ☐ no

"Were child protection services involved?"

☐ yes ☐ no

Details: ____

____

A9. INTERVIEWER: Ask Subject:

"Did your anger or violence have any effect on your relationships with others in your life?"

☐ yes ☐ no ☐ n/a

If YES, INTERVIEWER: Ask Subject:

"Did your anger or violence result in your relationship ending?"

☐ yes ☐ no ☐ unsure

"Was the effect of your anger or violence on your relationships with others in your life . . ."

☐ very negative ☐ somewhat negative ☐ neutral

☐ somewhat positive ☐ very positive

Details: ____

____

A10. INTERVIEWER: Ask Subject:

"Did your anger or violence have any effect on your job?"

☐ yes ☐ no ☐ n/a

If YES, INTERVIEWER: Ask Subject:

"Did your anger or violence lead you to quit your job or be fired or suspended?"

☐ yes ☐ no

"How many days of work did you miss?" _____ days

"Was the effect of your anger or violence on your job . . ."

☐ very negative ☐ somewhat negative ☐ neutral

☐ somewhat positive ☐ very positive

Details: ____

____

Violence and Anger History Interview Subject ID: ______________ Date: ______________

A11. INTERVIEWER: Ask Subject:

"Did your anger or violence have any effect on your finances?"

☐ yes ☐ no

If YES, INTERVIEWER: Ask Subject:

"Was the effect of your anger or violence on your finances . . ."

☐ very negative ☐ somewhat negative ☐ neutral

☐ somewhat positive ☐ very positive

Details: ____

____

A12. INTERVIEWER: Ask Subject:

"Did your anger or violence have any effect on your housing?"

☐ yes ☐ no

If YES, INTERVIEWER: Ask Subject:

"Did you lose your housing?

☐ yes ☐ no

"Was the effect of your anger or violence on your housing . . ."

☐ very negative ☐ somewhat negative ☐ neutral

☐ somewhat positive ☐ very positive

Details: ____

____

A13. INTERVIEWER: Ask Subject:

"Did your anger or violence have any effect on your studies?"

☐ yes ☐ no ☐ n/a

If YES, INTERVIEWER: Ask Subject:

"Were you suspended/expelled or did you drop out?" (check all that apply)

☐ suspended ☐ expelled ☐ dropped out ☐ no

"Was the effect of your anger or violence on your studies . . ."

☐ very negative ☐ somewhat negative ☐ neutral

☐ somewhat positive ☐ very positive

Details: ____

____

INTERVIEWER: Please proceed to item A14 on the next page.

Violence and Anger History Interview Subject ID: ______________ Date: ________________

A14. INTERVIEWER: Hand card to Subject and Ask:

"This card has a list of reasons why some people get angry or violent. For each reason please answer "yes" or "no" if you think this reason describes, in whole or in part, why you were angry or violent. Please rate how well each reason below explains why you were angry or violent, on a scale of **0** to **5**, with **0** meaning not at all, **3** meaning it moderately explains why you were angry or violent, and **5** meaning it explains extremely well why you were angry or violent."

Is this a reason	**You were angry or violent because . . .**	**Rating (0–5)**
☐ yes ☐ no	you were overwhelmed by your feelings SPECIFY FEELING(S)______________	
☐ yes ☐ no	you were criticized	
☐ yes ☐ no	you wanted to be taken seriously	
☐ yes ☐ no	you wanted to get revenge or punish someone	
☐ yes ☐ no	you thought someone you cared about might leave you	
☐ yes ☐ no	you wanted to make someone do something or stop doing something	
☐ yes ☐ no	you wanted to make someone understand how mad, afraid or hurt (**CIRCLE**) you were	
☐ yes ☐ no	you wanted to stop feeling bad	
☐ yes ☐ no	you wanted to get even with someone or to get revenge	
☐ yes ☐ no	you misunderstood the situation	
☐ yes ☐ no	you wanted to hurt someone before they could hurt you	
☐ yes ☐ no	your pride was hurt	
☐ yes ☐ no	you needed to show that you were right and they were wrong	
☐ yes ☐ no	you needed to defend yourself or someone else	
☐ yes ☐ no	you couldn't let go of your anger, even though you wanted to	
☐ yes ☐ no	you kept thinking over and over about a situation that upset you	
☐ yes ☐ no	you couldn't forgive someone for what they had done to you	
☐ yes ☐ no	you didn't know how to stand up for yourself any other way	
☐ yes ☐ no	you thought someone meant to hurt you	

Chapter 10

Treating concurrent substance use and eating disorders

CHRISTINE M.A. COURBASSON AND PATRICK D. SMITH

INTRODUCTION

There is a growing consensus in the literature that people with eating disorders often also struggle with substance use disorders. While either disorder tends to be difficult to treat, helping people with these concurrent disorders is particularly challenging. Most often, co-existing substance use and eating disorders are treated sequentially. However, addressing only one of these disordered behaviours at a time overlooks the relationship between the two. As a result, the symptoms of the problem left untreated may become more severe. We believe that treatment is most effective when it addresses both problems together.

At the Centre for Addiction and Mental Health (CAMH), we have developed an outpatient program that addresses substance use and eating disorders concurrently. In contrast to programs that focus on eating, weight and abstinence from substance use, our program educates clients about the interrelationships between substance use and eating disordered behaviours, as well as related issues and nutrition.

The program—an adaptation and extension of Linehan's (1993) work in dialectical behaviour therapy (DBT)—emphasizes skills training, including mindfulness, emotion experiencing and regulation, distress and urge management, interpersonal effectiveness and building balanced structure. Our program merges DBT with psychodynamic, constructivist and narrative principles. Preliminary data suggest that the treatment we offer can benefit clients, not only in terms of addressing problematic eating and substance use behaviours, but also in developing and enhancing a healthy identity.

In this chapter, we offer an overview of various conceptualizations and treatment approaches to substance use and eating disorders. We describe Dialectical Behaviour Therapy—Personal Construct (DBT-PC), the treatment program we developed and provide at the Eating Disorders and Addiction Clinic at CAMH. We present a brief case example to demonstrate the application of this treatment. Finally, we suggest future clinical and research directions specific to these concurrent disorders.

PREVALENCE

A recent report from the (U.S.) National Center on Addiction and Substance Abuse (2003) states that, compared to the general population:

- People with eating disorders are up to five times more likely to have problems with alcohol or other drugs.
- People who have problems with alcohol or other drugs are up to 11 times more likely to have an eating disorder.

Other studies suggest that:

- Between three per cent and 49 per cent of people who exhibit disordered eating behaviours also experience substance use problems (Bulik, 1987; Goldbloom et al., 1992; Hatsukami et al., 1986; Hudson et al., 1987; Mitchell et al., 1985; Pyle et al., 1981).
- Similarly, between one per cent and 32 per cent of people with substance use problems engage in disordered eating behaviours (Hudson et al., 1992; Jonas et al., 1987; Lacey & Moureli, 1986; Peveler & Fairburn, 1990; Schuckit et al., 1996).

The variability in these estimates is due to differences in the criteria used by researchers to assess eating disorders and substance use.

SYMPTOMS OF CONCERN

Anorexia nervosa

People with anorexia nervosa have an intense fear of gaining weight and are preoccupied by a distorted perception of their body. They intentionally lose weight or maintain their weight at 85 per cent below a weight that is healthy for their age and height. Women stop menstruating for at least three consecutive cycles.

People with anorexia may or may not engage in binge eating or purging. Binge eating is defined as uncontrolled consumption of a large amount of food, usually within a two-hour period. Methods of purging to prevent weight gain are extreme, and can include self-induced vomiting, excessive exercising, fasting and overuse of laxatives, diuretics, other medications and/or herbs (American Psychiatric Association, 1994).

Bulimia nervosa

People with bulimia nervosa engage in repeated binge eating and purging, approximately twice per week for at least three months. People with this disorder also tend to base their self-evaluation on their body shape and weight (American Psychiatric Association, 1994).

Eating disorders not otherwise specified

People may engage in problematic eating behaviours that do not meet all the criteria for a diagnosis of anorexia or bulimia but can nevertheless be serious and deserve significant attention. These are called eating disorders not otherwise specified.

Binge-eating disorders

Many people exhibit harmful binge-eating behaviours. Because of the prevalence and medical risks associated with binge-eating, the APA has proposed it as a research criterion; when more research on it has accumulated, it is expected to become a classification of eating disorders.

Substance use

The American Psychiatric Association has defined two categories of substance use disorders, *substance abuse* and *substance dependence*.

People with substance abuse disorders have a pattern of use that contributes to problems or distress that can affect several areas of their life for a 12-month period. They may continue to use substances even though they are aware of the problems substance use causes or worsens (American Psychiatric Association, 1994).

People with substance dependence experience distress or functional impairment and also have at least three of the following problems during a one-year period:

- needing to consume more of the substance to obtain the same effect
- withdrawal symptoms if they reduce or cease their consumption of the substance
- consuming larger amounts of the substance or spending a longer period of time using the substance than they had intended
- repeated desires and unsuccessful efforts to reduce or control their use
- spending a great deal of time trying to get, use and/or recover from the effect of the substance
- continuing to use the substance, even though they know it can have ongoing or long-term adverse effects on their health and functioning (American Psychiatric Association, 1994).

SHARED FEATURES OF SUBSTANCE USE AND EATING DISORDERS

AGE OF ONSET

The problematic behaviours that characterize eating disorders and substance use usually begin in adolescence—although they may onset earlier or later—and are usually chronic.

DENIAL

Both disorders feature intense denial (Krahn, 1991), which is often accompanied by feelings of shame and a desire for secrecy. Denial is a barrier that prevents people from seeking treatment and complying with treatment, and lengthens the duration of their disorders.

SHAME

Even when people with eating disorders and substance use acknowledge that their behaviours are problematic, they resist disclosure because of shame (Yeary & Heck, 1989). An experienced therapist who conveys a non-judgmental stance can help people to disclose such problems.

COUNTER-TRANSFERENCE ISSUES

Counter-transference issues may also be significant obstacles to treatment. These obstacles can be minimized with advanced knowledge of the disorders and increased experience in treating them (Katz, 1990).

DEFICITS IN EMOTION REGULATION

Deficits in emotion regulation are often the antecedents of eating disorders and substance use behaviours. People with these deficits learn to cope with stress by using drugs, alcohol and food, or by restricting their use of food. They experience a lack of control and a preoccupation with food and alcohol or other drugs.

OTHER SIMILARITIES

People with eating disorders and substance use cannot predict or control the onset and the duration of the problematic behaviours (Yeary & Heck, 1989). They continue to engage in these behaviours, even though they experience harm. As a result, they often drop out of treatment.

While eating disorders and substance use have similarities, we do not propose that they have a similar etiology. For example, people with eating disorders do not exhibit tolerance or withdrawal symptoms. They are not "addicted" to food. Like everyone, they eat because they need food in order to live. While having an eating disorder or a substance use problem has its own challenges, people with both disorders suffer the compounded difficulties associated with each condition.

CONSEQUENCES OF SUBSTANCE USE AND EATING DISORDERS

The physiological and psychosocial consequences of concurrent substance use and eating disorders vary, depending on the severity of the disorders and how long they last. The consequences range from mild impairment in social life to death. Anorexia nervosa, it should be noted, has one of the highest death rates in psychiatry (Crisp et al., 1992).

Physiological consequences

Medical complications resulting from substance use and disordered eating behaviours include:

- damage to the cardiovascular, respiratory, gastrointestinal, dermatologic, endocrine, renal, neurologic, musculoskeletal and metabolic systems (Brands et al., 1998; Hofeldt, 1999; Powers, 1999; Steele & Mehler, 1999; Waldholtz, 1999)
- damage to major organs
- for women who have low body weight, irregular menstruation, infertility and high-risk pregnancies (Goldbloom, 1993; Kaplan, 1993).

Psychosocial consequences

EMOTIONAL EFFECTS

The most prevalent emotional effects of concurrent eating disorders and substance use are anxiety, irritability, depression, apathy, mood fluctuations, agitation, difficulty sleeping, crying spells and sometimes anger and aggression (Brands et al., 1998; Hofeldt, 1999; Powers, 1999; Steele & Mehler, 1999).

ISOLATION

An important psychosocial consequence of eating disorders and substance use is isolation. Disordered eating behaviours include the desire to eat in secrecy or alone, spending great amounts of time exercising (usually done alone), a preoccupation with food and alcohol or other drugs, and withdrawal from friends and family. These behaviours all have a negative impact on social relationships.

Substance use can result in low mood, low energy and social withdrawal, which can also alienate friends and family, and result in isolation (Beary et al., 1986; Galanter, 1993; Hatsukami et al., 1986; Jonas et al., 1987; Westmeyer & Neider, 1988).

OTHER NEGATIVE CONSEQUENCES

Other negative consequences of these disorders include:

- poor attention, concentration and memory
- increased self-consciousness and self-defeating thoughts

- insomnia
- general weakness and fatigue.

Among the problematic effects especially related to substance use are:

- confusion
- unpleasant hallucinations
- tremors
- impaired judgment
- paranoia (Brands et al., 1998; Hatsukami et al., 1982).

If people with substance use and eating disorders experience negative consequences as a result of their behaviours, why do they continue? Initially, these behaviours make them feel better:

- Problematic substance use and eating behaviours can provide an escape from difficult situations and soothe negative emotions.
- Dieting and losing weight can provide an illusion of control when everything else is in chaos.
- Using alcohol and other drugs can provide social acceptance.

These satisfactions, however, are temporary. In the long term, as the cycle of bingeing, purging, restricting and substance use becomes more frequent, the positive effects last for shorter periods of time.

CONCEPTUALIZATIONS OF SUBSTANCE USE AND EATING DISORDERS

The various schools of psychology and psychiatry have different conceptualizations of substance use and eating disorders. For example:

- The psychoanalytic school views eating disorders as a result of concern with oral impregnation, Electra complex and other disturbances in the formation of the self (Bruch, 1973).
- The cognitive approach suggests that deficits in cognition—dichotomizing, overgeneralizing and catastrophizing—lead to problematic eating and substance use (Fairburn, 1981).
- Biological theories attribute these disorders to abnormalities in the hypothalamus (the region of the brain that controls hunger) (Garfinkel & Garner, 1982; Hudson & Pope, 1987).
- Family theories suggest that the disorders arise because of insensitivity from caregivers (Walden & Stunkard, 1987).
- Other theorists (Reid & Burr, 2000) have asked whether some eating disorders are "feminine addictions."
- Because many behavioural symptoms of eating disorders and substance use problems overlap (Woods & Brief, 1988), some propose that people with binge-eating problems may benefit from a 12-step program, as is commonly offered to people with substance use disorders (Yeary & Heck, 1989).

The emotion modulation perspective

The emotion modulation perspective suggests that substance use and eating disorders do not stem from disease, weight control or disturbed eating but from a deficit in emotion regulation skills. People with such a deficit may regulate their mood and sensations by restricting their eating or by using alcohol or other drugs (Castellani et al., 1997; Kornhaber, 1970).

For example, the person with anorexia is able to numb her emotions by not eating, and the person with bulimia may rid herself of intense and or distressful feelings by bingeing and purging.

Negative affect is a very frequent (if not the most frequent) antecedent of binge eating (Polivy & Herman, 1993) and people who binge regularly are aware that it can "anesthetize" their distressful feelings (Arnow et al., 1992). Self-regulation accomplished through meditation is related to a decrease in the frequency and severity of binges in women with binge-eating disorders (Kristeller & Hallett, 1999).

We argue that problematic eating, substance use, maladaptive decision-making and emotion dysregulation are all linked and interrelated. Each state increases vulnerability to another and can also lead directly or indirectly into another. DBT addresses the deficit in emotion regulation skills, reducing the client's vulnerability to problematic emotional states.

APPROACHES TO TREATMENT

Sequential treatment

Most often, treatment of concurrent substance use and eating disorders follows a step approach, which addresses the disorders sequentially. This poses two problems:

- First, the clinician must choose which disorder to treat first.
- Second, sequential treatment overlooks the complex relationship between the disorders (Yeary & Heck, 1989).

Clients do not learn how substance use influences eating or restricting behaviours and vice versa. They do not learn how substance use and eating disorders create or exacerbate other mental health problems. Clients do not learn ways to stop the cycle.

Some people in the field believe the substance use problem should be treated first, especially if it is severe, because it affects cognition and lifestyle, and interferes with addressing the eating disorders (Wilson, 1993). However, postponing treatment for disordered eating behaviour can decrease the effectiveness of the substance use treatment.

People with concurrent substance use and eating disorders have more problems in early sobriety and are more likely to relapse (Jonas, 1989). When clients are treated first for eating disorders, they often use alcohol and other drugs to self-medicate (Sutherland et al., 1993).

In our experience, we have found that when we address only the substance use behaviours, and these are controlled, the disordered eating behaviours worsen. Conversely, when we treat only the eating disorders, and the patients resume a healthy eating pattern, their substance use behaviours increase. Separate treatments do not address the relationship between these concurrent disorders.

Simultaneous treatment

An inpatient program developed by Sutherland, Weaver, McPeake and Quimby (1993) offers eating disorders treatment in conjunction with a program that addresses problem substance use. In this program, people with substance use and eating disorders are nutritionally assessed, given a dietary plan to follow while in treatment and participate in a series of psychoeducational sessions. Importantly, the program includes medical management, skills training, individual psychotherapy, and education about nutrition, eating disorders and substance use.

Although the program does offer treatment for substance use and eating disorders at the same time, these remain separate treatments.

Integrated treatment

We believe that, to be most effective, one treatment must address both problems, including the relationship between the disorders. With two treatments, clients may believe that one treatment is more important than the other. With one integrated, concurrent treatment, they are better able to understand the interrelationship between disordered substance use and eating behaviours, and how these behaviours influence their sense of physical and psychological well-being.

As yet, no outcome studies have been published that have evaluated the effectiveness of integrated treatment of concurrent substance use and eating disorders. In the most comprehensive report on substance use problems and eating disorders ever published, the (U.S.) National Center on Addiction and Substance Abuse (2003) states that research on the effectiveness of treatment for co-occurring eating disorders and substance use is lacking. Suggestions for research directions are discussed at the end of this chapter.

THE EATING DISORDERS AND ADDICTION CLINIC

At the Centre for Addiction and Mental Health (CAMH), we have developed an outpatient program that addresses eating disorders and substance use concurrently. We chose outpatient treatment because we believe that most of our clients' learning takes place outside of therapy, and that clients need to have the opportunity to apply their learning in their own environment. Clients come for treatment approximately twice per week for a minimum of 12 months.

Referral, assessment and admission to treatment

At CAMH, family doctors, psychiatrists, therapists or other clinicians may refer clients. Clients may also refer themselves. Clients are given a general intake assessment, and if concurrent problematic substance use and eating behaviours are identified, and clients are willing to enter treatment, they are referred to the Eating Disorders and Addiction Clinic.

The clinic's program co-ordinator then meets with the client to assess the severity of the client's eating disorders and substance use, to determine the client's motivation and eligibility for treatment, and to introduce the program structure and expectations.

Eligibility for treatment is limited to people with concurrent substance use and eating disorders who:

- are not currently receiving treatment for either disorder
- are not in a weight loss program
- do not show evidence of organic brain syndrome, mental retardation, psychosis or chronic suicidal intent or suicidal behaviours.

After the initial assessments, clients meet with a member of the clinic's treatment team for further diagnostic assessment to identify other mental health problems and other issues related to their concurrent disorders. The treatment team reviews the client's case and develops treatment recommendations. Clients then meet with an individual therapist for two to four sessions to establish personal goals and commitments within the program prior to starting the comprehensive treatment. Clients who do not enter treatment (or who later drop out of treatment) are given referrals for appropriate services within CAMH or in the community.

The treatment

Our program goes beyond focusing on healthy eating and addressing substance use issues to offer a comprehensive treatment process that helps clients meet their goals:

- addressing their eating disorders and substance use
- relating more effectively with others
- adopting a healthy lifestyle
- developing a more positive self-image and healthy identity
- improving their quality of life by developing skills that help them to know themselves better, handle feelings and tolerate distress adaptively.

The emphasis is on collaboration. Clinicians work with clients to help them develop new skills to better cope with emotions, stress and difficulties in relationships, to contribute to society and to develop a healthy identity. Two phases of treatment can be identified.

PHASE ONE

During the first phase of treatment, which usually lasts one year, clients learn to become more aware of their thoughts, emotions and behaviours, and to practise skills that help them to deal more effectively with stressful situations. Clients also meet with a dietitian, physician and nurse.

The modalities of the first phase of treatment are:

- one hour of weekly individual therapy
- a two-hour weekly skills-training group
- telephone consultations with a therapist, as needed.

Clients are weighed once per month, which provides exposure to being weighed without encouraging an obsession with weight. Every three months, clients draw a picture of how they view themselves in relation to their eating disorders and substance use. The drawing provides a basis for discussion between the client and the clinician on how to better target problematic issues.

Individual therapy

During weekly individual therapy sessions, clients present logs of their emotions, consumption of food and fluids (including alcohol) and other drugs. Together, therapist and client identify the antecedents of problematic behaviours and problem-solve to determine alternative ways of addressing the client's problems.

Skills-training group

The purpose of group sessions is to:

- heighten clients' awareness of their current patterns of thinking, feeling and behaving
- learn new skills to help them manage problems more effectively
- develop and practise new skills so that they may experience more success—and a greater sense of mastery—in their lives.

The weekly group sessions are led by two clinicians. The primary leader teaches the class and reviews the clients' homework with them. The secondary leader models appropriate behaviour, helps participants to regulate their emotions by coaching or other means, ensures that clients have the materials they need (i.e., paper, pencils, handouts, etc.) and ensures that the room is comfortable.

Nutritious snacks, such as fresh and dried fruits, and pretzels, and healthy drinks, such as herbal tea, are provided. This helps to maintain the participants' energy level and to decrease their vulnerability to becoming emotional due to hunger. It also provides exposure to food and normal eating. Clients are not obligated to eat. The food is set in the middle of the large table that the group sits around. Clients and therapists can help themselves, if they wish, at any time during the session.

We have observed that at the beginning of treatment, clients try to avoid looking at the food. As the treatment evolves, and clients see the group leaders model appropriate food intake each week, they venture to sample the snacks provided. Toward the end of treatment, the amount and frequency of clients' snack consumption are similar to those of the leaders.

Videotapes of each group session are available to group members who miss a session or to those who wish to review the session. For confidentiality reasons, the tapes are not taken out of our clinic.

Each group begins with leaders and clients engaging together in a two- to five-minute mindfulness exercise (Kabat-Zinn, 1990) to help clients ground themselves for the session. Each group session runs two hours, and is divided in half by a 10-minute break.

In the first half of the session, clients identify new or old skills they have used in the past week. Clients note what was helpful and what was not and devise a plan to improve their skills. If clients report that they used no skills, the group leaders ask the clients to describe difficult situations they experienced during the week and help clients to label the skills that they used, but did not identify. The leaders reinforce the use of skills with encouragement and praise.

Next, the clients' homework for the week is reviewed as a group. Each attempt and success is highlighted and reinforced by the therapist. As clients proceed with treatment, they also learn to reinforce each other. If a client does not complete the homework assigned, the leader labels it as therapy-interfering behaviour, and together they undertake a detailed analysis of what interfered with doing the homework and what could have helped. They establish a plan for the client to complete the homework during the following week.

The second half of the group session focuses on skills training, with each skill area taking two to eight sessions. The skill areas covered by the program are:

- mindfulness
- breaking the cycle of concurrent substance use and eating disorders and resulting problematic decisions
- building balanced structure
- interpersonal effectiveness
- emotion experiencing and regulation
- distress and urge management.

Mindfulness skills help clients develop awareness of their thoughts, emotions and bodily responses in the moment. We believe that being more mindful is an antecedent to understanding themselves and interacting more adaptively in their lives.

In sessions focusing on **breaking the cycle**, clients learn facts about eating disorders and substance use, which help them to identify problems related to these disorders and to learn ways to address the problems. In these sessions, clients also learn about the similarities and relationships between these problematic behaviours. Emotion regulation, body image, hunger patterns and healthy meal plans are addressed. (A dietitian conducts the session on the healthy meal plan.) Clients learn to identify their areas of vulnerability to problematic substance use and eating behaviours, and to become more competent in addressing these areas.

Sessions on **building balanced structure** help clients to set goals in the areas of time, work and relationships, and to commit to work toward meeting their goals. Clients with concurrent eating disorders and substance use often have rigid rules they follow in their lives. This module targets this rigidity with an emphasis on balancing structure with flexibility.

Interpersonal effectiveness skills help clients to become assertive in asking for what they want and in refusing unwanted demands. Clients learn to interact with others in a way that maintains their own sense of self-respect and is likely to obtain or maintain another person's approval and respect. In these sessions, clients engage in exercises in which they make requests and refuse requests, without being aggressive or passive.

Emotion experiencing and regulation skills help clients to tolerate emotions—a significant problem among people with eating disorders and substance use. These skills increase clients' control of emotions by achieving a balance between experiencing and accepting their emotions. Clients are encouraged to identify their negative processing of information and its consequences. They also learn to counteract their negative cognitions with alternative and more realistic ones.

Distress and urge management skills help clients to avoid engaging in disordered eating and substance use behaviours that arise out of emotional and physical distress. Clients learn to bear times of distress and to act in ways that are consistent with their goals. Clients also explore the connection between strong emotions, urges to engage in problematic eating or substance use behaviours, and other impulsive behaviours.

Telephone consultations

Our outpatient program recognizes that clients do much of their learning outside of the therapy environment. Urges to use alcohol or other drugs and to binge often occur in the evening, outside of working hours. Clients who need extra help can page a clinician 24 hours a day to receive skills coaching or to get help troubleshooting problems that may arise.

The clinician who answers a client's page first identifies whether or not the problem can wait until the next therapy session. When it needs to be addressed immediately, the therapist provides coaching. In our experience, clients rarely abuse the paging system. For those who do, the clinician automatically targets paging as problematic behaviour at the next therapy session, and the client and therapist discuss the issue and problem-solve together.

Conclusion of phase one

At the last group session, clients and staff mark one year in the program by sharing a potluck meal. We have found that clients take great care in selecting the food and drinks they contribute to the celebration and that they engage in healthy eating.

During this celebration, clients also participate in mindfulness exercises and share their experience of treatment. Clients are given diploma-like papers, stating that the Eating Disorders and Addiction Clinic treatment team congratulates them and wishes for them the achievement of a continually more mindful existence.

Once clients apply skills regularly and are in healthy control of their eating and substance use, they have completed phase one of their treatment. Some clients choose to end treatment at this stage. For others who want to explore other issues, the treatment shifts to phase two.

PHASE TWO

Phase two focuses on helping clients to identify their self-talk and negative way of seeing themselves and to address trauma-related issues. Treatment takes place primarily in a group format, although individual therapy is provided as needed. More process work is done, and principles from other theoretical paradigms are applied (e.g., psychodynamic, constructivist, etc.) In addition, art is used to elicit constructs of the self and the clients' problems.

Eating Disorders and Addiction Clinic—Case example: Kim

When she referred herself for treatment to the Eating Disorders and Addiction Clinic, Kim was 31 years old and lived with her fiancé. She had a three-year-old daughter with another man, who currently had custody of their child. At her assessment, Kim reported she had worked as a clerk for three months, but had taken medical leave for stress six weeks before arriving at the clinic.

Kim had an extensive history of inpatient and outpatient treatment, primarily for alcohol use, but also for bulimia nervosa, depression and two suicide attempts. She had participated in a variety of treatments, including cognitive-behavioural therapy, psychotherapy, counselling focusing on past lives and four months of daily psychoanalysis.

She indicated that she had only engaged in treatment for the sake of her family and that she had not completed any of her past treatments. In the 12 months prior to her assessment, she had experienced depression, her problematic eating behaviour had worsened and she had been raped.

Although Kim had never been overweight, she began dieting at age 13, and bingeing and purging a year later. She has been underweight ever since.

Kim grew up in an emotionally and physically abusive home. Her parents divorced when she was eight years old and her father remarried shortly thereafter. She missed her father, whom she saw only once every four months and during school holidays. She had been unhappy living with her mother and wanted to go and live with her father and her stepmother, whom she felt close to. However, she was aware that her mother was depressed and she felt guilty leaving her alone. She reported that her older sister had physically abused her, and that her mother had not protected her from the abuse. Kim reported that she has worried constantly since her teens. She stated that she found it difficult to control her worries, to concentrate, that she felt on edge and irritable, and experienced muscle tension and insomnia.

Her symptoms of bulimia worsened after her father's second divorce. She said she did not want to acknowledge her feelings of sadness and depression and coped with these feelings by studying and excelling in school. She won scholarships, completed a Bachelor of Arts degree and two years of a Bachelor of Sciences program.

Kim has had problems with alcohol since she was 21. She reported out-of-control drinking to numb her feelings. Her attempts to cut down and abstain had been unsuccessful. She had developed alcohol tolerance and experienced withdrawal symptoms when she tried to abstain. She had given up many social, occupational and recreational activities because of alcohol use and had experienced occasional blackouts at age 24.

Since her mid-20s, she has experienced weekly panic attacks characterized by palpitations, shortness of breath, abdominal distress, derealization (feeling detached from her environment), fear of going crazy and dying.

Kim reported that over the last 10 years she had experienced a depressed mood, hypersomnia, agitation, fatigue, feelings of worthlessness, inappropriate guilt and diminished ability to think. She also experienced chronic feelings of emptiness.

Kim's distress had significantly impaired her ability to work. She often missed work and did not perform her duties accurately, because she was hung over. She reported that she was not keeping her apartment clean. She had been arrested for driving while under the influence of alcohol and had spent a night in jail. She had had frequent arguments with co-workers and family and had withdrawn from their company. Her employer had recommended that she seek alcohol treatment.

Since Kim's symptoms worsened in the last year, the father of Kim's daughter had limited her access to their daughter. He was not willing to allow Kim to see her daughter until Kim's mood was more stable. As a result, Kim felt controlled by him and used alcohol and problematic eating behaviours to cope with her distressful emotions.

At intake, a series of problems were identified. The client met the criteria for anorexia nervosa bingeing/purging type, alcohol dependence, dysthymia, generalized anxiety disorder, panic disorder and borderline personality disorder.

The goals of treatment were to increase her mindfulness, emotion regulation, interpersonal effectiveness, healthy eating, sense of judgment, active problem solving and distress tolerance skills. Further goals included decreasing dysfunctional behaviours that impede the development of these skills. These behaviours included therapy-interfering behaviours and quality of life–interfering behaviours.

At the onset of treatment, her therapist considered it important that Kim monitor self-harm behaviours in case they resurfaced, even though Kim was no longer engaging in them. The therapist and Kim engaged in chain analyses of various behaviours to identify the vulnerability factors, precipitating events and links contributing to various problematic behaviours. The initial focus of treatment was on decreasing therapy-interfering behaviours (e.g. missing sessions, lying, lateness), substance use and problematic eating. Through learning and practising emotion experiencing and regulation, and distress management and urge management skills, Kim was able to use alternative ways of decreasing emotional reactivity.

At the beginning, Kim's sporadic attendance hindered treatment. She was often late for individual sessions or did not attend them at all. She also lied about her substance use and eating behaviour. Her sporadic attendance did not allow enough time to conduct behavioural analyses of her other problematic behaviours. Initially, the therapist rescheduled individual make-up sessions. Kim often missed these sessions as well, or cancelled them at the last minute. The therapist was concerned that scheduling additional make-up sessions was reinforcing Kim's lack of attendance. After addressing this hypothesis with Kim, the therapist stopped providing make-up sessions. This resulted in a somewhat more regular attendance in individual sessions.

When Kim shared how vulnerable she felt and asked for help, the therapist extended herself, to foster alliance. The therapist communicated that she took Kim seriously, and together they collaborated on a plan to help Kim be more skilful and consistent. The therapist validated Kim's feelings of vulnerability and provided positive reinforcement when Kim shared her difficulties. Telephone consultation was used when Kim needed coaching with the new skills in her own environment. The group leaders assisted Kim with skill acquisition in the group sessions.

Three months into treatment, Kim stopped purging. The frequency of her binges had decreased from twice per week to twice per month or less. She was able to eat a balanced diet, and she had reduced her alcohol use from excessive amounts every two days to moderate amounts approximately once per week. Her lying had decreased, and she started to identify feelings she experienced.

After a year of treatment, she rarely drank, and she ate a healthy diet, although she was still struggling with body image issues. Kim had learned to be in control of and to communicate her feelings. She no longer fought against herself—she fought against her negative self-process. She decided to continue the phase one work for another six months.

Future clinical and research directions

Client feedback and our data tell us that people with a 10- to 20-year history of eating disorders and substance use problems can benefit from this treatment program. In future research, randomized outcome studies should be conducted independently of CAMH, the treatment developer, to further evaluate the effectiveness of this treatment program for these concurrent disorders.

Comparing the effectiveness of this adaptation and extension of DBT to other treatment programs for a) alcohol or other drug addiction only, b) eating disorders only and c) an eating disorders program offered in conjunction with a substance use disorders program, would provide evidence of the effectiveness of the program. We hope research will show that people who receive this treatment are able to function more adaptively (i.e., are employed, maintain healthy interpersonal relationships and have fewer problems associated with either maladaptive eating or substance use behaviours). Follow-up studies should be conducted to identify whether the gains clients make while in the program are long-lasting.

Future investigations should also determine whether the effectiveness of our treatment for concurrent disorders differs for different eating disorders and substance use disorders. For example, would a person with concurrent bulimia and alcohol problems respond more favourably than a person with concurrent anorexia nervosa and cocaine use problems?

Unlike many other treatment programs, our treatment has shown a high rate of participant retention for one year. Research identifying variables that predict successful completion of the DBT-PC program would allow us to target these factors early in treatment. This would help us reduce the drop-out rate further and to enhance long-term treatment effects.

Paging and telephone consultation in our program enhance the immediacy of clinicians' responses to crisis situations (e.g., the urge to use drugs) outside of the therapy environment. Clients report feeling a sense of relief to know they can receive support at all times. Future investigations should explore how this paging system influences treatment success and if treatment success is reduced when clients have less access to a clinician outside of scheduled treatment sessions or no access at all.

The secondary leader of the group plays a primary role in modelling adaptive behaviour for clients, challenging dysfunctional behaviour in the moment and engaging in active problem solving and decision-making. It would be beneficial to determine how the secondary leader's role-modelling of skills influences the efficacy of the DBT-PC treatment program.

CLOSING COMMENTS

The comorbidity of eating disorders and substance use has been identified in the literature since the 1990s, and the need to offer a comprehensive, concurrent program for people with these disorders has become more widely recognized. However, clinicians trained in this domain are few. Reasons for this include a lack of empirically validated, concurrent treatment approaches and a lack of formal training opportunities.

Our preliminary data suggest that our treatment is effective. As further research validates the effectiveness of concurrent treatments, and training opportunities for clinicians become more available, clients will benefit, not only in terms of addressing problematic eating and substance use behaviours, but also in developing and enhancing the adoption of healthy identities.

REFERENCES

American Psychiatric Association. (1994). *Diagnostic and Statistical Manual of Mental Disorders* (4th ed.). Washington, DC: Author.

Arnow, B., Kennedy, J. & Agras, W.S. (1992). Binge eating among the obese: A descriptive study. *Journal of Behavioral Medicine, 15*, 155–170.

Beary, M., Lacey, J. & Merry, J. (1986). Alcoholism and eating disorders in women of fertile age. *British Journal of Addiction, 81*, 685–689.

Brands, B., Sproule, B. & Marshman, J. (Eds.). (1998). *Drugs and Drug Abuse* (3rd ed.). Ontario: Addiction Research Foundation.

Bulik, C.M. (1987). Drug and alcohol abuse by bulimic women and their families. *American Journal of Psychiatry, 144*, 1604–1606.

Bruch, H. (1973). *Eating disorders: Obesity, Anorexia Nervosa and the Person Within.* New York: Basic Books.

Castellani, B., Wedgeworth, R., Wootton, E. & Rugle, L. (1997). A bi-directional theory of addiction: Examining coping and the factors related to substance relapse. *Addictive Behaviors, 22*(1), 139–144.

Crisp, A.H., Callender, J.S., Halek, C. & Hsu, L.G. (1992). Long-term mortality in anorexia nervosa: A 20-year follow-up of the St. George's and Aberdeen cohorts. *British Journal of Psychiatry, 161*, 104–107.

Fairburn, C.G. (1981). A cognitive behavioural approach to the treatment of bulimia. *Psychological Medicine, 11*, 707–711.

Galanter, M. (1993). *Network Therapy for Alcohol and Drug Abuse.* New York: Basic Books.

Garfinkel, P.E. & Garner, D.M. (1982). *Anorexia Nervosa: A Multidimensional Perspective.* New York: Brunner/Mazel.

Goldbloom, D.S. (1993). Neurotransmitter, neuropeptide, and neuroendocrine disturbances. In A.S. Kaplan & P.E. Garfinkel (Eds.), *Medical Issues and the Eating Disorders: The Interface* (pp. 123–144). New York: Brunner/Mazel.

Goldbloom, D.S., Narjanjo, C.A., Bremner, K.E. & Hicks, L.K. (1992). Eating disorders and alcohol abuse in women. *British Journal of Addiction, 87,* 913–920.

Hatsukami, D., Mitchell, J., Eckert, E. & Pyle, R. (1986). Characteristics of patients with bulimia only, bulimia with affective disorder, and bulimia with substance abuse problems. *Addictive Behaviour, 11,* 399–406.

Hatsukami, D., Owen, P., Pyle, R. & Mitchell, J. (1982). Affective disorder and substance abuse in women with bulimia. *Psychological Medicine, 14,* 701–704.

Hofeldt, F.D. (1999). Gynecology, endocrinology, and osteoporosis. In P.S. Mehler & A.E. Anderson (Eds.), *Eating disorders: A Guide to Medical Care and Complications* (pp. 118–131). Baltimore, MD: Johns Hopkins University Press.

Hudson, J.I. & Pope, H.G. Jr. (Eds.). (1987). *The Psychobiology of Bulimia.* Washington, DC: American Psychiatric Press.

Hudson, J.I., Pope, H.G., Yurgelin-Todd, D., Jonas, J.M. & Frankengerg, F.R. (1987). A controlled study of lifetime prevalence of affective and other psychiatric disorders in bulimic outpatients. *American Journal of Psychiatry, 142,* 482–485.

Hudson, J.I., Weiss, R.D., Pope, H.G.J., McElroy, S.K. & Mirin, S.M. (1992). Eating disorders in hospitalized substance abusers. *American Journal of Drug and Alcohol Abuse, 18*(1), 75–85.

Jonas, J.M. (1989). Eating disorders and alcohol and other drug abuse: Is there an association? *Alcohol Health and Research World, 13,* 267–271.

Jonas, J., Gold, M., Sweeney, D. & Pottash, A.L.C. (1987). Eating disorders and cocaine use: A survey to 259 cocaine abusers. *Journal of Clinical Psychiatry, 7,* 435–439.

Kabat-Zinn, J. (1990). *Full Catastrophe Living: Using the Wisdom of Your Body and Mind to Face Stress, Pain and Illness.* New York: Delta Publishing.

Kaplan, A.S. (1993). Medical and nutritional assessment. In A.S. Kaplan & P.E. Garfinkel (Eds.), *Medical Issues and the Eating Disorders: The Interface* (pp. 1–16). New York: Brunner/Mazel.

Katz, J.L. (1990). Eating disorders: A primer for the substance abuse specialist. 2. Theories of etiology, treatment approaches, and considerations during co-morbidity with substance abuse. *Journal of Substance Abuse Treatment, 7*, 211–217.

Kornhaber, A. (1970). The stuffing syndrome. *Psychosomatics II,* 580–584.

Krahn, D.D. (1991). The relationship of eating disorders and substance abuse. *Journal of Substance Abuse, 3*, 239–254.

Kristeller, J.L. & Hallett, C.B. (1999). An exploratory study of a mediation-based intervention for binge eating disorders. *Journal of Health Psychology, 4*(3), 357–363.

Lacey, J.H. & Moureli, E. (1986). Bulimic alcoholics: Some features of a clinical sub-group. *British Journal of Addiction, 81*, 389–393.

Linehan, M. (1993). *Skills Training Manual for Treating Borderline Personality.* New York: Guilford Press.

Mitchell, J.E., Hatsukami, D., Eckert, E.D. & Pyle, R.L. (1985). Characteristics of 275 patients with bulimia. *American Journal of Psychiatry, 142*, 482–485.

National Center on Addiction and Substance Abuse. (2003). *Food for Thought: Substance Abuse and Eating Disorders.* New York: The National Center on Addiction and Substance Abuse at Columbia University.

Peveler, R. & Fairburn, C. (1990). Eating disorders in women who abuse alcohol. *British Journal of Addiction, 85*, 1633–1638.

Polivy, J. & Herman, C.P. (1993). Etiology of binge eating: Psychological mechanisms. In C.G. Fairburn & G.T. Wilson (Eds.), *Binge-eating: Nature, Assessment, and Treatment* (pp. 173–205). New York: Guilford Press.

Powers, P.S. (1999). Eating disorders: Cardiovascular risks. In P.S. Mehler & A.E. Anderson (Eds.), *Eating Disorders: A Guide to Medical Care and Complications* (pp. 100–117). Baltimore, MD: Johns Hopkins University Press.

Pyle, R.L., Mitchell, J.E. & Eckert, E.D. (1981). Bulimia: A report of 34 cases. *Journal of Clinical Psychiatry, 42*, 60–64.

Reid, M. & Burr, J. (2000). Are eating disorders feminine addictions? *Addiction Research, 8*(3), 203–210.

Schuckit, M.A., Tipp, J.E., Anthenelli, R.M., Bucholz, K.K., Hesselbrock, V.M. & Nurnberger, U.I. Jr. (1996). Anorexia nervosa and bulimia nervosa in alcohol-dependent men and women and their relatives. *American Journal of Psychiatry, 153*(1), 74–82.

Steele, A.W. & Mehler, P.S. (1999). Oral and dental complications. In P.S. Mehler & A.E. Anderson (Eds.), *Eating Disorders: A Guide to Medical Care and Complications* (pp. 144–153). Baltimore, MD: Johns Hopkins University Press.

Sutherland, L.A., Weaver, S.N., McPeake, J.D. & Quimby, C.D. (1993). The Beech Hill Hospital eating disorders treatment program for drug dependent females: Program description and case analysis. *Journal of Substance Abuse Treatment, 10*, 473–481.

Walden, T.A. & Stunkard, A.J. (1987). Psychopathology and obesity. *Annals of New York Academy of Science, 449*, 55–65.

Waldholtz, B.D. (1999). Gastrointestinal complaints and function in patients with eating disorders. In P.S. Mehler & A.E. Anderson (Eds.), *Eating Disorders: A Guide to Medical Care and Complications* (pp. 86–99). Baltimore, MD: Johns Hopkins University Press.

Westmeyer, J. & Neider, J. (1988). Social networks and psychopathology among substance abusers. *American Journal of Psychiatry, 145*(10), 1265–1269.

Wilson, G.T. (1993). Binge eating and addictive disorders. In C.G. Fairburn & G.T. Wilson (Eds.), *Binge Eating: Nature, Assessment, and Treatment* (pp. 97–120). New York: Guilford Press.

Woods, A.C. & Brief, D.J. (1988). Physiological factors. In D.M. Donovan & G.A. Marlatt (Eds.), *Assessment of Addictive Behaviors* (pp. 296–322). New York: Guilford.

Yeary, J.R. & Heck, C.L. (1989). Dual diagnosis: Eating disorders and psychoactive substance dependence. *Journal of Psychoactive Drugs, 21*, 239–249.

Part III

Approaches and Techniques

Chapter 11

Metacognitive therapy for concurrent alcohol use and anxiety disorder

TONY TONEATTO

Of all the co-occurring substance use and mental health disorders, the most prevalent combination is of mood and anxiety disorders and substance use, particularly alcohol. Approximately 50 per cent or more of addiction clients will have concurrent mood and anxiety problems; about the same percentage of clients of mood and anxiety services will have concurrent substance use problems.

Recent best practices documents, including Health Canada (2002), have identified a growing evidence base for assessing and treating concurrent mood and anxiety disorders and substance use disorders. For treatment, cognitive-behavioural therapies (CBT) have emerged as a best practice in this area.

While CBT principles can be effective over a wide range of co-occurring disorders, this chapter applies CBT principles to co-occurring anxiety and alcohol use disorders to illustrate specific, practical issues. CBT looks at the relationship between behaviour and cognition. Metacognitive therapy targets and modifies the distorted beliefs clients hold about their own mental experiences. (A recent article by Toneatto [2002] shows broad similarities between metacognitive analyses of anxiety and Buddhist philosophy and psychology.)

A functional relationship between anxiety and alcohol problems among clients in treatment has been shown in studies by Kushner et al. (2000) and by Brady and Lydiard (1993). The phobic anxiety disorders, especially panic disorder with agoraphobia and social phobia, are most often associated with alcohol problems.

Anxiety symptoms are sometimes caused by alcohol use. When this is the case, the usual first step (and sometimes the only one) is to treat the alcohol problem.

Once the drinking is controlled, it is common to find an almost complete remission of the anxiety symptoms. Such remission indicates a biological alcohol-induced anxiety disorder. When anxiety symptoms persist after the drinking is controlled, and appear to interfere with the successful treatment of the alcohol problem, it indicates a psychological relationship between anxiety and alcohol use. Metacognitive therapy can be used to address this condition.

Although empirically supported cognitive-behavioural treatments are available for anxiety disorders, and for alcohol use disorder (e.g., Anthony & Swinson, 1996; Miller et al., 1998), treatments designed specifically for concurrent anxiety and alcohol use are still in the early stages of development, and have not been evaluated for effectiveness. A study by Ormrod and Budd (1991) suggests that anxiety management training can help reduce anxiety and prevent relapse among people with drinking problems who have recently quit drinking. However, the people in their research sample were not formally diagnosed with anxiety disorders.

This chapter illustrates the role of metacognitive therapy in these co-occurring disorders, using the most common example that we see in our outpatient concurrent disorders treatment service: anxiety and alcohol use disorders. Clinicians and researchers are also given relevant background information and practical guidelines to participate in the further development of this treatment.

COGNITION AND METACOGNITION

Cognition is any conscious experience, including emotions, thoughts, images, memories, sensory perceptions and physical sensations. Cognition in the human mind is a continuous, highly complex process. Feelings can coexist with thoughts and images; sensations may include memories or fantasies. Thoughts may enter our awareness without any apparent stimulus, and then leave just as quickly with little active involvement on our part. Cognitions may be perceived as pleasant, unpleasant or neutral.

Nelson et al. (1999) divided cognitions into two different "types":

- Type 1 cognitions are those described above, such as thoughts, feelings and images.
- Type 2 cognitions, called *metacognitions*, interpret, judge or evaluate Type 1 cognitions. They can take the form of judgments (e.g., "I hate bad dreams") and attitudes (e.g., "feeling too much anxiety is dangerous").

Metacognition has been described as:

- beliefs and attitudes held about cognition, or as an active and reflective process that is directed at one's own cognitive activity (Allen & Armour-Thomas, 1991; Kluwe, 1982)
- cognitive activity for which other cognitive activities are the object of reflection, that is, "thinking about thinking" (Yussen, 1985)
- an activity, without which awareness of any other cognition, such as thoughts, feelings and memories, would be impossible (Slife, 1987).

The aspect of metacognition that concerns us most here is the activity of *evaluative beliefs* about other cognitions (Brown, 1987; Flavell & Wellman, 1977).

THE INFLUENCE OF METACOGNITIVE STATEMENTS

Metacognitive statements almost always refer to the self; this gives such statements greater behavioural or motivational effects than Type 1 cognitions. For example, a metacognitive statement that includes a self-reference and contains an evaluative judgment, such as "I hate the cold," is more potent in behavioural effect than the statement, "It's cold."

The degree to which a metacognition influences a person's behaviour depends on the value the person places in a metacognitive judgment, and on the intensity of the judgment. For example, the memory of an embarrassing moment may be interpreted with the metacognitive response, "I was stupid to say that." The effect of such a metacognition on behaviour can vary widely:

- One person might disregard the thought and pass it off, and continue to behave in the same way.
- Another might note the message and think, "That was a stupid thing to say; I should be more careful," and make appropriate alterations in his or her behaviour.
- Yet another might attach an intense negative significance to the metacognition. That person might think, "I really am stupid; they probably hate me; I should just keep my mouth shut." Such an interpretation might cause the person to withdraw from social situations, a behaviour that could have a negative effect on many aspects of the person's life.

MODIFYING METACOGNITIVE STATEMENTS

Type 1 cognitions, such as unpleasant memories or phobic thoughts, will occur even when someone wishes to avoid them. The way we interpret these thoughts, however, can be modified.

One way to modify metacognitions is by using alcohol or other drugs, which can depress or stimulate cognitive activity. Another way is through metacognitive therapy. Metacognitive therapy helps clients learn to distinguish their Type 1 cognitive experiences from their Type 2 interpretations, judgments or evaluations of the same experiences. They learn to identify which metacognitions lead to substance use, for example, and to modify these metacognitions through "non-judgmental awareness" of their thoughts.

APPLICATIONS OF METACOGNITION IN THEORY AND PRACTICE

Metacognitive variables have been widely used to understand how children acquire problem-solving skills, monitor and regulate their mental processes, and gain knowledge of their abilities, such as reading and academic performance (Berardi-Coletta et al., 1995).

Although interest in metacognition in clinical psychology has increased, applications to addictive behaviour have been few.

Several areas of research activity, however, are relevant to metacognition and its role in psychopathology. Recent work on metacognition and related constructs includes a special issue of *Clinical Psychology and Psychotherapy* (Wells & Purdon, 1999) devoted to metacognition and clinical psychology, and work by Wells (2000) on metacognitive models of anxiety disorders.

APPLYING THE METACOGNITIVE MODEL OF BEHAVIOUR TO CONCURRENT ANXIETY AND ALCOHOL USE DISORDERS

The metacognitive model of behaviour assumes that behaviour affects cognition and cognition affects behaviour. The most important consideration, in the metacognitive model, is how people interpret their cognitive activity, and how their beliefs determine their behaviour and subsequent mental activity.

In applying the metacognitive model to people with concurrent anxiety and alcohol use disorders, we look at how their beliefs fuel these disorders. For example: many people who use alcohol in a chronic and harmful manner believe that they cannot tolerate the *discomfort* caused by unpleasant cognitive states (Toneatto, 1999a, b). Alcohol alleviates their discomfort; it offers a way of *escaping or avoiding* their thoughts, and so its use is reinforced.

The key metacognitive belief among people with anxiety disorders is that they are in *danger*. Although there may be no real danger, stimuli are interpreted as dangerous and consequently, the person feels excessive fear or aversion. The person responds by taking extraordinary measures to *escape or avoid* the stimuli that arouse feelings of danger. Such a response may be behavioural (e.g., avoiding stimuli that are the focus of a phobia) or experiential (e.g., taking medication to reduce the intensity of stimuli).

The *discomfort* associated with chronic alcohol use and the *danger* associated with anxiety disorders are similar in that they elicit the same coping behaviours: *escape or avoidance.*

People who are anxious and unable to escape or avoid stimuli they interpret as dangerous may modify their internal environment by using alcohol. When trying to understand why alcohol is so often used by people to alleviate their anxiety, and how this alcohol use can itself become a disorder, we may consider the following variables that influence substance use:

- effect of substance
- speed of effect
- reinforcement (positive and negative).

Alcohol use

THE EFFECTS OF SUBSTANCES ON METACOGNITION

The key variable in a person's choice of any psychoactive substance, other than availability, is the impact that a drug has on specific cognitive states or metacognitions.

For example, someone who cannot tolerate boredom may choose a stimulant drug to create an excited cognitive state (and hence modify the metacognition from "*I can't stand boredom*" to "*I'm not bored anymore; this feels better*"). However, if a stimulant is unavailable or ineffective, the person may choose another drug, although the effect may be quite different. In the person unable to tolerate boredom, alcohol may depress cognitive activity to the point that boredom is no longer a concern (e.g., "*I am so drunk, I don't care about boredom or anything else*").

ALCOHOL AS "SELF-MEDICATION" FOR METACOGNITIVE DISCOMFORT

Alcohol may be used to relieve metacognitive discomfort in the same way that medications are used to relieve pain. When we have a toothache, a codeine pill can offer temporary relief. The potency and frequency of the dose is directed by the degree of pain experienced.

The relief it provides however, is palliative and brief; it cannot resolve the underlying condition. Trying to maintain the relief with alcohol leads to chronic use. Just as we all know that the person with a toothache needs to visit a dentist, people with cognitive distress often understand that interventions such as psychotherapy or psychiatric medications are needed to resolve their cognitive distress.

The interaction between alcohol use and anxiety is often viewed as self-medication, although *self-regulation* may be a more appropriate term (Toneatto, 1995). Such psychological functionality may be simple (i.e., co-occurrence of alcohol use and anxiety disorder but no other psychiatric disorder) or complicated (i.e., co-occurrence of alcohol use and anxiety disorder but with the presence of other mental health disorders or the use of other substances).

The matrix matching the short- and long-term effects of a psychoactive substance with the wide range of cognitive and metacognitive states yields a complex and detailed understanding of the interaction between a drug and mental activity. This understanding can be used in therapy to specify the timing and type of treatment for both the substance use and the mental health issues.

Speed of relief

Speed of relief is another critical variable in the decision to ingest a psychoactive substance. Psychoactive substances may be preferred to therapy because they act quickly, within seconds and minutes, whereas behavioural, social or cognitive interventions may take hours, weeks or months to modify cognitive or metacognitive states, if at all. Alcohol can be consumed as needed. It is a readily available and effective way to get rapid relief from cognitive distress. If its consciousness-modifying effects took several months to occur, people would be less likely to consume alcohol.

The need for fast relief may also affect the rate, type and quantity of alcohol consumed. Intense metacognitive beliefs may cause people to choose liquor over beer, drink rapidly by gulping or drink more than is appropriate in a social context.

Reinforcement

The most important function of alcohol is its ability to quickly and easily produce short-term changes in consciousness. Most social drinking is associated with feelings of enhanced pleasure and well-being; this is a positive reinforcement of alcohol's effects.

Problem drinking in people with concurrent alcohol use and anxiety disorders, however, is more likely to be associated with negative reinforcement: alcohol is consumed to change or eliminate distress and to suppress memories.

EXAMPLE: THE EFFECT OF ALCOHOL ON METACOGNITION

A woman who has been sexually traumatized may experience spontaneous unpleasant memories, sensory flashbacks and dreams. She may become overly sensitive to environmental stimuli conditioned to the traumatizing episode and seek to avoid or escape such stimuli, such as males who resemble the perpetrator, anniversary dates and so on.

The cognitions that define her anxiety will almost always be accompanied by several metacognitions that express aversion to these mental states. Examples may include "*I am afraid of these dreams,*" "*I keep seeing his face and I get really afraid,*" "*Today is the anniversary of the attack and I feel afraid I won't be able to get through it.*"

She may prefer not to experience these cognitive states but does not have remedial coping responses (or she is unwilling or unable to use them), and discovers that drinking alcohol makes her feel better.

Alcohol can affect cognitive states in at least two ways (Nelson et al., 1999):

- One way is for the alcohol to modify the Type 1 cognitive state directly. For example, the woman's traumatic memory is blurred, or the sensory anxiety symptoms are attenuated. The alcohol may transform the memories or images in such a way that they are rendered more benign, for example, by eliminating distressful aspects. This may lead to a revised and more acceptable Type 2 metacognition.
- The second way is for the alcohol to modify the metacognition directly. For example, the woman may conclude that the traumatic memories are not as disturbing as she thought, or that she is not afraid of men. At an extreme, this may produce a sense of "numbness" or detachment from cognition often valued by people who drink heavily and problematically (e.g., "*I remember very well what happened, but I don't really care, it doesn't bother me, it was long ago*").

Anxiety

DEFINING ANXIETY

Phobic anxiety disorders, such as agoraphobia, social phobia and simple phobia, are defined by excessive fear responses to stimuli.

Non-phobic anxiety disorders, such as panic disorder, posttraumatic stress disorder and generalized anxiety disorder, are characterized primarily by intense sensory/ cognitive symptoms, which produce fear and aversion.

In both types of anxiety disorder, the person takes extraordinary measures to escape, avoid or in some way eliminate the source of the distress. Such distressing stimuli (called anxiogenic stimuli) are, in reality, neither harmful nor dangerous, but are interpreted to be so by the person.

The metacognitive aspect of such interpretation includes beliefs about lack of ability to cope with symptoms, which in turn fuels the excessive responsiveness that is characteristic of anxiety disorders. With phobias, this responsiveness may manifest as behavioural avoidance; with non-phobic anxiety, it may manifest as experiential avoidance (through the use of medications, for example).

Not surprisingly, cognitive treatments for anxiety disorders often target the maladaptive assumptions that the person has made about anxiogenic stimuli. In effect, these treatments attempt to modify metacognition.

THE METACOGNITIVE MODEL OF ANXIETY

Metacognitive treatment for concurrent alcohol use and anxiety disorders views anxiety *phenomenologically*. That is, it looks at aspects of the anxious person's experience, and at how alcohol is being used to help cope with these experiences.

Anxiety has five components, which may or may not be equally present in an anxiety disorder. Most anxiety disorders include *sensory, cognitive, imaginal, affective* and *behavioural* components. The following table summarizes these components and some of their experiential aspects, and includes examples of how these aspects may be modified by alcohol or other drugs.

It is important to conceptualize anxiety phenomenologically, because people who have concurrent anxiety and alcohol problems are not using alcohol to cope with their anxiety *per se* (which is a concept), but rather with an aspect of their experience.

For example, a man experiencing the sudden, uncomfortable arousal of a panic attack may drink alcohol to modify his metacognition of danger and discomfort. The alcohol may have no direct effect on the sensory symptoms of the panic attack, such as increased heart rate or shortness of breath, and it may actually exacerbate them. But as the alcohol takes effect, the man may experience relief associated with the growing numbness and sense of detachment that results from intoxication.

PRACTISING METACOGNITIVE THERAPY FOR CONCURRENT ANXIETY AND ALCOHOL PROBLEMS

The metacognitive treatment presented here identifies and targets the key cognitions and metacognitions that inform the behavioural aspects of alcohol use and anxiety disorders (e.g., drug consumption, avoidance behaviour). The therapy is presented in

TABLE 11-1

Phenomenological dimensions of anxiety

COMPONENTS	EXPERIMENTAL ASPECTS	POSSIBLE EFFECTS OF SUBSTANCE USE
Sensory	Increased heart rate, breathing changes, hot flashes, chills Muscle pains, stomach upset	Detach from symptoms Suppress discomfort, numbness
Cognitive	Worry, thoughts of danger or dying Self-criticism Vigilance directed at people, animals or objects	Eliminate thoughts, numb thoughts Increase confidence, sedate
Imaginal	Embarrassment, humiliation Intrusive memories and images	Transform to praise Suppress or eliminate
Affective	Irritability, withdrawal, sadness, low energy or hyperarousal	Suppress or reverse symptoms
Behavioural	Avoidance, escape, pacing, erratic behaviour	Disinhibit, become more gregarious, sedate

three steps, but this is done primarily for clarity and ease of presentation. In actual practice, the treatment must be adapted to the unique needs of each client and may not follow this linear presentation.

Step 1: Addressing the alcohol problem

Few clients enter treatment having already reduced or stopped drinking; most are drinking excessively. Treatment should first try to help clients reduce their drinking. There are many reasons to target alcohol use first:

- Problem alcohol use can produce many psychiatric symptoms, especially anxiety and depression, which will diminish when alcohol use is reduced.
- When problem drinking continues, the person's resources and attention are severely compromised. This makes it difficult to adequately address any psychiatric condition or drinking-related problems.
- Problem drinking can harm many areas of the person's life, such as work, health, relationships, finances and cognitive functioning. Reducing alcohol use will alleviate the strain on these areas and re-establish relationships with others, whose social support may be needed during treatment and aftercare.
- To properly benefit from any therapy, the client's cognitive and mental functioning should be optimal. This is impossible when drinking continues to have a harmful effect on the brain.
- Problem drinking is essentially a behaviour, which can be easier to modify than mood disorders, such as anxiety and depression. When people have already begun to make

changes in their drinking behaviour, continuing to reduce alcohol use maintains this momentum and increases their motivation and optimism. Mood disorders are not as easily resolved, and the benefits of effort are not always immediately apparent.

The treatment of alcohol problems usually involves a treatment plan, which the therapist and client develop together. Goals are set to taper drinking, modify the drinking pattern, set a quit date and so on. The therapist then observes over time the degree to which the client is able to achieve these goals. If drinking is reduced significantly, and the client continues to have anxiety symptoms, then it is likely that the client also has an anxiety disorder. At this time, the therapist should proceed to treat the anxiety.

If attempts to modify drinking have failed repeatedly, the therapist must first determine if the problem is motivational. If this is the case, therapy should focus on assessing and, if necessary or possible, modifying the client's stage of change.

If motivation does not seem to be the problem, and the client continues to have trouble achieving his or her drinking goals despite a reasonable plan and time frame, Step 2 should be implemented.

Step 2: Metacognitive analysis of obstacles to reducing alcohol use

Because inability to reduce drinking may lie in cognitive factors, the goal of this step is to identify the client's beliefs about the relationship between alcohol use and the experience of anxiety. The therapist seeks to reveal:

- cognitive states that may be mediating the client's desire to drink alcohol (e.g., "*I feel very panicky*")
- the metacognitions that are preventing reliable reduction in alcohol use (e.g., "*I am too afraid of anxiety to not drink when I feel that way*"; "*I don't like feeling this way*").

"URGE STATEMENTS"

An effective way to probe cognitive factors is to ask clients about their urges or cravings to drink. A client's "urge statements" often express acute aversive cognitive states, such as intense anxiety, boredom or intrusive memories (Toneatto, 1999a, b).

QUESTIONS THERAPISTS CAN ASK

In addition to analysing urges, there are many questions therapists can ask that can help to reveal beliefs that make it difficult to refrain from drinking. For example:

- "What was it about being sober that made it preferable to drink alcohol rather than to continue to remain sober?"
- "What is difficult about remaining sober?"
- "What is the worst that could happen if you remained sober?"
- "Why not drink a coffee rather than alcohol?"
- "What would have had to have happened so that you would have decided not to drink alcohol?"

Therapists should aim for statements that clearly specify:
- which cognitive states are modified by alcohol use
- how the cognitive state is altered
- what cognitive and/or behavioural consequences would be expected should the cognitive state fail to be modified by alcohol use (Toneatto, 1999a, b).

For example, if the client uses alcohol to modify cognitive aspects of anxiety, such as worries or memories, it is important to discover whether alcohol:
- reduces the cognitive state
- changes the type of cognitions that occur
- initiates a more desirable cognitive activity
- reduces the concern about the ongoing cognitive activity.

In addition, if alcohol is not used, and the cognitive activity is not modified, what would the client expect to happen?
- being unable to tolerate the cognitive activity
- fearing the discomfort of continuing to think and feel this way
- worrying that the cognitive activity will not cease
- having concern for the effects of cognitions on sleep
- feeling suicidal and perhaps engaging in self-harm behaviour
- behaving impulsively?

CLIENT RESPONSE TO QUESTIONS

The statements clients make in response to questioning can be classified into several clusters, which may help the therapist respond to these obstacles.

Fear of discomfort

- "I can't stand boredom."
- "I hate feeling nervous."

Low frustration tolerance

- "I can't wait for the anxiety to go away on its own."
- "It takes too long to feel better if I don't drink."

Low self-efficacy

- "I can't function normally without alcohol."
- "I can't have fun without drinking."

Fear of judgment

- "I can't let other see how nervous I feel."
- "My hands were shaking."

Such beliefs may be interfering with a client's resolve to work toward his or her drinking goals, and indicate a need for therapeutic intervention. This may involve:
- modifying the treatment goal to allow more time for the client to adjust to not drinking

- therapeutic challenging of the validity of these beliefs, using evidence from the client's past experience
- correcting misperceptions about anxiety and other cognitive states.

Many of the cognitions expressed by people who are dependent on alcohol are similar to those expressed by people with severe anxiety. Regardless of whether a cognition leads to a decision to drink alcohol or to engage in phobic avoidance, clients need to develop more effective ways to respond to their own cognitive states. The metacognitive techniques discussed in Step 3 can help to achieve this goal.

Step 3: Metacognitive principles and non-judgmental awareness

Once the metacognitive beliefs that are interfering with the client's drinking goal have been identified, the next phase of treatment is to correct these beliefs.

To do this, the therapist can draw on the wide range of cognitive-behavioural techniques available to modify maladaptive cognitions. The metacognitive approach contributes to these interventions by encouraging clients to distinguish their Type 1 cognitive experiences from their Type 2 interpretations, judgments and evaluations of the same experience.

Type 1 cognitions are not always immediately avoidable. Unpleasant emotions, thoughts and images, for example, will always occur. However, Type 2 metacognitions are always modifiable, in the sense that the person can learn to experience (or describe) the cognitive state with minimal interpretive judgment ("non-judgmental awareness").

For metacognitive interventions to be effective, clients need to understand how problems coping with cognitive states and metacognitions may interfere with their ability to reach their drinking goal.

METACOGNITIVE PRINCIPLES

Cognitions are unavoidable. As long as we are alive and conscious, our minds constantly experience thoughts, feelings, body sensations, sensory perceptions, memories, images and so on. Cognitive activity is an expression of the minds' continuous creative capacity and responsiveness. The following metacognitive principles can guide the discussion with clients, and prepare clients for the metacognitive technique of non-judgmental awareness that follows.

i. Cognitions are temporary.

Cognitions emerge and fade, often with little active involvement on our part. Some may be little more than fleeting flashes, such as the scent of flowers as you pass by a garden, or the thought of a place you once visited. More enduring cognitive states, such as infatuation in a new-found love, or grief at the loss of a friend, may be prolonged, but these too are repeatedly interrupted with other cognitions, and eventually fade.

ii. Cognitions have no substance.
While the activities of our consciousness seem real, they are, in fact, difficult to define, locate or describe. They are like a television image, produced by electricity, capable of entertaining, horrifying or educating us, but they are an illusion; they are not real.

iii. Cognitions have only the power that we give them.
Unpleasant cognitions, such as frightening memories or fears, don't have any more power or control over what we do than the scent of baking bread, unless we let them. Some people respond to disturbing thoughts or feelings as though they were threatening or dangerous. They try to escape by drinking, or by avoiding situations that bring on such thoughts or feelings.

iv. Cognitions cannot physically hurt us.
We know that if you get bitten by a dog, it hurts, therefore running away from an angry dog makes good sense. But what happens in your mind can only tell you that you feel hurt; it can't hurt you any more.

v. Cognitions often indicate a need for change in our lives.
This is especially true for unpleasant cognitions, which serve the same function, psychologically, as pain does for our physical well-being. Pain in itself is harmless, though it is certainly unpleasant, and is highly effective at motivating us to do something about it. Similarly, unpleasant cognitions can serve to motivate changes in our behaviour, lifestyle, relationships and so on.

vi. Cognition does not determine action.
While it is difficult to control our cognitions (especially their onset), behavioural responses are almost always within our control. Whatever it is that produces feelings of fear is not the same thing that leads us to respond to that fear with, for example, avoidance or alcohol use.

DEVELOPING NON-JUDGMENTAL AWARENESS

When an aspect of anxiety emerges that clients find disturbing or fearful, therapists can use the metacognitive principles above to help clients to describe the anxiety as though it does not affect them, and thus separate the actual experience from their judgmental reaction to it. This technique develops "non-judgmental awareness," through which clients learn to experience the sensory, cognitive, imaginal, affective and behavioural aspects of anxiety as harmless and normal, although often unpleasant and undesirable.

To develop non-judgmental awareness, clients should be instructed using ordinary examples how a person's judgments can be easily separated from the pure sensory characteristics of the experience or object. For example, food aversions or music preferences are easily identified (e.g., "*I hate cauliflower*," "*I love techno*") and can usually be described separately from judgment (e.g., "*Cauliflower is bland*," "*Techno has a beat*"). Once clients can competently identify when they are expressing an evaluative judgment using non-clinical examples, then this technique can be applied to clinically relevant contexts.

The following is an example of a therapist helping to develop a client's non-judgmental awareness:

Client: When I have a panic attack, my heart starts to beat fast, my breathing gets shallow, and I think I'm going to die.

Therapist: But doesn't your heart beat fast and your breathing become shallow when you exercise? How is this different?

C: Well, when I exercise I know what's causing these changes, but during a panic attack it seems to come out of nowhere for no reason.

T: Other than not being able to connect the symptoms with a cause, does your heart and breathing feel any different from when you exercise?

C: I don't think so, no. I feel all sped up, like I just ran ten miles, except that, instead of feeling like I'm having a good workout, I feel like I'm going to die.

T: So what you're saying is that your heart and breathing are functioning in a normal way, but since they are functioning that way without exercising, it doesn't make sense. Because it doesn't make sense, you feel frightened.

C: Yes.

T: Let's think about how your mind is working when you have a panic attack, and to do that I'm going to use a couple of terms that help to describe different kinds of thought. One of these terms, *cognition*, describes the level of thought where your mind is simply aware of your heart and lungs working. These kind of thoughts come and go, sometimes for no apparent reason. But when you are having a panic attack, and you become aware of your heart and breathing, you think, "This doesn't make sense; I think I'm going to die." This response of confusion and fear to your awareness of your heart and breathing is called a *metacognition.* A metacognition attaches meaning to a cognition. What might help you with these panic attacks is to realize that you can change your metacognition. You can choose to regard your awareness of your heart beating and lungs breathing in any way you want. You can think that the way your heart and lungs are working is frightening, because it seems to be coming out of nowhere. Or you can think that your heart and lungs are working in normal way, just like when you exercise.

C: I guess my heart and lungs don't know the difference.

T: That's right, and if you give yourself a calm moment or two, your heart and breathing will return to normal.

As clients learn to experience their inner and outer environment without judgment, and allow distressing cognitive states to progress in a natural way, such cognitions become less disruptive.

Success with this technique requires persistence and practice. Clients may have a long history of constantly judging cognitive experience. Such a strong habit is not easily overcome. Therapeutic progress can be hastened if homework accompanies exercises such as the one in the example above. Homework allows new learning to occur, which can rapidly disconfirm the maladaptive metacognitive judgments.

Exposure treatments are among the most effective treatments for anxiety. This is because they correct metacognitive distortions in a very direct manner, through new experience. However, exposure without correction of metacognitive activity is less effective; it can also worsen the anxiety disorder. For example, people with panic anxiety are intensely exposed to sensory symptoms, but this exposure does not diminish the symptoms. What can diminish the symptoms, however, is learning to interpret these sensory responses—as nothing more than unusual and unpleasant activity of the body and mind, but in no way harmful or dangerous.

Because alcohol negatively reinforces the metacognitive beliefs about the danger and discomfort of cognitive states, clients must maintain a reduction in alcohol use throughout treatment for the anxiety. If an alcohol relapse occurs, the therapist will need to conduct a metacognitive analysis to identify which judgments about cognitive activity led to the client's decision to consume alcohol.

EXTENDING THE METACOGNITIVE MODEL

Although the illustrations here have been specific to anxiety symptoms and alcohol use, the model of metacognitive therapy has broader application, not just in treating co-occurring substance use and mood or anxiety problems, but also to the full range of concurrent disorders.

This chapter has illustrated how therapists need to be able to establish and maintain a therapeutic dialogue that is centred on the client's experience of his or her own problems. By developing an effective understanding of the context and nature of the problem behaviour, the metacognitive-oriented therapist can help shift the cognitive and metacognitive experience of the client. By making this shift, the client can see his or her problem as not so much of a problem, or as a problem that can be addressed in different ways.

Although concurrent disorders can be understood as having many causes and levels, one key value of the metacognitive approach is the way that it guides the therapist to connect with, understand, and align with the client to find behavioural alternatives that the client is willing to try out in real experiences. As these alternatives are applied, they begin to extend the client's self-efficacy, thus opening the client's horizons about healthier responses to very difficult and demanding circumstances.

REFERENCES

Allen, B.A. & Armour-Thomas, E. (1991). Construct validation of metacognition. *Journal of Psychology, 127*(2), 203–211.

Anthony, M.A. & Swinson, R.P. (1996). *Anxiety Disorders and Their Treatment. A Critical Review of the Evidence-Based Literature.* Ottawa: Health Canada, Cat. No. H39-388/1-1996E.

Berardi-Coletta, B., Buyer, L.S., Dominowski, R.L. & Rellinger, E.R. (1995). Metacognition and problem-solving: A process-oriented approach. *Journal of Consulting and Clinical Psychology, 21*, 205–223.

Brady, K.T. & Lydiard, R.B. (1993). The association of alcoholism and anxiety. *Psychiatric Quarterly, 6*(2), 135–149.

Brown, A. (1987). Metacognition, executive control, self-regulation and other more mysterious mechanisms. In E.W. Weinert & R.H. Kluwe (Eds.), *Metacognition, Motivation, and Understanding* (pp. 65–116). Hillsdale, NJ: Erlbaum.

Flavell, J.H. & Wellman, H.M. (1977). Metamemory. In R.V. Kail, Jr. & J.W. Hagen (Eds.), *Perspectives on the Development of Memory and Cognition* (pp. 3–33). Hillsdale, NJ: Erlbaum.

Health Canada. (2002). *Best Practices: Concurrent Mental Health and Substance Use Disorders.* Ottawa: Minister of Public Works and Government Services Canada, Cat. #H39-599/2001-2E.

Kluwe, R.H. (1982). Cognitive knowledge and executive control: Metacognition. In D.R. Griffin (Ed.), *Animal Mind—Human Mind* (pp. 201–224). Berlin: Springer-Verlag.

Kushner, M.G., Abrams, K. & Borchardt, C. (2000). Relationship between anxiety disorders and alcohol use disorders: A review of major perspectives and finding. *Clinical Psychology Review, 20*(2), 149–171.

Miller, W.R., Andrews, N.R., Wilbourne, P. & Bennett, M.E. (1998). A wealth of alternatives: Effective treatments for alcohol problems. In W.R. Miller (Ed.), *Treating Addictive Behaviours* (2nd ed., pp. 203–216). New York: Plenum Press.

Nelson, T.O., Stuart, R.B., Howard, C. & Crowley, M. (1999). Metacognition and clinical psychology: A preliminary framework for research and practice. *Clinical Psychology and Psychotherapy, 6*(2), 73–79.

Ormrod, J. & Budd, R. (1991). A comparison of two treatment interventions aimed at lowering anxiety levels and alcohol consumption amongst alcohol abusers. *Drug and Alcohol Dependence, 27*(3), 233–243.

Slife, B.D. (1987). Can cognitive psychology account for metacognitive functions of mind? *Journal of Mind and Behavior, 8*(2), 195–208.

Toneatto, T. (1995). The regulation of cognitive states: A description of cognitive model and treatment for psychoactive substance abuse. *Journal of Cognitive Psychotherapy, 9*(2), 93–104.

Toneatto, T. (1999a). A metacognitive analysis of craving: Assessment implications. *Journal of Clinical Psychology, 55*(5), 537–537.

Toneatto, T. (1999b). Metacognition and substance use. *Addictive Behaviours, 24*(2), 1–8.

Toneatto, T. (2002). A metacognitive therapy for anxiety disorders: Buddhist psychology applied. *Cognitive and Behavioral Practice, 9*, 72–78.

Wells, A. (2000). *Emotional Disorders and Metacognition.* Chichester: Wiley.

Wells, A. & Purdon, C. (1999). Metacognition and Cognitive Behaviour Therapy [Special issue]. *Clinical Psychology and Psychotherapy, 6*(2).

Yussen, S.R. (1985). The role of metacognition in contemporary theories of cognitive development. In D.L. Forrest-Presley, G.E. MacKinnon & T.G. Waller (Eds.), *Metacognition, Cognition, and Human Performance* (pp. 253–283). Orlando, FL: Academic.

Chapter 12

Interpersonal group therapy for concurrent alcohol dependence and interpersonal problems

JAN MALAT AND MOLYN LESZCZ

INTRODUCTION

In his study of human psychology, Sigmund Freud, the founder of psychoanalysis, discovered that some people repeat specific, self-defeating patterns of behaviour in their relating to others. Often these patterns create problems in people's lives, interfering with their ability to establish secure and satisfying relationships.

Such interpersonal problems are often found among people who are dependent on alcohol. Not only do interpersonal problems contribute to the psychological vulnerability that predisposes people to alcohol dependence; drinking problems also generate enormous relationship difficulties (Khantzian et al., 1990). It is well recognized that treatment of substance use problems demands attention to the client's social context (Galanter, 2001).

Interpersonal group therapy (IGT) helps people to modify problematic patterns of relating and to develop a more satisfactory interpersonal life. IGT draws on the fundamental principle of treating people in the context of their essential difficulties: clients are gathered together in an environment where they are likely to repeat their problematic patterns of relating. When interpersonal problems emerge within the group, the therapist and group members are given a unique opportunity. Rather than responding to the client's patterns as others have and adding to the experience of failure in relating, the therapist and group members use the techniques of IGT to help the client move toward change and growth.

IGT is optimally delivered with six to 10 clients, with a mix of gender and backgrounds but with similar levels of psychological stability. We recommend a program of weekly group therapy for a minimum of six months to one year in the acute phase of treatment, though optimal results in this treatment occur when it is delivered over several years.

The treatment and theory presented in this chapter are based on the work of Yalom (1995) and Yalom and Leszcz (2005) on interpersonal group therapy and Kiesler (1996) on interpersonal theory, along with the authors' own modifications of these approaches (Leszcz, 1992; Leszcz & Malat, 2001). IGT focuses on the here-and-now and on the interactions between members of the group, including the therapist.

The therapy presented here should not be confused with interpersonal therapy (IPT), developed by Klerman et al. (1984) to treat depression. IPT in a group context focuses more on what is happening in the client's environment outside the interactions in therapy, and avoids attention to in-session manifestations of interpersonal difficulty (Yalom & Leszcz, 2005).

Introducing a psychological approach to the treatment of alcohol dependence serves as a counterbalance to the potential overemphasis on treatment based on a disease model. The disease model regards alcohol dependence as a serious illness that is marked by loss of control, and that requires intensive supportive interventions such as inpatient treatment and long-term contact with Alcoholics Anonymous (AA). While it is important to recognize the merit of the disease model, too much emphasis on this approach minimizes individual complexity and differences (Gabbard, 1994). Our method strives to achieve a balance between the two approaches, focusing on individual psychology and personal responsibility for one's relationship world, while being mindful of alcohol dependence as an illness.

The psychological vulnerabilities of people with substance dependence have been noted by many authors, including Khantzian (Khantzian et al., 1990; Khantzian, 2001). He described this population as having four core psychological deficits, in:

- self-esteem
- affect tolerance
- self-care
- interpersonal functioning.

These difficulties reflect core problems in self-regulation, and have led some practitioners in the field to argue that substance use disorders can be best understood as attachment disorders (Flores, 2001).

When a client's psychological vulnerabilities and substance use disorders are addressed together at the outset of treatment, there are many potential benefits:

- Early identification and treatment of help-rejecting behaviours may increase the likelihood of the person's remaining in treatment.
- Discussions covering a broader range of the person's experience, beyond the substance use disorder, may be experienced by the client as more relevant to the totality of his or her daily struggles.
- Developing a greater capacity for affect tolerance and interpersonal relatedness may decrease the person's need to manage painful affects through alcohol use.

- The initial challenges of sobriety often elicit experiences of loss, guilt and re-examination of one's life, which are better tolerated with the help of meaning and understanding gained through psychological exploration.
- A psychological model that focuses on the study of repetitive, maladaptive patterns of relating reduces the risk of impasses and destructive interactions with treatment providers.
- Increasing the person's social support and relatedness by focusing on interpersonal functioning enhances the potential for durable sobriety by reducing isolation.

With any treatment, however, the benefits must be weighed against the risks. Psychological therapies that focus on characteristic maladaptive relationship patterns may increase the client's anxiety. Therefore, we have introduced a careful, step-wise approach to the treatment. In the early stages the focus is on increasing the structure within the group, with specific interventions to address group members' drinking and to help support their efforts toward sobriety. It is only in the middle stage of the group work that members are encouraged to give interpersonal feedback.

Another caveat is that we do not recommend administering this treatment to clients who are unstable, including those who are severely depressed and actively suicidal. Also, it is important that withdrawal symptoms be controlled, through either psychosocial or biological interventions.

Several authors have outlined group psychotherapy treatments that integrate a psychological focus with the disease model of substance dependence (Flores & Mahon, 1993; Khantzian et al., 1990; Matano, 1997; Matano & Yalom, 1991). The effectiveness of this model is supported by several studies and reports (Brandsma & Pattison, 1985; Brown & Yalom, 1977; Flores & Mahon, 1993; Kadden et al., 1989; Khantzian et al., 1990; Sandahl et al., 1998; Vanicelli, 1988; Yalom et al., 1978).

In addition, this approach is supported by a small, randomized controlled pilot study completed by the present authors (Malat et al., 1999a). That study compared the effectiveness of the IGT approach with that of structured relapse prevention (SRP), a psychoeducational and cognitive-behavioural approach, for people with concurrent alcohol dependence and mental health problems (Annis et al., 1996). Each group treatment was administered for eight weeks. IGT was delivered, in 16 sessions versus eight sessions for SRP, following a manual that the authors had designed for the study (Malat et al., 1999b).

The results were promising. IGT had significantly better rates of treatment retention (93 per cent versus 27 per cent, $p < .001$) and attendance (82 per cent versus 43 per cent, $p < .001$), in comparison to SRP (however, the SRP manual was not specifically designed for clients with concurrent mental health concerns). Also, members of the IGT group achieved significant reductions in drinking and other measures of mental health, which were maintained at eight-month follow-up. For example, the number of drinking days, heavy drinking days (more than five drinks in a day) and Brief Symptom Inventory scores were all significantly reduced. These results support our belief that people with alcohol dependence can benefit from psychological treatments, without necessarily succumbing to the hazard of increased drinking as a result of anxiety generated by increased personal awareness.

This chapter is divided into three sections. The first section outlines interpersonal theory, while the second describes how treatment follows from the theory. The third section describes the modifications made to IGT for people with alcohol dependence.

INTERPERSONAL THEORY

Contemporary interpersonal theory evolved from the concepts of Harry Stack Sullivan (1953), who studied the behaviour that emerges between people as they interact. Sullivan postulated the concept of the therapist as a "participant-observer" and the clinical interaction as the appropriate focus of therapy. As participants in the process of therapy, both the therapist and the client influence the behaviour of the other in a mutually reinforcing cycle. As an observer, the therapist focuses on how the client interacts in the current moment, not just on what the client says.

This approach provides much more information about a client's interpersonal style than the client is able to report directly. Body language, facial expressions, voice tone and the therapist's own subjective experience provide vital information about the client's relationships.

The cognitive-interpersonal schema

As a result of early childhood experience, each person develops a unique cognitive-interpersonal schema that operates as a covert "blueprint" for relationships, and that is aimed at maintaining "secure relatedness"—security and satisfaction in relationships with others and with the world around us—and avoiding anxiety (Safran & Segal, 1990). The schema consists of two elements:

- beliefs about the self in relation to others
- ways of behaving and communicating with others.

Behaviour follows beliefs and a self-perpetuating pattern unfolds.

A related aspect of interpersonal theory is the concept of "self-verification," which refers to the fact that people behave in their various relationships in ways that are familiar. They seek to bolster their sense of predictability, control and safety. These familiar ways of behaving persist, whether they reinforce in the person a positive or a negative self-concept (Giesler & Swann, 1999). Experiences of the self that are unfamiliar or linked with disapproval are typically avoided, since they may signal rejection and abandonment, and therefore cause anxiety.

For example, a boy whose parents are depressed and overwhelmed may learn that the only way to elicit a caring response, or to feel attuned to his parents, is to be quiet, subdued and depressive. If he becomes highly emotional, he feels threatened and expects to be sent away. As he grows older, he keeps a low profile—an interpersonal behaviour that has developed to maintain relatedness and avoid anxiety.

When a cognitive-interpersonal schema is maladaptive, the person can become trapped in it. Despite a wish for flexibility and growth, pathological patterns of relating may be deeply ingrained, blinding the person to other ways of relating, and leading him or her to continue to relate—and to be related to by others—in the same ways (Kiesler, 1996). The person's selective inattention to schema-disconfirming experience consolidates the status quo, and has the power to extinguish new interpersonal responses from others through the failure to recognize interpersonal reinforcement of new behaviours or experiences.

The interpersonal circle

Many factors combine to influence interpersonal interactions, including the nature of the social situation and the personal history of each participant. Because of this multiplicity of factors, it is difficult to predict precisely how people will interact in a given situation, but in general people show characteristic patterns of relatedness. Furthermore, the way one person behaves toward another pressures the other person to respond in a predictable way.

This pattern can be seen in the empirically derived "Interpersonal Circle." Interpersonal style is represented on two axes: affiliation, ranging from friendly to hostile, and control, ranging from dominant to submissive (Kiesler, 1996). A person's composite interpersonal behaviour may fall anywhere along each of these two intersecting axes, and will evoke a predictable response in another person. The behaviour of one person on the affiliation axis is typically matched in the other person; for example, friendly behaviour usually evokes a friendly response, and hostile behaviour is likely to evoke a hostile response. The person's behaviour on the control axis, in contrast, tends to evoke the *opposite* behaviour in the other person; for example, if one person behaves in a dominant manner, the other will feel pressured to take a submissive role, and vice versa. This interpersonal "pull" of a behavioural response is called "complementarity."

Complementarity helps to explain why a person with a rigid and repetitive maladaptive cognitive-interpersonal schema often complains of the same recurring problem in relationship after relationship. The person's schema also operates in the treatment situation, pulling the therapist or other group members to respond in a predictable way: the client relates in the same way that he or she has always related to others, unconsciously "testing" to see if the therapist or group members will respond as others have. This is termed the "transference test" (Weiss, 1993). The client's maladaptive schema may be either confirmed or disconfirmed by therapy, depending on whether the therapist "fails" or "passes" this transference test. To fail the test is to become engaged in the client's maladaptive relational style as others have; to pass the test is to provide a new, unexpected relational experience that disconfirms the client's long-held beliefs.

The maladaptive transaction cycle

As we have discussed above, the client's cognitive-interpersonal schema produces rigid, maladaptive interpersonal behaviours. These patterns are not readily altered by new experiences, and recruit predictable responses from others, generating a "maladaptive transaction cycle" (MTC). The following examples from group therapy sessions illustrate the three mechanisms that perpetuate this cycle:

- complementarity
- non-complementary antagonism
- selective inattention.

COMPLEMENTARITY

> Brian was afraid that if he got emotionally close to people, he would get hurt. When he drank, his fear of others decreased and he was able to achieve a false sense of connectedness.
>
> In the group, he was detached and aloof; he paid little attention to what was going on, seemed to have his mind elsewhere and did not become involved in group interactions. The other group members felt that Brian didn't care about them or the group. His behaviour puzzled and angered them, leading them to confront Brian and ask angrily, "Why are you here?"
>
> The group's response to Brian's behaviour was complementary: on the affiliation axis Brian's apparent hostility was matched by the group's hostility, and on the control axis Brian's quiet submissiveness evoked a reciprocal response of dominance from the group.

NON-COMPLEMENTARY ANTAGONISM

If the "pull" of complementarity is experienced as too controlling, the other person becomes frustrated and attempts to extricate himself or herself. This is termed "non-complementary antagonism."

> Jack presented as withdrawn and quiet during the initial group meetings. Drinking was a means through which Jack expressed his disappointment at others and gained relief from his suffering, since he lacked the interpersonal skills to elicit soothing responses from others.
>
> In the group, his initial behaviour did initially elicit warm, caretaking responses, particularly from the female members. However, his behaviour in the group did not change.
>
> By not reciprocating interest or concern, Jack extinguished others' interest, and the group members gradually withdrew from their interactions with Jack, confirming his belief that others do not care.

SELECTIVE INATTENTION

Selective inattention arises when a group member is being treated in a new, unfamiliar way, but neglects to notice and acknowledge it because the interaction contradicts his or her rigid beliefs about relationships and might generate anxiety and a sense of unpredictability.

> Lori had experiences that should have disconfirmed her maladaptive beliefs but, because of her high anxiety, she either did not recognize the significance of these experiences or dismissed it. Lori was so preoccupied with being rejected that she failed to notice the warmth and support of other group members. Alcohol was a trusted and safe "helper" when she was anxious—as opposed to people, whom she saw as being "rejecting."
>
> When the group first began meeting, she sat next to Dawn; then, after a few sessions, Lori playfully and pleasantly stated she would change seats for the sake of variety.
>
> Several weeks later, Lori admitted that she believed that Dawn was upset with her for changing seats. Dawn was surprised and responded that this was not the case. Although Dawn's behaviour toward Lori had been warm throughout the group, Lori failed to recognize that Dawn had given her no reason to believe she was upset. Lori brooded privately for several weeks before saying anything to give Dawn the opportunity to disconfirm her fear.

ELEMENTS OF INTERPERSONAL GROUP THERAPY

The therapist's observation of his or her own response to a group member's behaviour can reveal important information about the person's interpersonal problems, and bring clarity to "blind spots" in the person's self-report. However, when the therapist feels himself or herself responding to a group member's interpersonal behaviour, it is important that the therapist be able to tell the difference between consensual responses that are elicited by the person, and idiosyncratic ones that derive from the therapist's own cognitive-interpersonal schema. Only those elicited by the group member help provide insight into his or her MTC.

There is a risk that the therapist may become a full participant in the MTC, rather than retaining his or her observer role. Therapists, like others, may become "hooked" by the pull of a client's interpersonal behaviour. If the therapist responds to the pull as others do, then therapy can worsen—rather than solve—the person's problem. The process outlined below can help the therapist and the group members to become "unhooked," model the process of reflection (rather than reenactment) and disrupt the person's MTC.

The impact message

The first step is the therapist's exploration of his or her own covert response, or the "impact message" of the client's interpersonal behaviour. The impact message may be identified as consisting of four elements (Kiesler, 1996):

1. feelings evoked in the therapist by the group member (e.g., the therapist notices, "I feel angry toward this person.")
2. action tendencies evoked in the therapist toward the group member (e.g., the therapist notices, "I feel like rescuing this person.")
3. perceived messages evoked in the therapist by the group member—what the person seems to want the therapist to do or not to do (e.g., the therapist thinks, "It feels like this person wants me to take her side against her husband.")
4. fantasies or images the therapist has about what is going on with the group member (e.g., as the therapist lectures the member about coming late to the session, the therapist has an image of a parent scolding a misbehaving child.).

Metacommunication

Once the impact message has been privately explored and identified, the therapist attempts to link it with specific instances of the group member's interpersonal behaviours. These behaviours may be overt or subtle, verbal or non-verbal (including intonation, gesture and body posture). When the link is clear, the therapist elucidates the impact of the person's communication. This "communication about communication" is called "metacommunication." It sets the stage for group feedback and models for the group members the processing of relationship data.

Metacommunication is one of the main strategies that help the therapist identify and interrupt the MTC of the client in treatment. It is a core therapeutic tool in IGT. It is critical that the therapist metacommunicate with the group member in a manner that is collaborative, exploratory, clear and respectful, but intentionally tentative. It should avoid blaming or aggression.

In normal social communication, metacommunication is taboo. It involves a high degree of intimacy, authenticity and transparency, and demands a partial suspension of engagement in order for the communication to be described. Metacommunication may be seen by some people as a prelude to criticism and rejection, or as a controlling or critical intrusion on their autonomy and their freedom from having certain behaviours noticed (Yalom, 1995; Yalom & Leszcz, 2005).

In order to decrease the risk of negative enactments with group members, it is particularly important that the therapist reflect upon and process any intense feelings toward the group member before metacommunicating. The therapeutic alliance and group cohesion should be well established. The risk of the person's feeling judged, blamed or criticized decreases when the feedback is careful and considered, as in the example below.

Ron was in his early 50s, single and unemployed. He described many examples of his parents' unavailability and neglect, and his chronic difficulties in relationships—particularly with others losing interest in him. As Ron spoke of his difficulties, the therapist tried to listen but found himself growing detached and bored, as did others in the group. The therapist realized that he, along with the group, had become temporarily hooked in Ron's MTC and was responding exactly like others in Ron's life.

This became an important opportunity to get unhooked and to model reflection for the group. The impact message (in the form of feelings and action tendencies evoked in the therapist by the group member) was disinterest, detachment and neglect. The therapist focused on Ron's interpersonal behaviour to try to identify why he felt this way. He noticed that Ron spoke in a rapid, pressured fashion, leaving no room for two-way communication. A further impact message (in the form of a perceived message evoked in the therapist by the group member) was that Ron did not expect feedback. After some thought, the therapist was able to tell Ron about the impact of his patterns of interpersonal communication.

The therapist proceeded as follows: "Sometimes difficulties that people experience in their outside lives appear during their meetings here. This creates a unique opportunity to explore how things may go wrong. Is it all right for me to give you some feedback? As I listen to you speak, I notice that you change subjects quickly, leaving little room for me to respond; it feels almost as if you don't expect much feedback from us."

Ron responded that he changes the topic quickly out of fear that others won't respond, since that is what he usually experiences. Alcohol helped Ron to access some solitary enjoyment and distraction from these painful interpersonal anxieties. With sobriety, he needed to confront his interpersonal authorship of that which he assumed and dreaded—that others were not interested in him.

As he began to recognize how his own interpersonal behaviour elicited the very problem he feared, he slowly shifted his style, and the group felt that there was more opportunity to actually engage him.

Four key principles

IGT capitalizes on the group setting to bring about interpersonal learning and improve group members' self-understanding. With each person in the group playing a key role as a participant-observer, the group experience offers unique opportunities to illuminate maladaptive patterns of interpersonal behaviour. Four key principles, outlined below, underlie IGT treatment:

- group cohesion
- the group as a social microcosm
- working in the here-and-now
- the corrective emotional experience

(Leszcz, 1992; Leszcz & Malat, 2001).

GROUP COHESION

Interpersonal feedback and learning through metacommunication is a process that unfolds only when the members experience the group as cohesive. Group cohesion consists of two components:

- a sense of collaboration, acceptance and safety within the group, as reflected by an emotional bond of trust among members, and between members and the therapist
- a common experience of effectiveness and competence derived through working together at a task. When a group is cohesive, psychotherapeutic opportunities emerge.

For many people who are isolated and disconnected, the experience of being part of a meaningful group may in itself be therapeutic, in addition to setting the stage for interpersonal learning. The therapist strives to quickly create an atmosphere of group cohesion, and to maintain it throughout the life of the group. The first step is to take an active, structured approach that promotes a commitment to punctuality, regular attendance, confidentiality and respect. In every session, the therapist works to maintain a balance between stimulation of affect and cognitive understanding, and to model a warm, reliable, emotionally available and appropriately transparent therapeutic style. The therapist also models sensitive and respectful metacommunication, allowing the group members to learn how to give effective interpersonal feedback.

Group cohesion allows members to bring themselves as they genuinely are into the life of the group, and into the treatment process. In a cohesive group, each member feels included, and individual growth is encouraged. Individual members' attachment to and comfort within the group has been shown to contribute more to a positive outcome than the experience of the group itself having a positive working climate (Mackenzie & Tschuschke, 1993). It is the individual experience of connection that counts.

Out-of-group contact between members can have an impact on group cohesion, and so must be reported. Although members are allowed to help one another outside of group meetings, there is a risk that certain tensions and behaviours within the group may be diverted, taking away the opportunity for exploration and interpersonal learning. As tension builds in the group during its middle phase of interpersonal learning, members are tempted to talk in smaller subgroups outside of the group, where they may feel safer and unchallenged, but at the cost of undermining the sense of safety in the group. If this occurs, the primacy of the whole group must take priority.

THE GROUP AS A SOCIAL MICROCOSM

People's characteristic patterns of relating are, inevitably, reproduced in a treatment setting. The group functions as a social laboratory, in that it permits real-life study of interpersonal behaviour in an emotionally alive fashion. In the group setting, exploration of interpersonal style can go well beyond the limits of self-report. Further, the group members' perceptions compensate for any blind spots in the therapist's insight into the person's behaviour.

Clients are more likely to display their full repertoire of interpersonal behaviour in a group where there is unstructured, spontaneous interaction. Any and every behaviour within the group, including the behaviour of the therapist, is treated as a potential subject for exploration. Conflict, disappointment, anxiety and other interpersonal difficulties between group members are treated as learning opportunities. The group rarely *creates* interpersonal difficulties; rather the group, by functioning as a social microcosm, *illuminates* the difficulties.

WORKING IN THE HERE-AND-NOW

Working in the here-and-now is the core strategy of IGT; it is the engine that drives the group beyond simply offering support, advice and commiseration, and that opens group members to change. When a group works in the here-and-now, the focus is on the interactions between group members as they happen. This allows interpersonal behaviour to be experienced and illuminated, followed by reflection and cognitive integration.

Group members are likely to resist working in the here-and-now. One reason is that the focus on interactions as they happen is contrary to the style of communication we are used to—it is more intimate, engaged and anxiety provoking. Another factor is the emotional vulnerability and risk involved in both providing and receiving interpersonal feedback. To metacommunicate, the feedback provider must disclose his or her emotional response to the other person, without knowing how the disclosure will be received. At the same time, the receiver of feedback comes face-to-face with how his or her interpersonal style affects others.

Early in the life of the group, the therapist can counter the factors that lead to resistance by providing guidance and modelling on how to deliver effective interpersonal feedback. This helps group members learn how to metacommunicate with each other in a respectful, collaborative, non-condemning fashion. Members must learn that feedback need not be hostile and that it can provide opportunities for meaningful expressions of support and engagement, in addition to interpersonal learning. To be effective, interpersonal feedback must:

- clearly and honestly convey feelings or reactions to specific verbal or nonverbal behaviours
- avoid value judgments or opinions speculating about the person's behaviour pattern
- invite change, rather than demand it (Rothke, 1986).

Working in the here-and-now involves the therapeutic techniques of "activation" and "process illumination." Activation plunges members of the group into the experience of intimately relating in an emotionally alive, spontaneous manner. Activation stimulates group members, inviting them to take risks, express feelings, disclose fears and become fully engaged with one another in the group setting. To create an atmosphere of activation, the therapist encourages members to comment on specific reactions to each other. Discussion is redirected from outside issues to in-group themes, from generic to personal, from the vague to the specific.

Process illumination moves the group back into a self-reflective "loop" to clarify, interpret and cognitively integrate the activation experience. The therapist:

- actively intervenes following an interpersonal sequence to illuminate what happened and to help the members to integrate it cognitively
- models metacommunication
- synthesizes feedback from other group members to help the members integrate it
- highlights and endorses new interpersonal behaviours that challenge restrictive schemas.

Through process illumination, group members develop a more adaptive cognitive-interpersonal map to guide them in interactions outside the group setting.

The techniques of activation and process illumination are not distinct, and often interact and overlap with one another. For example, the therapist who gives a group member feedback is working in process illumination, but the person's unpredictable response to the feedback shows that activation is also at work. In another example, the behaviour of one group member giving feedback to another may in turn become the subject of process illumination.

Within any given moment in the group, multiple opportunities for feedback exist. The value of feedback depends on a number of factors, including the vulnerability and readiness of the particular group member and the developmental level of the group. The therapist often has to determine how and from whom feedback would best be provided at any given time. For example, in response to an interpersonal sequence in the group, the therapist may:

- deepen the process by inviting a member of the group to reflect on his or her own experience
- invite specified other members to comment
- provide feedback himself or herself
- open things up to the group as a whole.

THE CORRECTIVE EMOTIONAL EXPERIENCE

When a group member is fully engaged and authentic, and his or her interpersonal style is well illuminated, the therapist and other group members can help to move the person toward the "corrective emotional experience" (Alexander & French, 1946). Such an experience disconfirms the maladaptive beliefs a person has about himself or herself and about others in the group, and leads to the modification of the person's maladaptive cognitive-interpersonal schema.

The pull of complementarity can make it hard to disconfirm a group member's maladaptive beliefs. For example, if the person's behaviour is hostile, the therapist and other group members are likely to respond to the person with hostility, which may confirm—rather than disconfirm—the person's maladaptive beliefs that the world is uncaring and adversarial. For therapy to be effective, the group must resist total engagement with the client's provoking pull and instead seek a deeper, empathic appreciation of what is occurring within the person. The therapist's role is to model this capacity by providing non-blaming interpersonal feedback, and by working with the person to explore the beliefs that shape the behaviour.

The corrective emotional experience is not to be contrived. The principles of the corrective emotional experience are rooted in authentic engagement and are becoming a core aspect of contemporary relational models of psychotherapy (Mitchell, 1993; Weiss, 1993).

The therapist's awareness of each group member's cognitive-interpersonal schema allows the therapist to note interpersonal behaviours that are new, unexpected and inconsistent with the person's maladaptive beliefs. Such behaviours can be subtle, but may nonetheless indicate that the person is risking new behaviour and new forms of engagement. It is a key therapist task to ensure that group members do not stay hooked negatively and that the emergence of healthier communication is reinforced.

The process of disconfirming a maladaptive schema can be very moving for the group member. When the process is successful, the person's confidence, assertiveness and courage within the group can increase. As this emboldenment is welcomed and confirmed within the group, the client becomes more able and willing to transfer his or her learning to life outside the group.

Interpersonal learning

When the group is guided by the four principles discussed above, the process of interpersonal learning unfolds. The following series of steps illustrates this process for a particular client.

1. The client manifests his or her characteristic maladaptive style in the group social microcosm through verbal, paraverbal and non-verbal communication.
2. This stimulates reaction and hooked responses from others in the group.
3. Here-and-now exploration occurs: the group focuses on the client's experience and beliefs, and members give feedback about the impact of the client's behaviour.
4. This can lead to three possible avenues of change for the client:
   - Disconfirmation of the expected outcome of an interpersonal interaction leads to a corrective emotional experience and a modified cognitive-interpersonal schema.
   - An increased awareness of the client's own role in creating his or her interpersonal difficulties leads to a sense of responsibility and empowerment, and the capacity to make broader interpersonal choices.
   - The group's exploration of the client's maladaptive beliefs, including the developmental origins of those beliefs, illuminates what his or her beliefs are, and also increases the client's ability to distinguish the past, which can't be changed, from the present, which can.

5. New, more adaptive interpersonal behaviours emerge.
6. The client risks new interpersonal behaviour, and the response from the group is positive (or at least is not negative, as the client had expected), which deepens the corrective emotional experience. This solidifies the modifications of the client's cognitive-interpersonal schema and broadens his or her interpersonal repertoire.
7. An adaptive spiral emerges: changes demonstrated in the group begin to generalize in the person's life, including a greater feeling of boldness, greater self-awareness, greater engagement with self and others, and enhanced self-understanding (Weiss, 1993).

TREATING ALCOHOL DEPENDENCE WITH INTERPERSONAL GROUP THERAPY—KEY MODIFICATIONS

It is a significant clinical challenge to harness the power of the interpersonal approach while maintaining a close, structured focus on a client's drinking problems. Although excessive focus on interpersonal issues can jeopardize the progress made in reducing drinking, exclusive attention to reducing drinking fails to address interpersonal difficulties. Khantzian et al. (1990) argues that addressing interpersonal vulnerabilities safeguards against the client's "psychological relapse." This lies at the heart of relapse prevention in people with substance use problems. Providing IGT to clients with alcohol dependence requires skill in establishing a link between interpersonal problems and drinking. The therapist needs to know, based on the clinical situation, when to emphasize drinking and when to emphasize interpersonal issues.

Six key modifications to the earlier-noted principles are required to apply IGT to the treatment of concurrent interpersonal problems and alcohol dependence:

- Establish a link between drinking patterns and the MTC.
- Develop a core group norm for drinking goals.
- Provide regular, structured monitoring of drinking.
- Explore mild intoxication but do not tolerate disruptive behaviour.
- Carefully modulate anxiety levels to reduce the risk of relapse.
- Encourage and integrate participation in Alcoholics Anonymous.

These strategies are summarized below.

Establish a link between drinking patterns and the MTC

The therapist's search for links between the client's maladaptive interpersonal behaviour and his or her drinking problems begins with the first individual pre-group meeting, and continues until the final meeting. Over this time, the therapist continually develops understanding of how the client's interpersonal and drinking problems are linked, and communicates this understanding to the client. The following example illustrates the link between the MTC and drinking, which must be actively sought and highlighted through the therapy.

> Sarah, a successful professional in her late 30s, presented with alcohol dependence and frustrations in her relationships. Over time, Sarah revealed that she carried an entrenched view of herself as "damaged goods." Along with this self-view came a fear and expectation that if she were to expose her true self, others would be unresponsive toward her or would reject her.
>
> Sarah's interpersonal behaviour in the group alternated between domineering, compulsive caretaking and quiet, detached superiority. Although she wished her efforts to help others would be returned, she did not say anything or give any signals to indicate that she needed help or support herself. The predictable complementary response of other group members was to either passively accept her help or to pull away from her detached style.
>
> As a result, Sarah felt neglected and became increasingly frustrated, reinforcing her view of herself as "messed up." She attempted to soothe her "messed-up mind" by drinking alone at home in the evening, since she "did not deserve any better." Of course, this further worsened her negative self-image.
>
> Eventually, after several members confronted her about her limited engagement in the group, she risked talking about her fears and frustrations. She was surprised to learn that the other group members responded positively to her vulnerability and seemed to value her more than when she had only tried to help them. One member told her, "Before, you were above us like a queen on a throne; now I know more about you and find you more interesting and likeable." As Sarah became more effective in communicating her interpersonal needs for nurturance and support, both her compulsive helping and quiet detachment diminished, along with her drinking.

Develop a core group norm for drinking goals

Whether the goal is harm reduction or abstinence, IGT for clients with alcohol problems works best when all group members share the same drinking goal. Groups with a shared goal have several advantages over groups in which some members have a goal of controlled drinking, and others a goal of abstinence. For example, when a new group begins with an explicit shared drinking goal, members are able to relate through their common goal. This helps to develop engagement and trust among group members and to establish group cohesion, which is essential for interpersonal work. A shared goal also clarifies the drinking goal of each group member, which helps members to support and confront one another about their drinking.

Many clients wish they could drink in a controlled fashion, but fail to do so. In a group with mixed goals, members who continue to drink contribute to the frustration and envy of clients in early sobriety. A client whose goal was abstinence may rationalize during the early stages of a relapse that he or she has changed the goal to controlled drinking. For example, in one group, Mark started enthusiastically and reported that he had stopped drinking, but several weeks later he returned to drinking. When the therapist asked him about his drinking, Mark admitted that he had noticed other group members were not committed to sobriety and continued to drink. This frustrated him because he had had expectations of an abstinent group; furthermore, he did not want to stand out as being sober, but preferred to be "in the middle."

A group with mixed goals may develop a split between the "abstainers" and the "controlled drinkers," and may deteriorate into a polarized state, with each side denigrating, dismissing or envying the other. Such conflict over drinking goals may also result in one or more group members' becoming scapegoats, distracting attention away from interpersonal issues. For example, if a member with a maladaptive domineering, controlling style becomes the spokesperson for abstinence, it may be difficult to separate an examination of his interpersonal style from the conflict about drinking goals.

A lack of clarity about drinking goals in a mixed group may interfere with opportunities for interpersonal growth. For example, a client who fears being rejected as a failure may say her goal is controlled drinking, even though her genuine wish is to be abstinent. Because she is too ashamed to disclose her difficulties in remaining abstinent, she misses the opportunity to learn through sharing her failure, and to discover that she would be more valued for her genuineness.

Clients who refuse to agree to a group norm of abstinence are best served in a group that shares their goals. If a member of an abstinent group changes her goal and decides to return to drinking, the group should be invited into a dialogue with her about her reasoning. What are the advantages and disadvantages of drinking? What has led to this shift in her goal? Other members should be encouraged to share their opinions. Feedback about drinking and its risks may have more impact if delivered by other members struggling with the same problem.

If a client resumes drinking, the therapist should try to identify the factors behind the client's decision. For example, does this client's defiance or help-rejecting behaviour mask underlying shame or low self-worth? Does the person's decision to drink represent resignation in response to his or her hopelessness about achieving abstinence? If such factors are present, the client should be offered further support and help, in addition to the group. If the client remains firm in the conviction to return to drinking, he or she should be encouraged to think seriously about the decision. Continuing in the group is not viable in this situation. But before being discharged from the group, this client should be invited to return for two more group sessions to further explore the consequences of his or her action.

The struggles that unfold with such a client may also be taken as opportunities for the here-and-now exploration of other members' responses. For example, what is it like for them to deal with someone who refuses to go along with the group's plan? How do they experience witnessing someone's deciding to do something harmful to himself or herself? What is the impact on them of this member's being discharged from the group?

Provide regular, structured monitoring of drinking

Although spontaneity and lack of rigid structure are essential in an interpersonal group to help elicit members' characteristic interpersonal patterns, this approach can also make it easier for clients to conceal drinking. Therefore regular, structured monitoring of drinking is required.

Weekly self-report diary cards are one way to maintain a focus on drinking, without producing unnecessary embarrassment or shame through public disclosure to the group. Group members are expected to hand in their weekly diary cards to the therapist at the beginning of every meeting. The diary card records the number of standard drinks the person consumed each day, and whether the drinks were beer, wine or spirits. After the group members hand in their cards, they are invited, but not obligated, to discuss any difficulties they are having with alcohol. This process allows members to control the pace at which they work on their drinking, without having to discuss it in the group every week.

If a member repeatedly reports drinking on the diary cards but does not discuss it in the group, the therapist should explore what maladaptive beliefs may be stopping the person discussing relapses. For example, the client may harbour fears of admitting vulnerability and failure. The therapist should try to involve the person in an empathic dialogue by stating that he or she seems to be struggling with drinking. If the person continues to have difficulties talking about his or her drinking, the therapist should attempt to explore any concerns or fears the person may have about disclosing to the group. What does it mean to the person to be relapsing? What kind of reactions does he or she expect, and from which group members?

For example, Megan, in her early 20s, presented with a quiet, undemanding but attentive style in the group. She had significant difficulty in stopping her drinking, but feared other members would criticize her if she spoke in the group about her difficulties. This interpersonal pattern was common in Megan's life. She often attempted to resolve her anxieties in isolation, rather than risking censure by disclosing to others. Gradually, she became more comfortable discussing her drinking problems in the group, and realized that sharing vulnerability with others could yield new solutions and could sometimes alleviate distress more effectively than alcohol could.

Explore mild intoxication but do not tolerate disruptive behaviour

When the therapist notices or suspects that a group member has been drinking, the therapist should ask the person about it in a straightforward, non-critical fashion.

This lets the group member know that others notice when he or she has been drinking, which helps to counteract denial of the impact of drinking. A client who drinks before coming to a group session may be indirectly seeking help through his or her intoxication. The person may fear being rejected if he or she asks for help directly. By drinking, the person communicates helplessness without accepting the responsibility of asking for help (Gorad et al., 1971).

If the group member admits to drinking, the therapist has a dilemma, which may be shared with the group: the client's drinking is not helpful for the group, but the therapist nonetheless wants to be supportive to the client. Members are invited to explore the effect of having an intoxicated person in the group, and to decide together whether the person should remain. This dialogue draws out members' responses, and shows how they resolve a tense situation. The therapist might ask, "Does seeing this person intoxicated increase your sense of vulnerability or your urge to drink, or does it make you even more determined to achieve sobriety?"

If the group decides that the member should leave, the therapist should state that he or she hopes to see the person next week, and follow up with a phone call the next day. If the group decides that the member can remain for the rest of the meeting, it is the therapist's responsibility to limit the person's participation until he or she is sober and more ready to benefit from the group.

If the client is extremely intoxicated or disruptive, the therapist should ask the person to leave, pointing out that it would not be helpful for the client or the group if he or she were to remain. Again, the therapist should follow up with a call the next day and invite the client back to the next group. If the client continues to have difficulty arriving sober, the therapist may need to suspend the person's attendance and meet with him or her individually instead. It is important, though, that the client be re-integrated into the group as soon as possible.

Carefully modulate anxiety levels to reduce the risk of relapse

IGT for clients with alcohol dependence presents a dilemma: on one hand, realizing the potential of interpersonal learning requires that clients engage in anxiety-provoking experiences; on the other hand, such anxiety may increase the risk of drinking. Therapists can, however, minimize their clients' anxiety by means of carefully pacing the client's emotional arousal, with a particular emphasis on the early stages of the group experience:

- An individual pre-group preparation meeting between the client and the therapist helps anticipate and normalize many common anxieties about group treatment. Clients often fear rejection, forced disclosure or contagion by other group members' negative emotions; believe that group is a second-rate treatment; or have anxieties about confidentiality. This meeting can also foster a therapeutic alliance by building agreement about the goals, tasks and nature of the relationships in treatment.
- In the early stages of the group, the therapist provides structure through activities

and educative interventions, such as explaining how to give interpersonal feedback.

- In the early stages, there is a greater emphasis on the homogeneity of drinking problems and discussions of outside issues (there-and-then) than on group behaviour (here-and-now).
- To reduce the risk of relapse between meetings, the last few minutes of each group session focus on cognitive integration, winding down and troubleshooting. Group members are encouraged to help at-risk members develop short-term plans to remain sober. This should occur throughout the life of the group.
- If there is conflict or aggression between group members in the early stages of the group, prior to the establishment of cohesion, the therapist's task is to intervene quickly and ask the members to step back from the conflict. Group members *will* get hooked into each others' maladaptive patterns, and in the early stages they do not possess the skills to metacommunicate effectively. If members react spontaneously, destructive exchanges may result, compromising the safety of the group and inhibiting interpersonal exploration of difficult issues in the future. The therapist can model successful metacommunication by giving interpersonal feedback to those involved in the conflict.
- The therapist should help marginalized or withdrawn group members feel related to the group as early as possible, since their ability to function as part of the group will impact their long-term outcome. Group members who are withdrawn are, paradoxically, very noticeable to other members. Their silence is often a source of unspoken tension in the group, which contributes to their own anxiety and to the anxiety of other members, who worry about them.
- In order to help group members cognitively integrate the group experience, the therapist attempts to share his or her understanding of clients' cognitive-interpersonal schemas throughout the group treatment. A written summary at the beginning and the end of the group treatment may help group members process and integrate some of the group experiences in a calmer state, as opposed to the emotional intensity of the group process.

The following example illustrates how levels of anxiety within a group can be carefully modulated to allow for maximum interpersonal benefit, while minimizing the risk of relapse.

> Bob, who was in his mid-30s, dominated the early group sessions with many disclosures and a loud, aggressive interpersonal style. He interrupted other members and "talked over them" rather than listening to their feedback. Bob reported that outside of the group, people did not seem to listen to him. Drinking in social situations helped Bob temporarily forget how frightened he was of alienating himself from others.
>
> The therapist was concerned that the other members would become increasingly frustrated by Bob's style in the group, since their only options were either to respond aggressively or to drop out of the group. At this early stage, it was important to minimize the other members' frustration and to main-

> tain their participation and interest.
>
> The therapist decided to intervene by modelling interpersonal feedback to Bob. The therapist relied on the impact message of frustration and boredom that he was experiencing during Bob's disclosures. He said, "Bob, I'd like to take this opportunity to give you some feedback. Often, we get a window onto people's relationship difficulties in the group itself. I appreciate that you have presented yourself today in such an honest fashion. I now feel I have a better understanding of why people don't listen to you. As I was listening to you, I began to shut down a bit myself because I felt there was no space or time for my feedback. It seems that you fear that others won't listen to you, so you turn up the volume even louder. However, the louder you turn up the volume, the less people listen. But when you drink, you temporarily forget your fears of other people being turned off, and so you feel a little safer."

Note that the therapist links the interpersonal impact of Bob's disengaging the listener to, first, his specific behaviours of speaking loudly and not letting others get a word in and, second, the misuse of alcohol that follows. This intervention helped Bob recognize his own role in creating his difficulties. Following this intervention, Bob's domineering style subsided, and other members became more comfortable giving interpersonal feedback.

Encourage and integrate participation in Alcoholics Anonymous

IGT meshes well with the 12-step, mutual help group approach of Alcoholics Anonymous (AA). The principles underlying each approach have much in common (Matano & Yalom, 1991; Freimuth, 2000; Yalom & Leszcz, 2005). In addition, aspects of the 12-step approach are very similar to the interpersonal approach, notably:

- the shared emphasis on acknowledging interpersonal deficits and personal limits
- self-examination to initiate a process of repair
- maintenance of healthier, mutual, empathic relatedness.

The two approaches work well together in helping clients achieve abstinence and social integration. Group members should be actively encouraged to attend AA and to support each other in attending AA meetings during the group treatment. Note too that familiarity with AA language is essential for the therapist to retain credibility with clients. The main difference that needs to be emphasized and explained to clients starting an IGT group is the emphasis on interpersonal feedback between group members, which stands in contrast to the AA rule of "no cross talk" between group members.

CONCLUSION

This chapter introduces the use of psychological interventions to help clients with concurrent alcohol dependence and interpersonal problems. The theory and techniques described here are drawn from a rich base of literature in the fields of group psychotherapy, psychoanalysis and interpersonal theory. Applying these techniques creates a stimulating and rewarding environment in which clients learn about themselves and develop meaningful ways of relating to others, often for the first time in their lives. The client's goals are typically more ambitious than simply achieving sobriety: with the acquisition of new self-knowledge, clients are able to:

- access their potential to develop a more satisfying and integrated life
- repair interpersonal deficits that promote relapse, and
- repair interpersonal damage caused by their drinking problems.

REFERENCES

Alexander, F. & French, T. (1946). *Psychoanalytic Therapy: Principles and Applications.* New York: Ronald Press.

Annis, H.M., Herie, M.A. & Watkin-Merek, L. (1996). *Structured Relapse Prevention.* Toronto: Addiction Research Foundation.

Brandsma, J.M. & Pattison, E.M. (1985). The outcome of group psychotherapy of alcoholics: An empirical review. *American Journal of Drug and Alcohol Abuse, 11*, 151–162.

Brown, S. & Yalom, I.D. (1977). Interactional group psychotherapy with alcoholics. *Journal of Studies on Alcohol, 38*, 426–456.

Flores, P.J. (2001). Addiction as an attachment disorder: Implications for group therapy. *International Journal of Group Psychotherapy, 51*(1), 63–82.

Flores, P.J. & Mahon, L. (1993). The treatment of addiction in group psychotherapy. *International Journal of Group Psychotherapy, 43*(2), 143–156.

Freimuth, M. (2000). Integrating group psychotherapy and 12-step work: A collaborative approach. *International Journal of Group Psychotherapy, 50*(3), 297–314.

Freud, S. (1957). Remembering, repeating and working through. In J. Strachey (Ed. and Trans.), *Standard Edition of Complete Psychological Works of Sigmund Freud,* Vol. XII (pp. 147–156). London, U.K.: Hogarth Press.

Gabbard, G.O. (1994). *Psychodynamic Psychiatry in Clinical Practice.* Washington, D.C.: American Psychiatric Press.

Galanter, M. (2001). Network therapy for addiction: Bringing family and peer support into office practice. *International Journal of Group Psychotherapy, 51*(1), 101–123.

Giesler, R.B. & Swann, W.B. (1999). Striving for confirmation: The role of self-verification in depression. In T. Joiner & J.C. Coyne (Eds.), *The Interactional Nature of Depression* (pp. 189–217). Washington, D.C.: American Psychological Association.

Gorad, S.L., McCourt, W.F. & Cobb, J.C. (1971). A communications approach to alcoholism. *Quarterly Journal of Studies in Alcohol, 32*, 651–668.

Kadden, R.M., Cooney, N.L., Getter, H. & Litt, M.D. (1989). Matching alcoholics to coping skills or interactional therapies: Posttreatment results. *Journal of Counseling and Clinical Psychology, 57*, 698–704.

Khantzian, E.J. (2001). Reflections on group treatments as corrective emotional experiences for addiction vulnerabilities. *International Journal of Group Psychotherapy, 51*(1), 11–20.

Khantzian, E.J., Halliday, K.S. & McAuliffe, W.E. (1990). *Addiction and the Vulnerable Self.* New York: Guilford Press.

Kiesler, D.J. (1996). *Contemporary Interpersonal Theory and Research: Personality, Psychopathology and Psychotherapy.* New York: John Wiley and Sons.

Klerman, G.L., Weissman, M.M., Rounsaville, B.J. & Chevron, E. (1984). *Interpersonal Psychotherapy of Depression.* New York: Basic Books.

Leszcz, M. (1992). The interpersonal approach to group psychotherapy. *International Journal of Group Psychotherapy, 43*, 37–62.

Leszcz, M. & Malat, J. (2001). The interpersonal model of group psychotherapy. In V. Tschuschke (Ed.), *Praxis der Gruppenpsychotherapie* (pp. 355–369). Frankfurt: George Thieme Verlag.

Mackenzie, K.R. & Tschuschke, V. (1993). Relatedness, group work and outcome in long-term inpatient psychotherapy groups. *Journal of Psychotherapy Practice and Research, 2*(2), 147–156.

Malat, J., Leszcz, M. & Negrete, J.C. (1999a). *Time-limited, modified interpersonal group psychotherapy for the treatment of comorbid alcohol dependence.* Presented at the annual Canadian Psychiatric Association meeting, Montreal, 2001.

Malat, J., Leszcz, M. & Negrete, J.C. (1999b). *Time-limited, modified interpersonal group psychotherapy for the treatment of comorbid alcohol dependence.* Unpublished manuscript.

Matano, R.A. & Yalom, I.D. (1991). Approaches to chemical dependency: Chemical dependency and interactive group therapy—a synthesis. *International Journal of Group Psychotherapy, 41*(3), 269–293.

Matano, R.A. (1997). Interactive group therapy for substance abusers. In J.L. Spira (Ed.), *Group Therapy for Medically Ill Patients* (pp. 296–235). New York: Guilford Press.

Mitchell, S.A. (1993). *Hope and Dread in Psychoanalysis.* New York: Basic Books.

Rothke, S. (1986). The role of interpersonal feedback in group psychotherapy. *International Journal of Group Psychotherapy, 36*, 225–240.

Safran, J.O. & Segal, Z.V. (1990). *Interpersonal Process in Cognitive Therapy.* New York: Basic Books.

Sandahl, C., Herlitz, K., Ahlin, G. & Ronnberg, S. (1998). Time-limited group psychotherapy for moderately alcohol dependent patients: A randomized controlled clinical trial. *Psychotherapy Research, 8*(4), 361–378.

Sullivan, H.S. (1953). *The Interpersonal Theory of Psychiatry.* New York: Norton.

Vanicelli, M. (1982). Group psychotherapy with alcoholics. Special techniques. *Journal of Studies on Alcohol, 43*, 17–37.

Vanicelli, M. (1988). Group therapy aftercare for alcoholic patients. *International Journal of Group Psychotherapy, 61*, 620–630.

Weiss, J. (1993). *How Psychotherapy Works.* New York: Guilford Press

Yalom, I.D. (1995). *The Theory and Practice of Group Psychotherapy* (4th ed.). New York: Basic Books.

Yalom I.D., Bloch, S., Bond, G., Zimmerman, E. & Qualls, B. (1978). Alcoholics in interactional group therapy: An outcome study. *Archives of General Psychiatry, 35*, 419–425.

Yalom, I.D. & Leszcz, M. (2005). *The Theory and Practice of Group Psychotherapy* (5th ed.). New York: Perseus Books.

Chapter 13

The impact of concurrent disorders on the family

CAROLINE P. O'GRADY

INTRODUCTION

Deinstitutionalization and restructuring of the health care system in many countries, including Canada, have led to an increased emphasis on the importance of not only community-based health care providers, but also of informal caregivers.

In the case of mental health problems, families comprise a vitally important health care resource and are being acknowledged as the primary caregivers of relatives who are seriously mentally and emotionally ill (Boydell & Trainor, 1998; Hatfield, 1991, 1997; O'Grady, 2004; Pomeroy & Trainor, 1991). In Canada, up to 72 per cent of people with a mental illness are discharged to the care of their families—an estimated 40 to 60 per cent live with family members for part or all of their lives (Hatfield, 1997).

As the closure of hospitals and the trend of downsizing continue, families will increasingly play a major role in caregiving. Although family caregivers are a vitally important resource in community-based care, few families are prepared emotionally, physically or financially to accommodate the needs of a relative with serious and persistent mental illness (Hatfield, 1997). Such families bear enormous hardships when they assume caregiving responsibilities. These responsibilities, in addition to the nature and extent of the ill relative's various symptoms, can place much stress on families and often result in emotional, physical, social and financial burden (Aviram, 1990; Hobbs, 1997).

This chapter looks at the effects of concurrent substance use and mental health problems on family members. It looks at family members' challenges and needs, and the role they play in recovery, as well as looking at coping strategies, psychoeducation and empowerment for families. It concludes with a description of a study we conducted in the Concurrent Disorders Service at the Centre for Addiction and Mental Health. Throughout the chapter, we have also included first-person accounts from family members interviewed during a study on stigma, concurrent disorders, and family members (O'Grady, 2004); their voices speak eloquently of their challenges, strengths and hope.

THE IMPACT OF MENTAL HEALTH PROBLEMS ON THE FAMILY

Mental health problems can bring frightening changes in how people experience reality, which can affect their relationships and ability to function. They may begin to lose trust in close family members. Changes in perception and mood may sometimes involve paranoia and hallucinations, feelings of anger, drastic mood changes or overwhelming anxiety. It may become difficult for them to make even simple decisions, to complete plans or set goals. They may cut themselves off from the outside world and stop participating in activities that they once enjoyed. They may find it difficult to express their feelings and thoughts, and may retreat into their own inner world. Some people with mental illness become hostile, even with their families, and may act out verbally and in some cases physically.

THE IMPACT OF SUBSTANCE USE PROBLEMS ON THE FAMILY

Substance use problems have their own impact on family life. They can interfere with people's ability to follow family routines and meet their responsibilities. People may begin spending more time acquiring and using substances, and less time in their usual activities. The cost of using substances can become significant. In some cases, it can lead to job loss, which can create financial difficulties. Some people who use substances may act out verbally and physically.

CO-OCCURRING DISORDERS AND FAMILY LIFE

In addition to the individual effects of either substance use or mental health problems, coexisting mental health and substance use problems can more severely compromise a person's functioning in the areas of affect regulation, cognitive abilities, self-care, socialization, financial management, nutrition level, housing, recreation and employment.

Additionally, people with concurrent disorders often demonstrate more severe symptoms and sometimes less successful outcomes with disruptive behaviours, are less likely to comply with medication and other treatment, and attempt suicide more often in comparison to people with either disorder alone. They are twice as likely to be hospitalized as someone with a diagnosis of mental illness only (Mueser, 2002).

The daily work of caring for and seeking treatment for a relative with concurrent mental health and substance use problems, the financial burden, the feelings of loss, worry, anger, guilt and shame are all major sources of stress. Family members' lives often change dramatically as a result. Families often face:

- changes in roles and expectations
- emotional strain and social isolation, such as loss of companionship with the ill person, as well as friendships that might suffer
- if a spouse is affected, loss of intimacy, sexual relationship and a parenting partner
- emotional and physical exhaustion, due to the demands of caregiving
- preoccupation with the relative
- financial worries, due to employment issues and medical expenses
- difficulties in trying to understand the ill relative's treatment, encouraging the person to follow his or her plan, and determining where each family member fits in
- effects on other family members, such as siblings.

While many of these changes create stress, it's also important to recognize that some positive changes can and do happen.

THE FAMILY AS PRIMARY CAREGIVER

Caring for basic needs

The impact of concurrent disorders begins to affect every aspect of family life. Families who once had a safe and comfortable daily routine may find themselves on an emotional roller-coaster ride. When a person has concurrent mental illness and a substance use disorder, family members may find themselves assuming more responsibility for tasks such as motivating the person to keep up with his or her personal hygiene, and coaxing the person to get out of bed in the morning.

The need to monitor

Family members often worry about what might happen to their ill relative if he or she is left alone. They may be concerned that their loved one will:

- neglect his or her own physical care by forgetting to eat meals, or neglecting to take prescribed medications

- obtain access to more harmful drugs, or either consciously or inadvertently harm him- or herself during an acute episode of mental illness or dangerous use of substances
- place him- or herself in dangerous and possibly life-threatening situations while trying to buy drugs or by overdosing on drugs
- engage in criminal behaviour in order to access illegal drugs, and be arrested or hurt
- jeopardize his or her housing status by spending rent money on drugs or becoming involved in criminal activity to get money to buy drugs.

As a result, families often feel a desperate need to monitor the ill person most, if not all, of the time.

> Our son not only has schizophrenia, but he also uses drugs; he's been involved with gangs—and with the police. Half the time we're not sure if he's taking his medication—he gets mad if we keep after him to do simple things, like have a shower . . . we're so stressed as it is. We're trying to find out things, how we can resolve some of these problems. Sometimes I think I can't deal with it all.

When the single provider of the household income is also the primary caregiver, the need to monitor can lead to enormous financial consequences for the family as a whole, as well as additional emotional strain for the caregiver.

Consequences for the family

EMOTIONAL CONSEQUENCES

Family members may feel that their own lives are overshadowed by the illness. Some may find it almost impossible to calm themselves emotionally, to soothe their own anxieties, and to distract themselves from the strain of coping with their ill family member.

Family members may feel guilty if they take time to relax and care for their own emotional and physical health, and rebuild their own coping resources. Sometimes, they feel guilty if they experience resentment or anger about the situation. They may not allow themselves to admit that they are extremely tired, worn out, angry or bitter. Denying these emotions can lead to exhaustion, depression, isolation and hopelessness. In addition, their relationship with their loved one can begin to change.

ISOLATION

It is often a challenge for family members to find time to spend on their own interests and activities. They may begin to feel isolated from others who were once major social supports. They might feel that they do not have the time to maintain friendships, or they may be embarrassed or ashamed.

THE ILL RELATIVE'S RESPONSE TO FAMILY CONCERNS

To the person who has the concurrent disorders, the family's concern can seem like an invasion of personal life. This may lead to anger, rebellion and acting-out behaviours, which can exacerbate the person's mental health problems. Rebelling against what seems like the family's overprotectiveness, the person may end up in unsafe situations. This may form a repeating cycle: the family attempts to protect, and the person with the disorders reacts. This "preoccupation effect" costs everyone in terms of time, physical and emotional energy, and quality of life.

COMPASSION FATIGUE

Family caregivers give a great deal of themselves emotionally in the care of their ill loved ones and are susceptible to a condition called "compassion fatigue." In contrast to burnout, which is characterized by emotional withdrawal and decreased empathy, people with compassion fatigue feel that they can never give enough physically or emotionally.

For example, many family members may take the person's setbacks or relapses personally. Some feel that if they are not constantly thinking about the ill family member, they are somehow a lesser person.

> You become extremely protective of them [ill family members]. It takes incredible emotional energy.

When stress is unrelenting, emotional energy is depleted. Caregivers may become withdrawn from their meaningful world and begin feeling more irritable and overwhelmed. Formerly excellent caregivers can become discouraged, demoralized, cynical, depressed and anxious.

Self-care

It is essential that family caregivers understand the importance of self-care. If the family situation can't be changed, at least in the short term, the only recourse is to learn strategies for coping with physical and emotional stress, such as:

- following the basics, such as a good diet, exercise and sleep
- identifying and allowing oneself to experience a wide range of emotions
- developing effective ways of coping with feelings such as anger, resentment, bitterness, hopelessness, loss and grief.

Family members must learn to have compassion for themselves and to believe that they too deserve care from others. Many caregivers have difficulty believing that self-care is not selfish. They need to accept that they must care for themselves, so that they are able to care for others. They need to understand that they have the right to make choices based on their own values, beliefs and goals.

Seemingly insignificant ways of taking care of oneself, such as giving oneself time alone, in nature or in other places that evoke a sense of peace and timelessness, can help reduce stress. This may involve visualizing, meditating and learning how to relax the mind as well as the body. People can re-connect to their family and other support systems by having meaningful discussions once a day. Sharing joy as well as despair is also enormously powerful. To talk about our emotions, we have to be able to feel them.

FAMILY RECOVERY: THE POSITIVE ASPECTS OF CAREGIVING

It is important to acknowledge the challenges that family members face, but challenges represent only one aspect of the caregiver experience. Many people describe a renewed sense of closeness with their ill family member and an appreciation for the truly important things in life, such as connecting emotionally with another human being, having hope, overcoming extreme hardships and experiencing the journey of recovery along with their ill loved one.

> My son's illness, the whole thing, was just so devastating, and now we're a part of his recovery. It's just been so great for those of us who were along for the ride. I think it's been one of the most amazing experiences of my life, it really has been!

Recovery is a unique journey for each person, with its own rewards and perils along the way. It has been called a process, an outlook, a vision and a guiding principle. All the definitions are similar in suggesting the development of new meaning and purpose in life, as people grow beyond the impact of mental illness and substance misuse.

For people with concurrent disorders, recovery is a process—recovering their self-esteem, dreams, self-worth, sense of personal efficacy, pride, choice, dignity and meaning. For professionals and families, recovery is about treating the whole person—identifying strengths, instilling hope, and helping the person to function at an optimal level by taking responsibility for his or her own life. For family members, an important step in the recovery journey is realizing that people are people, before they are diagnoses, cases or clients. They are not defined nor controlled by their symptoms.

> As family members, we have an opportunity here to offer a lot of hope to other families going through the same thing. The general public seems to think that, once a doctor tells you your family member has a mental illness and a problem with drugs and alcohol, it's over—there's no hope; their lives are destroyed, and yours too. But it's so different now, so many people recover from concurrent disorders. And look at the research, the new medications and treatments—there have been so many advances. I know so many parents whose kids have gone back to university or have jobs—I mean, they're doing well. Mental illness and substance abuse doesn't have to mean that the person's life is over. So I think we need to give some hope to people.

> When people meet my son now, everybody is just so flabbergasted. And I think he offers such hope to sufferers and families . . . . People tend to want to talk to you about it. And we try. We try to help families whenever we can, and I think we give them a lot of hope. We get a number of families calling us over the course of a year. And either a social worker, or doctor, or somebody from the family support group—they've used our family as an example and say, "Their son is doing so well"—and then families say, "Can we come over and visit you?", and they come over and talk to my son. So we try to help; we try to give hope to other families.

EFFECT ON SIBLINGS

> You have lots of your own feelings about it, and then lots of feelings for your loved one: how is this going to affect their life, what's going to happen to them? There are so many things that just come pouring in. And you have concerns for their siblings, for your other children . . . . It can affect so many people.

Parents understandably spend a great deal of time and energy on a child with concurrent disorders. But their other children will also feel the impact of the disorders. Siblings may become afraid of developing a mental health problem, a substance use problem or both. They may worry about the stress and strain that their parents are enduring, and they may feel pressure to make up for what their parents have lost in their sibling.

At the same time, brothers or sisters sometimes resent the time that parents spend on their sibling. They may become angry to the point of acting out or distancing themselves from family members and friends. Sometimes, children who were close to their sibling may feel like they have lost their best friend. They may feel guilty that they have a better life than their brother or sister.

Siblings may also experience symptoms of anger, hostility or verbal or physical aggression from their ill brother or sister. These behaviours can evoke shock, dismay and a sense of abandonment and rejection.

> I remember being sort of teased as a child because I was so serious, so sombre. People told me that I acted like a middle-aged woman, a lot older than I actually was. It was impossible to explain to other people—you go to school after not sleeping all night, and after the police were at your house because of your sister's psychotic episode, and no one thought of dinner or anything like that because she overdosed, and your parents had to go to the emergency room with her—and then you go to school the next day and all the expectations are still on you. But you don't tell anybody anything; you just carry on as usual—you can't talk to anybody about it. Nobody will understand.

Taking care of siblings' needs

Parents can help their other children by:

- assuring them that the ill person's behaviours are symptoms of the illness and should not be taken personally, even though it may be difficult
- sharing their own feelings and encouraging their children to talk about how they feel and about how their brother's or sister's concurrent disorders are affecting them
- talking about how common it is for other family members to feel uncomfortable, embarrassed or ashamed of their relative's behaviours, symptoms and diagnosis
- helping siblings learn about major mental health problems and substance use problems and how these interact with and affect each other
- trying to spend time alone with siblings, talking and doing enjoyable activities
- if appropriate, discussing the issue of stigma and why it happens, as well as effective ways of dealing with it
- helping the children build a new relationship with their brother or sister and creating unique ways of being with their ill sibling.

CHANGING EXPECTATIONS

Family members who held expectations around education, career paths, marriage and children for their loved ones may find themselves having to dramatically modify their expectations.

For example, young adults who were previously involved in social activities, were achieving good grades in school, or were holding down a job and engaging in relationships with friends and families may gradually, and in some cases quite suddenly, begin to withdraw from other people. They may appear depressed, paranoid and apathetic, or they may begin to exhibit bizarre and frightening behaviours, such as talking to themselves and responding to auditory hallucinations. They may be overwhelmed when faced with formerly enjoyable and taken-for-granted activities, such as work or school, or even socializing and keeping up with self-care.

The process of changing expectations can involve much emotional pain, a sense of loss, grief, sadness and anger. Families may require a period of mourning for the kind of life they once expected for their ill loved one. The grieving process is similar to that of losing a loved one to a terminal illness, or of adjusting to a loved one's serious enduring physical illness.

> The whole family, we had so many other problems to face. I remember feeling grief and frustration and a sense of tremendous loss, for my daughter and for her potential.

STIGMA AND THE FAMILY

There has been much discussion about stigmatization of people with mental health and substance use problems. However, stigma also generalizes to their families (Lefley, 1987). This is called "courtesy stigma."

Having a person who has substance use and mental health problems in the household can affect family relationships with the wider community. Much has been researched and written about the burden of stigma and isolation on the family, and many resources are available on this subject (Biegel et al., 1994; Francell et al., 1988; Hatfield & Lefley, 1987; Loukissa, 1995; Ohaeri, 2003).

Forms of stigma

Stigmatizing behaviours have their roots in different misconceptions about substance use and mental illness. People may, for example:
- blame the family for causing the illness
- associate the family members with the frightening aspects of the illness
- avoid the family members to avoid the behaviour of the person who is ill.

BLAME FOR CAUSING THE ILLNESS

Despite evidence that a wide range of environmental and biochemical stressors may trigger psychiatric symptoms and substance use problems, including relapse, many families still feel blamed by the broader society for an adult child's concurrent disorders. Many have internalized this belief and live with deep shame and in relative isolation.

> Stigma can make parents hesitate to go for more help. But who can blame them? It only takes one really bad experience in the health care system and you don't want to go through anything like that again. When my husband and I took our son to a child psychiatrist, the psychiatrist blamed the behaviour on our parenting. Now, that sort of thing, being blamed, being told you have bad parenting skills, prevents many people from seeking needed treatment later. People think, well, there's no use going to those guys for help—they're only going to tell us it's our fault! Basically, we went away and never came back. We all just lived with it.
>
> I compare mental illness and addiction to Alzheimer's disease, because my mother-in-law felt comfortable calling up all her relatives and letting us know that her husband had Alzheimer's. No doctor blamed her. The community offered all kinds of support, and I think that's because they had known him to be a valid member of society, as a hard-working, neighbourly person, for 75 years. And as people get older, we expect some mental degeneration, right? Whereas with mental illness . . . my mother was partially blamed for my sister's schizophrenia, so she started hiding it from people.

ASSOCIATION WITH A CONDITION THAT IS MISUNDERSTOOD AND FEARED

Many people are frightened of mental illness and substance use disorders. One of our deepest dreads involves the loss of our mental abilities—to think and communicate, to make our own decisions and to set the course of our own lives. This fear can be associated not only with the person with the co-occurring problems but also with other members of the family. People close to the person with concurrent disorders may be devalued or shunned.

Goffman (1963) considers the people who are socially related to a stigmatized person. In many respects, their relationship leads the wider society to treat both the stigmatized person and those closely associated/related to the person as one.

> I would never tell any of my co-workers. Never. Because it would hurt me professionally—that's a fact. It's a spillover stigma. So at work, I have a separate circle of friends, and it's like a haven. It's the one place I can go that hasn't been touched by schizophrenia, and depression, and drugs and alcohol. If I were to tell those people [co-workers], then mental illness would take over that world as well. So, it's better to just have that barrier there between the two worlds, and then there's a threshold I can step over, to get over to this normal world. It's a refuge and a place of rest.

As a result of being associated with the illness, family members often rearrange their lives to avoid social situations. The isolation and lack of regular social contact can lead to depression, suspiciousness, hostility, anxiety and confusion (Goffman, 1963).

REACTION TO THE UNPREDICTABLE BEHAVIOUR OF THE PERSON WHO IS ILL

Severe mental illness and substance use problems can manifest themselves in ways that, according to societal rules, violate social norms of appropriate conduct. Such behaviour may further isolate the person's family and jeopardize relationships with friends, neighbours and the community (Lefley, 1987). Evidence of shame, guilt and fear can be found in narratives written about family experiences with mental illness.

Although ample evidence demonstrates that families undergo significant emotional stress overall as they struggle to cope with the unique challenges of caring for a person with concurrent disorders, there has been little research on stigma as a primary aspect of concurrent disorders in families (MacRae, 1999). This is surprising given the nature of many concurrent disorders, which can involve such problematic behaviours as delusions and hallucinations, poor hygiene, verbal outbursts, violence, anger and aggression, apathy and depression.

> I think a common belief is that people with mental illness are violent—you know how the media sometimes portrays people. And then you think, are my relatives concerned that my daughter will be violent? Let's face it, she is often inappropriate and really angry when she's not well, but she never gets violent

with people. But a lot of people associate mental illness with criminal behaviour in general.

Coping strategies to deal with stigma

Goffman (1963) describes people with disorders that are stigmatized and that cannot be hidden or disguised as "discredited," and those with conditions that allow people to "pass as normal" as "discreditable." Whereas the discredited may be confronted with problems of impression management, the discreditable may face difficulties of information management. "Enacted stigma" refers to actual discrimination, whereas "felt stigma" refers to the fear of such discrimination on the part of the stigmatized.

IMPRESSION MANAGEMENT

Family members sometimes cope by accepting the diagnosis and dealing directly with the negative attitudes they face. Strategies such as ignoring, downplaying or challenging negative attitudes and beliefs may help families feel a sense of success; they also help to enhance self-esteem and resilience. For many family members, accepting the idea that they cannot control other people's attitudes, beliefs and behaviour is emotionally liberating.

> You can't let negative people get to you. You just have to put on a suit of armour and face it. Stigma is everywhere—running away won't make it any better, for you or for your family. You have to be tough with things like this.

INFORMATION MANAGEMENT

As a result of felt stigma, people's first choice of strategy is non-disclosure and concealment of the diagnosis. It is possible to avoid courtesy stigma if the symptoms of the illness are concealed from others (MacRae, 1999).

Covering-up strategies are, however, stressful and may involve avoidance of face-to-face contact with others. Many stigmatized people who are attempting to pass the test of normality live in perpetual fear that their stigmatized attributes or condition will be discovered. Goffman (1963) calls this the fear of being discredited on the part of discreditable people.

> You give up a lot when you have to hide or keep your family member hidden. It's like self-enforced isolation. Your world shrinks to something you can manage. What you give up is that link to the rest of the world. You cut yourself off—it becomes "the outside world," and it's a dangerous place to go.

Having a supportive network of understanding and non-judgmental peers acts as a buffer against stigma and appears to be an important coping resource for family members. Family groups "serve as a protective circle" (Goffman, 1963), which may give members less reason to be concerned about embarrassment and stigma management.

THE RELATIONSHIP OF FAMILIES WITH THE HEALTH CARE SYSTEM

Gaps in the health care system

Families often find themselves assuming more responsibility for their ill loved one because of more systemic problems within the health care system. It is still common for mental health programs to refuse to treat people with concurrent disorders, or to treat only the mental illness. Similarly, some addiction treatment programs and facilities cannot address the mental health problem. People with co-occurring problems tend to fall through the cracks.

This has tremendous consequences for the families, who not only have to take on the caregiving responsibilities for their ill relative, but must also act as de facto "case managers." It is not surprising that family caregivers are frustrated by a system that has failed to make their needs a priority.

Relationships with agency staff

In exploring the nature of stigma as it is understood, suffered and survived by family members of people with severe mental illness and substance use disorders, one study found that, in addition to being disappointed with the lack of adequate programs for their relatives, families often see mental health and substance use agency staff as being unresponsive and uninformative. The majority of family members also commented on the pervasive lack of education and understanding about mental illness, substance use disorders and concurrent disorders, and about the experiences of families throughout the general health care system and the public service sector (O'Grady, 2004).

LACK OF RESPECT FOR FAMILY'S EXPERTISE

Participants in the above study noted that families are rarely viewed in a positive light, their strengths recognized, their opinions valued or their efforts to support and protect a mentally ill loved one acknowledged. They described being ignored, devalued, patronized and relegated to the status of bystander by health care professionals. In addition, they commonly reported feeling disrespected, blamed for their loved one's illness, excluded from consultations, kept "out of the loop" and discounted.

> I have felt resentful, for all the years I put in before the illness was diagnosed. How much time and how much agony, and how much worry, because this was a child who was not developing normally, and nobody listened to me! I was so angry over that—and I'm still angry.

> Having a loved one who is suffering from both a mental illness and a substance use disorder can represent a significant disruption in the lives of families and can have an enormous impact on overall family functioning and sense of well-being. People need to be able to call somebody when their loved one is in the hospital because of a mental illness or a drug problem. They need to be able to touch base and get information from someone. It's hard for people who don't know the system—like, what channels have to be manœuvred, or who to call when you have specific questions. There are so many roadblocks.

Many believed that being listened to in a respectful and truly caring manner would have made an enormous difference in their appraisal of their experiences with the mental health care system. Family members did not discount the professional and specialized training and expertise of mental health care practitioners but, rather, expressed distress over their own invalidating experiences as family caregivers within the system.

These experiences contrast with their experience with family self-help / mutual aid support groups, where knowledge is developed, disseminated and validated by peers in similar circumstances, a process that has been described as an empowering way of teaching and learning (Levine & Ligenza, 2002).

PARTNERS IN CARE

Families need to understand the nature and course of their relatives' mental health and substance use problems. Because gaps in the health care system often force them into the role of case managers, families must have the information that is essential to understanding their relative's treatment plan (Levine & Ligenza, 2002). Informed family caregivers can be valuable members of the treatment team.

However, many family members feel that they haven't received pertinent information about their loved one's diagnosis, prognosis or course of treatment, nor information concerning the availability of mental health, addiction and concurrent disorders treatment and support resources. In fact, in one recent study (O'Grady, 2004), many family members felt that many health care professionals perceived them not as partners, but as part of the problem. The majority of participants in the study acknowledged and understood the issue of confidentiality concerning their ill relative's condition. However, they remained frustrated with the lack of information about:

- mental health and addiction services in general
- the major signs and symptoms of various mental illnesses and substance use disorders
- effective modes of treatment for these conditions
- coping strategies for themselves as caregivers.

THE EXPERT KNOWLEDGE TRAP

An uncritical view of science, and a failure to recognize its limitations in understanding the human condition, often create an exaggerated view of professional expertise (Lefley, 1987). Kingsfisher and Millard (1998) found that staff often ignored or discounted the questions of family members, if those questions were perceived to arise from a lay rather than a biomedical understanding of illness or treatment.

This false distinction, between professional, "objective" data and the insights developed by people who live with and care for relatives with long-term illnesses, is often reinforced by the structure of health care settings and professional education and training.

Empowerment

Much of the current discussion about the need for family participation in health care decisions is based on a model of empowerment. In this case, empowerment refers to encouraging people to participate as equal partners in decisions about the health care they receive (Opie, 1998).

Health care professionals who adopt empowering practices:

- respect family members' abilities to make decisions
- value the input of family members in such decisions
- are able to relinquish control when families question or reject their advice.

However, empowerment may be used to disguise and sometimes even to justify paternalistic practices (Opie, 1998). Changing one's language is not sufficient to effect empowerment; there must also be profound changes in the complex power relations in practitioner–patient interactions (Paterson, 2001). In spite of their stated intention to foster participatory decision-making, practitioners often discount the experiential knowledge of families and fail to provide the resources families need to make informed decisions.

A study of empowerment in health care settings in New Zealand found that, although health care professionals believed that they invited and welcomed family participation, the families' input regarding decisions about the client's plan of care was limited to the agenda established by the health care team (Opie, 1998). Practitioners often assumed that family members held similar views about the goals and methods of illness management, without asking them to validate this assumption.

A spirit of collaboration between health care professionals and families will only be possible with mutual understanding and recognition of each other's strengths and areas of expertise. The hope is that, in a spirit of partnership and mutual respect, families will be accepted as expert, valued members of the treatment team.

Ways for health care professionals to work with families

Health care professionals in both the mental health and addiction fields may effectively help families of people with concurrent mental health and substance use problems in the following ways:

Be respectful

- Approach all interactions with family members in an empowering, respectful, compassionate manner, and in a spirit of partnership.
- Honour and value family members' experiential knowledge concerning their ill loved one.
- Avoid either implicitly or explicitly blaming or criticizing family members.

Offer support for the family

- Be as supportive as possible, and offer other potential avenues of support, such as family self-help / mutual aid groups; wherever possible, refer family members to concurrent disorders support/psychoeducational groups.
- Refer family members for counselling when it is requested.
- Educate families about the importance of caring for themselves and maintaining balance in their lives.
- Acknowledge and validate the ways in which family members cope; offer—in an uncritical and non-accusatory manner—alternative and potentially more effective ways of coping.

Listen to and acknowledge their concerns and feelings

- Acknowledge the difficulties inherent in caring for a loved with concurrent disorders.
- Encourage family members to identify and talk about their feelings (both positive and negative).
- Try to take a minute, and LISTEN to their concerns and questions.

Offer information and education on dealing with the illness

- Provide answers whenever possible—if you cannot provide answers, refer family members to someone who will be able to address their concerns.
- Provide education about concurrent disorders.
- Provide education about the high rates of relapse in concurrent disorders.
- Provide crisis information, such as telephone numbers and advice on how to talk to the ill family member in a crisis.

FAMILY PSYCHOEDUCATION

People who are providing emotional support, case management, financial assistance, advocacy and housing to family members with co-occurring problems need access to resources, information and support. Family psychoeducation groups are increasingly being recognized as an important link in a comprehensive system of care.

Concurrent disorders family psychoeducation:

- combines information about co-occurring substance use and mental health problems with training in problem solving, communication skills and developing social supports

- uses the expertise of both family and professionals
- aims to reduce family stress, develop coping skills and enhance personal empowerment for caregivers.

Early best practice evidence from the United States suggests that families of people who have concurrent disorders are best served with a combination of both peer support and psychoeducation tailored to their unique needs (Mueser, 2002). However, research from the mental health care field has also found that psychoeducation alone has positive effects on the quality of life of family members (Mueser, 2002). Effective group interventions have also been shown to improve overall family coping and an increased sense of hope (Bloom, 1990).

Research conducted over the past decade (Levine & Ligenza, 2002; Mueser, 2002; Solomon et al., 1997) has shown that patient outcomes also improve when the needs of family members—for information, clinical guidance and support—are met.

> When I first started in the family support group, I found myself listening to other family members who were doing really well and had been in situations similar to my own. So it's the hope—the giving of hope, that it really is possible to get through it, that no matter how tough it's been and how often the treatment has failed, that it still may one day succeed, that recovery is possible. And no matter how many people turn away from you, or what they think of you, things will get better.

THE CAMH CONCURRENT DISORDERS FAMILY PSYCHOEDUCATION PROJECT: OFFERING INFORMATION AND SUPPORT TO FAMILIES

An important component of family support / psychoeducational interventions includes offering opportunities for family members to share their feelings and experiences in a supportive, empowering and understanding environment with others who are in similar situations.

At the Centre for Addiction and Mental Health (CAMH), we have been conducting a family study within our Concurrent Disorders Service to compare: a. a concurrent disorders family support/psychoeducational group with b. an educational manual for family members of individuals with concurrent mental illness and substance use.

OBJECTIVES/HYPOTHESIS OF THE STUDY

The main objective of the study is to improve the overall quality of life for family members of people with concurrent disorders, by providing a peer support / psychoeducational group intervention. Our hypothesis is that combined peer social support and professional facilitator-led psychoeducation, both in a large-city institutional setting and within a smaller community agency, will result in improved quality of life for family members by:

1. providing opportunities for enhanced social support, self-efficacy, mastery, hope, and positive and effective coping strategies
2. reducing caregiver burden and the distress associated with stigmatizing experiences.

In addition, we hope to find out whether involvement in a weekly peer support, facilitator-led educational group will be more effective in achieving these aims than offering a family educational manual alone.

PHASE 1

During Phase 1 of the project, we conducted a focus group to find out what families needed. Needs that emerged included:

- information about various psychiatric diagnoses and associated treatments, especially psychotropic medication
- information about alcohol/drug abuse and dependence and how problematic substance use interacts with mental illness and with prescribed medication
- information about community resources for consumers and families
- crisis management
- effective family communication techniques
- self-care and coping with stress
- crisis management.

Results also suggested that family members preferred a structure that included both peer support and facilitator-led educational components.

PHASE 2

Using the results from the Phase 1 focus group, we began Phase 2: to design and pilot a support group intervention. The purpose of this phase was to evaluate the group content and format.

Ten family members participated in a 90-minute weekly support group for six weeks. The group provided educational material about concurrent disorders and allowed participants to share their personal stories, challenges and coping strategies.

At the end of the pilot phase, we completed open-ended qualitative interviews with family member participants, evaluating overall satisfaction with the group content and format. The principal investigator administered a series of quantitative instrument tools to participating family members during a one-to-one meeting before beginning the group intervention; these tools were administered again at the completion of the pilot study. These tools were designed to measure changes in:

- perceptions of social support
- feelings of personal mastery and empowerment
- sense of caregiver burden
- level of hopefulness
- degree of stigma.

PHASE 3

Phase 3, which will be completed by the fall of 2005, employs a randomized controlled trial to determine the effectiveness of a 12-week group intervention. This intervention consists of a one-hour peer support open discussion, followed by a 30-minute psychoeducational session led by the group co-facilitators. The educational content is based on primary areas of interest identified by family participants from Phases 1 and 2 of the study.

Family members at both the CAMH site and a community-based agency site will be randomly assigned to either the experimental intervention group or the control group. Each of the two sites will recruit 12 to 15 participants for both the experimental and the control groups, for a total sample size of 20 to 30 study participants per site. The control group participants will not take part in a support group; they will receive a comprehensive educational manual designed for family members.

Both the group intervention and the manual cover the following topics:

- introduction to concurrent disorders
- understanding substance use problems
- understanding mental health problems
- the effects of concurrent disorders on the family
- social support needs
- self-care for family members
- concurrent disorders treatment issues and approaches
- pharmacotherapies in the treatment of concurrent disorders
- crisis management
- stigma: a challenge for clients with concurrent disorders and their families
- relapse and relapse prevention
- recovery.

CONCLUSION

Family members and other persons involved in the lives and care of adults who have serious mental illnesses and coexisting substance use disorders often provide emotional support, case management, financial assistance, advocacy and housing to the loved one who is ill. Family members often have limited access to the resources, information and support they need. Research conducted over the past two decades in particular has shown that the outcomes for people with concurrent mental health and substance use disorders improve when the needs of family members—for information, clinical guidance and support—are met. Offering the appropriate components of family support and education appears to be an important determinant of positive outcomes both for family members and for the person who is ill.

Important components of family support / educational interventions include providing opportunities for sharing feelings and experiences in a supportive, empowering and understanding environment with others who are in similar situations. Effective group interventions have also been shown to improve overall family coping and an increased sense of hope.

REFERENCES

Aviram, U. (1990). Community care of the seriously mentally ill: Continuing problems and current issues. *Community Mental Health Journal, 26*(1), 69–88.

Biegel, D.E., Milligan, S.E., Putnam, P.L. & Song, L. (1994). Predictors of burden among lower socioeconomic status caregivers of persons with chronic mental illness. *Community Mental Health Journal, 30*, 473–494.

Bloom, J.R. (1990). The relationship of social support and health. *Social Science and Medicine, 39*, 635–637.

Boydell, K. & Trainor, J. (1998). *Community Mental Health Evaluation Initiative: A Longitudinal Study of Family Initiatives in Community Mental Health in Ontario—Project Proposal.* Toronto: Community Support and Research Unit, Centre for Addiction and Mental Health.

Francell, C.G., Conn, V.S. & Gray, D.P. (1988). Families' perceptions of burden of care for chronic mentally ill relatives. *Hospital and Community Psychiatry, 39*, 1296–1300.

Goffman, E. (1963). *Stigma: Notes on the Management of Spoiled Identity.* Englewood Cliffs, NJ: Prentice-Hall.

Hatfield, A.B. (1991). The National Alliance for the mentally ill: A decade later. *Hospital and Community Psychiatry, 27*, 95–103.

Hatfield, A.B. (1997). Families of adults with severe mental illness: New directions in research. *American Journal of Orthopsychiatry, 67*, 254–260.

Hatfield, A.B. & Lefley, H.P. (1987). *Families of the Mentally Ill: Coping and Adaptation.* New York: The Guilford Press.

Hobbs, T.R. (1997). Depression in the caregiving mothers of adult schizophrenics: A test of the resource deterioration model. *Community Mental Health Journal, 33*, 387–399.

Kingsfisher, C.P. & Millard, A.V. (1998). "Milk makes me sick but my body needs it": Conflict and contradiction in the establishment of authoritarian knowledge. *Medical Anthropology Quarterly, 12*, 447–466.

Lefley, H.P. (1987). Culture and mental illness: The family role. In A.B. Hatfield and H.P. Lefley (Eds.), *Families of the Mentally Ill: Coping and Adaptation* (pp. 30–59). New York: Guilford Press.

Levine, I.S. & Ligenza, L.R. (2002). In their own voices: Families in crisis—a focus group study of families of persons with serious mental illness. *Journal of Psychiatric Practice, 8*, 344–353.

Loukissa, D.A. (1995). Family burden in chronic mental illness: A review of research studies. *Journal of Advanced Nursing, 21*, 248–255.

MacRae, H. (1999). Managing courtesy stigma: The case of Alzheimer's disease. *Sociology of Health and Illness, 21,* 54–70.

Mueser, K.T. (2002). A family intervention program for dual disorders. *Community Mental Health Journal, 38*, 253–270.

O'Grady, C. (2004). *Stigma as experienced by family members of people with severe mental illness: The impact of participation in self-help / mutual aid support groups.* Doctoral Dissertation, University of Toronto.

Ohaeri, J. (2003). The burden of caregiving in families with a mental illness: A review of 2002. *Current Opinion in Psychiatry, 16*, 457–465.

Opie, A. (1998). "Nobody's asked me for my view": Users' empowerment by multidisciplinary health teams. *Qualitative Health Research, 18*, 188–206.

Paterson, B. (2001). Myth of empowerment in chronic illness. *Journal of Advanced Nursing, 34*, 574–581.

Pomeroy, E. & Trainor, J. (1991). *Families of People with Mental Illness: Current Dilemmas and Strategies for Change.* Toronto: Canadian Mental Health Association.

Solomon, P., Draine, J., Mannion, E. & Meisel, M. (1997). Effectiveness of two models of brief family education: Retention of gains by family members of adults with serious mental illness. *American Journal of Orthopsychiatry, 67*, 177–187.

Chapter 14

Concurrent disorders: A framework for working with couples and families

GLORIA CHAIM AND JOANNE SHENFELD

INTRODUCTION

When someone has co-occurring mental health and substance use problems, his or her family, partner or spouse are all usually affected. Caring about and for someone with mental health and substance use problems taxes the health and well-being of those in the support position, sometimes to the point that they feel they have little left to offer. Emotions among family members typically fluctuate between fury, pity, anxiety and grief.

Often, families also need support to better understand and respond to what is happening. This support includes recognizing and attending to their own thoughts and feelings, as well as to the impact of the person's illness on their lives.

Strong, healthy families are much better able to accommodate the person who is ill and to develop strategies to help. Family members, partners and friends can play a vital role in helping the recovery process.

The interrelationships of problems within families

Just as the person with concurrent disorders faces extra challenges, so the person's family carries additional burdens. This needs to be recognized and addressed, to develop the best helping response.

When working with families, it is sometimes hard to define who the client is. While only one person may present with a "disorder," other family members may also have substance use and mental health concerns.

Families in which there is either a mental health or substance use problem experience more stress and distress than do unaffected families. However, families in which there is a severe mental illness *and* substance use problems are four times as likely to have other members with severely disturbed affect than are families in which there is severe mental illness alone (Kashner et al., 1991).

In addition, there is evidence that levels of expressed emotion among family members are higher in families in which a family member has both a substance use problem and mental health issues (Turner, 1998). This is concerning, because higher levels of expressed emotion (e.g., anger, frustration, irritation) signal that the family members believe the person who is ill is in control of his or her symptoms. The presence of such beliefs, in turn, places a higher burden on the person who is ill, and predicts higher rates of relapse.

Studies indicate that people with concurrent disorders, and their families, report significantly lower family satisfaction than people with a single disorder (Dixon et al., 1995; Read et al., 1993; Silver, 1999). These studies also show that, compared to family members of people with a single disorder, family members of people with concurrent disorders are more likely to misuse substances and to experience depression and anxiety. Although the research is limited and sample sizes are small, these findings support our clinical experience. The context of the person with concurrent disorders within the couple or family, and the dynamics of this relationship, are highly relevant and affect treatment outcome.

That said, there is encouraging evidence that where the helping response includes the family as well as the person with the problem, better outcomes emerge for all involved (Barrowclough, 2002).

How families can be involved in treatment

Clients coming into treatment for substance use or mental health concerns are most often assessed and treated on their own, without any direct family participation in the treatment process. However, interventions with these clients have been shown to be more effective when the family is involved in either the primary or secondary mode of treatment (Stanton & Heath, 1997; Baucom, et al., 1998). Family involvement in treatment has also been shown to enhance treatment retention and outcome (Rubinstein et al., 1990; Ryglewicz, 1991; Selekman, 1991).

Helpful and relevant treatment of clients with concurrent disorders begins with understanding the client's whole biopsychosocial / socio-cultural–political context. This includes understanding:

- how clients define and regard their family and social networks
- how clients, their families and their social networks define and regard co-occurring substance use and mental health concerns.

Taking this holistic approach can identify issues that need to be dealt with in treatment.

Families can be involved in the treatment of concurrent disorders in many ways. The expertise required to implement these approaches varies, with more basic approaches being appropriate for all helpers, and some requiring more expert training in family counselling and therapy.

The following types of family involvement can be helpful in working with people affected by concurrent disorders:

- family involvement while the person with concurrent disorders is not in care
- family involvement independent of the care the person with concurrent disorders is receiving
- information sessions for the family, focused on the nature of the person's illness or problems, the plan of care and the challenges of recovery, including relapse prevention
- psychoeducation sessions to help the family work actively to support the person in treatment and recovery
- family counselling to help the family address and resolve issues related to the person's problems and relevant family circumstances that may affect his or her treatment and recovery
- family therapy in which the family becomes the client, working on problems they have identified and goals they want to pursue with expert guidance.

At the very least, families need:

- information about the specific substance use and mental health issues that are affecting them, including how these problems interrelate and interact
- information about the treatment process and the options that are available
- validation, not only as having been affected by the person's mental health and substance use problems, but also as having an important role to play in the treatment and recovery process
- support, which can be most valuable when it comes from other families facing similar challenges.

More direct interventions, such as counselling or therapy, can help families learn to cope more effectively, ensure that their own needs are met and improve family dynamics.

Most often, family interventions focus on either the mental health or the substance use problem. When clients have both disorders, one or the other is often ignored or, at best, is treated sequentially. For example, support and psychoeducation groups for family members of people with schizophrenia do not address substance use vulnerability and concerns, and self-help groups such as Al-Anon for family members of people with alcohol problems do not address mental health concerns.

Ryglewicz (1991) points out that instructional points or guidelines given to families of people with concurrent disorders may conflict. For example, family members of people with schizophrenia may be advised to reduce stress and modify expectations, while family members of people with alcohol problems may be advised to increase expectations, structured activities and accountability.

Psychoeducation, support groups and treatments that target the co-occurring disorders together can help families understand substance use and mental health concerns and the interaction between them. This understanding better enables families to make the necessary accommodations and to develop strategies to effect change. Family members can also help therapists, by corroborating or clarifying the client's information; in effect, supporting and facilitating the treatment process while also benefiting from therapeutic intervention.

This chapter looks at four levels of family intervention (in order of intensity):

- family orientation interventions
- family psychoeducation interventions
- family support groups
- conjoint family or couple counselling.

These levels are presented within a framework that helps therapists match families of people with concurrent disorders with the appropriate level of intervention. We also present a model of family therapy, the Integrative Couple/Family Counselling Model, that incorporates theory and treatment techniques from different treatment perspectives.

IDENTIFYING EFFECTIVE FAMILY-BASED TREATMENT APPROACHES

Baucom et al. (1998) conducted a comprehensive review and evaluation of couple- and family-based treatment approaches. They found that some family interventions appeared to reduce marital and family distress, as well as symptoms of the identified disorder. Their study looked at couple and family therapies that:

- address relationship issues thought to be related to the causes or maintenance of a disorder and/or its symptoms
- are disorder specific and focus on ways in which family members' response to the client's disorder may contribute to symptoms or interfere with treatment
- involve family members as helpers to the client, without focusing on relationship issues.

Their review identifies therapies that are effective with specific disorders, including:

- family-assisted exposure for obsessive-compulsive disorder
- behavioural marital therapy for depression
- community reinforcement approach for alcohol dependence.

A schema for grouping clients and family-based interventions

Identifying the type and level of intervention that is most suitable for individual clients with concurrent disorders and their families becomes clearer with the use of the following schema developed by Ryglewicz (1991). The schema identifies clients with concurrent disorders as fitting into the following categories:

SPMI + SUD
People with severe and persistent mental illness and diagnosable substance use disorders (dependence or abuse).

SPMI + SV
People with severe and persistent mental illness and substance vulnerability.

PD et al. + SUD
People with non-psychotic mental/emotional/personality disorders whose substance use disorder complicates or escalates their problems.

SUD + PS
People with substance use disorders whose recovery is impeded by psychiatric symptoms.

The level of family intervention must be congruent with the type and severity of the concurrent disorder. Table 14-1: Level of Family Involvement links the above schema with Boudreau's (1997) description of appropriate levels of family-based intervention for clients with substance use concerns.

Contraindications for family involvement

It is important to avoid making automatic assumptions about involving or excluding the family. In all cases, both the client and the family must consent to the family's involvement.

Family dynamics may raise safety issues contraindicating any family-focused work. Ideally, to best determine the appropriate level and timing of family involvement, the counsellor or therapist meets with each family member individually to explore the options. Other issues, such as members' own mental health or substance use difficulties, overwhelming anger or other negative dynamics, may also contraindicate current family's involvement.

If the client does not consent to family involvement in the treatment plan, families can be offered general psychoeducation about concurrent disorders and an opportunity to share their experiences with other understanding families. This type of family intervention is specifically designed to increase family coping and overall quality of life, and to reduce the family's level of stress.

FAMILY ORIENTATION INTERVENTIONS

Clients come into treatment in a variety of ways. Some seek or are brought for treatment on their own; others are accompanied by friends or family. If the client is

TABLE 14-1

Level of family involvement

LEVEL OF INTERVENTION	ACTIVITY	OBJECTIVES	TARGET GROUP
FAMILY ORIENTATION	orient the family to the philosophy and approaches of the service	• provide information and education • enlist family support	• families of people with severe mental illness and substance use problems • families of people with personality disorders whose substance use complicates or escalates their problems • families of people whose psychiatric symptoms interfere with their recovery from substance abuse
PSYCHO-EDUCATIONAL SESSIONS	provide education and information on substance use and mental illness suitable for target subgroup	• understand interaction between substance use and mental illness • reduce anxiety • assist in anticipating high-risk situations • develop coping strategies	• SPMI + SUD • SPMI + SV • PD et al. + SUD • SUD + PS
SUPPORT GROUPS	provide support and counselling	• reduce isolation • assist in coping • help family members to consider their own goals and needs	• SPMI + SUD • SPMI + SV • PD et al. + SUD • SUD + PS • family members who are able and willing to participate in a group that is oriented toward their own needs as well as those of the client
CONJOINT FAMILY OR COUPLE COUNSELLING	contract with each member of the family/couple for interventions aimed at resolving relationship problems related to substance use and mental illness	• improve family functioning • provide support for client treatment through resolution of related family problems	• SUD + PS • PD et al. + SUD • clients who have made some steps toward individual treatment for concurrent disorders • families that are stable, not in crisis

capable and there are no contraindications, the treatment provider should discuss with the client the possibility and benefits of involving the family in treatment.

If the treatment provider discusses, in a positive manner, the purpose and process of family involvement, along with the parameters of confidentiality, clients will often agree to invite their family or significant others into the treatment process. Clients who refuse family contact at the beginning of treatment may be open to it later on.

Family involvement begins with an orientation process. Family members often:
- have many questions about the problems of the family member in treatment
- have conflicting feelings and ideas about how and whether to be involved in treatment
- are reluctant to get involved, fearing blame, shame and reinforcement of hopelessness.

Family members need to be assured that help is available to them as much as for the identified client.

Family orientation is an opportunity to discuss:
- treatment philosophy and approach
- treatment options for the identified client as well as the family members
- information about the treatment process, including engagement in the treatment process, stages of treatment and expected length of involvement
- roles of the client, family members and treatment providers
- information about the identified concurrent disorders
- strengths of the client as well as individual family members
- sources of support.

Case example: Colin and Mary
Colin came for treatment for alcohol use. He also had severe depression, requiring hospitalization at times. His partner, Mary, attended his initial assessment and discussed the program and his treatment plan with the counsellor. Mary was given information about how she could support and help Colin as well as about treatment options for herself, such as psychoeducational groups for family members.

Mary was able to help Colin remember his group and individual appointments and help him get to treatment or let staff know if he was unable to attend. Due to his depression, Colin was sometimes confused about appointment times or the overall treatment plan, and Mary was able to work with staff to keep Colin attending the program and following through with treatment.

FAMILY PSYCHOEDUCATION INTERVENTIONS

Family psychoeducation interventions can be offered in individual or group sessions. The group format is preferable, as it provides a supportive context and a network for family members who are often isolated and depleted by the day-to-day difficulties of living with a person with concurrent disorders. From an agency perspective, the group format is also a cost-effective way to meet service demand.

Psychoeducation related to concurrent disorders should be content-focused and time-limited. (Long-term psychoeducation is more suitably labelled a support group, as described below.) The focus on content is crucial, because families usually have little general information about the client's disorders.

Group content

Content will vary, depending on group composition. Regardless of which disorders the group members are dealing with, the group can receive information about general principles, mental illness, problem substance use and substance vulnerability—particularly if the group comprises families of clients with severe mental illness and substance use problems. Such family members tend to be involved with treatment providers and may be more accessible than the families of clients with personality disorders, or whose psychiatric symptoms interfere with their recovery from substance use.

The content of psychoeducational groups that focus on either mental illness or substance use problems individually may give contradictory information. So, a main function of the group focused on concurrent disorders is to integrate guidelines for management, structure, coping and support that will help the client manage both disorders, as opposed to using strategies for one that exacerbate the symptoms of the other. For example, when family members encourage a person who is depressed to engage in social interaction, they must be careful to screen activities for risk for substance availability and use.

Group composition

Groups that target concurrent disorders may include families who are dealing with problems related to a range of disorders. This variety of issues may broaden the perspective and scope of the group, but may also dictate more generic content. The challenge for the therapist is to ensure that, although the content is general, it is relevant and useful.

Groups may include family members who have various relationships to the client (for example, parents, spouses or siblings of different clients in the same group). Although there are enough common issues to make this type of mixed group workable, a more homogeneous group composition is preferable. For example, parents of adolescents generally find that parenting concerns and responsibilities often take precedence over other issues, so a specific parents' group will likely be most helpful to them. Staff resources, client mix and the number of clients dictate the number and type of groups that can be offered in a particular setting.

Clients with personality disorders and substance use problems are often difficult to engage in treatment, and when they are in treatment, they often refuse family involvement in their treatment. Depending on other issues, such as a history of trauma in the family, this group may be the least appropriate for family involvement. When contact can be made with such families, and where family involvement is indicated, psychoeducation can help families understand and manage the issues, deal with their frustrations and support clients who may be disengaging.

As mental health care providers, consumers and family members learn more about the issues and impact of substance use problems, and as addiction treatment providers, clients and family members learn more about the issues and impact of mental health problems, these services will come closer together.

> *Case example: Mark and Elizabeth*
> Mark had been diagnosed with and treated for schizophrenia four years before initiating a relationship with Elizabeth, a fellow university student. He had been stable and compliant with medication and clinic appointments. He started smoking cannabis occasionally with Elizabeth and had some episodes of recurrent voices. Initially, Elizabeth attributed his relapse to stress and encouraged Mark to use cannabis to relax.
>
> Mark's case manager referred Elizabeth to a psychoeducational group at the clinic. Elizabeth talked about helping Mark to get better, and often asked staff when he would be cured. Through attending the group, she came to better understand the chronic nature of his illness and the impact of cannabis use on his symptoms. She found herself thinking about her own substance use and its potential impact on their relationship, as well as how Mark's ability to manage his schizophrenia might affect their relationship over the long term. Elizabeth joined a support group for partners of people with concurrent disorders to help her to continue to sort out these issues.

FAMILY SUPPORT GROUPS

Through support groups, family members develop ways to help the client, and, at the same time:

- learn to take care of themselves: to maintain healthy boundaries, develop coping skills and achieve their own life goals, hopes and dreams
- connect with others, air their emotions and learn about how others cope with similar situations
- reduce their isolation, and gain perspective on their own situation.

Family members may attend and benefit from such groups, whether or not the identified client in the family is in active treatment. As with psychoeducational groups, it is useful, when possible, to form groups that are focused on the same concerns. For example:

- severe mental illness and substance use problems
- personality disorders and substance use
- groups for different types of family members, such as parents, partners or siblings.

Support groups range from open-ended, drop-in self-help groups, which usually have different members from session to session, to brief, structured therapist-led groups, designed to raise awareness and generate discussion on a particular theme. These groups may be grounded in specific philosophical approaches and models, such as 12-step, abstinence-based models (e.g., Al-Anon) and harm reduction models.

Membership of both long- and short-term groups needs to be consistent and committed. Potential group members should be carefully assessed to ensure that they are suited to the type of group experience. Groups may be led by one or two therapists.

SHORT-TERM SUPPORT GROUPS

Short term, or brief treatment, support groups (six to 12 sessions) are suitable for family members of clients with all types of concurrent disorders (Selekman, 1991). Such groups help people focus on the issues facing their family and explore their own roles and responses. Brief treatments appear to be effective in engaging, motivating, creating a semblance of control and initiating change processes.

LONG-TERM SUPPORT GROUPS

Long-term support groups allow participants to apply themes and issues in the group situation to other parts of their lives, and to set personal goals. Long-term support groups can be particularly helpful for family members of clients with severe and persistent mental health and substance use disorders. These groups can help families to maintain stability and cope with chronic, relapsing conditions.

Common themes in support groups

Families of people with concurrent disorders often raise the same concerns, creating recurrent themes in group sessions.

SETTING BOUNDARIES

An issue that comes up often is the need for family members to set appropriate boundaries for the client, and also for themselves. For example, family members often present a history of escalating threats or ultimatums directed toward the client, which, though intended to effect change, have been ineffective due to a lack of follow-through.

Families also tell of taking on the client's responsibilities, in an effort to protect the client from the effects of his or her use or illness, but, in doing so, of having caused themselves too much extra work and stress and taken away responsibility from the client inappropriately. The group process can help members to initiate more comfortable boundaries and interactions with the client. The group also focuses on realistic and natural consequences for maladaptive behaviour, and empowers family members to engage in appropriate and effective action.

REFOCUSING ON FAMILY MEMBERS' NEEDS

Support groups can also help family members to refocus on themselves and their own direction. Family members often become stuck in a pattern of putting their own plans on hold until the client stops using and/or becomes "well." Accepting that the client may not change at all—or not as much or in the way that the family would like—can help family members examine what may be missing from their own lives. Such reflection might range from a broad focus on values and a way of life, to a more specific focus on issues related to career goals, how to spend free time and with whom to socialize.

UNDERSTANDING EMOTIONAL RESPONSES

Family members may also need help to understand their emotional responses to the client and how to express these responses in a controlled, constructive manner. Family members typically discuss moving from fury to pity and grief. Validation of this confusing range of emotion, having a space to express feelings and having help in understanding feelings are powerful benefits of the group experience.

UNDERSTANDING RESPONSIBILITIES AND LIMITS

Family members often see themselves as responsible for the client's problems. Sometimes family members work harder than the client to find solutions, and blame themselves when the situation does not improve. These family members need help to see that they themselves are neither the problem nor the solution. They describe "walking on eggshells," trying not to do or say anything that may cause a relapse.

Introducing the idea of choice and the client's potential responsibility can help family members understand the limits of their control. Strategies and plans must always be discussed in the context of what can be reasonably expected of the client, depending on the severity of his or her mental illness and substance use.

> *Case example: Sam and Janet*
> Sam's former wife, Janet, had bipolar disorder, which was complicated by the use of alcohol. They lived separately, but Janet phoned Sam often and relied on him almost daily for help in managing her life. She was unable to work, and Sam also helped her financially. Sam's business declined as a result, because he was unable to concentrate or devote enough time to his work. He saw little of friends or family, and felt he had no life of his own.
>
> Sam attended a six-week support group, which focused on setting boundaries and helping family members assess their own needs. He began to redefine his relationship with Janet and his response to her illness. He set boundaries on the practical and financial help he gave her, and encouraged her to use other supports more.
>
> As Sam withdrew his help, Janet began to rely on other forms of support, such as other family members and professionals. She also began to make changes in her alcohol use, which improved her bipolar condition.

CONJOINT FAMILY OR COUPLE COUNSELLING

Family orientation, psychoeducation and support are useful and effective ways to effect change in the family system without having the whole family present. At times, these three levels of intervention are incorporated in conjoint treatment as well.

Conjoint family and couple counselling or therapy (with families and clients together) is a forum for resolving problems, finding new solutions and intervening directly with the family system. Because this therapy engages families in intensive relationship counselling, the client with mental health and substance use problems must be stable, and all family members must function well for it to succeed.

INTEGRATIVE COUPLE/FAMILY COUNSELLING MODEL

Our approach to working with families incorporates the use of techniques and theory from different treatment perspectives. This is reflected in Figure 14-1: Integrative Couple/Family Counselling Model, which grew from scrutiny of our own practice in a family treatment team at the former Addiction Research Foundation (ARF, one of the founding partners of the Centre for Addiction and Mental Health). We have always worked with clients with a range of substance use–related problems, but in more recent years have seen a tremendous increase in the level of severity of presenting problems and in the incidence of comorbid substance use and mental health concerns. We adapted our model in response to these changes in our client population, and find that its multifaceted approach is effective in working with clients with concurrent disorders and their families.

This model has been developed specifically for use with families experiencing problems related to concurrent disorders and is well-suited to the range and depth of difficulties that can be present in these situations.

At the core of this model are **substance use** and **mental health**. These are the main targets of intervention and the presenting focus of family concern.

The four key areas of family functioning identified in the next circle are **values, strengths, relationships and transactions**. It is essential to understand these areas from the perspective of each family member, as well as from the perspective of the family as a whole. Exploring the family's **values** is important to understanding the family members' unique perspective and beliefs, and where they situate themselves in the socio-cultural–political world. Searching for and highlighting the **strengths** of the family can help to identify solutions to the presenting problem. Looking at the depth and quality of **relationships** in the family, as well as positive and negative **transactions** between members, is also important. In the circle surrounding family functioning, the four core areas are expanded and made more specific. Gathering information in these specific areas can help refine the therapist's understanding of the family system.

FIGURE 14-1

Integrative couple/family counselling model

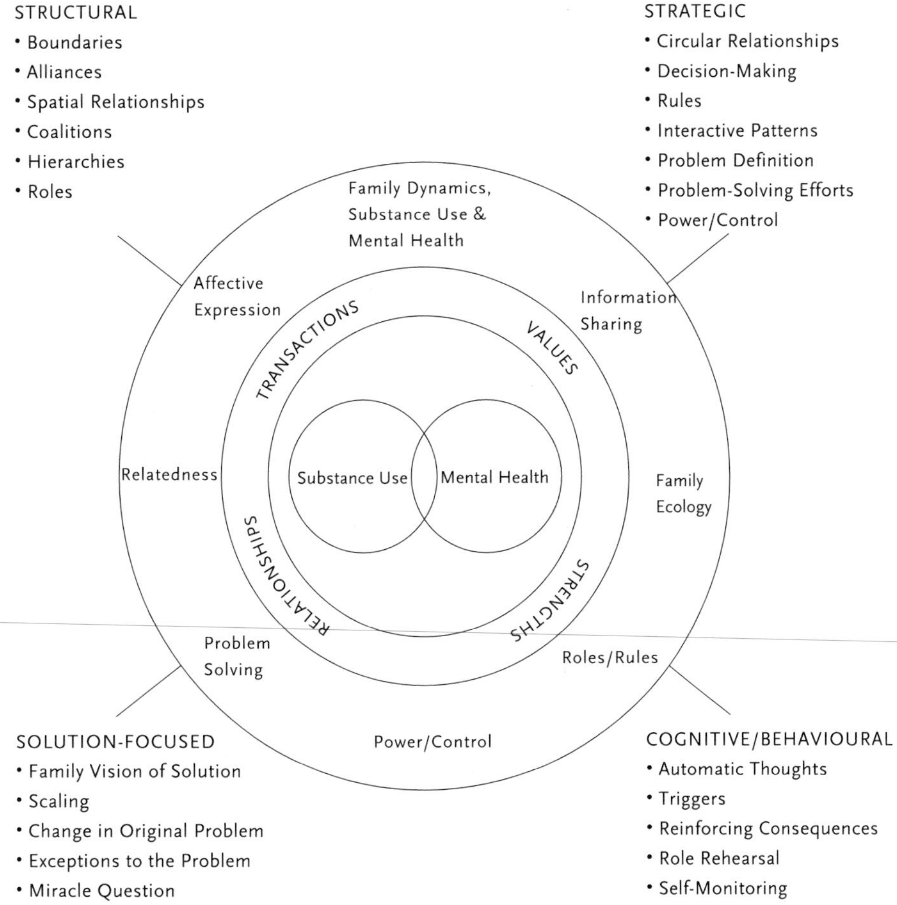

At the top of the circle, **family dynamics, substance use and mental health** refers to the unique meaning and role that these core identified concerns have in the family. Information about the substance use patterns of all members, history of substance use and mental illness in the family (including extended family), and values around and cultural context of substance use and mental illness are all important.

Information sharing refers to patterns of communication among family members. For example, who passes information to whom? Does the family have secrets? Is communication diffuse and unclear?

Family ecology refers to the family's context in terms of socio-economic status, including religion, education and community.

Roles/rules are the overt and covert operating patterns of the family, which may be organized as, for example, traditional versus modern or flexible versus rigid.

Power/control can be assessed along such parameters as shared versus dominant or democratic versus autocratic. It is crucial to determine whether violence or any form of intimidation is used and, if so, to assess for safety.

Problem solving may be flexible or idiosyncratic, and it is important to understand how different family members' styles may be similar or may conflict.

Relatedness refers to the degree to which the family members are close to or distant from each other.

Affective expression refers to how closeness, feelings and emotion are communicated. Whether the family is open or closed in this area may be affected by cultural and historical factors. This area of functioning should be placed into the larger context.

The hallmarks of the four treatment approaches that the model draws on are as follows:

- **strategic:** tracking and attempting to change key interactional patterns
- **cognitive-behavioural:** use of self-monitoring, and focus on identifying and addressing cognitions and overt, observable behaviour
- **solution-focused:** focus on strengths, small changes and creating solutions
- **structural:** attending to boundaries and coalitions.

Each treatment approach provides a unique orientation and allows the clinician to fully address all issues of concern, which could not be accomplished by the use of any of the treatment modalities alone.

The integrative model can be applied to many types of families, including:

- families in all stages of clinical contact from intake to termination
- families in various stages of the life cycle
- families of varying configurations (e.g., multicultural, blended, single-parent).

Further, other therapeutic approaches, such as narrative and existential, can easily be added, allowing for creativity and the matching of client/family style and need to therapist style, clinical judgment and mandate.

The model is non-prescriptive, and gives therapists many intervention options rather than limiting them to a particular technique for use only in specific circumstances. The interplay of clinician preference, agency factors and client strengths and needs will influence the application of the model.

Case example: Bruce and his family

Bruce is a 17-year-old whose parents brought him to the clinic due to concerns about his poor performance and attendance at school, stealing at home, lack of adherence to rules, and use of cannabis and alcohol. Bruce's family consisted of his mother, Carol, a nurse; his father, Tom, a manager in a hardware store; and his sister, Tanya, 21, a university student. Recent stressors on the family included Tom's long-term unemployment before getting his current job six months ago, and Carol's ailing parents.

Initially, Bruce was seen alone by the assessment therapist. The therapist found that Bruce was using cannabis almost daily and drinking heavily on weekends. Further assessment revealed that Bruce mainly used cannabis by himself throughout the day, to cope with overwhelming anxiety. Many of his school absences were related to his increasing social phobia. Bruce's alcohol use was associated with social situations, again mainly to help him deal with the stress of being with others. Following the assessment, the family was referred to a family counsellor.

At the family session, Carol presented as highly upset and vocal about her son's situation. In discussing how they had coped to date, she tended to take charge, while Tom withdrew and had little to say. Both parents compared Bruce unfavourably to his sister, who was an accomplished student and functioning well in university. Bruce was quiet and appeared sad and almost tearful at times, giving mostly one-word responses.

Further probing revealed a strong bond between Tom and Bruce. Tom himself had had some problems as a young man, drinking alcohol to excess and performing marginally in school. He had been able to overcome these problems on his own, and saw much of himself in his son. He was optimistic about his son's future and ability to "do what he needed to do," eventually. Tom was reluctant to intervene with Bruce, and saw his role as something of a friend or mentor.

In contrast and response to Tom's more passive approach, Carol tried to be very directive with her son. She tried to monitor all his activities and schoolwork, and most of their interaction was conflictual. She appeared angry and frustrated, both with Tom and Bruce. She relied on Tanya for most of her support, and was overwhelmed with the responsibility of caring for her parents as well. Until recently, she had also supported the family financially, and clearly felt isolated and tired.

The family therapist worked with the family in several ways. He labelled and addressed Bruce's anxiety and social phobia, creating for Tom and Carol a different context for Bruce's behaviour. After the therapist had strategically reframed the presenting problem, the parents were able to work together much more effectively. Once Carol saw Bruce as more "sad" than "bad," she began to respect and share Tom's viewpoint more, thereby situating herself alongside Tom in a united position of leadership in the family structure. This freed Tanya from her co-parenting role and allowed her to get on with her life tasks.

Bruce worked individually with his counsellor to reduce his substance use and understand both how his anxiety triggered his use and how his use ultimately exacerbated his anxiety.

In family sessions, Bruce was encouraged to talk about high-risk situations and triggers for use. To his surprise, as his parents' understanding of his struggles deepened, and they recognized that he was trying to make changes,

Bruce found that his parents were able to offer support as he developed coping strategies and moved toward achieving his goals. The counsellor also helped the family members gain a more positive view of their family by probing exceptions to problems and using these exceptions as building blocks to achieve their vision of a well-functioning family unit.

The integrative model gave the therapist a framework for assessing this complex family situation and drawing on various strategies and techniques to effect change.

FUTURE DIRECTIONS

Further research in matching family members and clients to the most appropriate level of intervention is necessary to use resources to greatest effect. Controlled trials of family interventions with specific groupings of co-occurring disorders, such as behavioural marital therapy for concurrent depression and substance use, would be useful to further refine treatment matching. Furthermore, most of the work to date has focused on a largely white, Western population. Addressing the myriad combinations and complexities of defining samples, given the complications of gender, race and ethnicity, will be a challenging but vital task.

CONCLUSION

Family issues are always present, even if the family isn't.
—Layne, 1990, p. 181.

This statement highlights both the power and the vulnerability of family. Families need to be considered and involved in the treatment process of clients with concurrent disorders. The pain of one family member has an impact on, and is affected by, all the other members. Treatment providers must engage families and mobilize them, where possible and appropriate, to help the client. Family members are often the only source of connection and support for clients who may be marginalized as a result of their mental health and substance use problems. At the same time, family members need support if they are to empower these clients to cope with the challenges they face.

The Level of Family Involvement framework (Table 14-1) can guide program planning and development, and the Integrative Couple/Family Counselling Model can be a framework for intervention. These frameworks are "works in progress," and we expect that they can be a foundation for family work in various settings, while further research is carried out to refine the choice of interventions for specific concurrent disorders.

REFERENCES

Barrowclough, C. (2002). Family intervention for substance misuse in psychosis. In H.L. Graham, A. Copello, M.J. Birchwood & K.T. Mueser (Eds.), *Substance Misuse in Psychosis: A Handbook of Approaches to Treatment and Service Delivery* (pp. 227–243). Chichester: John Wiley & Sons.

Baucom, D.H., Shoham, V., Mueser, K.T., Daiuto, A.D. & Stickle, T.R. (1998). Empirically supported couple and family interventions for marital distress and adult mental health problems. *Journal of Consulting and Clinical Psychology, 66*(1), 53–88.

Boudreau, R. (1997). Addiction and the family. In S. Harrison & V. Carver (Eds.), *Alcohol & Drug Problems: A Practical Guide for Counsellors* (2nd ed., pp. 407–418). Toronto: Addiction Research Foundation.

Boudreau, R., Chaim, G., Pearlman, S., Shenfeld, J. & Skinner, W. (1998). *Working with Couples and Families: Skills for Addiction Workers, Trainer's Guide.* Toronto: Addiction Research Foundation.

Dixon, L., McNary, S. & Lehman, A. (1995). Substance abuse and family relationships of persons with severe mental illness. *American Journal of Psychiatry, 152*, 456–458.

Kashner, T., Rader, L., Rodell, D., Beck, C., Rodell, L. & Muller, K. (1991). Family characteristics, substance abuse and hospitalization patterns of patients with schizophrenia. *Hospital and Community Psychiatry, 42*(2), 195–197.

Layne, G.S. (1990). Schizophrenia and substance abuse. *Journal of Chemical Dependency Treatment, 3*(2), 163–182.

Read, M.R., Penick, E.C. & Nickel, E.J. (1993). Treatment for dually diagnosed clients. In E.M. Freeman (Ed.), *Substance Abuse Treatment: A Family Systems Perspective* (pp. 123–156). Thousand Oaks, CA: Sage Publications.

Rubinstein, L., Campbell, F. & Daley, D. (1990). Four perspectives on dual diagnosis: An overview of treatment issues. *Journal of Chemical Dependency Treatment, 3*(2), 97–118.

Ryglewicz, H. (1991). Psychoeducation for clients and families: A way in, out, and through in working with people with dual disorders. *Psychosocial Rehabilitation Journal, 15*(2), 79–89.

Selekman, M. (1991). The Solution-oriented parenting group: A treatment alternative that works. *Journal of Strategic and Systemic Therapies, 10*(1), 36–48.

Silver, T. (1999). Families of persons with mental illness and substance use related disorders: Considerations for service delivery. *Administration and Policy in Mental Health, 26*(5), 361–367.

Stanton, M.D. & Heath, W.H. (1997). Family and marital therapy. In J.H. Lowinson, P. Ruiz, R.B. Millman & J.G. Ingrod (Eds.), *Substance Abuse: A Comprehensive Textbook* (3rd ed., pp. 448–454). Baltimore: Williams & Wilkins.

Turner, S.M. (1998). Comments on expressed emotion and the development of new treatments for substance abuse. *Behavior Therapy, 29*(4), 647–654.

ALSO CONSULTED

Epstein, N., Bishop, D. & Levin, S. (1978). The McMaster Model of family functioning. *Journal of Marriage and Family Counselling, 4,* 19–31.

Gregorius, H.H. & Smith, T.S. (1991). The adolescent mentally ill chemical abuser: Special considerations in dual diagnosis. *Journal of Adolescent Chemical Dependency, 1*(4), 79–113.

Guerin, P.J. & Chabot, D. (1992). Development of family systems theory. In D.K. Freedheim (Ed.), *History of Psychotherapy: A Century of Change* (pp. 225–260). Washington, D.C.: American Psychological Association.

Halford, W.K., Bouma, R., Kelly, A. & Young, R.M. (1999). Individual psychopathology and marital distress. *Behavior Modification, 23*(2), 179–216.

Journal of Marital and Family Therapy, 21(4). (1995). Special Issue on the Effectiveness of Marital and Family Therapy.

Kaufman, E. & Kaufman, P. (1992). *Family Therapy of Drug and Alcohol Abuse.* Boston: Allyn & Bacon.

Nichols, M.P. & Schwartz, R.C. (1998). *Family Therapy: Concepts and Methods.* Toronto: Allyn & Bacon.

Pressman, M.A. & Brook, D.W. (1999). A multiple group psychotherapy approach to adolescents with psychiatric and substance abuse comorbidity. *International Journal of Group Psychotherapy, 49*(4), 486–512.

Sciacca, K. & Hatfield, A.B. (1995). The family and the dually diagnosed patient. In A.F. Lehman & L.B. Dixon (Eds.), *Double Jeopardy: Chronic Mental Illness and Substance Use Disorders* (pp. 193–209). Chur, Switzerland: Harwood Academic Publishers.

Stanton, M.D. (1981). An integrated structural/strategic approach to family therapy. *Journal of Marital and Family Therapy, 7,* 427–439.

Szapocznik, J., Kurtines, W.M., Foote, F., Perez-Vidal, A. & Hervis, O. (1986). Conjoint versus one-person family therapy: Further evidence for the effectiveness of conducting family therapy through one person with drug-abusing adolescents. *Journal of Consulting and Clinical Psychology, 54*(3), 395–397.

Todd, T.C. & Selekman, M.D. (1991). *Family Therapy Approaches to Adolescent Substance Abuse.* Toronto: Allyn & Bacon.

Chapter 15

Concurrent disorders in young people

BRUCE BALLON

INTRODUCTION

Many youth experiment with alcohol or other drugs, but few develop problems as a result. When young people do develop severe substance use problems and present for treatment, a careful assessment almost always reveals other mental health problems as well. Like adults, youth may develop mental health problems as a result of substance use, or they may use substances to help cope with psychiatric symptoms that already exist. With youth, however, physical, social and spiritual factors related to their stage of life set them apart from adults, and can complicate treatment.

Researchers have only recently become interested in concurrent disorders in youth, and thus little systemic research evidence is available to draw on. However, here at CAMH we have clinical experience with the Youth Addiction Program, and an understanding of the research that does exist. We know enough to be able to offer helpful ways of approaching and treating this population, and to suggest avenues of further research.

This chapter focuses on concurrent disorders in adolescents and young adults, aged 14 to 24. It explores the nature of substance use and substance use disorder (SUD) in youth, as well as the mental health problems most common in youth with substance use problems. Many of the complex factors related to the assessment and treatment of concurrent disorders in youth are highlighted here, providing an overview of the issues for clinicians working with this population.

ADOLESCENT DEVELOPMENT

Adolescence is a stage of much change, with its own unique tasks, influences, processes and developments. Psychologically, youth grapple with emotion regulation, self-soothing and laying down a solid base of internally regulated self-esteem. Physically, hormonal changes affect mood and increase interest in sexual relationships. Socially, youth become more concerned with "fitting in" with their peers, and individuating away from the family.

During this period, a sense of connection with peers, family and society can help a youth to develop into a fully functioning adult with a strong, stable sense of identity.

When the developmental processes of adolescence are blocked, psychological growth may be hindered, causing damage to the person and leading to problems in life. Factors that may interfere with adolescent development include dysfunction within the family, SUDs or other psychiatric disorders. The dynamics of adolescence (e.g., experimenting with new peer groups, adjusting to emotional regulation changes, etc.) may accelerate the development of a SUD or other psychiatric disorder in youth for whom these factors affect development.

Some experimentation with boundaries, identity and social morals is normal in youth. However, certain behaviours—for example, self-harm, suicide attempts, problem substance use, regular vandalizing or fire-setting—fall outside of the normal range of adolescent development and indicate mental health issues.

SUBSTANCE USE AND SUBSTANCE USE DISORDERS IN YOUTH

Many youth in their high school years experiment with alcohol and cannabis, and more and more seem to be trying the "rave drugs," such as MDMA (ecstasy) and ketamine (Special K) than a decade ago. The 2003 *Ontario Student Drug Use Survey* (OSDUS), published by the Centre for Addiction and Mental Health (Adlaf & Paglia, 2003), reported that, of students in grades 7 to 12:

- 66.5 per cent have used alcohol in the past year.
- 29.6 per cent have used cannabis in the past year.
- 4.1 per cent have used MDMA in the past year.
- 6.1 per cent have used inhalants (not including glue) in the past year.

These figures indicate a significant increase in substance use among young people since 1993. American studies, such as NIDA's *Monitoring the Future*, show similar results (Johnston et al., 2002).

Experimenting with substance use is one of many behaviours that can begin in youth. Most adolescents use substances to express independence and autonomy, and the use does not progress to problem use or dependence (Bukstein, 1995; Newcomb, 1995). For some youth, however, substance use affects their social functioning, academic work and physical health, and causes their lives to deteriorate.

Substance use usually occurs as a result of social influence. However, substance use disorders (which include the DSM categories of substance abuse disorders and substance dependence disorders) are strongly tied to biological factors, and to internal psychological processes, such as self-medication to relieve unwanted emotional states. Studies show that both peer pressure and media influence can contribute to the development of mild substance use problems, but that youth who develop more severe problems have biological, psychological and familial factors that predispose them to substance use disorders (SUDs) (Weinberg et al., 1998).

The DSM-IV criteria for SUD were developed for adults, and do not always apply to adolescents (Bukstein, 1997). In presentation, SUDs in youth also differ from adult forms:

- Youth often present with more tolerance and fewer withdrawal symptoms and medical problems.
- Early onset of substance use, and intense and frequent use, may indicate a SUD.
- The more quickly a youth increases the frequency of use and amount of a substance used, the greater the risk that he or she will develop a SUD.
- With youth, polysubstance use is usually the rule (polysubstance use is less common in adults).

Studies estimate the rate of SUD among youth to be between 1.4 and 3.5 per cent, although true figures may be higher (Cohen et al., 1993; Lewinsohn et al., 1993; Warner et al., 1995).

In adolescent substance use, a spectrum exists that ranges from use to misuse to abuse to dependence. A clinician must be familiar with youth issues to distinguish where a young person's behaviour patterns fall along that spectrum.

Risk factors for substance use disorder in youth

Research data identifying risk factors for the development of SUD in youth are limited. The variables that have been most well researched as risk factors for SUD in youth include the following:

- psychiatric disorders, such as attention-deficit/hyperactivity disorder, conduct disorder, learning disorders, mood disorders, schizophrenia, eating disorders, anxiety disorders and somatoform disorders
- temperamental and biological factors, such as thrill-seeking, emotion dysregulation, disorders of behavioural self-regulation (e.g., deficits in planning, attention, reasoning, judgment, motor control, anger control / aggressive behaviour)
- low resilience, poor self-esteem, affect dysregulation (i.e., difficulty with controlling intensity of feelings, often linked to issues of coping /self-soothing) and low social skills
- having been sexually or physically abused
- family factors, such as mothers' prenatal alcohol use, parent(s) with antisocial personality disorder, genetic or adoptive parents with SUD, absentee or unavailable parents, mothers with depression and families with permissive attitudes toward drug use

- peers with conduct problems or substance use behaviours or both
- lack of positive role models, or idealization of poor role models
- social variables, such as low socio-economic status, problems in the community or neighbourhood (e.g., criminal or gang activity or both, and lack of safety)
- use of "gateway" substances, such as cigarettes, alcohol and cannabis.

This list is not exhaustive, as other theories, such as cultural variables, have not yet been adequately researched.

CO-OCCURRING SUBSTANCE USE AND MENTAL HEALTH PROBLEMS

Some mental health problems, such as attention-deficit/hyperactivity disorder, depression, anxiety, conduct and learning disorders, can emerge in childhood and later increase the risk that a young person will develop substance use problems. Other mental health problems, such as bipolar disorder and schizophrenia, tend to first appear in adolescence and young adulthood, as do substance use behaviours.

Studies of general and clinical populations have reported strong evidence of a link between mental health and SUDs among adolescents and young adults. One study showed a doubled risk for subsequent SUDs in adolescents and young adults who had earlier depressive or anxiety disorders (Christie et al., 1988). In another study, Cohen and colleagues (1993) found that half of those youth having at least one SUD had a co-occurring conduct, oppositional or attention-deficit/hyperactivity disorder.

Until now, no large-scale general population studies have examined the prevalence of coexisting psychiatric and substance use problems in adolescents. However, these problems likely co-occur as often in adolescent populations as in adults. One large study of adults found that 37 per cent with a substance use disorder also had another coexisting psychiatric disorder (Regier et al., 1990, as cited in Bukstein, 1995). Another U.S. study found that, depending on the drug involved, 41 to 66 per cent of those with a SUD had a co-occurring mental disorder (Kessler et al., 1996).

Here at CAMH, we looked at the assessment data of the approximately 250 youth who came through the Youth Addiction Services from 1998 to 1999. We found that many of these youth had concerns in addition to substance use. Our study showed that:

- 43 per cent of females and 28 per cent of males screened positive for depression.
- 33 per cent reported thoughts of suicide.
- 25 per cent reported at least one suicide attempt.
- 50.5 per cent of females and 26 per cent of males had experienced physical abuse.
- 50 per cent of females and 10.4 per cent of males had experienced sexual abuse.
- Among the clients who experienced abuse, 64.7 per cent of females and 37.9 per cent of males reported use of substances as a way to cope with the after-effects of trauma (e.g., the disruption of self, shame inducement, emotional numbing, etc.) (Ballon et al., 2001).

Psychiatric presentations

Other psychiatric symptoms often overlap with SUD symptoms, making it hard to determine whether psychiatric symptoms are induced by a SUD, or whether a psychiatric condition is concurrent with substance use. Psychosocial factors may also play a role, complicating the presentation even further. The most common psychiatric presentations that may co-occur with SUD include:

- attention-deficit/hyperactivity disorder
- conduct disorder
- bipolar disorder
- depression
- eating disorders
- learning disorders
- posttraumatic stress disorder
- schizophrenia
- social anxiety disorder.

ATTENTION-DEFICIT/HYPERACTIVITY DISORDER

Attention-deficit/hyperactivity disorder (ADHD) starts at an early age—symptoms must be evident before age seven for a correct diagnosis to be made. The hallmark symptoms of this condition are impulsivity, inattentiveness and hyperactivity. Children with ADHD often do not completely "grow out" of it and may later develop an ADHD residual syndrome (i.e., some symptoms persist in a lesser form). ADHD, conduct disorder and substance use problems are often linked. ADHD residual syndrome may be a factor in maintaining substance use.

Youth with ADHD often use substances such as cannabis to reduce impulsivity, although cannabis also increases inattentiveness. Chronic cannabis use can mimic the inattentiveness associated with ADHD, and so is sometimes misdiagnosed as ADHD. Ritalin™, the stimulant commonly prescribed to youth with ADHD, is the most effective treatment for ADHD symptoms, even in youth with substance use issues. However, Ritalin will not affect cannabis-induced cognitive difficulties, and the risk exists that this medication may be used or sold as a drug of abuse.

CONDUCT DISORDER

Conduct disorder is a personality disorder that manifests with:

- a lack of concern for other people's rights
- antisocial behaviours, such as lying, stealing and fighting
- risk-taking behaviours, such as polysubstance use and criminal activity.

Conduct disorder is often linked with ADHD and with the development of SUDs. Conduct disorder may have early onset, before adolescence, or it can appear in adolescence, with or without aggression. Some youth manifest conduct disorder behaviours to a lesser degree, with symptom resolution in early adulthood. Without intervention, however, youth with severe conduct problems risk developing strong antisocial/sociopathic tendencies that become fixed in adulthood.

In working with youth in the justice system, clinicians need to determine whether the crime a youth commits is related to conduct disorder or to a SUD. Youth who commit crimes to maintain their substance use patterns can often be diverted from further criminal activity with treatment for their substance dependence. If their crimes are extreme or violent, the youth need to receive treatment in a secure environment. Imprisoning such youth without treatment does not address their substance dependence, and often puts them in contact with true antisocial personalities, who then lead them to become more criminalized.

Substance dependence symptoms in youth with conduct disorder have been shown to differ in some ways from symptoms in those who do not have this condition. For example, youth with conduct disorder often develop dependence and withdrawal symptoms from cannabis, a drug that is generally considered to carry a low risk of dependence (Crowley et al., 1998).

BIPOLAR DISORDER

Because of the symptoms bipolar disorder shares with ADHD, the age of onset of this disorder is controversial. Most clinicians feel bipolar disorder doesn't fully manifest until age 12, whereas ADHD manifests before age seven. While the symptoms of ADHD are sustained, bipolar disorder manifests in discrete episodes of either irritable or euphoric moods alternating with depression.

People with bipolar illness may begin substance use at an early age. Substance use can cause bipolar symptoms to appear mixed (that is, showing both depressive and manic symptoms) or it can create a "rapid-cycling effect" (switching quickly back and forth from depression to mania). Substance use appears more often in people experiencing manic episodes of bipolar disorder than in people with any other psychiatric disorder. Those on manic highs may use stimulants to maintain the manic state and avoid or delay the depressive state. The chronic use of stimulants, however, eventually brings on depression. Clinicians may have difficulty diagnosing clients who use cocaine or other major stimulants until the clients have been abstinent for a time.

DEPRESSION

In youth, depression often manifests as conduct disorder behaviours, irritable mood and somatic complaints. As in adults, depression in youth usually causes initial insomnia (trouble falling asleep in the first place) rather than terminal insomnia (waking up early in the morning and not getting enough sleep). A decrease in school performance and social activities is also common.

Depression often manifests before the use of substances. With chronic use, most of the substances a youth uses to cope with depression, such as alcohol, cannabis or cocaine, eventually induce greater depression. This more severe depression is related to the decreased serotonin and induced amotivational states/apathy brought about by the substance use.

EATING DISORDERS

Eating disorders usually first appear in adolescence. They are often associated with the misuse of substances that can affect weight, such as stimulants and antinauseants, or with substances that can numb emotions, such as cannabis. As cannabis also stimulates appetite, youth with eating disorders often stop using it if they put on too much weight.

LEARNING DISORDERS

Impairment of executive cognitive functioning (e.g., abstract thinking, being able to order tasks, etc.) is associated with later SUD development (Beitchman et al., 1999).

POSTTRAUMATIC STRESS DISORDER

In teens, posttraumatic stress disorder can manifest with separation anxiety, preoccupation with death, perceptual disturbances and the development of a depressed mood.

A history of sexual and physical abuse is much more common among youth with SUD than in the general population. Many who report abuse also use drugs to cope with the trauma of the events. They may use the substances to modulate feelings of intense anger or self-harm behaviour, or both (Ballon et al., 2001).

SCHIZOPHRENIA

Symptoms of schizophrenia usually first appear in the late teens or early 20s. Some research has shown that people with schizophrenia who use cannabis heavily have a five-to-10 year earlier onset of schizophrenia, compared with those who have not used cannabis (Linszen et al., 1994; Linszen et al., 2001; Negrete & Gill, 1999). People with schizophrenia also use tobacco at a much higher rate than the general public, partially because of the blunting effects of nicotine on the side-effects of antipsychotic medications.

Psychotic symptoms may be induced by substance use, particularly stimulants such as cocaine or amphetamines. Cannabis may induce severe paranoia. Hallucinogens, such as LSD, usually cause visual effects, and chronic hallucinogen use can result in hallucinogen persisting perception disorder (HPPD, also known as "flashbacks"). HPPD manifests with visual pseudo-hallucinations, such as trailing effects, halos, and shifting movements from out of the corner of one's eye. Usually people with HPPD know they are experiencing unreal phenomena, unlike those who have a psychotic illness.

SOCIAL ANXIETY DISORDER

Social anxiety disorder usually manifests with school avoidance behaviours, poor self-image and social isolation. Initially, socially anxious youth may be protected from substance use, because they tend to avoid peers, who might give them access to drugs. However, once they try a substance that reduces their anxiety, such as alcohol or cannabis, they may begin to self-medicate. In the long term, however, substance use increases levels of anxiety and depression.

Diagnostic challenges

SUD and other psychiatric disorders often present differently in youth than in adults. Yet commonalities do exist. In both youth and adults, substances can induce psychiatric symptoms, and, as individuals with SUDs often have coexisting psychiatric conditions, the variety of presenting symptoms can be hard to classify into diagnostic categories. Many symptoms can be due to multiple causes.

Common diagnostic challenges may include the following:

- Delinquent behaviour: Is it depression? Addictive behaviours? Conduct disorder? Or a combination of them all?
- Psychotic symptoms: Are they substance induced? Is this schizophrenia? Is it HPPD? Is the fear justified by real threats to the person's safety? Is it a form of PTSD? Or some combination of them all?
- Self-harm behaviour: Is it substance induced? Is it a major depressive disorder? Is it bipolar disorder in a depressive phase? Is it addictive behaviour? Is it conduct disorder or another type of personality disorder? Or a combination of them all?

Case study: Joseph

Joseph, an 18-year-old male, had been imprisoned for robbing a bank, and was recently released on parole. Joseph was mandated by the courts to seek therapy for cannabis dependence and cocaine abuse. Before getting into drug use at age 15, Joseph had had no criminal behaviours. He presented as remorseful and guilt-ridden for his criminal actions.

In therapy, Joseph revealed that he had suppressed his realization that he had homosexual urges from an early age. He did so because his family, who were devout and strict, made it clear that they believed homosexuals were damned to hell. Joseph developed depressive symptoms and began to use large amounts of cannabis to avoid thinking about his situation. He tried to commit suicide several times. Eventually, he was introduced to cocaine, which he also used as a self-medicating substance. However, while intoxicated, he fell into a plan with adults who had true antisocial personality disorder, and robbed a bank to get money to buy cocaine. He was caught, and rather than receiving treatment, was sent to prison. While in prison, Joseph was raped once and tried to hang himself once. He then began developing links with other criminals for protection, which furthered his criminal outlook.

With concurrent treatment of his issues regarding identity, sexuality, depression and acquired substance dependencies, Joseph was able to change. He has now finished high school and is seeking to become a counsellor for youth.

Case study: Mara

Sixteen-year-old Mara presented with body image issues, self-loathing and a poor sense of self. She had experienced sexual abuse by a family friend from an early age, but her family did not want to acknowledge this had ever occurred.

Eventually, Mara began to use impulsive maladaptive coping mechanisms (i.e., quick-fix, short-term solutions to immediately feel better, rather than a healthier solution that doesn't result in self-destructive after-effects) to soothe herself. At age 13 she developed bulimia and used substances such as ephedrine to keep her weight down. She tried cannabis, which seemed to relieve her anxiety and eating disorder symptoms for a while, but attacks of the "munchies" from the cannabis led to weight gain, and she cut down the cannabis and redeveloped her eating disorder symptoms.

Concurrent therapy aimed at the eating disorder and cannabis dependence helped Mara deal with the symptom substitution, until she developed new psychiatric symptoms of self-cutting and self-burning to deal with stress. At this point, the trauma issues came to the fore, along with their impact on Mara's interpersonal development. Therapy aimed to address this issue, which had preceded the development of the other conditions.

Eventually, Mara began to develop new self-coping skills, learned not to blame herself for the abuse, and developed healthy relationships and set appropriate boundaries with people.

Case study: Lester

Lester was a 15-year-old male who abused numerous hallucinogens and presented with odd thoughts of believing people were constantly staring at him. He would sometimes hear voices calling his name. He had stopped using hallucinogens when the thoughts became overpowering. He switched to using alcohol and cannabis to try to calm his nerves. However, the symptoms seemed to get worse after a month of his attempting to "blot" them out with substances.

Lester's early history revealed that he was always a shy, introverted child who had difficulty developing friendships. His mother had brought him to many health care givers who said they could not diagnose Lester until he stopped all substance use. However, every time Lester tried to cut down his substance use, his psychiatric symptoms would worsen. He was afraid to go into hospital, and so received outpatient therapy consisting of addiction skills training and constant monitoring of his psychiatric status. Eventually, he was started on a low dose of antipsychotic medication, which resolved his symptoms and allowed him to feel comfortable enough to try to stop his substance use.

After a year without symptoms, Lester's dose of medication was reduced, but unfortunately his symptoms returned. He had developed schizophrenia.

ASSESSMENT FOR CONCURRENT SUBSTANCE USE AND MENTAL HEALTH PROBLEMS IN YOUTH

Considerations

As with adults, assessing youth with substance use and mental health problems is an ongoing process that requires continual updating as the client/patient follows (or does not follow) the treatment plan. The following points also need to be considered when assessing young people.

RESIDENTIAL TREATMENT

A proper initial assessment sometimes requires that the client be admitted to hospital or to a drug-free residential setting. Although adolescents do not often need withdrawal management, they do sometimes need a safe and positive contained environment to break the cycle of dependence.

DENIAL OF THE PROBLEM

Youth often deny the negative consequences of drug use, and are reluctant to think of a SUD as a condition that is implanted and becomes rooted within them. When taking a history from a young person, clinicians should talk to parents or guardians, and to other family members, friends, teachers and health care providers, with the client's consent.

RELUCTANCE TO DISCLOSE INFORMATION

Young people may be referred to treatment in various ways, or come for help on their own. Often, though, parents bring their son or daughter in for treatment, or the youths are mandated by the justice system.

Assessing young clients requires patience and therapeutic rapport. It often takes a few sessions before youth begin to feel comfortable and speak freely about what they are doing and experiencing. They may be gauging for confidentiality, waiting to be sure the therapist will not reveal anything to their parents or guardians, or, if their treatment is mandated, to their probation officer. To avoid possible disruption in trust, clinicians should present the rights and limits of confidentiality at first contact and at the start of an assessment.

Youth with substance use issues know they are breaking the law by using illicit substances. At our service, we have encountered many youth who started using substances at ages eight to 10. They were brought to various doctors for attention problems, depression and anger issues, but no one ever asked them about substance use. They never volunteered such information, because they were afraid they would be sent to jail.

PARENTAL INVOLVEMENT IN TREATMENT

In Ontario, the treatment of youth under 16 must involve a youth's parents or legal guardians. Youth who are 16 years or older can decide on their own treatment, unless they are incapable, or their treatment is mandated by the legal system.

Sometimes parents behave inappropriately by forcing (or preventing) an assessment, or trying to obtain information about their child without consent of the client. Such behaviour represents a breach of the clinician–patient relationship.

Often, young people do not want their parents to be involved in their treatment. When young people do not wish their parents to intervene, yet the parents want to be involved, the clinician should arrange support for the parents. Arranging parental support is also important when the parents are unable to get their son or daughter to go to therapy.

Instruments for assessment

No instruments have been developed specifically to screen for concurrent disorders in youth. Yet several adolescent- and youth-specific screening questionnaires, developed for either substance use or mental health, can be useful. Because SUDs commonly occur with other psychiatric disorders, screening measures should include an array of instruments to assess the many possible common problems.

SUBSTANCE USE

Instruments for screening adolescent SUD that are reliable and valid include the Adolescent Drug Abuse Diagnosis (ADAD) (Friedman & Utada, 1989), the Adolescent Diagnostic Interview (ADI) (Winters & Henly, 1993), the Adolescent Problem Severity Index (APSI) (Metzger et al., 1991), the Diagnostic Interview Schedule for Children (DISC) (Shaffer et al., 1996), the Personal Experience Inventory (PEI) (Winters & Henly, 1989), the Problem Oriented Screening Questionnaire (PESQ) (Winters, 1991), the Substance Abuse Subtle Screening Instrument (SASSI) (Miller, 1990), the Teen Addiction Severity Index (TASI) (Kaminer et al., 1991) and the Youth Self Report (YSR) (Achenbach, 1991).

MENTAL HEALTH

Many of the above measures, such as the DISC, include scales for assessing depression and anxiety. However, adding in screening instruments for other disorders, ranging from the childhood depression scales to the Children's Structured Clinical Interview for DSM-IV (KID-SCID), can help identify concurrent psychiatric issues.

More information on the assessment of concurrent disorders appears in chapters 1 and 2.

TREATMENT FOR CONCURRENT SUBSTANCE USE AND MENTAL HEALTH PROBLEMS IN YOUTH

Problems with substance use and mental health are often chronic, and even with treatment, may take years to stabilize. Relapses are common, and the intensity of need of young clients may increase and diminish repeatedly, requiring ongoing adjustment of level of support. Providing effective care to youth requires patience, and works best with a comprehensive case management approach. That means targeting not only substance use and mental health issues, but also the many other issues of an adolescent's life, such as family, vocation, recreation, housing and peer relations. Although youth can be particularly challenging to work with, the benefits of making interventions during a person's youth, before the sequelae of untreated mental health and substance use issues take their toll, can be quite rewarding.

While some of the issues related to treating concurrent disorders are the same for adults as they are for youth, the following are particularly relevant in working with youth.

Barriers to treatment

Psychiatric and substance use problems exist in every sector of the population, and clinicians thus need to be sensitive to issues specific to gender, age, sexual orientation and ethnicity. Groups who may have special needs include youth who:

- belong to ethnic minorities
- are homeless or street-involved
- are gay, lesbian, bisexual, transgendered or belong to other sexual minorities
- are pregnant
- are in the justice system.

Some youth with significant SUD and other mental health problems do not come for help due to various barriers. Youth who are street-involved, for example, have high rates of mental health problems, suicide attempts, self-injurious behaviour, SUD and HIV (Unger et al., 1997). The instability of their lives often prevents them from accessing the health care system. Another example is Asian youth, for whom using Western medical treatment facilities may bring shame.

Overall, many other factors and influences can act as a motivational barrier for youths. These include:

- fear of family finding out
- fear of revealing family secrets
- fear of being judged or criticized
- perception of the health care system as "cold"
- remaining in a precontemplative stage of change
- reaction to being mandated.

Case management

Young people can easily fall through cracks in the system. The current best practice in providing care to youth is the case management approach.

Ideally, one of the first people youth see when they come for help is the case manager, which should eliminate the need to tell their entire histories over and over again. The case manager acts as an advocate for youth, and is able to call upon a well-functioning multidisciplinary team to address the myriad issues associated with concurrent disorders. The case management approach aims to build the young person a network of support in the community, through services, family and friends.

The case manager needs to take into account all of the social, physical, substance use, mental, cultural and spiritual factors affecting youth.

Sometimes, basic needs such as food and shelter must be met before any form of treatment can be considered. A young person with mental health and substance use problems who is living on the street may not have a health card or the drug benefits coverage needed to get psychiatric treatment and medication. If the person is having a psychotic episode and has paranoid symptoms, he or she may not be willing to stay in a shelter or group home.

Street-involved youth have one of the highest rates of concurrent disorders. The stresses of homelessness likely intensify pre-existing conditions, and such youth may need to be stabilized in a psychiatric facility before trying other treatments.

Goal setting, harm reduction and motivational techniques

While a goal of abstinence is ideal in terms of minimizing the effects of substances, young clients are often reluctant to name abstinence as their goal. Pressing for a goal of abstinence too soon in the treatment process may overwhelm and alienate the young client, jeopardizing the therapeutic alliance.

With youth, it is often more effective to begin with "harm reduction" goals that aim to reduce the severity, frequency and adverse effects of substance use. Emphasis on improving functioning and lifestyle, rather than on stopping drug use, proves more effective in motivating youth to change.

That said, a clinician should promote the benefits of stopping use and finding constructive alternatives to substance use behaviours. At the same time, the worker must accept the difficulties and challenges involved in recovery. One strategy that can help is to encourage the client to set substance use goals—ideally abstinence—for specific periods of time, and then to review the pros and cons of stopping or reducing substance use, in order to set goals for the next period.

Treatment setting

When youth with concurrent disorders begin treatment, clinicians need to consider various factors in recommending the most appropriate and least restrictive environment for therapy. For example, while a withdrawal management service may be best for new clients who present extremely intoxicated or with severe withdrawal symptoms, they may initially only accept outpatient treatment. Later, once clients are more comfortable with therapy, they may be more open to withdrawal management. For youth with concurrent disorders, it is important to take a case management / long-term outlook in order to create the initial therapeutic alliance.

Many different levels of care exist, and, although not all are widely available, clinicians should try to create a spectrum of care. For example, clinicians may draw on resources such as an inpatient psychiatric ward, long- or short-term residential therapy, abstinence-based group homes, day therapy, intensive outpatient individual and group therapy, school-based programs, mutual help group meetings (e.g., Alcoholics or Narcotics Anonymous) or psychiatric groups, and occasional outpatient check-in meetings.

Approaches to treatment and support

Many of the different forms of psychotherapy and support for adults are also useful for youth. With youth, however, some special considerations exist.

FAMILY THERAPY

For best overall outcome with youth, the clinician should always consider family therapy as a primary or augmentative technique. Most youth are still involved with their families—a clinician must recognize that the bonds between a youth and his or her family are strong, even if they are bonds of anger. Clinicians must always work to maintain confidentiality and a therapeutic alliance with the youth, even when the family demands to know everything about their son or daughter.

Assessing the family and educating them about substance use and mental health are important. Occasionally, a clinician will come across a family that is too toxic to be involved in therapy with their son or daughter; for example, a family that is rejecting and negative, physically abusive, or where all members have major substance use problems they do not want to address. In such an event, the clinician needs to help the client develop other positive social supports and to work on setting strong boundaries with the rest of the family.

Most families, however, do have their children's best interests in mind. Even though some of their techniques may be maladaptive, they do what they believe is best, and are usually open to advice and support.

INDIVIDUAL THERAPY

Individual therapy for youth can consist of motivational interviewing, supportive measures, cognitive-behavioural techniques and insight-oriented psychotherapy.

Insight-oriented psychotherapy is only appropriate once a youth is not psychotic, is stable in terms of housing, is maintaining his or her drug use goal and has developed enough stress coping skills to be able to discuss intense psychodynamic issues.

DIALECTICAL BEHAVIOUR THERAPY

Dialectical behaviour therapy (DBT) can help to develop concrete skills and mindfulness techniques to address self-harm and chronic suicidal acts in youth with developing or fully formed borderline personality disorder behaviours. For more information on DBT, see Chapter 7.

12-STEP PROGRAMS

Some youth with abstinence goals respond well to 12-step programs such as Alcoholics Anonymous or Narcotics Anonymous. However, much older adults are often in these groups, and many of the developmental issues a youth faces are not dealt with.

When possible, treatment programs for youth should try to create peer groups based on shared characteristics, where feedback and support can come from peers in similar stages of treatment and development.

PSYCHOEDUCATION

Psychoeducation can also play a role in the treatment process. Throughout treatment, the clinician should weave in psychoeducation on the links between substance use effects and the creation or intensification of underlying psychiatric conditions.

CHANGES OF LIFESTYLE AND SOCIAL CONTACTS

Some youth become involved in drug trafficking to maintain their habit. Almost always, changing substance use behaviour means breaking from drug-dealing connections, along with a drop in financial status. Where money once flowed though their hands, these youth now have no cash, and perhaps a poor school record and few (legitimate) job skills. Skill-building programs, transition schools and vocational rehabilitation can help these youth to find new ways of living.

When a youth is caught in the justice system, clinicians sometimes need to fight to provide non-punitive therapy. It may become clear that the youth's criminal acts are directly linked to substance use. If so, the object is to get him or her as far away as possible from the antisocial behaviour that fills group homes and juvenile detention centres. Slowly, youth court diversion programs are being developed to create a good working alliance among the addiction, mental health and justice systems.

Social contact with peers who do not use drugs and with family is important for minimizing experiences that might trigger relapse into substance use. When youth give up substances and the activities associated with substance use, they often find themselves with large amounts of free time. This can trigger boredom. Exploration of a youth's dreams, goals and former hobbies can help direct the youth toward activities to take the place of substance use behaviours. Youth groups, school, sports and other physical activities, for example, can help fill the time and allay boredom. Adventure therapy (e.g., a camp experience blended with specific therapy goals) can be a helpful adjunct to other therapies.

CAMH services for youth

In our Youth Addiction Service clinic, primary and augmentative services for youth include:

- case management
- psychiatric consultation
- individual and group therapy
- day and outpatient treatment programs
- family therapy
- adventure therapy
- outreach programs.

The clinic offers two groups specific to the needs of youth with concurrent disorders:

- a group for youth with co-occurring substance use and mood and/or anxiety problems, which focuses on interpersonal issues
- a support group for youth whose co-occurring substance use and mental health problems (most commonly schizophrenia or bipolar disorder) have led to problems in life functioning.

A NOTE ON PREVENTION AND EARLY INTERVENTION

Research has shown a window of opportunity from first use of drugs to the development of SUD in adolescents (Beitchman et al., 1999). Clinicians who see the danger signs should try to intervene early. Addressing and treating other psychiatric conditions are also high priorities, as many psychiatric disorders are associated with later SUD development (Cicchetti & Rogosch, 1999). Other important interventions include:

- aiming at changing motivations and attitudes
- helping family functioning
- limiting gateway substances
- referring youth for specific help providers (e.g., psychiatrists, social workers, shelter providers).

Clinicians are increasingly focused on finding young people who are at risk and getting support to them before substance use and mental health problems begin to fully manifest. Currently, school-based interventions are the mainstay—research indicates success with some but not others.

Successful interventions that aim to prevent or delay substance use are interactive, harm reduction, non-didactic (i.e., interactive, flexible) programs that teach a combination of social resistance and general life skills (Botvin et al., 1995).

However, early intervention programs often do not reach the youth at greatest risk, such as those with disruptive behaviours who may have dropped out of school, those who have family problems, those who move frequently and so on.

We know that adolescents succeed best when parents are firm about their own values, make expectations clear, express a strong interest in their child, encourage autonomous behaviour, supervise activities and monitor whereabouts (McDermott, 1984). Thus, an important goal is to target parents to enhance parenting skills.

CONCLUSIONS

Clinicians who work with youth need to be aware that co-occurring substance use and mental health conditions are common in youth, and may even be becoming more so. Although very little research exists in this area, enough is available to have developed an approach to working with youth with concurrent disorders.

At the core of working with youth who have concurrent disorders is the spectrum of care offered by a holistic case management approach. Youth often need many interventions, and thus having a multidisciplinary team or contacts to weave together a concurrent therapy plan is essential. Early intervention, before the development of the substance use and mental health problems can fully manifest, often decreases the conditions' severity and course, and increases overall functioning.

REFERENCES

Achenbach, T.M. (1991). *Manual for the Youth Self-Report and 1991 Profile.* Burlington: University of Vermont, Department of Psychiatry.

Adlaf, E.M. & Paglia, A. (2003). *Drug Use among Ontario Students, 1977–2003, Findings from the OSDUS.* Toronto: Centre for Addiction and Mental Health.

Ballon, B., Courbasson, C. & Smith, P. (2001). Physical and sexual abuse issues among youths with substance use problems. *Canadian Journal of Psychiatry, 46*, 617–621.

Beitchman, J.H., Douglas, L., Wilson, B., Johnson, C., Young, A., Atkinson, L. et al. (1999). Adolescent substance use disorders: Findings from a 14-year follow-up of speech / language-impaired and control children. *Journal of Clinical Child Psychology, 28*(3), 312–321.

Botvin, G.J., Baker, E., Dusenbury, L., Botvin, E.M. & Diaz, T. (1995). Long-term follow-up results of a randomized drug abuse prevention trial in a white middle-class population. *Journal of the American Medical Association, 273*(14), 1106–1112.

Bukstein, O. (1997). Practice parameters for the assessment and treatment of children and adolescents with substance use disorders. American Academy of Child and Adolescent Psychiatry. *Journal of the American Academy of Child and Adolescent Psychiatry, 36*(10 Suppl), 140s–156s.

Bukstein, O.G. (1995). *Adolescent Substance Abuse: Assessment, Prevention and Treatment.* New York: Wiley & Sons.

Christie, K.A., Burke, J.D. Jr., Regier, D.A., Rae, D.S., Boyd, J.H. & Locke, B.Z. (1988). Epidemiological evidence for early onset of mental disorders and higher risk of drug abuse in young adults. *American Journal of Psychiatry, 145,* 971–975.

Cicchetti, D. & Rogosch, F.A. (1999). Psychopathology as risk for adolescent substance use disorders: A developmental psychopathology perspective. *Journal of Clinical Psychology, 28,* 3355–3365.

Cohen, P., Cohen, J., Kasen, S., Velez, C.N., Hartmark, C., Johnson, J. et al. (1993). An epidemiological study of disorders in late childhood and adolescence—I. Age- and gender-specific prevalence. *Journal of Child Psychology and Psychiatry, and Allied Disciplines, 34*(6), 851–867.

Crowley, T.J., Macdonald, M.J., Whitmore, E.A. & Mikulich, S.K. (1998). Cannabis dependence, withdrawal, and reinforcing effects among adolescents with conduct symptoms and substance use disorders. *Drug and Alcohol Dependence, 50*(1), 27–37.

Friedman, A.S. & Utada, A. (1989). A method for diagnosing and planning treatment of adolescent drug abusers (The Adolescent Drug Abuse Diagnosis Instrument). *Journal of Drug Education, 19,* 285–312.

Johnston, L.D., O'Malley, P.M. & Bachman, J.G. (2002). *Monitoring the Future National Survey Results on Drug Use, 1975–2001. Volume I: Secondary School Students* (NIH Publication No. 02-5106). Bethesda, MD: National Institute on Drug Abuse.

Kaminer, Y., Bukstein, O. & Tarter, R.E. (1991). The Teen-Addiction Severity Index: Rationale and reliability. *International Journal of Addiction, 26,* 219–226.

Kessler, R.C., Nelson, C.B., McGonagle, K.A., Edlund, M.J., Frank, R.G. & Leaf, P.J. (1996). The epidemiology of co-occurring addictive and mental disorders: Implications for prevention and service utilization. *American Journal of Orthopsychiatry, 66,* 17–31.

Lewinsohn, P.M., Hops, H., Roberts, R.E., Seeley, J.R. & Andrews, J.A. (1993). Adolescent psychopathology: Prevalence and incidence of depression and other DSM-III-R disorders in high school students. *Journal of Abnormal Child Psychology, 102,* 133–144.

Linszen, D.H, Dingemans, P.M. & Lenior, M.E. (1994). Cannabis abuse and the course of recent-onset schizophrenic disorders. *Archives of General Psychiatry, 51, 273–279.*

Linszen, D., Dingemans, P. & Lenior, M. (2001). Early intervention and a five year follow up in young adults with a short duration of untreated psychosis. *Schizophrenia Research, 51,* 55–61.

McDermott, D. (1984). The relationship of parental drug use and parents' attitude concerning adolescent drug use to adolescent drug use. *Adolescence, 19*(73), 89–97.

Metzger, D., Kushner, H. & McLellan, A. (1991). *Adolescent Problem Severity Index.* Philadelphia: University of Pennsylvania.

Miller, G. (1990). *The Substance Abuse Subtle Screening Inventory— Adolescent Version.* Bloomington, IN: SASSI Institute.

Negrete, J. & Gill, K. (1999). Cannabis and schizophrenia. In G.G. Nahas, K.M. Sutin & D.J. Harvey (Eds.), *Marihuana and Medicine* (pp. 671–681). Totowa, NJ: Humana Press.

Newcomb, M.D. (1995). Identifying high-risk youth: Prevalence and patterns of adolescent drug abuse. *NIDA Research Monograph 156*, 7–38.

Regier, D.A., Farmer, M.E., Rae, D.S., Locke, B.Z., Keith, S.J., Judd, L.L. et al. (1990). Comorbidity of mental disorders with alcohol and other drug abuse. Results from the Epidemiologic Catchment Area (ECA) Study. *Journal of the American Medical Association 264*, 2511–2518.

Shaffer, D., Fisher, P., Dulcan, M.K., Davies, M., Piacentini, J., Schwab-Stone, M.E. et al. (1996). The NIMH Diagnostic Interview Schedule for Children Version 2.3 (DISC 2.3): Description, acceptability, prevalence rates, and performance in the MECA study. *Journal of the American Academy of Child and Adolescent Psychiatry, 35*(7), 865–877.

Unger, J.B., Kipke, M.D., Simon, T.R., Montgomery, S.B. & Johnson, C.J. (1997). Homeless youths and young adults in Los Angeles: Prevalence of mental health problems and the relationship between mental health and substance abuse disorders. American Journal of Community Psychology, June 25(3), 371–394.

Warner, L.A., Kessler, R.C., Hughes, M., Anthony, J.C. & Nelson, C.B. (1995). Prevalence and correlates of drug use and dependence in the United States. *Archives of General Psychiatry, 52*(3), 219–229.

Weinberg, N.Z., Rahdert, E., Colliver, J.D. & Glantz, M.D. (1998). Adolescent substance abuse: A review of the past 10 years. *Journal of the American Academy of Child and Adolescent Psychiatry, 37*(3), 252–261.

Winters, K.C. (1991). *The Personal Experience Screening Questionnaire and Manual.* Los Angeles: Psychological Services.

Winters, K.C. & Henly, G.A. (1989). *The Personal Experience Inventory Test and User's Manual.* Los Angeles: Psychological Services.

Winters, K.C. & Henly, G.A. (1993). *The Adolescent Diagnostic Interview Schedule and User's Manual.* Los Angeles: Psychological Services.

Chapter 16

A concurrent disorders capacity-building initiative in a clinical program for people with schizophrenia

ANDREA TSANOS AND MARILYN HERIE

INTRODUCTION

Traditionally, a clear boundary has been drawn between approaches to the treatment of substance use and to the treatment of mental health problems. Substance use problems, when encountered in mental health settings, have often been viewed as an impediment to treatment, requiring referral to a specialist setting. Equally, in substance use agencies, mental health problems can present a challenge to clinicians who lack appropriate diagnostic and treatment expertise, and who often have limited access to psychiatric services. The gap between the two treatment systems has been exacerbated by a general lack of inter-agency communication and case co-ordination, by misunderstandings and misconceptions about substance use and mental health problems, and by lack of knowledge and tools to serve clients' complex and often challenging needs. Inevitably, clients with both substance use and mental health problems have become lost in the "grey zone" between two distinct systems.

In response to this gap in service options for people with concurrent disorders, there has been a growing awareness of the need to develop integrated and appropriate treatment programming. However, while agencies and programs now acknowledge that people with concurrent disorders are underserved, the mechanisms by which concurrent disorders services should be developed are still not well elaborated.

For example, of the 56 Ontario agencies that are willing to accept clients with concurrent disorders, only a few offer programs specifically tailored to this population. While many of these agencies have indicated that they intend to develop concurrent disorders programs in the future (Centre for Addiction and Mental Health, 2003), it is not clear how these programs will be developed, what kinds of programs are being considered, or how the intention to change at an organizational level will translate into changes in the approach of front-line staff.

This chapter is for policy-makers, program management and front-line staff, and is intended to provide a review of current literature and approaches to capacity building, as well as highlight lessons learned and potential barriers. We hope that the approaches outlined here will stimulate further development and system/program integration.

In 1998, the merging of two substance use and two mental health hospitals led to the creation of the Centre for Addiction and Mental Health (CAMH). This came about as a result of the Ontario Hospitals Restructuring Act, a policy directive that was intended to create more integrated client care while avoiding duplication of services.

Within CAMH, a small clinical program, the Concurrent Disorders Service (CDS), became a primary referral site for clients with co-occurring substance use and mental health issues, from across the organization and from the wider community. In the years following the CAMH merger, there has been a steady increase in the number of clients referred to CDS, particularly in the number of people with more severe mental health issues (for example, between 2002 and 2003, there was an approximate three-fold increase in client visits in the CDS subprogram that treats these clients). In responding to this challenge, CAMH faced a choice similar to that of the substance use and mental health systems as a whole: whether to create—or in the case of CAMH, expand—a specialist concurrent disorders stream, or to increase the capacity of the existing substance use and mental health systems and programs to work with these clients where they present for treatment.

Increasing the capacity of existing programs has generally been seen as the most client-centred and pragmatic option. It also avoids an unfortunate by-product of referring people to specialist settings: lack of follow-through by clients themselves, with the result that many clients are "lost" to the system when they are referred out. In addition, there is a recognition that specialist settings may be best reserved for the most complex clients (Department of Health, 2003; Substance Abuse and Mental Health Services Administration, 2003).

The concept of "broadening the base" of treatment services was first outlined in an influential report of that name released by the (U.S.) Institute of Medicine (1990). This policy document argued that people with substance use issues can often be best served in the community settings in which they present. The concept was initially applied to addiction services, but has important implications for the treatment of people with concurrent substance use and mental health problems. This approach was later integrated into Ontario's substance abuse policy (Ontario Substance Abuse Bureau [OSAB], 1999).

The concept of increased capacity in existing substance use and mental health programs builds on this notion. In this approach, a comprehensive integrated service system would be created by building on the strengths of the current services and programs. When needed, new services and programs could be developed that would be evidence-based or be innovations with a high likelihood of success (Arizona Integrated Treatment Consensus Panel, 1999).

These two strands of policy and program development—broadening the base of treatment services and increasing capacity in existing services—have become known in a new but growing literature as "capacity building." In this context, concurrent disorders capacity building means developing knowledge, enhancing existing programs, and creating new and innovative approaches to serve clients where they present. This literature draws on a varied base of theory and research, including motivational psychology, organizational change, the diffusion of innovations and the transtheoretical model of change.

Given the emergent nature of capacity-building theory, research and applications, we urgently need concrete strategies and research-based best practices. This chapter outlines the overall capacity-building framework as it is currently conceptualized, and illustrates how it has been applied at the level of front-line practice in CAMH's Schizophrenia Program, a large clinical program. The chapter includes a case study that illustrates both the strengths and the challenges inherent in capacity-building initiatives, and concludes with some general reflections on lessons learned, implications for future efforts, and areas for further research.

STRATEGIES FOR CAPACITY BUILDING

Capacity building has been defined as the "development of sustainable skills, organisational structures, resources and commitment to health improvement in health and other sectors, to prolong and multiply health gains many times over" (Hawe et al., 2000). Concurrent disorders capacity building occurs at the systems level, at the agency or program management level, and with front-line staff (Robinson et al., 2001). The specific components of capacity building are:

- **organizational development:** processes that ensure that the structures, systems, policies, procedures and practices of an organization reflect its purpose, role, values and objectives, and ensure that change is managed effectively (NSW Health Department, 2001, p. 10)
- **workforce development:** a process initiated within organizations and communities in response to the identified strategic priorities of the system, to help ensure that the people working within these systems have the abilities and commitment to contribute to organizational and community goals (p. 12)
- **resource allocation:** an economic process . . . that requires the technical efficiency to minimize the use of available resources (which could be used elsewhere) and allocate efficiency to ensure that the mix of goods and resources yields the greatest benefit (p. 14)
- **leadership development:** the process of fostering the characteristics of leadership within programs and across organizations (p. 16)

- **partnership development:** the encouragement of joint ventures, collaboration, alliances, intersectoral collaboration and coalitions between different agencies and programs (p. 18).

Not surprisingly, the greater complexity of system-level change means that it tends to be slower than program-level change. However, in the absence of existing programs for people with concurrent disorders and given the great need for services, working at the system level alone may not be sufficient. A more pragmatic approach involves working at macro level (systems), mezzo level (programs) and micro level (front-line staff) simultaneously. The case study outlined in this chapter focuses on change at the program and staff levels.

Building on current knowledge

One of the key lessons learned in *Strategies for Developing Treatment Programs for People with Co-occurring Substance Abuse and Mental Disorders* is that programs "build on their current knowledge, skills, and strengths while expanding gradually" (Substance Abuse and Mental Health Services Administration, 2003, p. 5). In individual programs where a skills gap exists, this may often mean that capacity-building strategies emphasize "workforce development," or continuing professional education and follow-up support. Clinical programs are heterogeneous with respect to knowledge and skills about concurrent disorders, so a careful assessment of existing levels of expertise and experience, readiness to change, and barriers to implementing new programs is key.

The first (and perhaps most crucial) step in capacity building involves forming a partnership with the target program management and staff. A strategy that emphasizes existing skills and tailors capacity-building efforts to the identified needs of programs and staff has a greater likelihood of success than a "top-down," prescriptive approach.

Capacity-building efforts need to focus on high-quality, evidence-based skills and clinical tools. At the program level, workforce development "encompasses methods of improving individual professional functioning . . . [by] ensuring that opportunities to develop individual skills, knowledge and attitudes are of high quality, effective and well utilized" (Roche, 2002, p. 10). Workforce development strategies in isolation are unlikely to bring about sustainable change; however, when linked to other capacity-building initiatives and formal and informal learning strategies, this approach can result in greatly enhanced service capacity and the development of new and innovative programs. Formal learning strategies can include mentoring schemes, certificate programs, and college and university courses; while informal strategies such as encouraging and supporting people to take on new responsibilities give program staff a chance to acquire and apply new skills.

Implementing change

Like many people, organizations and institutions tend to resist change or change very slowly. Often, the dissemination of new knowledge and clinical applications is complicated by the need to influence both practitioners and the organizations in which they work. Practice behaviour is often strongly influenced by organizational policies, procedures, values, routines and resource configurations (Rosenheck, 2001). Like treatment planning, workforce development initiatives are generally more effective if they take account of clinicians' (and programs') readiness for change.

The transtheoretical model of change (Prochaska et al., 1992), which is used to assess clients' readiness to participate in treatment, has also been advocated for use in assessing organizational readiness for change (Velasquez, 2000). This model, which is well known in the substance use field, proposes five stages in the process of behaviour change:

- *precontemplation* (not yet considering change or unwilling to consider changing)
- *contemplation* (ambivalent about change)
- *preparation* (ready to make a decision to change)
- *action* (implementing change)
- *maintenance* (maintaining change).

At any time organizations, like individuals, may "relapse" and return to an earlier stage in the change cycle. One major implication of this model is the need to use different strategies for each of the stages of change. For example, people or organizations in the precontemplation or contemplation stages may benefit from considering the costs and benefits of change, leading to increasing awareness of discrepancies between their core values and their current behaviours. The goal in working toward change is to "tip the balance" in favour of movement to the next stage in the change process.

Several guidelines to identifying stages in interpreting and applying research-based knowledge (knowledge exchange) have been developed. *The Change Book,* developed in the United States by the Addiction Technology Transfer Center Network (Center for Substance Abuse Treatment, 2000), was specifically designed to help administrators, staff and educators in substance use and mental health agencies implement change initiatives at the agency level. *The Change Book* outlines a 10-step process for planning, implementing and evaluating a change strategy at the organization level:

1. Identify the problem.
2. Organize a team for addressing the problem.
3. Identify the desired outcomes.
4. Assess the organization or agency.
5. Assess the specific audience(s) to be targeted.
6. Identify the approach most likely to achieve the desired outcome.
7. Design action and maintenance plans for your change initiative.
8. Implement the action and maintenance plans for your change initiatives.
9. Evaluate the progress of your change initiative.
10. Revise action and maintenance plans based on evaluation results (p. 9).

One unique aspect of applying the transtheoretical model to organizations and programs is that readiness for change may differ within programs and among front-line staff. In addition, management may be unwilling to make changes to existing programs and strategies while staff are eager to make changes, or vice versa. Therefore, any assessment of organizational and program readiness to change should take into account this potential variability. Identifying change "champions"—key people who carry influence and credibility within the organization or program—may help facilitate knowledge exchange. Finally, the goal in capacity building should be to support and encourage incremental steps toward enhanced services and programs, rather than sudden, wholesale change. A realistic approach should consider the organizational and individual stages of change.

Barriers and incentives to change

BARRIERS

While there is a growing consensus that substance use and mental health programs need to develop the capacity to deliver integrated treatment to clients with concurrent disorders, a number of barriers have been identified. These include:

- differing educational and experiential requirements across the substance use and mental health fields
- limited acceptance of the harm reduction approaches that are necessary to engage many clients
- different policy, planning, funding and governance streams (Health Canada, 2001).

When CAMH was founded, substance use and mental health practitioners, along with clients and their families, expressed concerns about the integration of substance use and mental health treatments. Table 16-1 (below) presents a summary of these concerns. Many of the fears identified (e.g., concerns about increased stigma, the dilution of already-scarce resources, and declining standards of care) are common to both fields. In order for capacity-building efforts to result in sustainable change, these issues must be carefully considered.

INCENTIVES

In contrast to the potential barriers noted above, there are also a number of compelling "positive expectancies" regarding the integration of mental health and substance use treatment into concurrent disorders services (Smith, 2003). These include:

- better acceptance of clients with concurrent disorders
- better care for clients with concurrent disorders (i.e., clients who need intensive concurrent treatment for their substance use and mental health issues could receive care from staff who have appropriate background and qualifications to serve them)
- increased opportunities for professional development for front-line staff and students
- improved screening and identification of substance use issues in clients receiving mental health treatment, and better screening and identification of mental health issues in clients receiving substance use treatment

TABLE 16-1

Concerns about the integration of substance use and mental health services among staff, and clients and their families

SUBSTANCE USE PRACTITIONERS, AND CLIENTS AND THEIR FAMILIES	MENTAL HEALTH PRACTITIONERS, AND CLIENTS AND THEIR FAMILIES
Integration could introduce new stigma (e.g., substance use clients not wanting to be labelled as "mentally ill").	Integration could introduce new stigma (e.g., mental health patients not wanting to be identified as "addicts").
Fewer resources may be devoted to what different stakeholders view as critically important (e.g., clients, families and service providers in the substance use field fear that there could be decreased emphasis on substance use in general).	Fewer resources may be devoted to what different stakeholders view as critically important (e.g., mental health workers, clients and families fear that there could be decreased emphasis on people who have serious mental illness and are the most difficult to treat).
Holistic care (which characterizes the substance use field) could be diminished and become more "medicalized."	Standards of care could decrease (i.e., if mental health workers are expected to address substance use problems in clients, but feel they do not have adequate training, then clients may receive less than optimal care).
Substance use will get "lost in the shuffle" because of the greater size of mental health field.	There could be "de-skilling" of staff, whereby the unique contributions of each discipline (e.g., psychology, social work, nursing) are diminished or downplayed.
If substance use is subsumed under mental health, substance use services will not retain their relevance to the substance use field at large.	

- a "critical mass" of expert resources, from both the substance use and mental health systems, brought to bear on problems of concurrent disorders
- better clinical co-ordination between two previously unco-ordinated treatment systems
- more opportunities for advances in the substance use and mental health fields to reciprocally inform and benefit client care
- opportunities for developing, providing and disseminating evidence-based care (e.g., brain imaging of people with primary cocaine addiction; motivational interviewing and strategies for increasing treatment compliance for mental health clients)
- opportunities to advocate for clients and families with a collective voice, and to join forces to reduce the stigma associated with substance use and mental illness.

Organizations or programs trying to develop integrated services can highlight these benefits in order to address concerns about the effect of integration on client care, resources and stigma. However, an abstract consideration of the anticipated costs and benefits of concurrent disorders capacity building may not be sufficient to create the necessary conditions for a commitment to change. It is important to recognize that programs exist within unique social, economic and political contexts that may either constrain or create opportunities for change. In addition, an understanding of the leadership dynamics inherent in programs can help in the planning and execution of capacity-building initiatives. The next section articulates some of the major contextual and leadership factors in program-level capacity building.

Workforce development at the program level

CONTEXT

For program-level change to succeed, it is helpful to anticipate the contextual factors that may have an impact on the readiness and sustainability of program and practitioner change:

> Context refers to the range of physical, economic, political, organisational and cultural environments within which a program sits. "Context" is often thought about as the environmental constraints on a program that are generally not amenable to change. Programs never exist in isolation. Context can have a negative or positive impact on a program and is ever changing. Practitioners need to be aware of and be ready to respond to changes in context. (NSW Health Department, 2001, p. 6)

In other words, it is insufficient to approach programs as isolated entities; rather, changes in program development and delivery must be linked to the broader system. Numerous questions may be raised that highlight the complexity of contextual factors in the implementation of program-level change. For example:

- Will the development of a program's capacity to offer integrated concurrent disorders services lead to an influx of client referrals from a system in which these resources are in short supply?
- Will new and innovative programs divert resources from existing and essential services perceived to fit more closely with a program's mandate?
- To what extent do staff regard concurrent disorders treatment as a part of their personal and professional capability?
- How will external partners and clients regard the program's enhancements?

These "environmental" issues are critical. "Workforce development strategies represent an important component of building the capacity of an organisation or community. However when developed in isolation from other capacity-building strategies, they are unlikely to bring about effective and sustainable changes in work practices" (NSW Health Department, 2001, p. 12).

LEADERSHIP AND PARTNERSHIPS

Leadership and partnership structures, too, can influence the success or failure of capacity building. Programs and organizations need a healthy mix of simultaneous top-down commitment and bottom-up influence.

Top-down commitment is required at the program level, demonstrating endorsement and support from senior management that concurrent disorders integration is a priority. Similarly, "buy-in" from the front-line staff level is equally important. Collaborative leadership from the training provider, as well as from management of the program being trained, allows sharing of responsibilities. This kind of active participation at the program management level demonstrates commitment to the initiative, and plans are included to backfill the duties of staff who participate in training activities, to enable them to be free to attend.

Bottom-up influence refers to front-line clinicians' being active champions of the concurrent disorders integration and training agenda. Their ideas and involvement must be solicited and encouraged at all phases. With buy-in and support from both team members and management, the hope is that a culture shift will begin to take shape such that clients with concurrent disorders will be routinely identified, and will receive customized integrated treatment.

SUMMARY

The framework for capacity building at the program and staff levels takes into account theories of organizational change, dissemination research and motivation. By assessing readiness for change and focusing on interim, achievable goals, it is possible to tailor capacity-building initiatives to the unique needs of individual programs. Identifying the barriers to, and benefits of, integrating mental health and substance use services, as well as identifying the contextual and leadership factors, helps to ensure that change efforts are made more relevant to the learning needs and service priorities of staff and programs.

A CASE STUDY: CAMH'S CONCURRENT DISORDERS CAPACITY-BUILDING INITIATIVE

The following case study gives a practical illustration of the principles and issues discussed above. It discusses a joint initiative of the Concurrent Disorders Service and the Schizophrenia Program, both at CAMH, that aimed to implement concurrent disorders capacity building at the program level.

Background

The impetus for developing concurrent disorders capacity at CAMH arose from a combination of contextual and resource issues. First, after the merger at CAMH, there was increased demand for integrated concurrent disorders treatment. The interim model at CAMH for treatment of clients identified as having concurrent disorders was to simply refer them to the Concurrent Disorders Service. Given the high proportion of clients presenting with both substance use and mental health issues, there was a significant and increasing burden on the limited number of staff working in the Concurrent Disorders Service.

As a consequence, increases in the client wait lists for treatment, ranging from three to 18 months for most of the specialized treatment services, were no longer acceptable or sustainable. Second, this model was no longer in keeping with the long-term vision of CAMH's capacity-building strategy, which stated that all clinicians in the organization (from both the Addictions Program and the Mental Health Programs) develop a Level I competency (see Table 16-2, on page 383, for competency criteria) for the optimal care of clients with concurrent disorders.

Given the need to assess, plan and deliver effective, comprehensive care for clients with concurrent disorders, this lack of shared, organization-wide basic competencies in the substance use and mental health areas was a concern for CAMH management and program leaders. Finally, it was recognized that clients should be offered integrated treatment in the programs where they are already receiving services, since this is where they have already established relationships with staff and are most comfortable. In summary, integrated concurrent disorders treatment was recognized as offering better overall care, and also fit the longer-term vision and expectations of CAMH.

This section outlines the capacity-building initiative as a five-step process. It details:
1. selecting a pilot program
2. planning and goal setting
3. developing and implementing an evaluation strategy
4. developing curriculum and designing workshops
5. implementing the initiative.

The section ends with an exploration of "lessons learned" and implications for future capacity-building efforts.

Step 1: Selecting a pilot program

CAMH's concurrent disorders capacity-building strategy began in 2000 and is ongoing. In order to improve understanding of what "works" in capacity building, leadership staff from the Concurrent Disorders Service proposed a pilot test with a focus on the needs of a particular program. After the pilot study was evaluated, the approach could be refined and the capacity-building initiative carried out across CAMH as a whole.

The criterion for selecting a pilot program was straightforward: where was CAMH's largest proportion of clients with concurrent disorders? This criterion was regarded as an indication of greatest need for internal capacity building. Therefore, the Schizophrenia Program was selected for the pilot study, since roughly 50 per cent of people with severe mental illness will meet criteria for a concurrent substance use disorder in their lifetime (Ontario Ministry of Health, 1994; Regier et al., 1990). The Schizophrenia Program has 465 inpatient and outpatient clinical staff. This program includes numerous inpatient and outpatient programs, satellite clinics, and two Assertive Community Treatment (ACT) teams. The pilot program included a mix of staff from all of these groups.

Staff learn best when they have the opportunity to discuss their work with other clinicians or with their supervisors over time, using a team approach (Torres et al., 2001). Training the Schizophrenia Program with a "team-as-a-whole" model allowed staff who do similar work, and see similar clients, to participate in this process together.

The needs of clients with concurrent disorders in one program (such as the Schizophrenia Program) may differ from those of clients in another program (such as an anxiety program). While some treatment interventions will be relevant in numerous contexts, many require adaptation to best fit the needs of each unique client population (Health Canada, 2002). Thus, training and follow-up support were customized to the clinical issues and concerns of staff in the Schizophrenia Program.

Step 2: Planning and goal setting

In order to engage with staff and program managers from all levels, a planning group was formed, comprising staff from both the Concurrent Disorders Service (CDS) and the Schizophrenia Program, with representation from both clinical and management staff of the two programs. The planning group, co-chaired by the manager of the CDS (Andrea Tsanos, one of this chapter's authors) and a manager from the Schizophrenia Program, recognized that a cohesive core team of dynamic and highly motivated people was required to implement the initiative. This team, a subset of the planning group, became known as the capacity-building team.

As part of their planning, the capacity-building team needed to reflect a broad spectrum of philosophies of care (such as harm reduction and a biopsychosocial perspective on substance use and mental health problems). To address the five major goals of capacity building outlined in the previous section, it was important that a close and collaborative partnership develop between the CDS and the Schizophrenia Program for the capacity-building team to be effective. It was recognized that while the CDS planning group members had expertise in concurrent disorders treatment and program development, the Schizophrenia Program managers and staff were expert on the program's organizational opportunities and constraints, strengths and weaknesses among clinical staff, and client needs. The planning group was designed to link these areas of knowledge, to build "ownership" within the Schizophrenia Program of the process and outcomes, and to ensure that the concurrent disorders capacity-building initiative closely reflected the Schizophrenia Program's needs and priorities.

The intended outcomes of this phase of the concurrent disorders capacity-building initiative were to:
- enhance client care
- distribute the clinical capacity to work with clients with concurrent disorders more broadly across CAMH, by providing continuing professional education in the development of Level I competencies
- support the Schizophrenia Program staff who were members of the capacity-building training team so they could train colleagues within their program
- advance the agenda of concurrent disorders integration within CAMH.

Accordingly, there were three major tasks that the planning group had to address in the early stages of the capacity-building initiative:
1. developing and implementing a concurrent disorders needs assessment of front-line clinical staff
2. developing the concurrent disorders training curriculum and selecting a clinical training team
3. setting goals, identifying indicators and articulating desired outcomes.

These tasks are outlined in greater detail below.

NEEDS ASSESSMENT

The planning group developed a needs assessment survey, which was administered to the entire Schizophrenia Program in 2001 (see Appendix 2 of this chapter: "The Training and Support Needs Questionnaire"). The needs assessment provided useful information on, for example, current methods of responding to clients with concurrent disorders, as well as staff members' self-assessments of:
- their knowledge of concurrent disorders treatment issues
- their competence in treating concurrent disorders
- the importance they attach to integrated concurrent disorders treatment, and their interest in it.

This step incorporated a number of the principles outlined by Kraft et al. (2000). However, while useful, their approach to implementing organizational change seemed too prescriptive, and was therefore modified to better reflect the planning group's collaborative approach.

The needs assessment survey received a 26.2 per cent response, suggesting that caution should be used in judging the representativeness of the responses. This noted, the results suggested that staff wanted:
- more information about concurrent severe mental illness and substance use disorders
- practical skills training to work effectively with these clients
- improved links between the Schizophrenia Program and the Concurrent Disorders Service.

The data from the needs assessment also provided a general "snapshot" of staff readiness to change their ways of practising. Although most stated a high level of interest in developing skills in this area, this was not consistently the case. These results suggested the need for the planning group to incorporate capacity-building strategies aimed at people at various stages in the change process (i.e., precontemplation, contemplation, preparation and action). The results also signalled the existence of potential attitudinal and resource barriers within the program.

SELECTION OF CLINICAL TRAINERS

Assembling a highly skilled and responsive training team was another major task for the planning group. It was recognized that since the first step in workforce development would be to disseminate new knowledge and clinical skills, the ability of the training team to engage with front-line staff and build motivation was of critical importance. Therefore, the planning group developed a list of essential qualities and characteristics to guide the selection of clinical trainers. These skills included:

- previous training experience on which to draw in facilitating groups at various stages in the change process
- skill in communicating new knowledge to an experienced group of clinicians (e.g., knowledge and application of core adult learning principles, such as respect for participants' experience and existing knowledge)
- ability to facilitate skill building (e.g., experience in facilitating group and individual practice of skills, and the ability to link theory with practice)
- continuing involvement in direct clinical practice, which increases trainers' credibility and permits them to incorporate their own clinical examples
- knowledge of instructional design principles and applications, so that trainers could respond to a variety of learning styles by incorporating interactive and engaging activities
- excellent communication and teamwork, and the willingness to collaborate with participants in developing and exchanging knowledge and skills.

Clinical trainers were drawn from a variety of backgrounds, including psychiatry, psychology, social work, nursing and occupational therapy. The roles of the training team included education, consultation, clinical supervision and follow-up to support the various units and services within the Schizophrenia Program. The broad range of roles should be noted, since clinical training represented just the first step in capacity building. After this step was completed, the training team needed to be able to act as an ongoing resource to the clinical staff, in order to monitor and help consolidate new clinical skills.

The planning team anticipated that including Schizophrenia Program staff in the training team would enhance the credibility of the training, and would provide role models for the workshop participants. The program staff's familiarity with their colleagues and clients would allow them to customize the training to meet participants' needs. It was also anticipated that the long-term objective—sustainability in continuing training and development—would be enhanced by the Schizophrenia Program trainers leading ongoing professional development initiatives. The New Mexico train-the-trainer curriculum is a good model that has increased access and clinical competency

(New Mexico Department of Health, 2002). It represents an efficient use of resources and broadens the pool of potential trainers.

GOAL SETTING

The process of goal setting was a third major task for the planning group. The desired outcome of the capacity-building initiative was two-fold:

- to increase knowledge and skills in integrated concurrent disorders treatment among front-line staff
- to enhance client care through the development of enhanced clinical practice and services.

Outcome indicators included:

- an objective assessment of knowledge and skills at various points in the capacity-building process
- evidence of enhancements to existing clinical programs
- start-up of new services for clients with concurrent disorders.

This process of linking goals, indicators and outcomes is a core feature of the capacity-building framework outlined in the first section of this chapter. A detailed and carefully executed evaluation strategy was, therefore, critically important. At a minimum, it was intended that all clinicians in the Schizophrenia Program would develop Level I competencies in treating concurrent disorders, with a small but hopefully influential minority developing Level II competencies. (Table 16-2, below, outlines criteria for both levels of competency, and includes an illustrative vignette for each). These latter clinicians would then be well positioned to act as "innovation champions" within the program, and would be key in sustaining and further developing capacity for integrated concurrent disorders treatment.

Step 3: Developing and implementing an evaluation strategy

As mentioned above, the planning group recognized the importance of evaluating the effectiveness of each stage in the capacity-building process, in both quantitative and qualitative terms. This feedback would provide important feedback to the trainers and would allow for refinement and improvement of subsequent trainings. Additionally, the evaluation was designed to measure the effect of the training on the participants' knowledge and skill level.

Two members of the planning and training team with specialized knowledge in clinical evaluation spearheaded this component of the capacity-building strategy. The evaluation involved a brief questionnaire (a modified version of the Training and Support Needs Questionnaire [TSNQ]; Maslin et al., 2001) completed by participants before and after participating in the workshop. Staff were also asked to participate in a 10-minute, qualitative, audiotaped interview shortly after the initial training session (this feedback is outlined under "Step 5," below).

TABLE 16-2

Criteria for Level I and Level II concurrent disorders competency

LEVEL I: CONCURRENT DISORDERS–CAPABLE	Concurrent disorders–capable clinicians provide a minimal level of integrated substance use and mental health services for clients. Concurrent disorders–capable *mental health* clinicians would typically be capable of helping clients who also have substance use problems, providing the concerns are of low severity. Similarly, concurrent disorders–capable *substance use* clinicians would be capable of helping clients who also have mental health concerns of low severity. Staff in all substance use and mental health programs should have knowledge and skill in the following areas regarding concurrent disorders: • attitudes and values about substance use and mental illness (including stigma) • identification (recognition, screening) • assessment of substance use and mental health problems and their relationship, but less advanced than the specialized diagnostic assessment required in Level II • treatment planning • referral • provision of Level I treatment interventions (e.g., motivational interviewing, harm reduction, relapse prevention) • case management and supportive care.
Level I client vignette	A client with a single psychiatric disorder and a single concurrent substance use disorder. This client has a diagnosis of schizophrenia and is connected to the Schizophrenia Program at CAMH. He has a psychiatrist and a case manager through the program, and antipsychotic medication is part of his treatment plan. The client has disclosed that he uses crack cocaine in binges, particularly when his monthly cheque arrives. This substance use has led to negative consequences in his mental health, and stands to place his living accommodation in jeopardy because substance use is not permitted in the supportive housing in which he lives. The client recognizes the consequences of ongoing use, but still values the enjoyment and escape he gets from crack. He is open to receiving help to explore his concurrent disorders issues further, but feels ambivalent about giving up use entirely.
LEVEL II: CONCURRENT DISORDERS–SPECIALIZED	Concurrent disorders–specialized clinicians are those who provide fully integrated substance use and mental health treatment to individuals with a high severity of both issues. Staff working in Level II programs (e.g., a concurrent disorders program, such as CAMH's Concurrent Disorders Service) should be skilled in the following areas: All Level I competencies noted above, plus: • specialized assessment methods (e.g., Structured Clinical Interview for DSM-IV [SCID]) and procedures

(continued on next page)

LEVEL II: CONCURRENT DISORDERS—SPECIALIZED	• delivering specialized therapies and modules (e.g., dialectical behaviour therapy—which incorporates aspects of Eastern and Western philosophies—in combination with cognitive-behavioural therapy; treatment focuses on enhancing behavioural skills, including regulation of emotions, distress tolerance and interpersonal functioning). • providing concurrent disorders consultation to Level I staff • providing clinical training and education in the assessment and treatment of concurrent disorders • conducting clinical research in concurrent disorders in collaboration with scientists and practitioners in the substance use and mental health fields.
Level II client vignette	A client is seeking treatment who has received multiple psychiatric diagnoses (both Axis I and Axis II) over the years, and who engages in polysubstance use (i.e., alcohol, cannabis, cocaine and opioids). Previous psychiatric diagnoses have been inconsistent and at times contradictory. They have included dysthymia, panic disorder and posttraumatic stress disorder, while borderline personality disorder has been a consistent diagnosis. While this client has had numerous assessments and admissions to the mental health system (most notably in psychiatric emergency departments), she unfortunately has not been linked up to ongoing follow-up and treatment. Her repeated efforts to get help have met with rejection and with exclusion from various treatment programs—either due to her ongoing substance use, or to recent self-harming behaviour related to her active and ongoing suicidal ideation. Her substance use has resulted in repeated admissions to substance use programs, spanning withdrawal management, outpatient treatment and residential treatment. However, the substance use counselling she has received has not addressed her concurrent psychiatric issues, which has left her feeling that the true complexity of her issues has been inadequately understood. She has been told she has high case management needs, and requires intensive treatment resources, which programs have claimed they are not able to offer at this time. This has left her feeling like a "system misfit" and has reinforced her feelings of hopelessness and despair.

The evaluation results (O'Grady & Tsanos, 2005) are available and being prepared for publication submission. Preliminary analysis of the data suggests that the evaluation results have yielded highly favourable ratings on all aspects of the training. More specifically, following the training, a statistically significant number of respondents reported:

- greater knowledge of the issues related to concurrent severe mental illness and problematic substance use
- greater sense of competence in dealing with this client population
- increased appraisal of the importance of concurrent severe mental illness and problematic substance use

- increased interest in this client population
- increased sense of satisfaction in working with this client population
- better working knowledge of concurrent severe mental illness and problematic alcohol/other drug use
- clearer sense of their responsibilities in working with this client population
- greater ease in finding someone to help them with clients who have concurrent severe mental illness and problematic substance use
- greater recognition that working with clients who have concurrent severe mental illness and problematic substance use was, in fact, part of their professional role.

Step 4: Developing curriculum and designing workshops

The training team, in collaboration with the planning group, developed an overall strategy of knowledge exchange (i.e., a concurrent disorders capacity-building curriculum), and designed the initial workshops. This process was informed by the results of the needs assessment, and incorporated areas of interest and gaps in knowledge and skills that were identified by front-line staff. For example, the workshop content emphasized the treatment of clients with severe mental health and substance use problems, the subgroup of concurrent disorders clients with whom the clinical staff of the Schizophrenia Program primarily work.

In addition, the workshop content reflected evidence-based best practices in concurrent disorders treatment (Health Canada, 2002), and prominent U.S. research and practice guidelines (Minkoff, 2001). Three members of the planning group attended a five-day symposium on integrated treatment models for concurrent psychiatric and substance disorders (Minkoff, 2001; See Appendix 3 of this chapter, "Minkoff Symposium, 2001," for symposium overview). The symposium enhanced the trainers' skills related to concurrent disorders in people with severe mental health problems.

Principles of instructional design and adult learning were integrated into the curriculum development and workshop design. Clinical demonstrations (using videotaped and live role playing by trainers) illustrated clinical concepts and applications, and opportunities for small group work and skill-building provided practice. Clinicians from the Schizophrenia Program were asked to submit cases in advance of the training, so that real-life clinical vignettes could be built in to illustrate key concepts and skills.

The training team also created a resource binder for participants, which included copies of the presentation material, recommended readings in concurrent disorders, a comprehensive concurrent disorders reference list, information on agencies that will accept referrals of clients with concurrent disorders, and information about assessment measures. The participant package was intended as an ongoing resource for clinicians' use as they implement new skills and clinical tools with clients.

The core of the training consisted of a two-day workshop, for which participants received a certificate of completion. A team of seven trainers facilitated the workshops. Each trainer facilitated (or co-facilitated) one module, so as to provide a rich and varied array of clinical styles, perspectives and disciplines. While clients were not directly involved in the training, videos were used (with client consent) to demonstrate therapy sessions and to represent client perspectives.

Day one covered a number of key issues in concurrent disorders, including:

- an introduction to concurrent disorders (prevalence, importance, attitudes and values)
- screening and assessment
- motivational interviewing with clients with severe mental health and substance use problems.

Day two covered:

- pharmacotherapy
- stigma
- treatment approaches.

The two-day workshop was followed by clinical support from CDS clinicians for the Schizophrenia Program staff who were most enthusiastic and motivated to implement concurrent disorders programming (the project "champions"). This support included a follow-up opportunity, known as the CDS Action Trainee Program, which allowed staff who completed the two-day training to attend the CDS to acquire *in vivo* experience of the facilitation of a concurrent disorders group.

This experience is achieved by observing or even co-facilitating an established therapy group—led by two co-facilitators from the CDS—for clients with concurrent severe mental health concerns and substance use problems. Thus, the Schizophrenia Program clinician acted as a third facilitator of the group, making direct clinical interventions with the clients. As part of the traineeship, participants also attend a debriefing session after the group session, along with the group's regular co-therapists, thereby allowing them to consolidate their learning and to reinforce skills and interventions.

The CDS Action Trainee Program involves eight weekly group sessions. Interested staff are required to obtain their supervisor's approval to take the time away from their clinical program. This opportunity has helped demystify the process of facilitating a concurrent disorders group.

Step 5: Implementing the initiative

The planning group recognized the importance of contextual factors in the successful implementation of the capacity-building initiative. In order to better understand the potential issues related to context (such as organizational and resource issues, staff attitudes and readiness to adopt new tools and techniques, and the broader implications and impacts of enhanced client services), a preliminary pilot phase took place in two clinical subprograms within the Schizophrenia Program. After these contextual factors and their potential repercussions were assessed and adjusted for, the initiative was rolled out across the overall Schizophrenia Program in the second phase of implementation.

Up to the time of writing, 243 staff members (52 per cent) had participated in the workshops. As noted above, staff evaluations have consistently yielded highly favourable ratings on all aspects of the training. Six clinicians from the Schizophrenia Program completed the CDS Action Trainee Program after participating in the two-day training. Staff who acquired this follow-up training reported finding its applied nature helpful, and said it gave them confidence to believe they could offer a similar intervention in their program.

Following the second phase of the capacity-building implementation, two treatment groups for clients with concurrent disorders were started in the Schizophrenia Program. The first, located at a satellite clinic in the community, was co-facilitated by a member of the CDS and a clinician from the Schizophrenia Program who had completed the Action Trainee Program. The second group, located on-site at CAMH, was facilitated by a clinician from the Schizophrenia Program with the initial support of a CDS clinician, who was replaced after three months by another Schizophrenia Program clinician. This approach allows Schizophrenia Program staff to become self-sufficient in offering the group. Nonetheless, after cycling out of the group, CDS staff continue to offer consultation and support to their Schizophrenia Program colleagues in running these groups.

IMPLEMENTATION CHALLENGES

Despite the positive accomplishments of the capacity-building initiative, this process also illustrated some of the challenges inherent in trying to change clinical practice in a multi-level organization. While most clinicians in the program recognized that they needed to learn about working with clients with concurrent disorders, a significant number were at the precontemplative or contemplative stages. These clinicians expressed some of the concerns about concurrent disorders integration outlined in the first section of the chapter, such as concern about the diversion of resources to new treatment applications, and about their lack of knowledge, skills and comfort in working with substance use issues.

The planning group anticipated that the clinicians at the action stage would see the workshop as the first step in building the skills they needed to work with concurrent disorders clients, and that they would be ready to take advantage of the opportunities provided by the CDS action trainee program to acquire practical experience. It was expected that those in the precontemplation or contemplation stages would begin to feel more comfortable with the idea of integrating substance use and mental health services within their program. However, not all staff appear to have perceived the training as important, as indicated by the difficulty in meeting the target attendance of 40 to 45 people per session. Several practical problems contributed to this result:

- Pressures of day-to-day responsibilities made it difficult for supervisors and managers to attend a two-day workshop. Because managers were underrepresented at the workshops, some front-line staff questioned the importance of the training.
- Budget pressures made it difficult to find backfill pay for agency staff to cover clinical responsibilities, so that nurses could attend the workshops.
- Initially the training was mandatory for some staff members and not for others. Some staff members questioned, and perhaps resented, this inequity.

- When the Schizophrenia Program decided to make the workshops "optional but recommended" for everyone, some staff perceived that the training was not a priority now that it was no longer mandatory.
- There were a number of changes in leadership in the Schizophrenia Program and consequently in the shared leadership of the planning team. This contributed to inconsistent messages to staff about the importance of the concurrent disorders initiative, and interfered with the momentum.
- Finally, staff from both programs have heavy demands on their time. CDS staff are involved in many other internal and external concurrent disorders training projects. The Schizophrenia Program had intended to hire several therapist/trainers who could focus on the concurrent disorders initiative but, because of competing demands on resources, this was not possible. As a result, CDS staff delivered about 70 per cent of the training. The objective of having Schizophrenia Program staff take complete responsibility for within-program concurrent disorders training has still not yet been achieved. Consequently, fewer resources have been available for follow-up learning activities such as ongoing supervision and mentorship, and the roll-out of concurrent disorders training to other CAMH clinical programs has been slower than anticipated.

Lessons learned

The combination of small gains offset by ongoing contextual and attitudinal challenges is not unusual in efforts to disseminate new knowledge and skills (Rogers, 1995). As noted earlier, change takes time, and occurs in incremental steps. The capacity-building initiative was intended to guide future efforts by building on elements of success and learning from those areas that were less successful. Therefore, we end by exploring some of the "lessons learned" and implications for future capacity-building efforts. Also see Appendix 1 of this chapter ("Concurrent Disorders Capacity-Building Activities"), which offers a number of practical options for programs wishing to implement concurrent disorders capacity-building initiatives, based on our experience of trying to do capacity building with very few resources.

CONDUCT A FORMAL PROGRAM ASSESSMENT

A realistic approach to capacity building should consider both organizational and individual stages of change. The organization-level assessment should account for the potential variability in motivation to change among different levels of the organization. For example, front-line staff may see the need to make changes to existing programs and strategies, while supervisors may be more resistant to change. Asking staff to participate in an assessment of the organization can often be a first step to gaining their commitment to a change initiative.

CUSTOMIZE TRAINING

It is important to customize the training to the unique needs of the clinical staff. A brief needs assessment may not be sufficient to determine current core competencies, desired areas for training and unique needs of the program. A more comprehensive instrument may better gauge staff needs and preferences, allowing material to be customized accordingly (thus following the adage, "Start where the client is"). In addition, it is important to ensure a high response rate to the needs assessment to protect against selection bias. Given the disparity we found between participant interest and actual participation, this is clearly an important consideration.

Since needs can differ significantly among staff in the same program, consideration should be given to developing training at several different levels. For example, offering introductory and advanced workshops would better take into account the range of pre-existing knowledge and skills among front-line staff. In addition, it may be helpful to involve more front-line clinical staff in developing the training content and format, and to offer a greater variety of training formats (e.g., self-study, clinical observation, online learning).

PROVIDE CLEAR AND ACCESSIBLE FOLLOW-UP OPTIONS

Following training, clinicians learn and adopt new skills best if they have opportunities for practice and reinforcement (Drake et al., 2001). Booster sessions, and training sessions for new staff, should also be made available. As one clinician noted, "We need to plan for the long term—people can't learn it all at once. They need time to change the way they work and the services they offer. The training should be offered as a menu of continuing education."

ENSURE LEADERSHIP BUY-IN

A consistent commitment and a consistent message from program management is essential. Organizations need a mix of top-down and bottom-up commitment to change. Collaborative leadership from both management and front-line clinical staff is ideal. Leaders should be committed, among other things, to providing support and recognition for concurrent disorders trainers. Trainers may be recognized and rewarded in various ways, such as:

- sending out an e-mail to the entire unit, service or team after a training event to acknowledge contributions
- providing a certificate recognizing the person's status as a concurrent disorders trainer or champion
- creating a bulletin board that features photos of the educational event and accomplishments of specific trainers or champions.

ENSURE THAT INNOVATIONS ARE BOTH RELEVANT AND IMPORTANT

The way the training is positioned will influence staff's motivation to participate. Clinicians report that they are particularly motivated to learn a new practice if they believe it will help them in a clinical area where they currently feel ineffective. Making the training mandatory may cause resistance on the part of staff who are not motivated to participate—yet if training is optional, it may appear that it is not a management priority. Without high levels of staff participation, it may be difficult to achieve a critical mass of skill development that will result in substantive, sustained change.

MAKE TRAINING ACCESSIBLE

The project budget should account for the cost of covering the responsibilities of staff who are attending a training event. If staff cannot be released from clinical duties to attend workshops and follow-up activities, some of the content can often be delivered in other ways, such as online learning, which has a growing array of courses in concurrent disorders.

STANDARDIZE TRAINING CURRICULUM

The training content and curriculum should be standardized to ensure consistency. The curriculum should adhere to Health Canada's best practices (2002), and the content should be as evidence-based as possible. A shared vision among addiction and mental health treatment providers, with a consistent terminology and treatment philosophy, will help to promote a common understanding of the essential components of an integrated approach to care for people with concurrent disorders. Further, staff will be more motivated to attend concurrent disorders training if it is accredited or certified. This requires formal curriculum development and credentialling.

It has been suggested that a "concurrent disorders toolkit" be developed and disseminated (which would include clinical practice guidelines in the form of manuals and training tapes) to ensure consistency in training content, and that subsequently another toolkit be created for specific concurrent disorders populations (e.g., people with severe mental health and substance use problems) to ensure consistency in service delivery. Several U.S.-based toolkits have been developed (e.g., Minkoff & Rossi, 1998; New Mexico Department of Health, 2002). However, these resources reflect the managed care environment in the United States, and so an Ontario-specific toolkit is recommended to address regional and local differences, and to take into account ethnocultural diversity (Butterill et al., 2003).

INVOLVE PEOPLE IN RECOVERY AS PART OF THE TRAINING

Although the planning group did not directly include clients in the training workshops, this idea was suggested in the qualitative interviews and evaluation. There are a number of roles for consumers, but among them, the most profound is to incorporate their personal story/stories of recovery into the training; this often inspires and motivates professionals, and lends an important perspective that, participants state, makes a lasting impact. When it is not possible to include clients' input directly, videos (used with clients' consent) can be used to demonstrate assessment interviews or therapy sessions, and to represent client perspectives. As well as being part of the training team, clients can play a valuable role in advocating for services, participating on planning committees and evaluating services. These contributions typically have a profound impact on participants.

CONCLUSION

The preceding discussion has outlined a general framework and approach to capacity building based on the available literature, as well as a case illustration of a workforce development initiative at CAMH. However, the limited amount of research and theory to guide capacity-building efforts means that there is still much to be done before clear guidelines and directions can be definitively established. In addition, the nature of capacity building affirms the unique needs of each system, making ongoing adaptation and flexibility of primary importance.

The approach taken in the case study, and the accompanying lessons learned, should be regarded as tentative directions, as opposed to definitive conclusions. As in any new area, further research is needed to provide a more definitive template on how to proceed. Nonetheless, the experiences discussed in this chapter seem to support the importance of tailoring intervention strategies to organizational, programmatic and individual readiness to change, the need to adapt the approach to various contextual factors, the necessity for partnership and collaboration, and the critical importance of evaluation. Throughout this experience, it has been evident that engaging staff attitudes and beliefs, in addition to skills, is critical. Introducing a new approach to treatment, such as integrated treatment for clients with concurrent disorders, challenges established attitudes, as well as requires that clinicians acquire new knowledge and skills. As one participant from the Schizophrenia Program remarked, "It's encouraging to know of all that is happening . . . in the area of concurrent disorders—this area seems to have been shunned for some time—I feel that I have been given permission to carry on with my shift in attitude (re: concurrent disorders) and therefore in the direction of my practice."

Overall, identifying a need for enhanced service is insufficient, in itself, as a catalyst for change. Capacity building requires considerable planning, commitment, resources and expertise to be effective. However, given the increased emphasis on evidence-based practice, responsiveness to client needs, and accountability in the health care field, capacity building is poised to become a major contributor to program development and organizational change. For clients with concurrent substance use and mental health issues, these developments cannot come soon enough.

ACKNOWLEDGMENTS

The authors express gratitude to the staff in the Schizophrenia Program who agreed to be study participants and who provided feedback on the modified Training and Support Needs Questionnaire, and to those staff who shared their comments and feedback on the workshop evaluations. We also thank all the members of the planning group and training team for the concurrent disorders capacity-building initiative.

REFERENCES

American Association of Community Psychiatrists. (2001). *AACP Position Statement on Program Competencies in a Comprehensive Continuous Integrated System of Care for Individuals with Co-occurring Psychiatric and Substance Disorders.* Dallas, TX: Author.

Arizona Integrated Treatment Consensus Panel. (1999). *Providing Integrated Services for Persons with Co-occurring Mental Health and Substance Use Disorders: Implementation Plan—Phase 1.* Phoenix: Arizona Department of Health Services.

Butterill, D., O'Shea, M. & Leclerc, P. (2003). *Building a CD Action Plan: Report from the CAMH Concurrent Disorders Provincial Forum.* Toronto: Centre for Addiction and Mental Health.

Center for Substance Abuse Treatment. (2000). *The Change Book: A Blueprint for Technology Transfer.* Rockville, MD: Addiction Technology Transfer Centers.

Centre for Addiction and Mental Health. (2003). *Concurrent Disorders Priority Plan.* Toronto: Author.

Department of Health. (2003). *Dual Diagnosis Good Practice Guide.* London, UK: Author.

Drake, R.E., Essock, S.M., Shaner, A., Carey, K.B., Minkoff, K., Kola, L. et al. (2001). Implementing dual diagnosis services for clients with severe mental illness. *Psychiatric Services, 52*(4), 469–476.

Hawe, P., King, L., Noort, M., Jordens, C. & Lloyd L. (2000). *Indicators to Help with Capacity Building in Health Promotion.* Sydney, Australia: NSW Health Department.

Health Canada. (2002). *Best Practices: Concurrent Mental Health and Substance Use Disorders.* Ottawa: Minister of Public Works and Government Services Canada, Cat. #H39-599/2001-2E.

Institute of Medicine. (1990). *Broadening the Base of Treatment for Alcohol Problems.* Washington, DC: National Academy Press.

Kraft, J.M., Mezoff, J.S., Sogolow, E.D., Neumann, M.S. & Thomas, P.A. (2000). A technology transfer model for effective HIV/AIDS interventions: Science and practice. *AIDS Education and Prevention, 12*, Supplement A, 7–20.

Maslin, J., Graham, H., Cawley, M., Copello, A., Birchwood, M., Georgiou, G. et al. (2001). Combined severe mental health and substance use problems: What are the training and support needs of staff working with this client group? *Journal of Mental Health, 10*(2), 131–140.

Minkoff, K. (2001). *Behavioral Health Recovery Management Service Planning Guidelines: Co-occurring Psychiatric and Substance Disorders.* Bloomington, IL: University of Chicago.

Minkoff, K. & Rossi, A. (1998). *Co-occurring Psychiatric and Substance Disorders in Managed Care Systems: Standards of Care, Practice Guidelines, Workforce Competencies, and Training Curricula.* Washington, DC: Center for Mental Health Services.

New Mexico Department of Health. (2002). *A Strengths-Based Systems Approach to Creating Integrated Services for Individuals with Co-occurring Psychiatric and Substance Use Disorders.* Santa Fe, NM: Author.

NSW Health Department. (2001). *A Framework for Building Capacity to Improve Health.* Sydney, Australia: Author.

O'Grady, C. & Tsanos, A. (2005). [Evaluation of a Capacity-Building Staff Training Initiative in Concurrent Severe Mental Illness and Substance Use Disorders]. Unpublished raw data. Centre for Addiction and Mental Health.

Ontario Ministry of Health. (1994). *Ontario Health Survey 1990: Mental Health Supplement.* Toronto: Ontario Ministry of Health.

Ontario Substance Abuse Bureau (OSAB). (1999). *Setting the Course: A Framework for Integrating Addiction Treatment Services in Ontario.* Toronto, ON: Author

Prochaska, J.O., DiClemente, C.C. & Norcross, J.C. (1992). In search of how people change: Applications to addictive behaviors. *American Psychologist, 47*(19), 1102–1114.

Regier, D.A., Farmer, M.E. & Rae, D.S. (1990). Co-morbidity of mental disorders with alcohol and other drug abuse. Results from the Epidemiological Catchment Area (ECA) study. *Journal of American Medical Association, 264,* 2511–2518.

Robinson, S., Gomes, A., Pennebaker, D., Quigley, A. & Bennetts, A. (2001). *Co-occurring Mental Illness & Substance Abuse: A Service Review.* Perth: Centre for Mental Health Services Research Inc.

Roche, A.M. (2002). Workforce development: Our national dilemma. In A.M. Roche & J. McDonald (Eds.), *Catching Clouds: Exploring Diversity in Workforce Development in the Alcohol and Other Drugs Field* (pp. 7–16). Adelaide: National Centre for Education and Training on Addiction.

Rogers, E.M. (1995). *Diffusion of Innovations* (4th ed.). New York: The Free Press.

Rosenheck, R. (2001). Stages in the implementation of innovative clinical programs in complex organizations. *The Journal of Nervous and Mental Disease, 189*(12), 812–821.

Smith, P. (2003, March). *Setting the course and making it happen: Concurrent disorders.* Presentation at the Centre for Addiction and Mental Health, Toronto, ON.

Substance Abuse and Mental Health Services Administration (SAMHSA). (2003). *Strategies for Developing Treatment Programs for People with Co-occurring Substance Abuse and Mental Disorders.* Washington, DC: Author.

Torres, R.T. & Preskill, H. (2001). Evaluation and organizational learning: Past, present, and future. *American Journal of Evaluation, 22*(3), 387–395.

Velasquez, M.M. (2000). The application of the Transtheoretical Model of Change to addiction technology transfer. In Center for Substance Abuse Treatment (Ed.), *The Change Book: A Blueprint for Technology Transfer* (pp. 52–53). Rockville MD: Addiction Technology Transfer Centers.

Chapter 16: Appendix 1
Concurrent disorders capacity-building activities

The most commonly cited barriers to introducing integrated concurrent disorders treatment into a substance use or mental health program include limited time, money and resources. The following is a list of concurrent disorders capacity-building activities that require no additional financial resources at all. These approaches can be useful either as stand-alone efforts or as important adjuncts to the training recommendations for concurrent disorders capacity-building training, noted above.

Performance objectives: Build a professional concurrent disorders learning goal into staff's performance objectives for the coming year.

Concurrent disorders action traineeship at CAMH: Staff can apply to this program to have an *in vivo* learning experience in concurrent disorders.

Experiential learning: The kind of experience that comes from observing clinical work with concurrent disorders clients and being immersed in a concurrent disorders work environment is invaluable. Creative ways of obtaining experiential learning include:

- shadowing a staff member who works in an integrated concurrent disorders treatment program (e.g., CAMH's CDS)
- arranging a "staff swap" to obtain cross-training in substance use and mental health (For example, staff from different agencies, or managers from the same agency, could arrange for one of their addiction therapists to work in a mental health program for an agreed period [e.g., six months], and vice versa. After completing the exchange, the staff can then bring back their concurrent disorders knowledge and skills to their "home" location.)
- if cross-training is not possible, seconding a staff member to a program such as the CDS that practises integrated concurrent disorders treatment (while the home program would lose this person for the duration of the secondment, this investment might be worthwhile for the sake of the knowledge and skill he or she would bring back to the home location).

Concurrent disorders group co-facilitation: Have a novice concurrent disorders clinician co-facilitate a new group in the unit or service, along with a clinician who is more experienced in concurrent disorders.

Application of clinical knowledge and skill: Following concurrent disorders training, start to apply what has been learned with clients, and discuss in supervision.

There is no need to wait to become an "expert" before working with concurrent disorders clients.

Concurrent disorders "champions": This is a term to describe a staff member who is intrinsically motivated to learn more about concurrent disorders. Ideally, he or she can also serve as a trainer. The champion will endorse concurrent disorders approaches with the team, and make sure that principles learned are not forgotten but are integrated into clinical practice. Champions should not be merely volunteers; this role should be a formal part of their job description and reflected in their performance objectives and annual performance review.

Concurrent disorders journal club: There is a growing literature on concurrent disorders, as well as various concurrent disorders listservs, both in Ontario and elsewhere in North America. Staff should be encouraged to read more about concurrent disorders and to share articles with each other. A formal extension of this strategy is to start a monthly concurrent disorders journal lunch club.

Introduction of concurrent disorders issues: Discussions of concurrent disorders issues should take place in team meetings and in clinical meetings such as case rounds.

Supervision, consultation or mentorship: This should be in place for staff whose caseload includes clients with concurrent disorders. A multidisciplinary team of experts should be available to clinical staff regarding concurrent disorders issues. As stated previously, clinicians learn best through incremental learning and ongoing feedback and support, which help ensure that knowledge and skills are not lost over time.

Chapter 16: Appendix 2

The Training and Support Needs Questionnaire

Code number:__________

The Training and Support Needs Questionnaire (TSNQ)

Please answer all 7 questions

Name: ____

(*Please Note:* Your name will be kept confidential—only the code number in the upper right hand corner will be used to identify you.)

Professional Designation/Role: ______________________________

Service/Team: ______________________________________

1. If applicable, how long have you been working with clients who have a severe mental illness and who also use drugs and/or alcohol problematically?

   ____

2. In the past, how have you personally dealt with clients who use alcohol and/or drugs problematically and also have a severe mental illness?

   ___ Referred to specialist service
   ___ Tried to work jointly with other professionals
   ___ Focused primarily on the mental illness
   ___ Focused primarily on the drug/alcohol use
   ___ Other (please describe) ______________________________

3. In the past, how has your service or department dealt with clients who use alcohol and/or drugs problematically and also have a severe mental illness?

___ Referred to specialist service

___ Tried to work jointly with other professionals

___ Focused primarily on the mental illness

___ Focused primarily on the drug / alcohol use

___ Other (please describe) ________________________________

4. How do you rate your knowledge of the issues of combined severe mental illness and problematic alcohol/drug use?

0 ________ 1 ________ 2 ________ 3 ________ 4 ________ 5

(0 = no knowledge ; 5 = expert knowledge)

5. How do you rate your competence in dealing with clients who have a severe mental illness and also use drugs/alcohol problematically?

0 ________ 1 ________ 2 ________ 3 ________ 4 ________ 5

(0 = none ; 5 = expert)

How do you rate the importance of combined problematic drug/alcohol use and severe mental illness?

0 ________ 1 ________ 2 ________ 3 ________ 4 ________ 5

(0 = irrelevant ; 5 = essential)

6. Please state how strongly you agree or disagree with the following statements by ticking the appropriate circle:

	Very Strongly Agree	Strongly Agree	Agree	Neither Agree Nor Disagree	Disagree	Strongly Disagree	Very Strongly Disagree
I am interested in the nature of combined severe mental illness and problematic drug/ alcohol use.	O	O	O	O	O	O	O
In general, one can get satisfaction from working with clients who use drugs/alcohol problematically and also have a severe mental illness.	O	O	O	O	O	O	O
I feel I have a working knowledge of combined severe mental illness and problematic drug/ alcohol use.	O	O	O	O	O	O	O
I have a clear idea of my responsibilities in working with clients who have a severe mental illness and also use drugs/alcohol problematically.	O	O	O	O	O	O	O
If I needed to, I could easily find someone to help me with clients who have severe mental illness and use drugs/alcohol problematically.	O	O	O	O	O	O	O
I feel it is part of my professional role to work with clients who have severe mental illness and use alcohol/ drugs problematically.	O	O	O	O	O	O	O

7. Do you feel you need additional support to enable you to work with clients who use alcohol and/or drugs problematically and also have a severe mental illness?

___ yes ___ no

What might this support entail?

Thank you very much for your participation!

Chapter 16: Appendix 3
Minkoff symposium, 2001

NEW ENGLAND EDUCATIONAL INSTITUTE

Symposium: **Treating Individuals with Co-occurring Psychiatric and Substance Disorders**

Presenter: **Kenneth Minkoff**

18th Annual Cape Cod Summer Symposium (June, 2001):

This symposium has been designed to provide an intensive course on the treatment of individuals with co-occurring psychiatric and substance disorders. Research-based principles of successful treatment intervention will be discussed in the context of an integrated model for service delivery. This model uses a common language for treatment that is relevant to both the substance field and the mental health field.

Symposium participants will learn how to incorporate this model into the process of clinical assessment, treatment matching, psychopharmacology, and the development of practice guidelines for this population. Participants are invited to participate in an open clinical forum in which in-depth case discussions will be facilitated.

Monday

The Problem of Co-occurring Disorders

Development of the Integrated Model

Identification of Principles of Successful Treatment Intervention

Application of this Model to Both Practice Guidelines and System of Care Design

Tuesday

Screening and Assessment of Individuals Who May Have Co-occurring Disorders in Either Mental Health or Substance Treatment Settings

Individualized Treatment Matching, Treatment Planning and Treatment Interventions, Including Motivational Enhancement Strategies

Wednesday	Designing and Planning Contingency Management Interventions
	Principles of Psychopharmacology for Individuals with Co-occurring Disorders, Applicable for Either the Prescriber or Non-Prescriber
Thursday	Design and Implementation of a Comprehensive, Continuous, Integrated System of Care for Individuals with Co-occurring Disorders
	Application of the Model to Developing Change at the System, Program, Clinical Practice and Clinician Competency Levels
Friday	Clinical, Programmatic and Systemic Case Consultation
	Strategies for Level of Care Assessment and Treatment in Managed Care Systems

About the authors

BRUCE BALLON is a psychiatrist at the Centre for Addiction and Mental Health, where he also is a clinical education specialist in the Concurrent Disorders Service, and the consultant to the Youth Addiction Service and the Problem Gambling Service. He is the addiction education co-ordinator for the Addiction Psychiatry Program in the University of Toronto's Department of Psychiatry, as well as an assistant professor for the University of Toronto's Faculty of Medicine. His training includes a B.Sc. in genetics, his MD, a Psychiatry Specialist degree and two fellowships: child and adolescent psychiatry and addiction psychiatry. He has received numerous awards for his work in psychotherapy, education and the humanities, and for his writing. Dr. Ballon is a sought-after speaker for national and international meetings, and his work has been published in academic journals. He has a special interest in different forms of media and their relationship with addiction and mental health issues; his work in this area has included designing a variety of novel psychoeducational and therapy initiatives involving the use of film, television, the Internet, creative writing and art, and he has been a consultant and adviser to television and film productions to help create accurate portrayals of psychiatric and addiction elements. He has also created games dealing with mental health and addiction issues, which have garnered him awards from the Games Manufacturers Association, international literary associations and academic associations.

GLORIA CHAIM, MSW, RSW, is beginning a new appointment as deputy clinical director in the Child, Youth and Family program at the Centre for Addiction and Mental Health (CAMH), where she will focus on families and addiction and mental health integration. Gloria has worked in the substance use treatment field for over 20 years and has prior experience in community mental health settings. Most recently, she was a project manager for the Pathways to Healthy Families Program at the Jean Tweed Centre, on a secondment from CAMH, where she was then the clinical director of the Assessment and General Treatment Program and Addiction Treatment Program for Special Populations. She has focused on clinical work and research, as well as training and education, as they relate to her areas of special interest—primarily youth, families and couples. She is particularly interested in integrating research, training and education to facilitate program development that will meet the needs of special population groups that are frequently underserved.

CHRISTINE M.A. COURBASSON is the head of the Eating Disorders and Addiction Clinic at the Centre for Addiction and Mental Health (CAMH). She received her PhD in clinical psychology from York University. Subsequently, she received a post-doctoral fellowship at CAMH, investigating the psychological determinants of resiliency and treatment success in people with substance use problems, conducting assessments and providing treatment to people with concurrent disorders. She holds a status appointment with the Department of Psychiatry at the University of Toronto and is also an adjunct faculty member at the Adler School of Professional Psychology in Toronto. She is involved in training clinicians in the application of dialectical behavioural therapy for substance use and eating disorders. Her clinical and research interests include the treatment of concurrent substance use, eating disorders, depression, anxiety and personality disorders; coping with stress; mindfulness; resiliency; expectancies; and the role of the self in eating disorders. She has received many awards, has authored scientific articles and book chapters, and has lectured on a variety of topics related to her clinical and research interests.

LAUREN DIXON, MSW, RSW, has been a therapist in the Eating Disorders and Addiction Clinic at the Centre for Addiction and Mental Health (CAMH) since 1999. She also worked for over two years in the Dialectical Behaviour Therapy (DBT) Clinic at CAMH. She obtained her degree in social work from Columbia University in 1995 and has worked in both inpatient and outpatient mental health, with individuals, groups and families. In addition to clinical work at CAMH, she has contributed to program development and research. Lauren has collaborated on training in using DBT treatment strategies for clients with concurrent substance use and eating problems and on the use of mindfulness in treating eating disorders.

SHIRA GREEN, MSW, RSW, received her Master of Social Work degree from the University of Michigan in 2001. She is currently a therapist in both the Dialectical Behaviour Therapy Clinic and the Anger and Addiction Clinic in the Concurrent Disorders Service at the Centre for Addiction and Mental Health. In addition to her clinical work, Shira has been involved in the development of outreach, education and training programs for family members, consumers and health care providers, with a focus on borderline personality disorder and concurrent anger and addictions.

MARILYN A. HERIE has been a therapist and project leader at the Centre for Addiction and Mental Health (CAMH) since 1992, and is currently an advanced practice clinician in the Concurrent Disorders Unit. She is also an adjunct professor at the Faculty of Social Work, University of Toronto; social work co-ordinator of the Collaborative Program in Addiction Studies at the University of Toronto; and sessional instructor at Ryerson Polytechnic University. Her focus at CAMH has been on the development and dissemination of research-based practice protocols and, more recently, on the development, facilitation and evaluation of online courses. In addition, Marilyn is a clinical trainer and therapist specializing in the group and individual treatment of adults with substance use problems. She facilitates workshops in such areas as motivational interviewing, addiction treatment, presentation/facilitation skills and cognitive-behavioural therapy. She has co-authored books, book chapters and articles in scholarly journals, on brief treatment, alcohol dependence, relapse prevention, dissemination research and online learning, and has presented at academic conferences throughout Canada and in other countries. She received her doctorate in social work at the University of Toronto, where she conducted research on web-based continuing education for therapists and health care practitioners.

LORNE KORMAN is the head of the Anger and Addiction Clinic at the Centre for Addiction and Mental Health and an assistant professor in the Department of Psychiatry at the University of Toronto. He received his doctorate in clinical psychology from York University. His research interests include the study of emotion in psychotherapy and integrative approaches to the treatment of concurrent anger and addictions.

MOLYN LESZCZ is an associate professor and head of the Group Psychotherapy Program in the Department of Psychiatry at the University of Toronto. His academic and clinical work has focused on broadening the application of group psychotherapy within psychiatry. His recent research has focused on group psychotherapy for people with schizophrenia, substance use disorders, and medical illnesses, such as cancer and HIV, and he recently completed a large, multi-site, national clinical trial in the application of supportive expressive group psychotherapy for women with metastatic breast cancer. He has published on integrative and interpersonal approaches in group psychotherapy and group psychotherapy applications for geriatric depression and for medical illness; recent articles and chapters have appeared in the *International Journal of Group Psychotherapy*, *Group*, the *New England Medical Journal*, the *Canadian Psychiatric Association Journal*, the *Comprehensive Review of Geriatric Psychiatry* and Kaplan and Sadock's *Comprehensive Textbook of Psychiatry*. Dr. Leszcz has been awarded a fellowship in the Canadian Group Psychotherapy Association, and has received teaching awards at the University of Toronto. Currently, Dr. Leszcz is co-writing, with Dr. Irvin Yalom, the fifth edition of *The Theory and Practice of Group Psychotherapy*.

JAN MALAT is a staff psychiatrist at the Centre for Addiction and Mental Health, in the Concurrent Disorders Service. He is the head of the Integrative Group Psychotherapy Clinic, which specializes in delivering group treatment to patients with concurrent disorders. Dr. Malat's research interests include the application of psychodynamic group and individual psychotherapy in concurrent disorders and early sobriety, particularly long-term effects of treatment.

SHELLY MCMAIN received her PhD in clinical psychology at York University in 1995, where she specialized in psychotherapy research. A registered psychologist with the College of Psychology, Dr. McMain is currently the head and founder of the Dialectical Behaviour Therapy Clinic at the Centre for Addiction and Mental Health and an assistant professor in the Department of Psychiatry at the University of Toronto. Her clinical and research interests and activities include psychotherapy for the treatment of concurrent disorders, treatment of borderline personality disorder and substance abuse disorder, dialectical behaviour therapy, and an evaluation of the relationship of psychotherapy process to treatment outcome.

SUZANNE MORROW, MSW, RSW, has been a therapist in the Concurrent Disorders Service at the Centre for Addiction and Mental Health (CAMH) since 1997. She uses an integrated approach to provide individual and group therapy to clients who have substance use and mental health issues. She has a special interest in clients with severe mental illness. Before working at CAMH, she worked as a social worker, supervisor and manager in several community agencies and hospitals. She enjoys teaching students, and is an adjunct practice lecturer at the University of Toronto's Faculty of Social Work.

VICKI MYERS, MSW, RSW, has been a therapist in the Concurrent Disorders Service of the Centre for Addiction and Mental Health (CAMH) since 1997. Her area of special interest is working with people who have concurrent severe mental illness and substance use problems. In addition to her clinical work with individuals and groups, other activities include training and educating social work students and other health care professionals, and involvement in various clinical research studies. Her previous clinical experience includes working with individuals and groups in the Youth Addiction Service at CAMH and at the Community Older Persons Alcohol Program (COPA). She was instrumental in implementing Project CARES, a joint program of COPA and The Family Services Association of Toronto that involved caring for at-risk older adults with substance misuse problems, by providing caregivers with addiction resources, education and support.

JUAN CARLOS NEGRETE, MD, DIP.PSY., CSCMQ, FRCP(C), is a professor of psychiatry at McGill University, Montreal. He founded and directed for many years the Addictions Unit of the Montreal General Hospital's Department of Psychiatry, where he still serves as their senior psychiatric consultant. He has taught on the subject of addictions at McGill for more than 30 years; he was also head of the Addiction Psychiatry Program at the University of Toronto and the first medical director of the Concurrent Disorders Service at the Centre for Addiction and Mental Health. Dr. Negrete plays a leading role in the field of addiction; he has been expert consultant for the World Health Organization, president of the Canadian Society of Addiction Medicine, zone director (Canada and international) of the American Academy of Addiction Psychiatry, and chair of the addictions section of the Canadian Psychiatric Association.

CAROLINE O'GRADY, MN, PHD, is an advanced practice nurse and clinical researcher at the Concurrent Disorders Service of the Centre for Addiction and Mental Health (CAMH). Her PhD dissertation focused on the stigmatizing experiences of family members of individuals with concurrent mental health and substance use disorders. Caroline has worked for many years in both the mental health and addiction fields. She is a member of a CAMH recovery reference group committee and is an adjunct professor within the Graduate Department of Nursing Science at the University of Toronto, where she teaches a masters-level nursing course, "A Recovery Paradigm for Mental Health and Addictions Systems of Care." She is the principal investigator on a number of research studies within the Concurrent Disorders Service at CAMH, including a randomized controlled trial comparing the outcomes of a support psycho-educational group with an educational-manual-only group for family members of people with concurrent substance use and mental health disorders. She is also co-principal investigator on a study evaluating the effectiveness of a two-day health professional educational forum focusing on the prevalence, screening and assessment and treatment of persons with severe mental illness and substance use disorders.

LORNA SAGORSKY originally trained in physical therapy in South Africa, graduating in 1962. She joined the Addiction Research Foundation (one of the founding partners of the Centre for Addiction and Mental Health) as a senior therapist in 1980, specializing in stress management for inpatients and outpatients. In 1990, she transferred to the brief treatment division of general addiction services, which she managed from 1997 until her retirement in 2004. In 1998, Lorna received training in teaching motivational interviewing, an integral part of brief treatment. She has conducted numerous workshops for a wide variety of audiences. She was also Toronto manager/clinician for the Back on Track program (Ontario's remedial measures program for impaired drivers), and revised the manuals used in the program.

JOANNE SHENFELD received her MSW from the University of Toronto in 1986 and has been with the Centre for Addiction and Mental Health (CAMH) for 15 years. Joanne has extensive clinical experience working with individuals, couples, families and groups in the field of addiction. She has been involved in research and program development, as well as training and education through CAMH. Currently, Joanne is the service manager for CAMH's Family and Youth Addiction Services. Recent projects include a study and treatment manual on brief therapy for couples, book chapters on youth and family interventions, and a treatment manual on family support and addiction. Joanne is also involved with the Family Initiative project at CAMH.

WAYNE SKINNER, MSW, RSW, is the deputy clinical director of Addictions Programs at the Centre for Addiction and Mental Health (CAMH), where he leads the concurrent disorders capacity-building team, along with other projects directed at knowledge exchange and skill development. He is an assistant professor in the Department of Psychiatry, and an adjunct senior lecturer in the Faculty of Social Work, at the University of Toronto. He also directs the Addiction Studies Program in Continuing Education at the University of Toronto's St. Michael's College and teaches in the School of Social Work at York University. Wayne worked at the Addiction Research Foundation (one of the founding partners of CAMH) for over 20 years as a clinician, program director, consultant, research collaborator and educator. Since 1996, he has played a lead role in concurrent disorders, directing the development of the Concurrent Disorders Service at CAMH. He is currently involved in research on supporting families affected by concurrent disorders, along with collaborations on treating anger and addiction, telecounselling for problem gamblers, and recovery processes through mutual aid fellowship and peer support.

PATRICK SMITH received his PhD in clinical psychology at the University of Nebraska, where he received specialty training in substance abuse. He was awarded a Fulbright Research Scholarship to the University of Canterbury in Christ Church, New Zealand, where he studied cross-cultural aspects of problem drinking. Dr. Smith completed his predoctoral internship at the Yale University School of Medicine with his primary placement at the Substance Abuse

Treatment Unit. He was awarded a National Institute on Drug Abuse (NIDA) post-doctoral fellowship that he also completed at the Yale University School of Medicine's Department of Psychiatry. He has received various awards and has held many senior clinical and administrative positions. Dr. Smith has clinical experience in providing individual, group and family therapy in the areas of substance use and mental health. His clinical research interests are in the areas of substance use, specifically alcohol and other drug expectancies and adolescent substance use and mental health, eating disorders, smoking cessation, and cross-cultural factors in substance use and mental health.

TONY TONEATTO is a research scientist in the Clinical Research Department of the Centre for Addiction and Mental Health. He received his doctorate in clinical psychology from McGill University, Montreal, in 1987 and is a registered psychologist. He is an assistant professor in the departments of Public Health Sciences and Psychiatry at the University of Toronto. His research interests include concurrent alcohol use and psychiatric disorders, treatment of problem gambling and natural recovery from substance dependence.

ANDREA TSANOS, MA (PSYCH.), has over 10 years' experience as a clinician, educator and administrator, and is currently an advanced practice clinician on the Concurrent Disorders Capacity-Building Team at the Centre for Addiction and Mental Health (CAMH). Andrea received her MA from McGill University. Since 1994, she has worked as a therapist and then manager in both the Concurrent Disorders Service and the Mood and Anxiety Program at CAMH. Currently, she provides individual and group therapy to clients with concurrent disorders, with a special interest in clients with severe mental illness and addictions. She has also served as a therapist in clinical research studies, and is currently a co-investigator for a study evaluating the effectiveness of a concurrent disorders capacity-building workforce development training initiative in the Schizophrenia Program at CAMH. Andrea is also a clinical trainer; she currently teaches an online course, "Introduction to Concurrent Disorders," has facilitated numerous workshops, and provides other forms of concurrent disorders capacity-building training to addiction and mental health professionals interested in developing clinical competency in working with concurrent disorders.